Hippopotamus Sea;

My Viral Sobriety

By: Jared Bryan Smith

Published by: Books For Free, LLC.

First Published 2010

Copyright © Books For Free, LLC.

Editor: Barton Wright, Book Cover Design: Sharline Bramucci

ISBN: 978-0-9845955-0-1

Contact Books For Free, LLC., J. Brandon Wright, Founder, For bulk sale pricing; Brandon@booksforfree.com

Printed in the United States of America

This book is dedicated to Rand Hopkins, who told me I was a writer, and that it would help to heal. RIP Rand and thank you.

"Moreover, I, on my side, require of every writer, first or last, a simple and sincere account of his own life, and not merely what he has heard of other men's lives; some such account as he would send to his kindred from a distant land; for if he has lived sincerely, it must have been in a distant land to me."

-Henry David Thoreau, *Walden*

Hippopotamus Sea

Moon Rocks in the Loony Bin

The first time I was checked into the loony bin, I was carrying three rocks. In my deluded mind that July in 2006, they were a moon rock, a space rock and an earth rock, the latter I was certain was also an ancient arrowhead. I'd found them all in my gravel driveway. I was shaking, paranoid, and still drunk even though I hadn't had a sip in the several hours I'd been waiting in the lobby to check into the Dekalb County Crisis center, which others would later give me a reality check about, and refer to as the "loony bin!" They were right and I was loony. When I heard the rocks clamor onto the counter after emptying my pockets, my uncle said "Traveling light, aren't we?" My only possessions were one Rolex, one wallet, the clothes on my back, and three rocks.

When I emptied the contents of my camouflage shorts, a sane person would have seen three very common, non-identical rocks, the kind you see every day in your yard or driveway. Not symmetrical, not very triangular even. But to me, a psychic CIA deep cover agent in training, these were perfectly triangular rocks that were hard to let go of. They were my weapons, in case any Al-Qaeda were just around the corner. The delusions I was living with sound ridiculous to me now, but they were real and quite serious at the time. However comical they are to me now, at the time they were scary as hell.

My uncle, my brother, and my sister really wanted me to check into the loony bin immediately, but I definitely still had some reservations. Fortunately they were adamant, and having three adults sign you in, makes it happen in Georgia. The way my uncle persuaded me though, is still amazing to me. The fact that he quasi-understood my delusions well enough to sell me the idea is fascinating in its own right. That I bought it, even more so.

"Bryan, if you are in psychic training for the CIA, who do you think sent us here? Don't you think you talked just a little too much to your brother about the work you've been doing? Don't you think they want you to check in here, right now, just like this so he can witness you check in?" My Uncle Jack delivered it with all the sincerity of a 5 star general.

How could I dispute such a brilliant argument? If my uncle did believe I was a psychic CIA agent in training for a deep cover mission to Afghanistan, then I sure as hell babbled a whole hell of a lot to my brother about my super secret mission! Of course! I was only here at Dekalb County Crisis to play the part, to completely disqualify all the Top Secret information I'd divulged to my brother! How silly of me! Why didn't this occur to me sooner?

It's really hard to keep state secrets on a Crown Royal and amphetamines diet. It finally made sense to me! So we sat there, my uncle, my brother, and I for a long time, my sister had returned to work after signing me in. They interviewed me with my brother and uncle there, my uncle eyeballing me to make sure I didn't weasel out of the qualifications for admittance, for which I was batting a thousand. I lied straight to the nurse's face when she asked if I drank liquor. "No," I said, to which my brother said "You ordered six Crown and Sevens last night right in front of me!" Oh yeah, except for when I had witnesses. I admitted to it, but still didn't fully acknowledge I drank liquor too much. This was just a dog and pony show so my brother wouldn't believe I was in the CIA. It was important for my cover, so I just kept playing along. In my mind, I was being debriefed.

We went back out to the lobby, and my brother left around that time. So I sat with my uncle at Dekalb County Crisis for several more hours while they found me a bed. I began to go into what I now know is detox, but at the time just thought I was going even more insane. Shaking, shivering, voices in your head, hundreds of them, a ludicrous committee. Ranging from full blown hallucinations to implied innuendo. I thought my uncle was an angel and then five minutes later he was the devil. I twitched, thought insane thoughts, I listened to an orchestra of voices in my head, all telling me to do conflicting things, and I sat on my hands and waited to go into the loony bin. The CIA wanted me to, and alcoholic junkie I may be, but by God I'm a patriot! I'll await my bed to convince my brother I'm nuts. For God and Country!

They say if AA doesn't fix your drinking, it'll certainly ruin it. I, too, found this to be the case. Nine months before I checked into the loony bin, I'd tried AA for about 28 days -- well, exactly 28 days. I'm an executive recruiter and have worked for some pretty good companies in Atlanta. At the time of my first AA experiment, I'd already owned two of my own recruiting companies, but had drunk them into the ground and now worked for CV Confidential and was about to be fired for not showing up to work for a week. So I begged for a second chance and offered to go to AA as a buffer to being fired. I smoked weed every day, thinking I was original and that I'd fool everyone, but it's all been done in AA. I found out later this is called the Marijuana Maintenance program. It didn't work for me either. I did find a girl that could deal with an alcoholic, though, and who also had some pointers as to how to work through your alcoholism, mainly through other medications from the doctor, so they're OK. Adderall was her drug of choice. The shrink wouldn't give it to me, as after just a few questions he could tell I was an alcoholic. Not to be discouraged, I went to a general doctor who hooked me up, and I was off to the races.

Now I'd tried other combos before. You name it I've done it, other than crack. But meth and ice kept me up for days on end, the year of opiates had caused me to go through hell on withdrawal so I'd sworn them off, and coke was just ten minutes of fun for three weeks of hell. Not that I hadn't given all these drug combos their chance, I just knew from repeated pain that none of those combos worked for me. Adderall and drinking, though, that combo worked perfectly -- for about nine months, when I suddenly found myself being checked into the loony bin by three of my very busy family members. When I was in there, I called one of my best friends, Adam Archer. Three days before, I'd called him from the Ritz Carlton, while playing the drunk big shot, now I was calling him from a loony bin. "Only Jared Bryan Smith," he said. "From the Ritz to the Nuthouse in three days," and he laughed uncontrollably.

So the Adderall had worked wonders on my ability to work with a hangover, but it also fed my appetite for the drink. Like a mini coke binge every single day, with me drinking the uppers away every night. Well, I guess for me, it took about six months of binge drinking and 60 milligrams of Adderall a day to drive me to the edge of paranoid schizophrenia.

I know that I was insane now, looking back, but I was the last to know then. The rocks were the first proof I had that I was nuts. After three days in the insane asylum, I checked out, and the rocks they handed back to me were clearly just regular rocks. Not the Moon Rock, Space Rock, or Earth Rock. Just rocks. The other huge indicator I had was the jigsaw puzzle they had inside the loony bin. I'll never forget it. It was as clear to me as the image of those perfectly triangular rocks were. It was a big puzzle of shiny Christmas tree decorations, and after spending the first several days organizing the other nuts in the place to help me, we finally pieced together the border of the puzzle. This being done, we could begin filling in the inside. The only problem was that the cover of the puzzle box didn't match the picture. I looked at it for hours on end trying to match it up, and it just wouldn't match. The problem, of course, wasn't the top of the puzzle box, it was me. I had lost the ability to see the true from the false. In madness, we literally see things differently than others see it. It was like living in a different dimension.

When I was 11 years old, my father committed suicide because of alcoholism. I thought he'd gone nuts. I never realized until well after I was sober that the two went hand in hand. Late stages of alcoholism and paranoid schizophrenia, with full blown hallucinations, both visual and audible, as well as paranoia beyond belief, are all part of detoxing or living with late-stage alcoholism. My father had lived to be 37 before he found it necessary to blow his head off with a .357, and I always had a lingering doubt that I, too, may have to deal with alcoholism someday, but not this soon. Not at 28 years old.

After six months or so of being a drunk, Adderall-addicted nutcase for CV Confidential, they'd eventually let me go. I'd started my third recruiting firm in Atlanta and named it Seek and Employ, Inc. The CIA delusion stemmed from a client I had who asked me innocently enough to find them Arabic-speaking auditors. I was still a Fortune 500 executive recruiter, and one of my clients in particular, a Fortune 100 international conglomerate, had a need for auditors, CPAs who spoke Arabic and were born in the States, to audit their many overseas facilities. Well, this slowly went in my head, from me trying to recruit candidates for a job to my telling people I suspected it was CIA related. Before I knew it, I'd told so many people my conspiracy theory, that in my drunk, amphetamine driven, deluded mind, I believed it myself, and I was posting ads worldwide for this job order, to recruit potential Al-Qaeda and try to get into the States. I started off thinking it was a possibility, but it would grow in my mind as I drank and lost touch with reality.

Also, something happened that fueled the flames in my fragile little pickled mind. Three resumes sent to me from London, Egypt, and Rome matched the Arabic names I found in an article online about a thwarted jetliner takeover attempt by Al-Qaeda in England, during that summer of 2006. By God, I was a superhero! I was so deep under cover they hadn't even told me I was undercover! They were just tapping my computer, and letting me advertise on Craigslist worldwide and reaping in the results! I was a patriot, a lifesaver, and an All-Around Great American! This calls for a drink! By God, this calls for a binge! This line of thinking led me down a very dark, chilling path. The elation soon turned to paranoia that for this scheme to work, they were literally tapping my phones, every keystroke, and sending people to follow me everywhere. It also incidentally turned into the delusion that I was Al-Qaeda bait, trying to invoke a response. So I began carrying around knives. Drinking with a loaded gun always at my side, and of course the rocks, when a knife or gun is just too damn obvious.

Around this time, a Colonel in the US Marine Corps began talking to me at North River Tavern, in Sandy Springs. I let him crash at my house one night, and I told him how much of a patriot I was and how I'd been recruiting Arabs for my Fortune 100 client, but how really it was for the CIA, which by now I believed adamantly. I told him I'd love to be embedded in a unit in Afghanistan, and lo and behold, he said he could make it happen, and could even get me a grant to do so. So now, I'm a super secret undercover hero, and also an agent in training to go to Afghanistan to do God knows what, drinking and drugging more and more every day. Until just a few days before the 4th of July, 2006. That's when the direct psychic connection to the CIA really opened up. That's when rather, I began to believe the voices in my head to a certain extent. I often times negotiated with them. For instance, the first really crazy thing I was ordered to do by the new committee in my mind was to carve the microchip out of my ankle. Well, I got the knife. I even looked at the scar from where Grady Hospital had rebuilt my ankle after a skateboarding accident, and then in a modest retreat in the direction of sanity, I negotiated with myself. I decided that the satellites wouldn't be able to track the microchip in my ankle as long as it was underwater. So a few nights before the 4th, I began drinking with my foot underwater in the bathtub. This would obviously throw the satellites off. Now don't go asking the logic of how you can be simultaneously training for and hiding from the CIA. Obviously the CIA was just testing the uplink device, to see if I could hear them or not. That is about the logic I was running with at this stage, always drunk, always high, now half the time with my foot submerged in the bathtub as I drank.

July 3rd, Caroline Gerard, the poor girlfriend of mine I'd picked up at the AA clubhouse moths before, who was still debating as to whether I was insane or not, was still enjoying the benefits of dating an only mildly ridiculous psychotic. She would soon leave, but as of yet had dealt with my shooting guns in the house directly at a brick chimney, listening to bullets and brick shrapnel ricochet, throwing knives, and all-around insanity. On July 3rd, though, I picked up the pace. We went to the Ritz Carlton on Peachtree and I bought a $900 dollar room. I'd just closed some deals with my third company, oh yes, and saved a 747 or two from going into the ocean,

9

so we were going to celebrate. They put us on the top floor of the Ritz, obviously because we were important, most likely because of my CIA connections, I thought. This was all pretty impromptu as we'd only left the house to go shopping, and had ended up drunk at Phipps Plaza at the Tavern and gone to the Ritz when I decided I was too drunk to drive home. Two DUI's and numerous close calls had at least made me paranoid about some of the right things.

Once we were there, we ordered a case of Budweiser's, iced down, placed in a huge brass bowl, as if we were white trash royalty, and I went and picked up a Rainbow Family hippie, or so I believed, to buy some shrooms from, and we drank until about 5 in the morning, finally passing out for an hour or so. At about 7 or 8 in the morning, we awoke to a HUGE black helicopter flying directly outside our window. I mean I could see the pilot's eyeballs and they were definitely Feds of some sort. The significance of a black helicopter to the truly paranoid really can't be overstated. To have one right outside my window must have sent God laughing into a tailspin, because it freaked me the hell out! Being paranoid already, it couldn't possibly have been that they were there to provide security for the famous Peachtree Road Race, though I'd acknowledged the possibility. The fact that they hovered directly outside our room was definitely a message! We left the hotel room and beelined to the car. I dumped the shrooms in a Porta-Potty and we hauled ass back to my house. We slept most of that day and when we awoke we had just enough time for us to make it to Mountain Park to watch the 4th of July fireworks. We both felt like we'd slept way too long for it to still be the 4th, but we just chalked it up to time travel and headed for Mountain Park. As a professional black out drunk, I'd long ago written off huge gaps of time by time travel, it was the only thing that made sense.

Crazy thoughts were coming hard and fast once we got to Mountain Park for the fireworks show. We were both drinking, of course, but I remember her bitching so much I thought she must not be human. "She must be a robot. You should kill her!" The committee was getting louder and crazier. And then I thought, "No, don't hurt anyone, just run!" So I took the less evil of the two options and left this poor East Cobb uppity girl in this little niche of Atlanta called Mountain Park. I ran first to a few old neighbors I used to know in the area, and then I bolted like a madman, ran for the nasty ass lake and swam through it until it turned into a creek. I followed the creek, keeping my foot under water, of course, to hide it from the tracking satellites, following the creek path all the way through Brookfield West, the country club neighborhood I'd grown up in, keeping my foot submerged, untraceable, like a ninja! I maneuvered the way out to King Road, from where I walked to the closest Taco Mac. From there I called a cab and went home. All part of the mission.

I drank a little more and then woke up with the voices full blaring. For some reason they told me to go to Chattanooga. I had no idea why. My brother lives in Chattanooga I thought to myself, but I really didn't know why the hell I was being summoned to Chattanooga, to save my life. Must be a CIA mission. All I could do was follow orders I guess, pop some more amphetamines, and do what I'm told. So I hopped in my little white BMW 318 and I hauled ass to Route 75 northbound. I got off at an exit up 75 and saw one uniformed Military Police guy at a gas station on the way up. We stayed near each other on the entire ride up, and that was all the vindication I needed in the world to rest assured that I was just following my psychic CIA orders. Hawks seemed to be everywhere as well, and I was positive they had cameras in their eyes, trailing me. When I arrive in Chattanooga, I check in to a motel with the simple name Motel. That's it. I then walked to the Marriot where I also checked in. That's how spies roll, I guess.

Once I was in the Marriot bar, and had ordered a Crown and Seven, even though I didn't drink liquor, the news began announcing that North Korea had launched some missiles. And here I was summoned to Chattanooga, a town surrounded by mountains and powered by the gravity of water, the Tennessee Valley Authority, and in my head it was the perfect place to survive a nuclear blast. Surely this was no coincidence. More fuel for the flame. Now I was on a short list of VIP's who, when the CIA wanted their topnotch talent to survive the nuclear holocaust, were alerted via psychic hotline, of course. Also, Fox News stated that intelligence agencies were concerned about a group of Hezbollah infiltrating the Mexican border to attack anywhere inside the US, so keep your head up, the news said. To me, that meant: go hang out in as many bars as possible and keep an eye out for Hezbollah-looking grunts. Roger that, over and out. I was thinking and speaking military speak and jargon to the best of my ability to anyone who would listen, scary-eyed, drunk as ever.

When I met my brother at the Marriot and told him about the accumulation of events, my saving a jetliner, being connected to Langley via the psychic drunk hotline, and my dodging the North Korean missiles, my incredible intelligence must have gone right over his head, because he came right to the bar and he looked at me like I was a nut! He did his best to humor me and even took me out to dinner with his wife, which in my state of mind was a dare, to say the least. This must have been where I had the six or so Crown and Sevens he inventoried for the detox center the next day. After I told him and his wife they needed to procreate on orders from the CIA, and made several other ridiculous statements, he and I left his poor wife and went to another bar, where I kept a drunken eye out for Hezbollah guerillas potentially attacking Chattanooga, Tennessee.

Eventually he left me at a bar near the Marriott and went home, and thankfully at some point called my uncle confused as to what he should do, and rightfully so. I'd said a lot. At one point I think I asked him to take me into the woods and put a bullet in my head to stop the voices. That was, of course, in between the messages I was delivering and that was probably the closest to the truth of how I felt. I think I felt that I would be better off with a bullet in my head, than with 15 voices going off all at once.

He and my uncle plotted to get me into Dekalb County Crisis as soon as possible, and the next day they confronted me in the street, and on my way to the nuthouse I went. It was the beginning of the end of my drinking. Thank God.

The Long Road There

I didn't go insane overnight, it took 17 years of drinking and drugging to become the paranoid delusional nut I described in these last pages. When I finally did get sober for the final time on December 24th, 2006, I had attempted the program my own way several times over with not so great results. When I finally did it the way it was suggested -- got a sponsor, prayed specifically for strength to stay sober through the day, and thanks once I had, called my sponsor every day, began working the steps, and began going to 90 meetings in my first 90 days -- the urge to drink and drug left me almost instantaneously. The voices in my head went away almost as rapidly.

And then the next challenge appeared before me. I was diagnosed hepatitis C positive. The first time I heard someone in the rooms of AA mention it, I didn't even hear them correctly. I heard Hippopotamus Sea, and I was so fuzzy, I disregarded it as unimportant. I heard lots of strange things those first few months, as my mind was just a haze. I'd continue hearing about it in the rooms, though, and eventually I heard it correctly, hepatitis C, a blood disease that just so happens to attack the organ my vice required to filter alcohol, my liver. Though I'd only used needles once in my entire life, I asked the doctor to test me for it. At first he told me, "No, that's a drug addict's disease." I asked him to kindly check anyway, and sure enough, I was sick.

He told me the cure was twelve months of Interferon treatment that was most closely described as low-level chemotherapy. I'd watched my mom go through five years of chemotherapy before she died of cancer, and I was scared to death. I was scared of being an outcast forever. I was scared I'd be alone for the rest of my life, branded hep C positive, and I was scared it was going to kill me. My doctor told me it could take me five years to die or it could take twenty, but I would eventually need a new liver and mine was already very dysfunctional with my liver enzymes through the roof. My urine had been a deep dark brown for almost a year, and it had hurt to pee for a while, but I'd just written it off as being caused by too much drinking. When I'd finally quit drinking and my urine stayed that nasty color and it still hurt to pee, and my whole side of my body ached constantly, I knew something was badly wrong, I just hadn't known what. Had I not been in AA, and heard other members talk about hepatitis C in those rooms, I don't know if I'd have ever found out. The doctor also told me people with criminal records were not the highest on the list of liver transplant patients, and oh brother, I had a record. After just being relieved of the burden to drink, it was the last thing I wanted to hear. I thought a lot about how I'd gotten there, and just what I'd done to deserve this. After much thought, I'm a lucky man and life isn't fair. If it was, I'd be dead and buried, serving a life sentence, or worse.

The story I present to you from here on is not one of bold, ego-establishing tall tales, but that of an angry young man who had a traumatic event happen to him at a young age, and who stayed angry for years. It's about a punk fuck-up, who thought the world owed him something. It's a humbling statement of how I was, what happened and what I'm like now. It's an apology to some and an explanation to others. It's a thank you to Alcoholics Anonymous, and ultimately, I hope that it gives hope to some alcoholic, drug addict like me who has just found out he has hep C and thinks his life is over. Because it isn't. Most of the miracles in my life have felt like a punch to the gut at first, and so was finding out I was hep C positive. But the reality is I contracted a disease that attacked the one organ my primary vice required, the liver. And had I not gotten it, I don't know that I would have stayed sober. For me, it had to be life or death for me to finally get sober, and get that first year of sobriety under my belt. I had to be at the precipice, at the crossroads of my soul, and then and only then did I get real honest, real fast, and learn to live the program and stay sober.

The most ridiculous of my delusions are also the funniest too me now. They are ego driven, and the madness is funny to me in retrospect. That the CIA would need a repeat DUI offender with ruined credit to conduct its missions! When they checked me into that loony bin, I thought I was connected to Langley via a psychic connection and they were giving me orders to do their bidding one thought at a time! I'd really lost it. I had ridiculous evidence heaped upon even less stable assumptions and illusions to support all of my lofty hallucinations, but I'll come back to how whacky and out of hand these eventually got. They weren't just the byproduct of drugs and alcohol, though that was the nuclear fuel that drove them. They were the culmination of many years of anger, hatred, resentment, and finger pointing.

They started with the suicide of my father when I was 11 years old, the ultimate surrender, in my eyes, to the disease of alcoholism. My anger and resentments began for me around that time probably peaking around 2006 after my mother finally lost her brave battle with cancer. Within two weeks of her leaving this harsh world I had lost my mother, my father, my girlfriend of a considerably chaotic three-and-a-half years, and the medicine I was using to cope with it all, opiates. When she died, I quit opiates on my own using alcohol and Xanax to fight the withdrawal, but from that time forward, my drinking no longer even had a semblance of its prior control. I've met more than once person, whom after Dr. or even Hospital ordered morphine, lost all control over their drinking, and I'd be willing to bet that future generations will find more data regarding that aspect as well as genetic predispositions, but for me, I probably had it coming. In 2004, after my mom died, all control was lost, and within two years I was stark, raving mad, eventually leading me into the loony bin. It wasn't fun, or hilarious as I can make it sound now, it was the scariest time of my life. I'll try to capture my life up to the point I brought you in, what happened, how it got even worse, and what it's like now.

I will talk about Alcoholics Anonymous, though I won't share any names or break anyone's confidentiality, as that is actually against their policy, as well. But fortunately, another policy states my membership is only dependent upon my desire to stop drinking, so if they can't kick me out, I don't see how I can write this without speaking of it. I would rather share with you my solution than tiptoe around Captain Obvious and insult the reader's intelligence.

Just as those rocks were different shapes in the world's reality than they were in mine, the puzzle pieces didn't match the cover, and the CIA were communicating with me by thought, so was my alcohol and drug problem. Delusional. Not the main issue. My world was a mess. Einstein said "You can't fix a problem caused by a level of thinking with the same level of thinking." He was right. You can't fix a broken thing, your brain, with a broken thing, because your brain is, for all human concerns, broken when you come into Alcoholics Anonymous. Here's how I got there.

Childhood With My Father

I thought at the time I had a pretty good childhood, but looking back I had quite a bit of oddball behavior long before the traumatic events of my father's death. Not so odd in relation to other alcoholics I've met since getting sober though. For instance, when I was a toddler, my mom told me I once cracked the childproof lock on some pink medicine I enjoyed, and having enjoyed one sip, I'd snuck back into the fridge, and drank the entire bottle, forcing her to rush me to the emergency room to have my stomach pumped. I also remember wondering about death quite a bit for a child, once asking my dad if I had ever lived before and if I were to die would I live again. I was about 7 years old, and he was shocked, and told me what he knew about reincarnation and quizzed me about what I knew. Shortly after that philosophical discussion with my dad, my mom walked in on me in our kitchen holding the biggest knife we owned to my chest. I remember just being curious, not depressed.

I was also overly infatuated with girls from an early age. My mom caught me playing doctor with Kelly Rogers at age 5, and I repeated that business as often as possible with any girl that would let me. My mom was horrified, but my dad, drinking Budweiser in a can on the front lawn, thought it was hilarious. "Son, I remember a girlfriend I had that I used to go sneak a quick look at from time to time, but damn son, I was 16 years old!" and he laughed his jovial happy drunk laugh. He was great when he was great, but the happy drunk laugh would keep coming less and less, and the ominous stares, and screaming and yelling would ultimately replace that awesome laugh over the years, as his disease of alcoholism would get worse. Still, though, my behavior, with or without his drinking, was already a little odd long before any major tragedies, and in retrospect, our entire family was already a bit dysfunctional.

The funny thing about living in a dysfunctional home is as a child if you don't know any different, you think everybody's family is just as dysfunctional. On the outside everything was pretty much the same, I mean all our neighbors had about the same amount of stuff as we did, same style of houses, same cars. My dad was an atheist as far as I could tell because he barely ever went to church when our mother dragged us every single Sunday. He once told me "Son, never shine another man's shoes," which I would later find directly clashed with what I'd learned of Christ washing his disciples' feet. My mother would strong-arm him into church for Christmas and Easter, though, and once or twice he played drums for the church, though they used full drum sets less in the 80's than they do nowadays. The day they finally joined RUMC to become members, I remember my dad had gone to church and then gone to work, selling houses. Laying on his bed later that evening he said that the same day he'd joined the church he'd sold five homes and asked me "Do you think God did it?" I said I didn't know and he laughed and said "I don't know either." He'd thought about the coincidence at least, but he wasn't sold on God, I could tell.

My dad used to say we were Upper Middle Class, whatever that is supposed to mean. My first indication that things weren't exactly the same as my friends was that I never wanted to go home. I remember staying at the house of a friend, George Donaldson, and never wanting to go home to my mom and dad fighting. George's dad was straight out of a Norman Rockwell painting. I still tie my fishing hooks the way he taught me to. I couldn't get my dad to ever go fishing with me. I did notice George's dad was at his baseball games, and my dad was never there, but at the time I just didn't think much of it, and I think my mom would cover for him, saying he was working and she couldn't get him to take off. I couldn't get my dad to do much of anything but the occasional drunk driving mission through country roads with the moon roof open in the Cadillac to go get candy at midnight. When I did have friends over, this is what he would do to make himself the coolest dad ever. And it worked. My friends loved him. Keith York, Shane Oleander, who is now dead to this disease as well, and George Dickinson are the only friends I remember that knew my father. He died too early for most of my friends to have ever met him. But the Cadillac rides were the top end of his benders. The bottom end included screaming and yelling at the top of his lungs over silly chores not being finished, painful scoldings over unavoidable childhood blunders. My mom would swear physical violence took place frequently, though to this day I can't recall any specific details. She would claim I'd blocked it out and truthfully, I just don't know. I once cut my finger open with a Swiss army knife he'd given me for my birthday and he screamed and yelled at me over it as though I'd done it on purpose.

The ultimate realization that my home was dysfunctional came when I was walking home from Shane Oleander's house and I stopped halfway home and began crying right there in the street. The mystery of whether he was going to be in a good or bad mood had lost all its shine and I was just miserably afraid. Although my dad had those cool moments, his moments were just as apt to be verbally abusive and screaming and yelling at my mom, and I found myself spending lots of time by myself in the woods, or trying to spend time at other friends' houses. There was a distinct moment in time that I remember when I was basically told by Shane Oleander's mother that I needed to go home, and a fear welled up in my stomach. I remember clearly walking home as slowly as humanly possible, and thinking for the first time that this was not normal. I'd seen other friends cry about not being at home. I knew they looked forward to going home at the very least and I absolutely dreaded it. I eventually stopped crying and went home anyway, worried about getting in trouble with my mom, but that memory has stuck with me for a long time. In later life, when I've feared going home, something has clicked inside me. There's something seriously wrong with not wanting to go home, and I've used it as a barometer for my life more than once.

Towards the end of my dad's life it was super obvious why I wouldn't want to go home. I guess I was roughly 10 years old when my dad really went over the edge with his drinking. I stayed up listening to him talk on the phone many nights previous, and I'd heard about his DUI's and his arrests. One conversation sticks out in my head vividly. He was reading an Alcoholics Anonymous pamphlet to Bob Kleff, one of his infamous drinking buddies. They would talk for hours and at this time my dad had escalated from just drinking lots of beer that I recalled in the earlier memories, starting at around 5 years old, to then drinking lots of Piña Coladas with loads of rum in them. They looked like milkshakes and I probably stole more than one or two sips from them, but was still revolted by the taste at that age. Ah, if only that had lasted. So he was on the phone reading down the list of possible indications that one is an alcoholic. He and Bob were laughing their asses off about how ridiculous this list was. "If you HAVE to have a drink for New Year's Eve. If you've ever had a drink to ease the pain of a hangover from the night before. If you'd ever been in trouble with the law because of your drinking," and so on. He thought they were so funny, but even at the age of 8 or 9 when he was reading that, I could hear a bit of fear in his voice. I remember thinking clearly that he fit all those categories and that it didn't sound too funny, but I knew better than to correct my father. I honestly don't remember him hitting me ever, but my mom says it happened quite a bit. I don't know how much of that is exaggeration or justification for divorcing him, or how much I've simply blocked out. I know I have a lot of unexplained scars and I know I was scared of him, and I know he did verbally abuse us both. Regardless, I kept my mouth shut when I overheard that conversation.

Before he would get uncontrollably sick there were lots of signs he was headed in the wrong direction. My mom would spend hours crying, sometimes in the house, but often she would walk out into the woods and cry and pray, where I would follow her silently and watch. He was unpredictable, and it was maddening to watch her suffer. One time a year or so after we'd moved to Roswell, a considerable upgrade from our first home in Norcross, she dinged the garage with her beat up old station wagon. He came home, screaming and yelling and throwing a fit, over a tiny ding in the wood paneling of the garage. The tirade lasted hours. Then a few months later, three kids running wild, I think my brother Carson darted out of the station wagon at the last second as she was backing out of the garage again, leaving the door open, so that when she reversed she not only ripped the door almost clean off the station wagon, she almost took out the wall separating the two garage door entrances. Fear instantly came over her face and I was immediately scared for her as well. She began panicking, crying, calling friends, pacing the driveway in a frenzy. Eventually she mustered up the courage to call Morris, my dad, and just face the music, telling him the worst. We were all scared for her, and watched her apprehensive, filled with fear. When she told him, he just laughed, said not to worry about it. It was insane, there was no logic to his reaction, no right or reason, it would have almost been easier to understand if he'd gotten mad.

Just a few months later, on my brother's birthday, I crashed my bike accidentally into the same stupid garage, and you'd have thought I burned the whole house down. It was unpredictable. That memory becomes hazy for me as well, because it got so bad. After being screamed at, berated in front of all my brother's friends, and heavy-handedly marched to my room, I took a little miniature hammer that was in my room, and I began hitting myself in the head numerous times, over and over again until I had obvious bumps all over my scalp. I went to my mom's room after a while and had her feel my head, and she of course accused my dad of beating me. Amazing manipulation for a child. The fight went on for days, and quite honestly, aside from the bike, I can't remember what's real and what's not from that story. So much was told and retold by my mother over the years, I've really lost a point of reference on what happened and what didn't. I believe he was verbally abusive, and a little rough handed and being a manipulative, vengeful victim, I banged my head up to get him in trouble and get my mom's attention. My mom would later counter that memory and say he'd definitely beat me that day giving me those bumps on my head, and I created the self-inflicted story to protect my fragile little psyche. Same as I can't remember why I've got a huge gash scar on my forehead, she would later tell me. Short of hypnosis I guess I'll never really know. Regardless, it was all a little less than stable and it was progressively getting worse.

A year or two later he'd leveraged quite a bit to start a new business, Roswell Realtors, and buy a large house in Brookfield West, the country club I remember all the cool kids lived in and I'd wished for ages we'd move to. Right after we moved in there, shit starting hitting the fan. He began drinking nonstop. It had progressed from drinking beer all day to the Piña Coladas, to now just chugging vodka at the kitchen table. The fights were intense and daily, and my mom cried a lot as did I, and my little brother and sister. She had three children with this man, and here he was clearly losing his mind. He made my house a living hell that year. It was fifth grade. I remember beginning to really act out around this time, though I didn't know why at the time. James Floyd, a skater kid, wanted to fight me because I'd made fun of his poor mother for being our bus driver. I wish he'd kicked my little snobby ass, but he didn't. He received a beating the likes of which if my 12 year old son inflicted on anyone else I'd have a shrink talk to him. I guess James and everyone involved in that little scuffle thought that a fight consisted of a few shoves. Herein lies some evidence that I knew what a punch was. I punched James in the face hard several times until he was bleeding all over the bathroom floor. He complained of having a metal plate in his head, so I picked him up and put him in a head lock and slammed his head into the bathroom wall. I was mean, I was cruel, and I don't know where it came from. James Floyd has also since died of addiction related issues, and I wish I'd been more kind to him back then. Who knew we would have so much in common?

By then though my dad had certainly crossed the threshold and I didn't want to bring friends home anymore, period. By fifth grade the ups and downs of an alcoholic father had turned into only the downs. I remember waking up to go to school and seeing him drinking at the kitchen table. When I'd come home from school he would be watching CNN at first, and ranting and raving madly at the television. He was absolutely disgusted that they would repeat the exact same 30 minute segment over and over. I can still get irritated by that monotony but his ranting was just lunacy. "Brainwash Bryan, over and over again! Watch now that 30 minutes is over it will start again!" And he would go from laughter to tears over and over again. For months this continued, and then it got even worse. He began watching the TV without the TV on. He would have the exact same ranting sessions, the same big worded diatribes with CNN, but now, the TV was off. I lost all hope in him at this point. Now I really didn't think he would get better. I didn't think he was an alcoholic, I just thought he was nuts. Obviously the urge to stay away from home stayed strong.

Eventually I remember my mother telling us that he was going away to get help. I had no real idea of what this meant at the time, but she did share that he had been checked in somewhere by herself, my uncle and my aunt. That it took three people to check him in, and that he would only be in there a few days, but that there was hope. I wasn't buying it still. After that he would supposedly go to Alcoholic Anonymous meetings every day. I do remember getting a little bit of hope out of this, though it was all so vague that I didn't know what to think. Mostly I remember thinking he was just absolutely insane and beyond the possibility of help. I remember thinking, yeah he's an alcoholic, but he's also absolutely crazy. What do we do about that? How are Alcoholic Anonymous meetings going to help him think the TV is on when it's really off?

This went on and off for a few more months throughout the winter of 1988-1989 or my 5th grade year. There must have been a lot of talk about the Alcoholics Anonymous meetings because there is a moment in time that stands out vividly, and would stand out in my head for years to come. Eventually when I had my moment of clarity, this moment stood out in time above much chaos and confusion. It was lucid and clear as day. We were at the Roswell Recreation center, and my brother had a basketball game. How my mother kept us in such domestic trivialities while this chaos went on is incredible and ultimately speaks volumes of my mother and her desire for everything to be status quo. So there is my dad, miserable at this game, and we walked outside where I recall everything clearly. I hugged him and said, "Why don't you quit drinking and go to the AA meetings?" He looked me in the eyes, with real fear in them, and said, "They don't work. As soon as I leave the meetings I go right to the store to get more to drink. Alcohol is everywhere." The fear in his eyes was so real, and so concentrated that I've never quite been able to get it out of my mind. I don't think I really associated it with alcoholism at the time, but more or less with insanity. I really just thought he was nuts. That statement, though would be a reason why I didn't try AA for many years. It didn't work, my dad had told me so quite clearly with a real fear in his eyes. I often felt like my dad gave me far too much information, but this would have wider implications than his telling me there was no Santa Claus in first grade.

That was in the winter, but things got worse. My poor mother began training to be a real estate agent. Here begins a resentment, one of my first. I remember clearly asking her why we didn't just move to a smaller house, but she was so adamantly against going backwards that she was almost insulted that I'd mentioned it. It made sense to me, but she abhorred the idea. And so she was training to be a real estate agent. Simultaneously, she had kicked my constantly drunk father out of the house and he'd moved back in with his parents in Daytona, Florida. I later learned he'd just increased his drinking down there, and gone deeper and deeper into insanity, if that were possible. I would soon learn that it was.

He began calling the house. Night and day, relentlessly, and every time the phone would ring my poor mother would run somewhere and cry. Occasionally, she would pick up the phone, speak with him, and then cry. More than one phone was destroyed. It was incessant, he would call day in, day out, twenty or more times and eventually she'd had it. She packed us all up and we went on an extended tour of every relative we had in the southeast. For at least a month or so, we were on the road, visiting relatives. I later learned she was having attorneys set up a restraining order and the like. When we returned, the calls had stopped for a while, and my mom began her real estate career wholeheartedly. This required that we get a baby sitter, and the first one we had was Dagmar Thorngood. My brother and sister and I must have been hell to watch over already. Add an insane, alcoholic, stalker father into the mix and my mom must have given this poor girl a hell of a pep talk to stick around. The insanity of my father had gotten worse. We all knew he wasn't supposed to be around the house at this time, but one day we all came back from a trip to Target or some such, and there was my dad, drunk at the kitchen table in all his madness, with about five different bottles of liquor in front of him.

He was out of his fucking mind at this stage. I remember him crying and coming at me with tears in his eyes, and then I remember Dagmar screaming at the top of her lungs to get Carrie and Carson into the car while I stopped my dad, and was confronting him. I think I was telling him, quite disrespectfully to quit bothering us, and stop calling us. It's very vague, but I remember there being a bit of a conflict in the garage as he stormed out drunk towards what used to be his little atomic family. It was no longer. Dagmar and I rushed my little brother and sister into the car, hauled away at top speed, and my mother was contacted shortly thereafter. I later learned he was arrested at the scene for violating a restraining order and he'd be in jail for a long, long time. We would later hear from my mom that he was there to kill us all and put us out of our misery, but I never really knew whether to believe that or not. Once she'd kicked him out, the stories had gotten pretty lopsided against him. Now, though, I think it's possible, seeing how far off the edge he'd gone. This must have been early August of 1989 or so. He wasn't in jail for more than a day or two, and the calls began again. Speaking to him on the phone, I would take advantage of his ludicrous state of mind. Cussing him out as disrespectfully as humanly possible, just because I could and of course because I was so tired of all the drama, and watching my poor mom suffer through it all. I was 11 years old and I was cursing out my father for not letting us have a trampoline and other such insults he'd propagated upon our childhood, outside of the realm of his lunacy. For instance, there was more than one dessert I'd missed that I now took full advantage of in order to get my verbal revenge. He was so weak and pitiful that he was letting his 11 year old boy say things that just two years prior would have put him into a rage. He was weak, and he was pathetic to me at this point, he was a nuisance. Life had been better when he wasn't calling 30 times a day and we were all looking forward to him not calling that whole time he was supposed to be in jail, but someone let him out. So here he was calling.

Now also he'd gotten so depressed that he was discussing the merits of suicide with me. More than once he said "I should just commit suicide. This drinking is just slow suicide I should just do it, man up and do it." Well after a while, this started to sound like a great idea. I didn't want to hear from him anymore. I didn't want to hear the man I used to idolize and worship, discuss how his only option was to kill himself. I didn't want to hear my mom cry the next time the phone rang. I didn't want the cops called anymore. I didn't want him to die, but I didn't want to live like this anymore either.

One day, he called again, I think it'd been going on a few weeks in August, and I'd heard it all. We'd talked for hours, or rather, he'd rambled and rambled for hours and I'd heard it all. I picked up the phone. My mom teared up and left the kitchen, and I said, "Dad, why don't you just do us all a favor and kill yourself?" And I meant it. What kind of sick bastard lets that be the last thing you hear your son say before killing yourself? A sick alcoholic, that's who. It was the last words I ever got to say to my dad. He shot himself with a .357 on August 22, 1989. I hate that day, even 20 years later.

People are so irritating when someone dies. To this day I hate anyone who claims friendship they didn't have with someone who just died. My dad was a prick for the last two years of his life, and he died alone, holed up in a hotel room all by himself, but damn you should have seen the funeral. You'd have thought he had his own television show. You'd have thought he worked miracles. I guess he must have been a nice guy before he lost his mind, because a lot of people were there saying a lot of stupid things.

I remember my Uncle Greg Mendolson taking me to the side and telling me exactly what a .357 caliber bullet would do to a person's head. He explained quite technically, that a bullet of that caliber would cause such a large hole on the backside of the head with such force, that it would then suck the rest of the head clear off of his head, leaving my dad completely headless or as he explained, decapitated. Hurray, new vocabulary! So that when people said he'd blown his head off, they were being absolutely literal. Then I remember him asking me "Why would he do that?" over and over again, a little drunk himself at the time, and I remember thinking, I don't know. Why did he do it, and why are you telling me the grotesque details of his entire head coming off? He told me all this and then explained that that is why it had to be a closed casket funeral. Of all the stupid things people said to me the days following my dad's death, that was the one statement that stuck out as the most ludicrous. When he told me he'd killed himself in a Red Roof Inn, and having just explained just how much of his head must have hit the roof, I couldn't help but chuckle, and wonder if in my Dad's sick insanity, he'd played one last joke. The Red Roof Inn, since he'd planned on splattering the roof red. This, sick as it is, has cracked me up on more than one occasion. The ultimate prankster, I thought, romantically almost, though in reality, he was so far gone, the irony was probably just a coincidence. I don't think he meant any harm, I think he was just as confused as me and of course drunk. I forgave him almost instantly but it stuck with me.

I'll tell you who I didn't forgive, though. Dan Jones, my soon to be stepfather who was there at the funeral and my mom had been dating him. I'd even told my dad about Dan Jones once or twice in our long conversations when I was in the taking advantage of my drunk dad stage, just to piss him off. Well he was at the funeral, and it pissed me off quite a bit. Dan Jones could have been Gandhi, walked on water, freed the slaves and died for my sins, and I'd have still hated whoever was there at my dad's funeral and would soon replace my father as my mom's husband. Hell, they weren't even officially divorced yet as I knew it. If they were, it was still very fresh and I was pissed. I hated him instantly and it took me years to get over it. In fact it was one of the biggest resentments I had to work through when I got sober, but when I did forgive him, totally and utterly, and love him for who he is, it was like a huge boulder lifted from my shoulders. He really is a good man who was just put in a rough situation and I did very little to ever make it any easier for him. But back then it was a pure, clean, hatred. Instantly and without real cause, he just wasn't my dad, and my dad was gone forever. So go to hell Dan Jones. The worst kind of anger is seemingly justified and I would hold onto those emotions toward him for years. An alcoholic can hold a grudge, right or wrong, and despite his kindness and effort, I would hate that man just underneath the surface and visibly for years to come.

Leading up to my dad's death of course, my mom had been trying to sell her first house as a real estate agent. She was struggling with every ounce of her strength for us to stay in the country club home we'd all become accustomed to living in and she didn't want to downgrade as I suggested and had even hoped for rather than see her stress this much. I mean every phone conversation was about money. There were debt collectors from my father's failed business, there was the mortgage company, every month we were under threat of foreclosure and I was just old enough to grasp how dire the situation was. Also it was just a stark polar opposite of the financial freedom we'd all experienced while my dad's alcoholism was catching up to him, for me from the age of 5-10 or so, we'd been fairly well off. Upper Middle Class, as I was told, with annual vacations to Hilton Head and the like.

So it had been financial dire straits for almost a year. I'd be lying if I said that we weren't all just a little relieved when my dad died. I mean, he'd tried to kill us, or so my mom said to get the restraining order, though I don't remember it. But still the phone calls, the drama, the waiting for him to die. When he died, I was at first shocked, then sad, then relieved, then angry. I stayed angry from there on out. So right about the time the relief was kicking in we found out that he had a huge life insurance policy and that our financial troubles were over. My mom told us right out that she would be collecting about $750,000 in life insurance. In my skewed mind I remember Dan Jones showing up more and more after that. I thought he was a gold digging opportunistic son of a bitch from that point on. I may have been 11 but I knew what the relief of money was. I mean I still held that a lot of my dad's insanity had been the direct result of the money problems. They weren't, but I certainly thought that from time to time. I immediately associated Dan Jones's ever-increasing presence with my mom's new found money, regardless of the truth, in my hateful, prejudiced mind, this became a fact. One of my first major resentments, real or not, started from the very beginning of our knowing each other.

By the summer of the next year, my mom came back from a date with Dan one night to tell us how excited she was that Dan Jones had asked her to marry him. I remember thinking, well that sucks. She wouldn't hear of it though. She was so excited, and she wanted me to be excited and I just wasn't. She did manage to get my little brother and little sister excited about it though. I simply couldn't. I didn't like him, and I thought he was after her money. My brother and sister didn't see the problem with him, but I resented him from the very beginning. I really don't think it would have mattered who it was. I would have hated whoever tried to fill those shoes period. Dan Jones was just the lucky guy I guess. I was vaguely excited about having another baby sister for some reason, I think mainly because I remember my mom and dad hoping and praying to have their third be a girl, and when Carrie came they were ecstatic, so though I was not keen on Dan Jones at all, his daughter, my soon to be sister didn't bother me too much at all, and Terry's name, even rhymed with Carrie, so it seemed to be fate. It wouldn't dampen my resentments towards Dan Jones though, she would just be another little sister to torture, as big brothers will.

I had to miss an all-star baseball game to go to their wedding. Strike two. Strike three was when I saw my mom and new stepdad kiss. In my head, this guy would be public enemy number 1 for life, I thought. For the rest of her life, anytime I saw them have any amount of affection I would get and hold a new resentment. Alcoholics can hold a grudge, my friend. Spoken or not, it may be there just underneath the surface for decades upon decades, and I'm no better. To me I guess it was rubbing it in my face what was fundamentally wrong in the first place. Had I accepted their marriage, my life would have been much easier. But that would have been too easy, and I'm an alcoholic. I can complicate anything and usually do.

Resentments and rebellion building, I began acting out

almost instantly, even more so than I'd already done. I mean Shane Oleander and I had been in the principal's office a couple of times together, but now I would take it to a new level. I knifed a kid's bicycle tire at school, got caught shoplifting at Oshmans, and began sneaking into my mom and Dan 's room every night when they were sleeping. With an air of superiority I would creep into their bedroom at night and rummage through Dan 's wallets, play with his Beretta 9 millimeter, and generally just snoop through everything he and my mom owned. Eventually I came across some tapes that my mom had hidden in the closet. When I played them I found them to be tapes my father had made just before blowing his head off. Several hours of drunk ramblings in which he apologized, ranted, cried, begged for another chance with my mom, then seemingly remembered he was about to kill himself and would become prideful, superior to the human condition almost, since he'd found a way out. I couldn't stop listening to them, and they made me angry, sad, guilty, you name it. They weren't all that sane, and didn't make much sense as he was belligerently drunk in all the audio tapes, but he did apologize profusely for abusing my mom and me, crying "Why would I hit such a sweet little boy. I'm so sorry, Meredith, I'm so sorry." That was really the first real evidence I had of him being abusive to me, as I truly don't remember any of it, and that isn't exactly proof, as he was wasted throughout the entire tapes, and my mom could have implied all that in his last months of insanity, and he just incorporated it into his guilt. Who knows, but I certainly took it at the time as an excuse for me to do anything and everything. The tapes rambled on about how could she have divorced him, and begun dating Dan Jones, who as always was an easy target? Hearing my dad angry with Dan Jones, and him being beyond the grave, made it all the more justified for me to have a resentment towards him as well. It seemed the only right thing to do, to carry on that jealousy and hatred on my father's behalf. I would eventually lose those psychotic pre-suicide ramblings and I wish my mom had lost them before I got my sneaky hands on them. I still don't remember being beaten or abused, but those tapes telling me otherwise gave me fodder and excuse for years to come. They would simultaneously justify ridiculous behavior and my unfair resentment to Dan Jones, to my mom, and even God himself, and they just couldn't have been helpful to a 12 year old kid, trying to find himself, and trying to understand his place in the world, and how his father had been torn from it. Those tapes played a large part in the nourishment of my darker side.

To add to all the drama around the time of my father's death I was diagnosed with a heart murmur. My mom's dad had died of a heart attack at 48, and her favorite writer, Lewis Grizzard, had the exact same heart complication we found out about, and though alive at the time had written extensively about the pain of open heart surgery, and my mom had absorbed it all. He would later die, fueling her worries about her little boy's eventual health issues. But at the time we found out, he'd just had a few major operations surrounding it, but it still somehow made it personal for my mom. She became downright panicky about my heart murmur. We went to several heart doctors who told her a variety of things, but most seemed to agree, I would need massive open heart surgery by the time I was 25. It was scary but what was scarier was that we didn't have health insurance for me at the time because the doctors found it as my dad was in his downward spiral and of course wasn't paying those pesky health insurance bills, thus it became a pre-existing condition. Now that we had money from the life insurance, the insurance companies wouldn't insure me because it was a pre-existing condition. That freaked her out a lot. Cory Black's dad told me, "Don't worry about it, son, if anything happens to you, I'll pay for it personally," and that settled it for me, but my mom remained freaked out about it for years. Once the rebellion and anarchy of my youth really starting kicking in full steam, I would begin stealing her Benson & Hedges cigarettes, or pick them up off the street. I can honestly remember the moment I smoked my first one thinking "I wonder what it's like to be addicted to something." It was a half mile from my house at the bottom of a steep paved hill, in between Shane Oleander's house and mine, and my sister was walking with me. Right out of the gutter and into my lips, and Carrie's eyes bulged, young, but not unaware of the bad I was doing. That was a piss-poor decision at age 12 years old or so. My God, it pissed my mom off to no end. "You have a heart condition!" she would scream! "You're going to kill yourself, just like your father!" I must have heard that a million times over, but I kept on doing it, disobeying her, hiding it at first, and then later, blatantly in the house, in front of her, wherever. It didn't take me a long time to get addicted to cigarettes, against all the advice of everyone in my family, but I wouldn't listen. At 12 years old, in our society, it immediately made me a liar and thief. I had to lie to my parents constantly, and I had to begin stealing the cigarettes, or stealing money for them, constantly. It's subtle, but it happens, and once you've begun down that path, those little things begin adding up. Smoking was a terrible mistake, but it certainly wasn't my first obsession.

Obsessing About Sex

The first thing I can really remember obsessing about was having sex. I'd always had girlfriends up to this point, but in 7th grade, upon first laying eyes upon Anne Marie Clark, I had a new goal. Man, what I wanted was to conquer those mountains she so early had begun to flaunt in the school cafeteria. She was probably doing her best to cover them up, but to a 12 or 13 year old boy, she may as well have been nude. I was obsessed instantly. And I wanted more than just those as well, as by now, I'd seen a porn or two in Corey Black's basement, and I intended on at least imitating what I'd seen these grown adults get so worked up over. I saw her at the Roswell Recreation after school one day and immediately asked her out. She said yes and so we were going out and things were going well. After a month or so I think I began negotiating to have sex with her. She was very reluctant at first but I put in the extra work, talking to her at school and on the phone day and night. I must have passed a thousand notes. Then she would come up with new objections, like that I would dump her after we'd done the deed. Had she known of my addictive tendencies she would have been well aware that I would not abandon the powerful drug of sex, but quite the opposite, demand it repeatedly over and over again, in more and more ways, in stranger and shadier places and circumstances, until I eventually self destructed the good scenario we had going. It took me seven months of talking late into the evening, much to the chagrin of my mother, and her parents. We talked on the phone for hours daily, and I probably passed her 17 thousand notes, of a romantic and begging nature. Probably mostly begging, as my technique wasn't quite honed at this point. First base, or french kissing came quickly, second base was maybe a month or so into it, but the coveted third and the Holy Home Plate, took some serious bargaining. I think I would have promised her my soul had she asked for it. She tortured me for seven months, saying no, while I bragged to my friends about my booby excursions, but eventually, seven months into our going out, we got down to brass tacks.

Needless to say, I had absolutely no clue what the hell I was doing. I knew that condoms still didn't fit, but I wasn't about to let that get the better of me. I'd grow into those eventually, but it was by no means an indicator that perhaps I was too young to be having sex. I just knew, by God I would be the first to do it, and I would be awesome at it, and I thought of little else until it happened. Not knowing how it worked was a slight problem though. I mean, I knew where to put it, I just had no idea when it was finished, or how. The first time we did it I simply remember putting the oversized condom on, getting it in (maybe) making a few slight stokes, and then declaring a mental victory. I had done it. Mission accomplished. I had had sex. I was my own personal hero. The only downside to this was that MOST if not ALL of the negotiations with Anne Marie had been regarding my vow of silence regarding this most sacred of events. I had sworn up and down, down and out never to tell a soul. So frightened was she that the entire school would find out, I think I even took a blood oath. So my victory remained a silent one, I could tell no one. Not that there was much to tell about my prepubescent awkward sex event, but still, to me it was huge, and I couldn't tell a soul. I didn't let it bother me too much, though, I was 13, I had a girlfriend and we had had sex! The funny thing is, as mental of a victory as it was, physically it was a letdown. You see, nobody had ever taught me to jack off, or what an ejaculation or coming even was. That first time with Anne Marie I didn't even come close -- hell, I didn't know what it was or meant. In retrospect, I guess we never watched porn all the way to the money shot.

Shortly thereafter I was at Shane Oleander's house and we were all enjoying some stolen cigarettes for the buzz they gave us, (though I don't remember actually getting a buzz, just saying that I did) and me, James Price Watson and Kyle Foster were all talking about how much jacking off we did, and I was of course agreeing and even bragging about how much I did it as well. But I didn't know what the hell they were talking about. Shane explained the ritual, and basically the nuts and bolts involved a porn magazine, some Vaseline, and rubbing your penis for about five minutes until the "come" came out of it. I bit my tongue the entire time but wanted to scream at the top of my lungs, "Me and my girlfriend had sex!" but I was sworn to secrecy. I of course agreed that I "beat off" all the time, eventually went home, and began scrounging around the house for the materials required. I came up with a Victoria's Secret catalog and some Neosporin. Close enough.

I did this ritual for what must have been an hour and a half with absolutely no effect but a little sticky stuff coming to the tip of my penis, so eventually I just resigned to the fact that that must be "come" and I had in fact accomplished the mission. It wasn't that thrilling, and in the following days I walked in on my mom watching an Oprah episode that discussed how some of the Victoria Secret's models were actually transvestites, and I was immediately disgusted, and wanted some clarifications on this and whether it affected me. But it was a little too embarrassing to ask her, and God knows, my friends weren't about to hear about it. I let it go, but I still don't look at those Victoria Secret's catalogs. Sounded like a homosexual ambush to me and I've been wary ever since.

So I'd had sex, and I'd "jacked off" and neither were all that great. My talk time probably tapered off with Anne Marie having accomplished the mission, but eventually I ended up back over there and we were doing the deed again. She must have known I'd done it all wrong or maybe women just have sex for different reasons, but she wanted to do it again, so why not? We were in her bedroom and this time after I flopped the rubber back on my poor little pecker, she rolled me over and got on top of me. We could hear her parents walking up and down the hall of her small little house. She went back and forth repeatedly for a long time and then all of a sudden, it started feeling really good. I mean different from the Neosporin and the Victoria's Secret magazine, different from the "sex" we'd had before, I mean it really started feeling fantastic! I couldn't believe how good it was feeling, it was phenomenal. And then without warning and out of the blue, BOOM, BANG, POW, my penis had exploded! I threw her off me to check to see what had happened! I expected to look down and see a bleeding stump, I literally thought my poor pecker had fallen off, the explosion was unlike anything I'd ever felt in my entire 13 years of life! It was incredible, it was magical, it was really sex! This is why it was such a big deal! I felt relieved to see my little pecker doing just fine, the oversized condom still intact, and now I felt like a MAN! I had come!

From there on out "jacking off" began working as well. Now that I knew what the actual goal was, and to stay away from the gay porn of Victoria's Secret, I must say I was into advanced jacking off before too long and I mean not once or twice a day, but easily five or six times daily. It's probable that 13 year old boys' peckers would stay smaller than condoms, were it not for the amount of pulling and stretching they perform upon them once they realize the goal. Jacking off, and as much sex with my girlfriend as humanly possible became my way of life. Once I realized what an orgasm was, I was a maniac for years. I think most addictive personalities are, and for that matter, probably just most boys, but what do I know. I know I overdid it, that's for sure.

In the spring and summer of 7th grade, Anne Marie and I had sex everywhere two 13 year olds could be alone for five minutes or more. We did it at the Roswell Rec, the local recreational park and hangout, quite a bit, just because she lived nearby and I could scam my mom into letting me spend hours at a time up there. The poor Roswell Rec was made love on under the bleachers, during and after basketball games. In the umpire booths of every baseball field in the park, over six or seven of them, and when occasionally every one of those was locked, we'd just do it in the woods. We were in love. And I'm an addict. I'm addicted to whatever you got and in 7th grade, before alcohol, before pot, I was addicted to sex. One time, and the event that broke my vow of silence, we were having sex in the umpire booth, and the entire football team came to practice on the baseball field in which we were getting it on. We could either wait it out or walk outside and be busted. One of us had to get home soon, and it was probably me, but the poor thing and I walked out of the umpire booth to the entire football team laughing their asses off at us, her head down in shame and messed up hair, me with my dumb, shit eating grin, and internal victory. About a week or two before, someone had looked in Anne Marie's purse and found her birth control pills, and I knew that everyone knew, but I don't think she did quite yet at the time. Within a week she did, and it was drama. The good news was that everyone knew anyway, and I could now break my code of silence without it being too much of an anchor on my conscience. I told my best friend Shane Oleander shortly thereafter.

That summer was an endless cycle of sneaking out, walking about 10 miles each way to go to Anne Marie 's house, and often times her walking over to mine, just to have sex. Usually addicts will go to any length to get a fix, and that was my fix at the time, before the drugs and drinking.

My poor mother would eventually find out about our sexual adventures first hand, in the worst way possible for any mom I'm sure, by walking directly into my room as her 13 year old naked son was mounting his 13 year old girlfriend. She screamed and yelled and didn't leave the room until we were both clothed, red with rage, never stopping her screaming at us to even breathe it seemed. Almost foaming at the mouth she snatched Anne Marie's hand, once she'd awkwardly put on her clothes, and marched her, dragging her at some stages by the arm, out to her car, and promptly drove her home. Anne Marie later told me the car ride home was absolute hell, my mom bashing all men without mercy, telling her to break up with me and remain celibate, join a nunnery, and so on. Anne Marie went home crying to her mom who promptly called my mom and gave her an earful, defending her daughter, of course, and telling my mom she could have handled it with a little more delicacy. This set the stage for animosity between our two families for years to come, as I assure you, my mom wasn't about to apologize. I was embarrassed, but it all just helped fuel the rebellion which was already burning by this stage.

Rebel Ouija Cause

Another rebellious thing we did in the summer of 7th and 8th grade was to play with Ouija boards. We created the boards ourselves, figuring they more likely to work that way. It was fun and we thought it was pretty harmless. We did it a lot to absolutely zero result, and then one day Josh Daugherty and I were messing with one in his bedroom. Stone cold sober, we both felt the thing move. Whether it was our overactive imaginations or not, I don't know, but it was creepy to us both, and it began telling us it was a spirit, giving us its name, and telling us a short story of its experience of existence during the middle ages. Josh and I both freaked out, both accused the other of making it move, and eventually we just threw the board away. That story by itself would have been forgotten long ago, had Josh's mother not awoken us at the butt crack of dawn the next morning and rushed us to Service Merchandise to buy us crucifixes. She didn't tell us why at first, but when we arrived at the store it was an hour before it opened, so during that time she explained her panic. "Last night I dreamed there was a demon standing over your bed, dark and intent, staring down at your souls. I woke up sweating and I just knew I had to do this." It was all very eerie and strange, coincidental and scary, so I wore that gold crucifix she bought us both for years to come. I wouldn't think of that again for years, but that experience and Josh's mom's fear, did put a stop to our Ouija board explorations. I'd never put much stock in demons, but her fear was real, and it would stay with me how moved she'd become.

But despite the small bouts of rebellion over that summer, when 8th grade started, my school career continued to go very well. I was in advanced mathematics, TAG, or Talented and Gifted, and I recall getting straight A's for the most part. I remember in particular, the fall of 8th grade, my mom and stepdad were thrilled when I came home from the first quarter with straight A's. They were proud and it was agreed that a birthday and good grades celebration was in order for the next day, and they dropped me off at the house of a friend, Josh Daugherty. This had to have been a school night, because the next day I would have my first hangover, and it would be in school. I would also not have a memory of what I did the day before.

Somehow a collection of us 8th graders were all gathered at Anne Hamilton's house, a pretty, albeit awkward redhead who'd just moved down from New Jersey. I remember Josh Daugherty, myself, Chris Tulane, Angie Hamilton, and Anne Marie Clark, my girlfriend, who is now my favorite, one and only ex-wife. Anne's parents had a liquor cabinet, and I think the girls began by taking a few shots. I don't know why, and I don't know how it came to pass, other than me just trying to be a big shot, or be the coolest one in the room, but I began my drinking career by proceeding to down 16 shots in a row, without puking them up...yet. I then took my girlfriend into the garage and had what I remembered as fantastic sex on the weight bench downstairs in the garage. Walking back up those stairs is my last conscious memory of that day. As for my poor parents, they arrived at Josh Daugherty's a few hours later and I was passed out in the driveway, smelling of puke and piss. They took me home and I awoke to find myself with a horrendous headache, naked in my own bed, not knowing how I'd arrived there. I got to school and found out the awful details.

I had apparently cussed everyone out at least once or twice, calling one of my good friends "LD" for learning disorder, because I was just oh-so-clever. Chris Tulane took it like a champ, though, and was the chief instrument in getting me into the shower to hose me down, after I had pulled out my little 13 year old pecker and pissed all over poor Anne Hamilton's living room. Not wanting to miss a spot, I was informed, I stripped naked on the second pass, starting pissing on the couch and ran through her living room to make quite certain I distributed the urine fairly, across all her furniture. This cycle continued for several hours, I'm told, pissing on important things or people, stripping naked, puking, being thrown in the shower, and making the world quite certain of what a jackass I was, until I eventually passed out. It should also be noted that the very close friend of mine whom I superiorly called "LD" now beats me at Facebook Scrabble every single time we play...but I digress. I truly don't remember a lick of that first drunk.

I was told the next day so much damning information, with a smile on the teller's face that it began to be told as a joke, like it was a cool thing. I was appalled at first, but suddenly I was the talk of the entire school, in a manner that seemed to entertain everyone, and therefore made me cool in a sense. I didn't feel cool, and if Chris Tulane had decided to beat my ass I'm sure the story would have been told differently. But he didn't, and so the story was an instant hit, it seemed. Still, I was mortified those first few days. After a while, though, I just felt like a bad ass for drinking 16 shots and surviving. At least, that's what I thought, and this being a disease of perception, thus began the lies. I was now a hero in my own head for pissing all over Amy's house and telling my good friend he was stupid. I still don't remember anything of that entire day, but it really isn't important. What I did with the blackout and following story is more important. The fact that I was first quite sincerely offended by the tales of this Dr. Jekyll and Mr. Hyde story, but within a few hours or days had twisted it in my own head to believe it was not only OK, but part of the Jared Bryan Smith persona or mystique -- that fact speaks volumes for what alcoholics do to justify their behavior, and how instantaneous it was for me in my case. Within a few days, I was ready to drink again.

Drugs with the Doors

It's remarkable but true, that for an eighth grader it is easier to get pot, LSD, or even cocaine than it is to get alcohol. From the time I saw The Doors with Val Kilmer, I began immersing myself in everything possible, Jim Morrison related. I obsessed as only addicts can obsess. I read his biographies, I listened to every CD I could get my hands on, including American Poet and I watched that Oliver Stone movie obsessively. I thought LSD would be the magic event that changed my life. It would end up changing my life, but not in a good way, and lo and behold, I did not become a rock star, though I did write a ton of rambling, not so great poetry. Here's a sample gem. I thought it proved I was a genius poet for a long time. Josh Daugherty had somehow scored some Dexedrine, or amphetamines, when I wrote this and I believed it proved beyond a shadow of a doubt I was destined to be a writer. Now when I read it, I see it as an atheist's justification, and crudely written at that:

Unknown Origin

As I stand here, lying down,
Things confused, stars and ground.
Revolution of endless thought,
Crowds my mind rejecting the taught.
Books by men who want, not by men who wander,
Reading in circles of theories, leaving souls who ponder.
Childish game, considered and watched,
Yet answers appear rhetorical,
Always there but not historical.
Thoughts of demons, murder, rape,
Sustained in mind, yet penetrate,
The boundaries known within our space,
Found observed through tattered lace,
Of Unknown Origin, or unwanted,
Prison of souls, tortured taunted.
Gleaming eyes and casual lies.

Unnecessary train of thought wandering aimlessly;
Royalty of Gods, and yet she stood there painlessly.
Flames spread with no emotion,
Planets collide with no commotion.
Science unknown, religion explains,
Some men gain, all men get,
One man earns, time to forget.
Block out life, except no answers,
History beckons of repeat,
Sanctuary's sacrifice, men kiss others feet.
God's of mind and curiosity,
Laugh at mortal's ferocity.
Invention of Gods' created by ignorance, or boredom?
Of philosophy, science and such.
Jesus found in man's own mind:
Created by,
Denied by,
Executed by,
And now is praised by: ignorance or boredom.
Not known where again,
Is explained with simple reasoning:
Unknown Origin.

-JB Smith

Years later, after my son was born and I again believed in God, I would change the name of that poem to **Unknown Origin. Lost** and I think the poem needs no more explanation than its new title. For eons, though, I thought that drivel was a thing of flawless beauty, despite being told by more than one English teacher it simply was not. You see, this and many other garbled nonsensical poems would allow me the delusion of a grandiose, undiscovered artist, ever so common among addicts, whether they be a writer, musician, painter, etc. As a writer, a poet, a romantic in my mind, I would use them to seduce women throughout middle school, high school, and even into my twenties, with less and less success as time marched on. A high school girl was much more apt to be moved by them, than women after my divorce at 22, but still occasionally they worked. More relevant though, was their effect on me, their sheer ego inflation. These poems would become the building stones of my artist persona in my own mind, the hidden genius, always allowing me to fall back on my "work" when my alcoholism got out of hand. I've met more than one addict with the artist defense. Mostly musicians. After all, aren't all great artists supposed to struggle with addiction? It is very convenient, and from the poem above, one can tell, doesn't take much of a foundation to establish.

It was spring of eighth grade when I first tried LSD. I remember taking it right before lunch and wondering if it had worked or not. "Am I tripping, am I tripping?" I asked Melissa a couple of times before it hit me like a brick. Once you're tripping on LSD, you need not ask anyone if you are or not, I assure you, you will know. Finding my classes was a challenge, but I remember sitting in science class first, debating with the teacher the validity of the Cheshire Cat Moon, which she emphatically denied existed, and me howling in laughter at her, demanding it did in fact exist, and why wasn't it in this book? To this day I wonder about that. Then again, the book I remember may not have even existed, so strong were those first trip's hallucinations.

Reading class became even more interesting. I wasn't quite capable of reading, but I was giggling for the entire period, and Roger Wallace, a classmate and friend of mine from baseball little league, somehow had begun entertaining me to no end. He grabbed two pens and was flicking the pen caps at me simultaneously and the trails created kept me in stitches the entire class. He did it over and over. Trails were entertaining the first few times I tripped. I would pay any amount of money in the world to get rid of them now, almost 20 years later. Trails, for the inexperienced, are the visions you see while on LSD (and apparently for decades later), that seem to slow time down. A hand waved in front of you will seem like 20 or 30 hands while you're tripping. You see considerably fewer hands years later, but the effect is still ever-present. I guess it would explain why they don't let you become a pilot after you've done LSD. Your vision is never quite the same.

It was fun those first few times, though, and I won't deny having a blast several times on LSD. With a church-going family, on several occasions, I would end up still awake Sunday from tripping Saturday night, wracked with fear that my mom would find out, and I would go to church still tripping, feeling like shit. The peaks were fun but coming down off of acid sucked. I spent many sleepless nights from then until I was 18 or so from doing LSD filled with fear over the irrational and rational alike. What I wouldn't give to know how my mind thought now without it. LSD intertwines with my story quite a bit throughout the years.

So in eighth grade, I had truly transformed from a popular jock to a druggie Jim Morrison wannabe. By then I worshipped Jim

Morrison. Read every biography, listened to everything I could get my hands on, and thought LSD had helped me "Break On Through to the Other Side." I almost studied the lyrics of American Poet, I so wanted there to be a meaning in there, hidden so that only I could find. I remember Chris Tulane accusing me of injecting LSD, and I laughed at how dumb that was, but the essence of what he was saying was true, I had changed that year. I spent my weekends trying to get LSD and doing it whenever we got the chance. At this point we began hunting down weed a lot as well. We didn't have much luck at first and unfortunately we ended up with a lot of oregano several times in a row, mostly from Devon, a black guy who looked three years older than all of us from failing grades so often. So we decided to make it to our first Dead show, where we definitely thought we could score some good weed.

Our plans to make it to that Dead show in 8th grade didn't include our parents, though I'm sure I'd stolen the cash for the tickets right out of my mom's purse. I didn't get permission because I knew it would be denied, but a few months before the show, Josh Daugherty, Patrick Elliott, and I paid cash at Turtles and scored some excellent seats. The Saturday of the show, my mom was supposed to be showing houses and was in and out of the house hastily, busy selling homes as an agent, before I sprang it on her at literally the last second. She said no, rather dramatically as was her way, and I of course only escalated the tension when I flipped out, screaming, yelling, so enraged I began crying. I walked back into my room, in a rage, ashamed I was crying in front of my friend Josh, and mad as hell at my mom. Out of nowhere, without any thought at all about it, I punched a hole through the window of my bedroom with my bare hand. When I pulled my hand back out, violently and without thinking it through, my wrist snagged on two jagged edges, tearing out holes in my forearm that looked like two drawn smiles, bloody, large gashes. I began to bleed everywhere. Coming to my senses I walked back to my mom's bedroom passing through the long hallway. The blood left on that hallway wall, had been sprayed on according to my heartbeat in an up and down pattern, making a graph chart of my pulse. It was bad, I was losing a lot of blood as it sprayed for a minute or two before I got something on it. My parents first rushed me to a little medical center we thought would be fast, and they told us to get to a real hospital, that I could bleed out with a gash that deep. That was a scary mad dash down Route GA 400 to Northside Hospital, as my mom realized the gravity of the situation. We got there in time, though, and they gave me blood and 30 some odd stitches later, we left the hospital and my mom wanted to go get a drink. They gave me pain meds, and as she drank her scotch, she forgave me, and I felt weak, and thankful she'd been there to take me to the hospital. With a drink or two in her, I asked her to go to the Dead show the next day, and she said yes, exhausted, spent, tired of fighting with me, worn down. I'd gotten my way, after behaving like a sheer lunatic.

Everything I remember about that first show was magical. Josh Daughtery, Patrick Elliot, and I got high with Patrick's brother Ethan on the way down to the Omni in Atlanta, and as I recall he gave Patrick a little bit and then went off on his own. We couldn't find a way to smoke it as we were all rookies in the art of joint rolling, and none of us had a pipe or bowl. We started asking around and we finally found a hippie near the railroad tracks that was willing to loan his bowl for our weed. We began smoking it and we all got a few hits before two cops came through some bushes into our semi-isolated area by the railroad. Josh yelled "5.0!" and gangster as Patrick and I were, we knew that meant police. The hippie that lent us the bowl to smoke out of, did not. We darted out of there, hearts racing, high as kites. Patrick and Josh got away clean, and I tried to blend into the crowd of hippies dancing. The cop grabbed me by the arm and I played dumb, saying I'd been dancing and eventually he let me go. I snuck back after we had cleared the scene to see the police going through that hippie's duffel bag, and they were removing huge bags, of white powdery substances. I don't know if it was coke or heroin or what, but that hippie messed up by smoking with us. He could still be in jail for all I know. I laughed and said "I guess he doesn't know what 5.0 means." We were having a blast as they arrested this guy in front of our eyes. The entire show gave me a sense of limitless possibilities. I didn't have a ticket as I'd been in the hospital the day I'd bought a ticket for, and Ethan Elliott had told me to raise my hand and say "I need a miracle," and though it sounded like he was screwing with me, I was the only one without a ticket, so after walking around for 20 minutes after the show started, I thought I'd give it a go. Sure enough on the second or third try someone just handed me a ticket. They were even good seats. A miracle indeed I thought. I walked into a magical world of fellow pot smokers dancing in circles seemingly entranced by the music. The seats next to me were filled with hippies from Humboldt County, CA they told me, and we got high, high, high, and smoked some amazing weed, and they even burned some hash with me. The music was incredible, the people were all nice and loving, and I felt like I belonged. This was it, these folks knew how to party, and I began to dance like a gypsy. I had the time of my life up until that point and it began a mystique around the hippie culture I would grow to love. Something magical you could almost touch, but never quite get your hands on. An illusion I would chase, and build and mold, and love for years.

We still didn't have too many ways to get weed, though, and Devon, the token black drug dealer at our middle school, kept selling us the shakey oregano. We must have fallen for it three or four times. Patrick's brother wouldn't sell it to us, so I think this is around the time we all began huffing gas, breathing in Scotchgard fumes, making our selves pass out and other random thrill seeking highs. To pass out we would grab our ankles, breathe in deeply 40 times or so, then stand up rapidly, put our thumbs in our mouths, and blow. Inevitably it makes you pass out. Why we did this is beyond me. It gave us headaches, as I recall, but there were some strange thoughts produced right before you would pass out. I liked to believe they were from another life, but I think that was just romance. I think I'm just an alcoholic, I like to set buildings on fire, and then go inside them. This is just another level of that behavior.

Little Five Points and Paideia

Around this time my good friend Josh Daugherty and I figured that Little Five Points in Atlanta was as good as place as any to find a drug dealer that wouldn't sell us freaking paprika. To this day I'm able to conjure things up after thinking of them long enough. Finding our first real drug dealer was similar. We went down there to find someone to sell us weed, and within an hour of being in Little Five Points, a man approached us and asked us "Hey boys, you want to smoke a joint?" Did we ever! We walked to the parking lot behind Little Five Points and thus began our interaction with a man by the name of Roberto Morena, who would become an influential person in my life. That joint was incredible, though, and we got high, pocketed the joint, and got high from it several times after that once we'd get home. He gave me his number as well and said if we ran out to call him again. Within a few days I was on the phone with him, and he would drive from Decatur to Roswell to bring me my weed. It was good weed too, and Josh Daugherty went through his savings that summer buying us smoke and burning it right up. When Josh ran out of money, I began stealing cash right out of my mom's purse. We would get high and I'd feel my chest hurt, ever conscious of my heart condition, scared I was going to have a heart attack like my mom kept telling me. But I'd go right on doing it despite the fear, and despite having to steal the cash out of her purse every single time, without remorse. This pissed her off to no end, but she always kept cash in there, so it never was a problem to score. I would rationalize the theft by telling myself it was my dad's 750k anyway. I could have rationalized nuclear holocaust to stay fucked up.

So ironically around the same time, my mom, probably in a cloud of denial, moved me from the public school system to Paideia, a college preparatory private school, supposedly one of the best in Atlanta, thinking I was just surrounded by the wrong kids. Little did she know I was almost always the ringleader. The irony was that it brought me closer to Little Five Points, and thus to my dealer, Roberto Morena. I did my best to do well there, though, and I did the first two semesters, but by the third semester, I was smoking a quarter bag a week and getting shit faced drunk every time I could. By this time, too, Roberto Morena was fronting me an ounce or two at a time and I was selling it back in Roswell. I was also selling acid, that I hooked up with from Paideia as well. It was obvious too that I was a drug addict to everyone but me. I remember my mom making me go see a drug counselor, and I usually went to those sessions with a few ounces of weed in my book bag that I would pick up from "Bob" as we called Roberto, before I left for my long MARTA ride home. In effect, my poor mom's strategy to get me away from drugs, landed me right smack dab in the middle of Little Five Points. I had my drug dealer Bob right down the street, and those rich kids had the best acid in town. I was transporting all kinds of stuff back to Roswell, and it sold very easily up there, because quite frankly, it beat the oregano-paprika mix Devon kept trying to sell us.

My usual commute in 9th grade began at the ass crack of dawn. From Roswell, my mom would drive me to the Mansell Park and Ride, where I would await the bus to take to the Lenox train station in Buckhead. That in itself was a 20 or 30 minute ride. From the Lenox train station I would wait for the notoriously slow and unreliable MARTA train to get there. To this day, it is the worst overall public transportation I've ever experienced in terms of reliability. From Lenox I would ride down to North Avenue, where I would depart the train and take the MARTA bus again to get to my school, 20 minutes or so with stops from that train station. It was a long ass haul and I have a few funny stories from it, including my first arrest.

One time, I was very tired exiting the North Avenue train, and with my hippie curly hair, and torn clothes I thought were so cool, I fell asleep waiting for the bus to arrive. I woke up around 10 PM or so with a bunch of change and a few bills in the coffee cup next to me. I had passed successfully for a bum. I thought it was hilarious at the time, but little did I know how close I would come to becoming just that. My mom thought that story was funny, and it also gives you an idea of the raggedy ass skater clothes and general hygiene I'd come to adopt by the middle of my 9th grade year.

First Arrest

The time I was arrested, though, was not quite as funny to her. We really had been to the dentist that morning so I was running late for a legitimate reason. We didn't know truancy was against the law, otherwise I'm sure my mother would have forced me to carry a doctor's note. When I reached the Lenox MARTA station that morning it was around 10 AM, so I was noticeably late, and as I walked down to the train platform I probably looked like a street urchin. A big black woman MARTA officer came up to me and asked why I was "truant". In all honesty, I had no idea what she was saying. She repeated it several times, "Why you truant!" in a brusque, loud manner and I snapped, being more than a bit venomous. "Why don't you speak English lady, I can't understand you?!" She was not amused.

This black woman grabbed me by my little scrawny, attitude-filled ass by my little white ear, twisted hard as she could and without saying another word, marched me across the platform in front of a hundred witnesses, up the escalators, all the while I was apologizing like a little boy. "Please, I'm sorry, please let go, please let go!" We got to the little mini MARTA Cop station up there and she planted my ass in a seat, closed the door which I heard lock with a loud clang, and quickly explained her situation to the other three or four MARTA cops in there. They asked me why I was late and I told them a likely story, I'd been at the dentist. They asked me what school I went to and I said "Paideia". Unfortunately either I couldn't spell it, they couldn't look it up properly or it wasn't in the phone book, because the next thing I know they're calling Fulton County Police Department to take me down to Juvenile Hall. This was not good at all. My mom was going to be less than thrilled. I tried to get them to spell Paideia again but they had stopped buying what I was selling, regardless of it being the truth, and I overhead the confirmation of a police escort to take me to Juvenile prison. Now I'd been caught shoplifting once before and been released almost instantly, slashed some tires and been in a few fights, but I'd never gone to jail or been arrested formally and I really did begin to panic sitting in that chair, thinking of how I was going to explain this bullshit to my mom. Right about then another MARTA cop opened the door and came in the little office. I saw that door open and smelled freedom. I was the closest one to the door and the person who just entered had made it half way across the room as it slowly closed. I seized the opportunity, jumped up and hauled ass!

Now the Lenox MARTA station in Buckhead actually connects to an office building with smartly dressed executives going about their business. On this day in the early 90's, if one of them was in that expensive looking lobby, they would have seen a short and scrawny homeless looking white kid running through the lobby at breakneck speed, stealing glances behind him as he ran smiling in victory. The large black MARTA police woman behind me must have been a good 250 pounds and, hell, I'd run the Peachtree Road Race, I was home free! And then she starting yelling, "Stop him, stop him!" The dumbfounded faces of executives went from shock to determination and I remember thinking "This is bullshit, they think I robbed a bank and I'm just late for school." About that time a freaking mailman, of all people, seized the initiative and threw a huge bag of mail at my feet. It was like a cartoon, the bag exploded, mail went everywhere, and the mailman jumped on top of me until the huge black woman caught up breathing heavily, and threw some cuffs on me behind my back. It was the first time I ever had cuffs on me and they sucked. All the Buckhead business executives applauded as they brought me to my feet, twisting the knife of humiliation deep in my gut. The walk of shame through that lobby back to the station was bad, but Juvenile was worse.

I'm not trying to make it a race issue, but race definitely played a part of my personal terror when I went to Juvenile. For one thing, a black woman had in my inexperienced mind just abused the hell out of me. Later I would learn that all cops do that, every time you get arrested white or black. But by this time in my life, I really had been raised very southern, so in all honesty black people scared me. To get admitted in Juvenile at age 14 or 15 in ninth grade was traumatizing. In the Atlanta area, Fulton County included Roswell, where I lived, so it wouldn't be the last time I visited Juvenile, but as an introduction it was pretty eye opening, scary. I was put into a holding tank that time around 11 AM or so with about five or six other big black guys. I was scared to death. I didn't suffer any beatings that day, but I sure did in my imagination the entire time I shared that cell with them. I couldn't understand what they were saying most of the time, and I did my best not to make eye contact. The guards let me call my mom and she answered but she had a closing for her real estate career and didn't pick me up until 5:30 or so that night. I was furious. She had blamed me, for good reason, and she came after she was done with her business. My anger with her began with my stepdad, Dan Jones, but it definitely grew that day.

Ninth grade is when my drinking and drug use began to become habitual and obviously detrimental to my life. Though I would somehow block it out, most everyone around me would know. Paideia was a good school, a lot of students went on to Ivy League colleges after attending. My mom was trying her best to break the downward spiral she saw so clearly in my life choices and I guess she'd hoped putting me in that school would get me away from a bad crowd. Unfortunately for her, and ultimately for me, I was the bad crowd. My first semester, straight A's, despite the long MARTA commute. Introduce steady marijuana use, and the second semester was B's and C's. Begin smoking weed every single day without fail, and by spring D's and F's. It was so obvious to everyone but me.

One of the greatest lies an addict tells himself is that everything is just fine. Another, more cunning and baffling, is that my drug of choice, mainly weed and LSD at this time, were actually making me smarter. Especially with pot, "It makes me more creative, or it connects me to the universe" and for me and my unchecked imagination "I feel like it's making me psychic." I honestly believed that by doing mass amounts of LSD, I'd opened up previously closed channels, and by smoking weed, I would keep those channels open. For me there was just an unspoken mysticism about weed, a feeling of superiority even, "It makes me super-intelligent, you just couldn't understand." Never mind that my grades were plummeting and it caused me to be a criminal, and an outcast in my own home, that was just how the outside world measured success, I justified. I had risen above such trivial measurements. I would listen to the Grateful Dead, just on the verge of total nirvana, practically a shaman I believed, and life crumbling to pieces around me, ascend to a higher plane that you, or the outside world, just couldn't understand. So long as I didn't run out of drugs, because then I'd turn into a common thief until I got high again. Once returned to my artificial Zen, stoned, I was on the verge of total enlightenment. I felt it was just around the corner, so stealing was always justified, anything was. Propagating the magic and mystique around all this drug use was our drug dealer, Roberto Morena, a Columbian who was incredibly charismatic, and continually brought us beer, gave us weed, and shared philosophy, politics, and even magic. He used to say we weren't even in the first grade yet, and there was so much more to learn, with a mystical gleam in his eye. I believed it, because being high, it just always felt like there was this great untold truth just below the surface, waiting to be discovered. He also talked about Jedi Mind tricks, fooling the police, and backing it up by showing us books explaining science's discovery of telepathy through brain waves, alpha and gamma he said. They were amplified with THC and LSD, it was a fact he said. Once, albeit while high, he told me he'd share with me telepathy and to this day I can still say I distinctly remember his voice in my head, clear as day, telling me something I didn't want to hear, but heard none the less. Then he told me the sentence out loud, and I was blown away. Maybe it was just a parlor trick, I don't know, but I guess I bought it all hook, line, and sinker. It was all such a romantic, grandiose idea, that there was more than meets the eye to this world, and I was finding it out, using drugs and thoroughly enjoying myself in the process. I guess I was always searching for a spiritual experience and temporarily found one through drugs, always just a bit further than my grasp.

Roswell's Finest

That was really before I'd started dealing drugs heavily though. But by the spring of 9th grade, Bob began fronting us weed and I was dealing pretty regularly and therefore never ever ran out of weed or money. At some point that spring, my mom began tapping my phone, and recording hundreds of phone conversations with all of my friends. Most of my friends were buying weed from me at this point, and then of course there were the long conversations with Bob, my drug dealer. My mom later told me that Paideia had asked her to tap my phones, but that seems unlikely now, and there's no telling where the truth lied in this matter. We were fighting almost daily now, and at least I knew better than to have my drugs in the house at this stage. I kept my weed in the woods in a foxhole I'd dug out. When someone would call, I'd go get the pot, measure it out in the woods, and meet the customers back at my house briefly, opening the window to my room, giving them the drugs and then pocketing the money. For this reason at least, when I came home one day that spring to see two unmarked cars in the driveway, and went into the house to meet a uniformed policeman and Narcotics Detective Officer Cantone searching my room, I was able to breathe a sigh of relief. They would find nothing. Little did I know how crooked police could be. I was smiling cockily as they tore everything in my room to shreds, because the drugs were in the woods.

And then that prick pulled out a knife, pointed it at me, and said, "I bet I know where they are." He stabbed my mattress and sliced it open, end to end, then put his hand deep inside with my mom and stepdad watching and me wondering what he was up to. He pulled out a bag of roaches, used marijuana joint butts, and smirked triumphantly. It was outrageous. I always smoked from a bowl or water bong, because I still couldn't role a joint. I was innocent by technicality, but guilty as hell regardless, and they were going to make me pay one way or another. I still didn't know how bad it was about to get until they took the little bag of roaches, sat me down in my mom's office chair and began playing the tapes of me selling weed to at least ten of my closest friends that went to Roswell High. They then went into the criminal background of my dealer, Roberto Morena. I had spent a lot of time talking to this guy, visiting his house, and though I knew he was an oddball Columbian drug dealer, I really didn't know much else about him. I knew that he scared me. The police told me he had a long criminal history, including child molestation, and other not so illustrious charges. I was disgusted, yes, but at the same time, more scared of him than I was of the Roswell police. The long and short of the conversation was that the Roswell Police department demanded I wear a wire and buy drugs from the guy. I told them "hell no". Regardless of what they told me about the guy, he had not tried to molest me at all, and though he was a whack job, he was still my friend, or so I thought. Not to mention I was scared of what he may do to me afterwards. I also hated those cops. They had already planted weed in my house and were now asking me to be a narc. It went against everything in my gut and I refused. So they began to get nasty. I'm 15 years old and these cops threaten me as best they could. "If you don't narc on Bob, we're going to call everyone on these tapes and tell their parents that you are a narc, that you have been selling drugs to their children and have been a narc this entire time for us." So it was literally be a narc for them, or they would tell my friends I was a narc. As an added incentive, if I didn't narc on Bob I would be charged with possession, intent to distribute, distribution, and a host of other bullshit charges, and I'd go to jail again, right now. I was so angry I just told them to fuck off and they took me to jail again. Juvenile. Time number two, as I recall. I WAS 15. The cops had planted weed on me, and then blackmailed me. Resentments abound!

I was out of Juvenile relatively quickly that time, but when I got out, the police had followed through on their threat. They called all my friend's parents and told them I was a narc. They called Roberto Morena and threatened him with charges of some sort, so that he too no longer wanted to talk to me. But the absolute worst thing they did, that I felt the guiltiest about, was calling my girlfriends parents at the time, not Anne Marie, but a girl I knew from church no less, and playing the God awful tapes of me bragging about having sex with her. She was an incredibly beautiful, very innocent young girl and her parents got to hear the lust filled, boasting story of how I'd had sex with her, and basically treated her like shit. I remember feeling bad after telling the story to my friend Josh Daugherty over the phone and it had stuck with me, though I laughed as I told the story to him. To find out they had played that tape of me gloating to her poor parents, was a reality shock. Of all the things on those tapes, I felt most ashamed for that. I didn't mean the things I'd said or the manner in which I'd said them, but there they were, for the Roswell Police Department to share with whomever they like. I hope she reads this book one day and knows that I was sorry then, and am sorry now. Regardless of their intentions, Detective Cantone and the Roswell Police could have handled the situation with a modicum of delicacy. They enjoyed telling her parents this stuff, and it had to be traumatic for her, and utterly unnecessary. It would fuel my resentments towards government and society even more. The more I fought, the more I lost.

So everyone in Roswell thought I was a narc at 15. After a few months it became evident to Bob that I hadn't narced him out and as long as I called him from a different phone and said nothing illegal, I could continue to get my weed, and continue to sell it, though my customer base had changed dramatically. The Roswell parents were able to prevent a lot of interaction, but the skater kids in Mountain Park and surrounding areas were still pretty excited about my weed, so the whole debacle basically made me hang out with the more hard core drug users at the time, the skaters. It wouldn't be long before I was wearing the absurdly baggy jeans, listening to rap constantly, and skateboarding myself.

The court date for the marijuana the Roswell Police had planted on me came up in the middle of the summer. I brought a book just in case I was sentenced to jail. I'd been in enough to know how boring and maddening sitting in a cell could be. The book was The Key to Rebecca by Ken Follett, who is still one of my favorite authors. My mom and I were still fighting like cats and dogs, and at this point it was just all out war all of the time. I wanted to smoke weed, and she wanted me to quit. I was self righteous and ridiculous, but I was 15 and not giving up, so we screamed and yelled at each other constantly. I said awful things, loudly and constantly. I'm ashamed of those absurdities still. They installed an alarm from ADP that I quickly learned to bypass electronically which pissed her off to no end, and they put a dead bolt on their door, to stop me from invading her purse. I'd copied the key within a week of its installation. So it

46

shouldn't have been so shocking to me that when the charges for the weed possession were dropped by the prosecution, because the marijuana was so old, that my mom would yell at the Judge in open court and say, "But he's a drug dealer, he deserves to go to jail!"

I was almost laughing at my luck, that they had tested the weed and it was so ancient I was being released, and I felt like John Gotti, bulletproof! I grinned right up until the Judge said, "You could deny custody and he would become a ward of the state, which would put him in Juvenile right now, until a suitable home could be found." The Judge, not knowing how battleship hardened she was, did not expect her to do it, but my mom was so pissed off, and I'm sure the smirk on my face wasn't helping. "Then I deny custody." I was indignant. I didn't say a word, but I clutched onto my book. The bailiff handcuffed me and off I went. My mom didn't have a shred of regret over it. She glared at me victoriously.

Naked in Juvenile Hall

I spent 11 days in Juvenile for absolutely 0 charges, simply because my mom denied custody, and though I can look back and forgive her for it now, I remained pissed at her for years afterwards because of it. I read that book backwards and forwards during that two weeks in Juvenile. It kept me sane. To add insult to injury, my mom told the judge that my father had killed himself, and that I should be treated with special precautions. In effect this meant I would be on suicide watch this time, and anytime following that I visited Atlanta's illustrious Juvenile prison. Suicide watch means that you walk around butt ass naked because you could use your clothes to hang yourself. I was already the smallest kid in Juvi, and white, but now, are you kidding, I'm the smallest, only white kid in Juvenile forced to walk around the facility naked while everyone else is wearing clothes. How the fuck this loophole of insanity existed is beyond me, but my fears of fights intensified upon this visit. Every time I left my cell to piss or shower, I walked past at least 20-30 big black guys, who inevitably made fun of my small little white pecker. Then I would get to the bathroom and try to piss while being yelled at, laughed at, pissed on, or smacked in the back of the head. It was hell. I still can't piss in stalls next to other people.

It still amazes me that in some bureaucrat's demented logic it made sense to say "Hey your dad killed himself, therefore you're especially mentally unstable, so for your protection, in all our bureaucratic wisdom, it would be best if you were forced to walk around all the fully clothed Juvenile prisoners, naked." But that's the way it was, so on top of the humiliation of incarceration at 15, and the fear of being the only white kid in an all-black facility, I was forced upon day one to surrender all my fucking clothes. My resentments towards authority were blossoming beyond belief.

At some point during this visit, I saw a friend of mine from high school about 100 feet away, and being completely desensitized to my own nakedness I yelled "Vijay, what's up man?", and walked by all the other inmates naked, to go shake his hand.

"Bryan Smith, why the fuck are you naked?" Vijay smiled wildly.

"Suicide watch," I said glumly, remembering my plight.

He laughed his ass off. He was released before me and was able to tell all the kids from our school of the only other white kid he saw in Juvenile, and how I was butt ass naked. When I got out we became pretty good friends from that funny story. Eventually, the mother of a friend of mine, Lauren Hunt, threatened my mom that she would take custody of me. I think I must have called anyone and everyone during the twenty minutes they gave me to use the phone, and somehow Lauren's mom Patricia forced the issue. Under threat of losing custody of me, my mom retook custody of me and I went back home for the remainder of the summer. When she got me out of Juvi, she did feel bad. She asked if I wanted some clothes and I said "Yes, I'd like some from Little Five Points." I wanted new baggy skater clothes that she hated. Feeling guilty I guess, we went there, to Stratosphere, a skater shop, and when they wouldn't take my mom's credit cards, only cash, she said "Well I tried, we're going to the GAP." So we went to the GAP where I bought oversized yuppie clothes to try to look like the cool skater all my friends were emulating now, and therefore I was trying to be as well. GAP wasn't exactly Stratosphere, but it would have to do.

My poor mother tried everything. When Juvenile didn't work, she'd try more therapy. When therapy didn't work on me alone, she dragged the whole family in. One therapist suggested tough love. That was probably the prick that had her tap my phones, come to think of it, but who knows. I do know this particular expert suggested I go to Outward Bound. While I was gone on what they told me would be a camping trip, my parents threw away literally every possession I had accumulated through childhood. They painted my room yellow, and told me it was all for a "fresh start."

I was livid upon returning. I would later learn the therapist believed that yellow walls would make my acid trips "bad" and therefore no fun, which is, incidentally, a bullshit theory. And I never really did figure out why they threw away everything of mine. Everything I'd ever written or drawn, all the baseball cards I'd collected, tons of books I'd read, everything. It all had something to do with identity awareness or some new bullshit 1990's therapeutic crap. They left the mattress the cops had destroyed, though. But I wasn't in an identity crisis, I was just an addict alcoholic. After three weeks in Outward Bound, hiking, marching, rock climbing, canoeing the Chattooga River, and a three-day solo in the woods jerking off, as soon as I got to the airport before I got back to Atlanta, I snuck a beer out of the airport lounge and stole a pack of smokes from the drugstore.

The Outward Bound trip had slowed me down temporarily, just like jail, but nothing could stop my self-destruction. I didn't even get a chance to experience their psychological experiment with my stuff and the new wall color before I was fucking up again. I was an addict, and not in need of new paint or possessions. God bless her for trying, though, I just wish she'd tried rehab. In all her experiments, rehab was never one of them, though in retrospect it seems the most obvious. Still, sobriety is for those who want it, not for those who need it.

The Roswell Rec

I was expelled from Paideia, or at least asked not to come back. That was fine with me because I wanted to end the long MARTA ride everyday anyway. After a few months, most of my Roswell friends began talking to me again, though they still wouldn't take my direct phone calls, I would maneuver and run to the Country Club to call folks. At 15, we were all worried about phone taps now. Patrick Elliott and I began hanging out at the Roswell Rec a lot and we began hanging out a lot with Devon, our previous purveyor of oregano, and a friend of his by the name of Charles Lewinski. In the first quarter of 10th grade at Roswell High, we would go to the Roswell Rec a lot and smoke weed in the woods. I didn't know Charles very well, but I loved the sound system in his car, and we were all quite ghetto fabulous listening to Pharcyde, Cypress Hill, Ghetto Boys, and what have you with his four 8-inch subwoofers in the back of his Civic. We all became friends, smoked a lot of herb together and occasionally would get 40's from the mini ghetto Roswell had off Oxbo Road, where Devon lived, and would get drunk in his cockroach-infested apartment. It was literally a mini ghetto. There was one building of slums right off Oxbo Road and some low rental apartments nearby, but we spent a lot of time hanging out there and of course at the Roswell Rec. The Roswell Police messed with us all the time. They arrested us down there and called our parents telling them we were hanging out in a known crack area. I remember laughing at that, because we only smoked weed and drank beer, but it was a real concern I'm sure to everyone else. It must have scared my parents to death. The police had searched Charles's car and shredded the seats, pocketed his weed, and stabbed one of his speakers, but we were all just happy we didn't get charged, and the cops just stole the drugs instead, and had called our parents, par for the course by then.

A few weeks before the serious drama with Charles Lewinski, we were all smoking weed at the Rec. We were in a circle and I remember he was double hitting my joint which was pissing me off. He said, "Man, I really want to kill my dad." To which in all my empathy I said, "Shut the fuck up and pass the God damn joint." I really thought he was kidding. Never mind that we listened to enough Ghetto Rap to brainwash the KKK, forget that he had showed us his .38 caliber gun and I had even waved it at one of my friends, DJ Van Gilden, for some God-forsaken reason. I can't even remember why now, I just simply didn't see it coming. After Charles's stepdad died, by gunshot wound to the head, things began to get VERY serious again. He was brought in first I remember and then they released him after searching his car and house. We later learned they bugged both. The police then took us all into custody, Devon, Patrick Elliott, Charles and I, and questioned many others trying to piece together what had happened. Having been royally ass raped by the Roswell police not a few months before I did not cooperate at all. I didn't say jack shit for the first two or three of several hours-long interrogation sessions they subjected us to. It wasn't until they had already charged Charles Lewinski with murder, and I'd read the statements of the others implicating him that I finally gave in, under threat of obstruction of justice, and after consulting with my stepdad's attorney. How I got involved in a murder investigation at the age of 15 was completely the result of having friends because of drugs. Otherwise I'd have never even hung out with Devon and Charles. Charles was eventually convicted of manslaughter and did some time, though he's out now. I think there was an underlying reason for his stepfather's death, though I never learned it and it was never any of my business. It did reinforce my hatred of the police again though. Those interrogations were intense, filled with threats, and scary. I hated the cops from before, but this experience certainly
50

didn't help. My parents were, of course, once again appalled. I had become desensitized. I was always high on weed and didn't care about much at all, quite honestly.

Independence High and Felix the Cat

So a few weeks after Charles was arrested I got into some more trouble at school. On top of the murder investigation, which I'm sure didn't make us a hit with the faculty, we'd been almost caught smoking weed outside the school, when the smoke from our joint had gone through an open window. We'd evaded trouble that time, how I have no idea, but we were searched, our lockers tossed, and stern warnings given. Shortly thereafter, the volleyball coach confronted me in the cafeteria, when I'd left the lunch table and thrown away my trash and set down my tray. He marched me back to the table I'd left and told me to clean up all my friends' trash, who had simply left it all there, and departed the cafeteria. I told him no, and he grabbed my arm and began marching me out of the cafeteria, where I completely lost my temper and began cussing him out at the top of my lungs, using every cuss word in the book, and pushed him off of me at the same time. I'd been showing my mom this uncontrollable, verbally abusive temper time and again, which had ultimately landed me in Juvenile, but I'd never done it in school and much less to a school faculty member. I had zero impulse control. The entire cafeteria stopped and stared as his face reddened with anger. He grabbed my arm again and did march me out of the cafeteria, me cussing and screaming at the top of my lungs. My mom was called from the principal's office, and I was suspended for seven days, which somehow turned into my being expelled. I hadn't even lasted a quarter at Roswell High School.

I was forced to enroll at Independence High School, where you could smoke cigarettes, and take classes at your own pace. It was great for a drug addict too. You could leave campus, go get high, come back and nobody would ever know the difference, or care. I actually passed a ton of classes as well, since you could read the curriculum, then simply take a test for the entire quarter. I passed something like 15 classes that first quarter, which they told me was a state record. I was very proud of that record for years, until I found someone who had passed 11 in a quarter and was told the same bullshit. A state record, ha! They probably told all us flunkies that. That year I met Faust Santino, who had the best LSD I'd ever found. He called it white blotter, and said the Rainbow Family made it. I didn't care who made it, I loved it. Every time I would get some fronted to me, bad shit would happen. I'd usually get a sheet or two, a sheet of acid is 100 hits total, though I'd never sell it all without consuming at least five or so.

Though I always managed to make a profit with the drugs, I was never what you would have called a successful drug dealer. This was because I would usually do too much, get freaked out, and either get in serious trouble, arrested, or something. One time I had sold a bunch at a friend's house, and Patrick Elliott and I decided to meet up with Faust Santino to go smoke some weed. We were tripping pretty hard when he told us he would be at his friend's apartment and that if we wanted we could meet him and his girlfriend there. When on LSD or any drug for that matter, time can have a way of getting away from you. We took a cab out to Faust Santino's friend's house late in the evening, and by the time we got there, to a small apartment complex in Alpharetta, we were tripping pretty damn hard on Felix the Cat LSD, and all I could remember about the directions were that inside the apartment complex was one of the only units that had Christmas lights up, in the middle of the summer. So we were able to find the apartment despite our tripping so hard. We knocked hard on the doors, and two guys answered, and let me tell you they didn't look happy. They did let us come in, though, and use the phone, telling us Faust had left hours before. Patrick and I both tried to page Faust repeatedly but the same error message kept coming up saying that the pager network was down. Our new hosts were not impressed or amused. We were both very talkative and high as kites. Eventually Faust's friends, whom I would later learn were his suppliers, ran out of patience, and began asking us not very politely to leave. Patrick and I both knew we'd get arrested for being out too late as we were both only 16 and we didn't want to go. He finally pulled out a Glock pistol and told us to get the fuck out of his apartment. It was the first time a gun had been pulled on me related to drugs, but it wouldn't be the last. I was scared to death, but Patrick just kept running his mouth. I thought for sure we were going to get shot, because Patrick simply wouldn't relent. "That's not cool motherfucker," and all kinds of other tough ass shit was coming out of Patrick's mouth, meanwhile this big gun toting guy is pointing a weapon at us.

Eventually we made it outside and began hiking. We were in Alpharetta, not very far from Faust's house, but hallucinating, and high as could be. Felix the Cat was some strong acid. Also, I remembered about this time that I had a sheet of LSD in my pockets from the batch Faust had fronted me earlier. We ran through the shadows out of the apartment complex, and into the backyard of a nearby house. There, Patrick and I looked through the woods that we were pretty sure would get us to Faust's house. It looked like a haunted forest. Tripping hard staring into the darkness of that forest scared the shit out of me. I was so frightened of walking through that jungle, that I'd have rather died right then and there. Patrick and I stared into the abyss for quite some time, and eventually I just talked Patrick into us taking the road, and inevitably getting stopped by the police, arrested, and our parents called. Patrick knew his parents would be pissed he was with me, and I knew my parents would be pissed period, but man those woods looked scary as hell on LSD. We threw the sheet into the woods, and began hiking down the road. The very first car was a police cruiser. She stopped us, and I asked if she had any water. She said she would ask the questions and I went into some rambling tirade about it being a violation of our United Nations Human Rights, and Patrick just rolled his eyes and begged me to shut up, which I simply was incapable of doing. I rode that poor, poor policewoman for an hour or two before she got us to the station, all the while obsessed about my United Nation given rights, and ultimately water. It was Patrick's first time in jail I think, but I'd been quite a few times already at this stage, and welcomed it to the unknown of that hallucination fueled forest. Our parents were at the police station within the hour. The next morning, without a wink of sleep, still tripping on acid, Faust and I had to go search for the sheet I'd discarded in the woods. I'd spent the entire night awake and worrying that it would be gone and he'd want to kill me for losing all the acid he'd fronted me. He came and got me while my family was at church, and we walked right into an unsuspecting suburbanite's back yard, found the tinfoil-wrapped LSD and left, all within five minutes. My parents, at this point, didn't know what to do with me. I raised hell like they could have never imagined.

Florida, Spring Break, and Meth

For Spring Break that year, while everyone else had planned out a trip, Lauren Hunt, David Lane, and myself found ourselves plotting at David's house, snorting huge lines of meth and talking a million miles a minute, certain we were solving all of Earth's problems, no less. David was a major drug dealer in our eyes. Lauren had found this winner, and he always had pounds of weed and multiple eightballs, which are the standard unit of measure for hard drugs like cocaine and meth. An eightball is generally a few days worth of consumption between a group, but in the end they could disappear in a night. It was my first experience with meth, and though I'd balked at first, eventually I was right there, madly plotting with them about God only knows what. Eventually we brainstormed a trip to Florida, quite suddenly and on a whim. Lauren and I must have sold it with finesse as we somehow got permission to go from our parents. David Lane had a pound of weed and several eight balls of meth and at first had been too paranoid to leave the house, much less drive to Florida. Somehow again, Lauren and I convinced him of a plan that was flawless. What plan involving eightballs of methamphetamines, a pound of weed, and a car ride to Florida, could possibly have flaws? We convinced David, the paranoid drug dealer, that if we removed all the seeds and stems from the pound of weed, that in the unlikely event we were pulled over, we could just roll down the window, release the weed into the air, and poof, the fine dust of marijuana would disappear! Like I said, flawless.

Thus, the night before we left for Florida all three of us obsessively and compulsively removed every fragment of non leaf product from that pound of weed, reducing it to a fine mist-like substance, fueled by methamphetamines, which were new to me, but that I was adapting to just fine. They sure could make me focus! It took all night, but we did it, and convinced it was a foolproof plan, David would allow me to sit in the back holding the drugs the entire ride down to Florida. Right before we left Atlanta, a friend of David's, Trent, called and was having a rough time, as his dad had tried to kill himself the night before, and he really wanted to get out of Dodge. So, he offered to drive, and came and picked us up, making it a foursome down to Florida.

The first few days weren't too bad as the drive down was uneventful, and we never had to implement our ingenious strategy. Arriving in Daytona, unfortunately we soon found out we picked the weekend of the Daytona 500, so all the hotels were booked, and we were forced to press on. By then we'd been up two or three days straight, and an hour or so south of Daytona we finally found a room and we all four piled inside. We snorted a bunch more meth, smoked some huge blunts out of the pound of weed we'd refrained from on the journey down, and we hit the beach. David bought us all body boards, as he was the only one with any real money, and having not slept, shortly after dawn we all hit the waves. It seemed like we'd been in the water for an hour or so when the sun began to set. Lauren had left the waves early and was on the beach, so that when David, Trent and I walked up, she freaked out and screamed "You're all blue!" the water had been cold but I hadn't thought about the danger, being so amped up on meth, but after she said that I looked at Trent and David, I realized she wasn't lying at all, we were all blue from being in that pre-summer springtime Atlantic ocean water for twelve hours straight. Our solution of course, was alcohol. What doesn't alcohol fix? We went and got some beer, got drunk, got stoned, and repeated the whole crazy adventure the very next day and the next after that, having a blast, tearing those waves up non-stop.

At some point someone from the beach invited us to a party. We were supposed to follow a VW bug, and somehow, maybe it was the being awake for five days straight, Trent lost the VW in traffic. A few blocks later, he sees a VW and we begin following it. There was a small discussion as to whether it was the same VW, color, make, and so on, but not much, and it was soon forgotten when it became evident from Trent's following this VW, that it must, in fact, be, the right VW. I remember doubting it was the same car, but then forgetting about four seconds after I registered the thought. My mind was no steel trap by this stage of the binge. We finally pulled into a driveway that had a bunch of cars in the driveway, and therefore "must be a party!" We all stormed into some stranger's house, four of us, geeked out of our minds, to find a fat man sitting in his white undies, watching the TV show Cops. "Where's the beer?" I said, still acutely oblivious to our mistake. "Get the fuck out of my house!" It was chaos, we were a complete wreck.

We were six days into our meth binge, without so much as a wink of sleep when the impossible happened. We ran out of meth. Completely out of our main drug, we were forced to fall on our backup, marijuana, and we rolled a huge blunt out of the fine mist we'd created out of his pound. It was a beaut. Until we smoked it, we were at each other's throats, out of drugs, sleepless -- cranky doesn't begin to explain. But after smoking the Marley sized monster, we all mellowed out, smiled, and even apologized for being short with each other. Ah, peace. Right up until there was a knock on t he door.

I peered through the peephole, already paranoid, to see a policeman standing there in all his authoritarian glory. I turned to David "It's the cops!" Through the haze and smoke from our blunt I saw the fear in his eyes light up.

"Flush the weed!" David said, scared as we all were.

"Are you sure?" I was just as scared of losing our drugs.

"Yes, flush it or were screwed, look at the smoke." David pointed to the fog in our little motel room.

The smoke had saved us, and then damned us, we would

open that door and that cop would immediately know we'd just burned one and he'd search the room, and we were all going to jail. So I followed David's orders and I flushed probably 2/3rds of a pound of weed right down the crapper of that crappy little motel room, sad as I did the deed.

David opened the door once it finished flushing and the cop said "Hi, have you guys noticed or seen a stereo around? Your neighbor left one out at the pool and now it's gone missing, did any of you see anything?" He smelled the weed and rolled his eyes a little bit, but didn't mention a word about it, as we all watched, examined, paranoid, sleepless, and filled with fear.

"Nope." David mustered.

"Ok, well, let the front desk know if you see anything, we're letting everybody in the place know. Have a good night." And the cop walked to the next door, performing his duty, ultimately uninterested in us whatsoever.

David closed the door slowly, rage building in his face, and once closed, immediately began yelling at me.

"But you told me to flush it!" He knew it was the truth and eventually he would shut up about it, but we all felt pretty freaking stupid. We were screwed and we knew it. The weed had been the only thing keeping us sane, and it would go downhill from there, quickly.

Completely and totally running out of drugs drove us all to madness, and I mean fast. The next day, seven days awake or thereabouts, we decided to call it quits and head back home. Right before we left for Atlanta we pulled into the gas station to fill up. David and Lauren went into the gas station and blatantly stole a bunch of 40 ounce beers and when they got back into the car all hell broke loose. Trent began screaming at them both saying the cashier had seen them steal the beer, and the clerk was in there staring us down quite obviously. As Trent was yelling, I saw Lauren steam up and I knew Trent was in for it. This woman had a vengeance in her, and I'd seen it first hand, more than once.

"Well at least my dad didn't try to kill himself!" She broke his rant with that one, and somehow even managed to offend me at the same time. It had no relevancy, no bearing at all, but we were mad, hadn't slept in eons, and we were all angry. It set Trent off, though.

SMASH! He punched his hand as hard as he could right into the windshield, crushing a huge dent into the glass, cracking and splitting it from the driver's side to the passenger's side. What's more, he was bleeding all over the car, and had left a bloody mark on the windshield itself. I got out of the car dying laughing. Now we were really fucked, we couldn't drive home in this piece of shit now.

At that precise moment, as Lauren stormed out of the car and paced frantically around the parking lot, screaming and yelling at Trent, as he bled, and I was laughing now sitting on the curb, a police cruiser rolled into the parking lot, and for the first time in my life I was happy to see the police. Hell, even happy at the prospect of being arrested, at least I would get some sleep, I thought. That cop took one look at the massive cluster-fuck we presented, and turned around and sped off. I figure now, he must have been close to getting off, and what he saw in us was just a lot of paperwork. Maybe he just didn't like the owner of the convenience store, I'll never know. We were a mess, though, and that cop driving off, was just nuts.

David, Lauren, and I walked to the nearest hotel where I surrendered, abandoned the circus and called my mom for help. As hard ass as she was most of the time, when it came down to it, she never failed to bail me out when I really needed it. She bought me a plane ticket home and didn't even press too hard for explanations. I was a hot mess, but damn was I glad to get home. I wouldn't touch meth again I swore to myself. And would even stay true to that for many years. At home in Roswell when I finally fell asleep, I'd been awake for seven whole days. I wonder what that does to a teenager's brain permanently?

On Social Security at 16

Around this time, one night, I stole my mom's Honda Accord and drove over to Lauren's house. We were all drunk as hell and tripping on acid again when I thought it would be a great idea to go driving the car around, hauling ass through the back roads of Roswell. Down Cox road where my biological dad used to take us out, and along those dirt roads that run parallel to Cox. It was Anne Marie, Lauren Hunt, Josh Daugherty and me in the car that night, and I remember I was going 95 miles an hour. I know this because in the split second it took me to look down and check the speedometer and look back up, I'd drifted to the side of the road. I felt one tire go over and I jerked the wheel putting the little Honda into a spin going entirely faster than we should have. How we didn't die is a pure miracle. The car did a 360, then spun another 180 to take an oak tree squarely in the trunk. The spin must have slowed us down considerably and the tree hitting the back of the Honda instead of head on, spared all four of us our lives. We all got out without a scratch. I don't know how we weren't hurt or how the car was even able to drive away. Not one of us had a seatbelt on and yet not one of us had a scratch. I look back now and think of the Footprints prayer when I think of this. The three of them called a cab and I limped the damaged car back to my mom's house, rolled it down the driveway and prepared the most asinine story imaginable, and I determined to stick to my guns. At this point it was all out war with my mom, and I didn't intend on going to jail. I wiped the car completely from trunk to gas pedal for fear of incriminating fingerprints, and I left the car straddling the driveway and the pavement of the road. It was ridiculous, but I was deathly afraid she'd send me to juvenile again, this time for a felony. The cops came again that morning, she didn't believe me, of course, but I lied through my teeth, and out of desperation somehow didn't get punished. They did search for prints and found nothing. It was all coming so fast for her now she just didn't know what to do, and I don't blame her, I was a hellion.

Shortly after my grand theft auto incident, and narrow escape from death, my stepdad had come to me late one night, and offered me $500 to run away and go live with one of my girlfriends, as he put it. I was couch surfing at age 16 due to my inability to follow even the most basic semblance of the rules, like not stealing from my mom's wallet, or her car whenever I felt like it. I was a spoiled rotten brat, and I felt justified in all my behavior from some unknown reason, though I'd always fall back on the money my dad left her through life insurance, my hatred for Dan Jones, or even by now, my artist defense. Addicts are amazing rationalizers. What my stepdad hadn't foreseen was that if I wasn't living at home, I was eligible to receive my dad's social security checks, which were roughly 750 bucks a month, a small fortune to a kid. Within a month of being out of the house I was cashing those checks, MUCH to the chagrin of my mother, and immediately buying drugs to resell them. That summer with one of those checks I bought a sheet of LSD and we were out partying and selling the hits wherever we went.

You can buy a bunch of acid with $750 of social security money, and Josh Daugherty and me, and two other girls had gone to some party off Roswell Road to go sell the doses. We sold roughly 50 hits, and I had a pocket full of cash. When we left that party, two cop cars got behind us immediately. They pulled us over a few miles down the road from the party and we pulled into a gas station. They came to the passenger side window and a female officer tapped on the window with a billy club. Tripping, and paranoid, but probably rightly so, I grabbed all the LSD in my pockets and threw the doses into my mouth and began swallowing. They pulled me out of the car and then the female officer put her billy club around my throat to stop me from swallowing, and I instinctively flipped her over my shoulder, using the club as leverage. About that time I saw three more cruisers pull in and I felt a big thud hit me in the back of my head. Once I hit the ground, I could see my friends staring at me in shock as club after club began hitting me all over my body. They must have hit me twenty or thirty times. I was hurting from my ears, mouth, nose, and eyes. And I was high as a kite. I had eaten most of the acid, but I somehow spit out four hits. Enough to go to jail for a long time as each hit carried a maximum sentence of 5 years locked up. They picked me up off the ground and put my face on the hood of one of the cruisers. I felt like my face was burning off. I'm not sure if it was the actual temperature of the hood, or if the LSD just made me think it was burning, but it felt as though my face would ignite at any moment. They were screaming and yelling at me at the top of their lungs, and I was beginning to get higher and higher as the potent acid hit my bloodstream. One of the bigger of the now ten or so cops that were there, picked me up from the hood of the cruiser. Sneered at me, reached his hands down into my pants and grabbed my dick, balls and all, squeezed hard enough to make me cry out and then used his other hand to grab my throat. Another cop opened the door to the cruiser and they threw my punk ass into the back seat of the cruiser, by my balls and my throat. Even on close to 50 hits of LSD, a grown man squeezing your balls hurts like hell, and isn't something you soon forget. More than the pain, it was humiliating to the core. I watched from the back of the squad car as there was cash scattered across the parking lot, and the cops went around individually pocketing every last dollar.

They drove us down to the North Annex building right off of Roswell Road, and they called all the other kids' parents and let the parents see me, as they picked up their children, my friends who'd been along for the adventure. Every single one of the other parents teared up when they saw me. I looked like hell, bruised up, two black eyes, and blood out of every orifice. Still, I was so high I was smiling and laughing at the police. I was a stupid ass kid.

They took me to Grady Memorial Hospital where I tried to stall as long as humanly possible in fear of going to Juvenile again. The first thing I remember is the nurse trying to draw blood, and my veins moving in my arm, as she tried to poke me. She would look at me and right when the needle went towards the vein, it would jump to the right or left, and I would laugh hysterically, driving the poor woman up a wall. It went on for twenty or thirty minutes and she must have poked my arm a dozen or more times, each time, to see the vein move away, as if I controlled it. That's what happened in my mind anyway, God only knows what was really going on. She eventually spiked a vein, laughed in triumph and I watched the blood fill up in the tube tripping on 50 some odd hits of LSD, wondering if my soul was in there somewhere.

Then the policeman wanted me to urinate for a drug test and in my rebellion I was determined not to give in. Left in a room while tripping on acid with just a glass of water, eventually you're going to need to piss. I lost that mental battle with the cup of water, inevitably, finally caved in and went into the little bathroom with the cop guarding the door. As soon as I was in the bathroom I looked up and saw the tile ceilings. Immediately I jumped up on top of the toilet and lifted the tile. I could have easily escaped except for one thing: that crawl space looked scary as hell. It reminded me of the darkness of that forest not long before; on LSD, dark spaces can become anything. All I could think about was what would happen if I fell through and landed right in someone's open heart surgery mess and they died, and it was all my fault? I surrendered, got back down, pissed in the cup and handed it to the cop outside. He gave it to the nurse. We went on the space ride back to Juvenile again. I say a space ride, because if you've ever done mass amounts of LSD and gotten in a police car, you'd know they may as well be space cruisers. Their dashboards look like the consoles to interstellar galactic warships. Or at least they do on acid. And these cops were hauling ass, for the first time I enjoyed a police escort. And then we got to Juvenile.

I was so beat to hell and back that for the first time ever, I wasn't fucked with while I was in there. Also, my mom didn't know I was there yet so they didn't put me on suicide watch. My beating was a badge of honor in there that time and nobody messed with me at all. I stayed in my cell through the whole weekend, staring out the window, watching a helicopter take off and land, still seeing the trails from its last departure when it would return, for three days straight. I didn't sleep and I didn't eat. When they came to get me for court I was still tripping my balls off and it felt like just a few hours had passed, though I'd watched the sun set and rise more than once. They walked me down to the courtroom, and when I came into the courtroom, the judge was actually someone I'd seen on WSB TV a few weeks before. My mom was in the courtroom as well, and when she saw me and my damaged face she began to cry. Before I even was called to the bench for my court case, I yelled out, because I was still just out of my mind on LSD, "Judge Hatchett, I saw you on television last week and you were beautiful!" Now if I hadn't been a 16 year old cute kid, who just received the worst beat down she'd ever seen in those courtrooms I doubt this would have worked, but she called me in front of all the other case files, and she asked, "Well thank you, where did you see me again?" I said I saw her on Channel 2 and thought she looked even better in person than she did on TV. She actually smiled and then asked what happened to me. I told her I'd gotten caught up with the wrong kids, and she looked through my already long file and smiled. "Now listen son, I'm going to give you a break. I'm going to put you under house arrest from here until your 17th birthday, and I'm going to drop all these charges if you can stay out of trouble from now until then, but if you mess up, you're going to big boy jail with all these charges and whatever additional charges you'll have, do you understand me?" I did, and nodded my head, and she let me go. It was something in the neighborhood of four felonies and five misdemeanors that she was dropping. It was a freaking miracle. I don't know how it happened, but once again God smiled down on me and had some mercy.

I went home to my Uncle Jack's, as my mom still wouldn't have me, and I slept for what felt like an eternity. When I woke up I'd hoped it had been a nightmare, but it wasn't I was still black and blue all over. I spent that entire rest of the summer on house arrest, and out of trouble. Big boy jail scared me... for a while.

After several months of house arrest, living with my uncle, somehow my mom let me move back in, and even bought me a car, which would have been around the fall of my junior year. When I turned 17, I immediately started fucking up again. We all dosed some acid at Vijay's house where I tripped so hard I couldn't remember a thing. Everyone else took a hit or two, and I had to have five. The next day they told me I pulled my dick out and pissed in the corner of his room because I was too scared to leave his room and walk the ten feet to his bathroom. That entire night was basically a blackout though and I've been meaning to catch up with Vijay and Tim Pelosi about that. I say it was basically a blackout, but I do remember crazy hallucinations of me traveling through the span of my life, and not just the one I'm living now. I went through past lives, watching from a distance, in warp speed mode, ending up as a particle of the universe, ever expanding, speeding into nothingness, a part of it all, and traveling at the speed of light or faster. I settled down to see my life back on earth again just in time to see me being killed by AK-47 gunfire, and burned in a funeral pyre. It was wild. Once I witnessed my death, I became a part of a huge oak tree, spent some time in what must have been hell or purgatory, but not forever, and ended up returning to the energy that made up the universe. That's what happened in my head. What happened on Earth was that I pulled out my wiener and pissed all over Vijay's room. Once again I'd gone overboard. Everyone there, Vijay, Tim Pelosi, and Mike all had about one or two hits, but I had to play the big shot and took five.

Theft and Lies

In Mark Twain's autobiography he tells his brother that he should write one, and be honest, make an honest account of all the fool things he had done, which Twain claimed had never been done up until that time. When it was finished and Mark Twain was reading it, he looked to find the painful and distinctly un-heroic events and found "they had turned themselves inside-out and were things to be intemperately proud of." In an effort to not do what Twain's brother did, I have to bring to light some of the more disgustingly shameful things I did as a teenager that absolutely had no sense in them, and usually caused me more pain and suffering than anyone could know.

I seemed to have easily glossed over, through this drunk-a-log of my early drinking career, is how much I stole from people, including those close to me and strangers alike. The first thing I was ever caught stealing was sunglasses from Oshman's in Brannon Square in Roswell. I was with my friends and I think it was the summer between 5th and 6th grade, and I was caught and the police were called. I cried like a little girl. Hell, I was only 11. The police came and called my parents who had to come and pick me up in front of Shane Oleander, Kyle Foster, and David Tulane. It was not a proud moment.

Even before that, though, I remember stealing from my dad's wallet when he would get drunk, and we'd be in Hilton Head, and damn it I deserved some salt water taffy. That's the thing about my stealing, I never felt guilty, I was always justified in my own head. From early on. Suicidal thoughts by 7 years old, and a klepto by 11. I should have known I was destined by an alcoholic drug/addict, I had all the early signs.

Moving forward in time, once the pot and drinking got heavier, the stealing was on. I stole money from my poor mom's wallet like it was my own personal ATM. She'd accuse me and I'd lie to her face. Over and over. I'd have CD collections of everything Jimi Hendrix ever recorded from Turtles, and she'd wonder, briefly I'm sure, how I'd gotten them. But it was to get much worse before that got better. I began breaking into houses throughout my neighborhood around 13 or so. I mainly looked for liquor and beer, as I began doing it more often, I would get braver and braver. Getting a rush sneaking into someone's bedroom, going through their closets while they slept, looking for anything valuable I could get my hands on, but never really getting off with much. I mostly lifted beer, porn and occasionally I'd get lucky and steal a gun, to sell to some pot dealer. I did that once with a shotgun that was later pulled on a friend of mine, and I decided against stealing any more guns.

Worse were the times my pathetic ass got caught. The first time we were trying a tactic I'd heard about from some other drug addict, about throwing pieces of a broken spark plug into a car window so that the window would break silently. Well, it didn't break silently, and I ended up having to use a rock. I broke in the window, and then very unprofessionally removed the stereo from the car using a screw driver and about as much skill as a drunken monkey. I think I ripped crucial wires, because I remember the eventual buyer being pissed that I'd done it wrong. Worse, I talked to so many people about the hot stereo that it leaked back to Barry Denver, the victim, that I'd done it. They were a grade or two above me and got wind of it fast, and came down on me hard. I remember being at the Rec and about a dozen or so big guys pushing me around demanding I get the radio back or they were calling the cops. So I bought some time and got the radio back, much to the chagrin of whoever the hell I borrowed the money from to buy the thing back, and of course the guy I'd sold it to already. It was bad, but I told him the same thing about the cops, and he was obliged to take his money back. Of course, I had already spent the money on weed or beer or something dumb. When I went to give Barry his radio back, he was still pissed. Apparently I'd done some serious damage to the unit, because I had no earthly idea of what I was doing. I don't remember how it all came to pass exactly, but I remember there being a dozen or so big guys, once again, this time in Patrick Elliott's kitchen and they were all screaming at me. Somehow I talked Barry Denver into going into the basement, just the two of us. And then, somehow I got him to go back upstairs to ask Patrick something, at which point I ran like a schoolgirl wondering how the hell I'd gotten away from twelve guys intent on beating me up. I also wondered what the hell I was doing to put myself in ridiculous situations like this. I remember wondering why I kept getting in trouble. It was always obvious, always right there in my face, but I could never see it. I was once again a pariah at Roswell High School after that. Not that I'd ever rebounded socially from the narc accusations, but from here on out, I'd be a narc and a thief in the eyes of my peers.

Another not so proud moment I've glazed over, and I don't remember the exact timeframe but I want to say it was the spring before being put under house arrest, I organized and then took part in a robbery on Dylan Sublime's house, a musical prodigy that grew up in my neighborhood, who actually ended up being a well known musician, even writing the music to an Apple commercial among several other amazing accomplishments. We were simply out of weed one day, and by now I was at the notorious Independence High where we could check in and out at will. I got a guy named Shane, and my friend Mark Robertson, to go with me and to kick this poor guy's parents' door down, and then we stormed up to his room and stole a bunch of expensive musical equipment. We were seen leaving the scene and the cops were on us quickly. I denied ever being a part of it, and somehow, probably by God's grace, I was the only one who didn't get charged. I denied it outright, and even with two statements of my two friends against me, I somehow walked away without getting charged. It didn't do much for my popularity, though, not that I cared. If it didn't get me fucked up, I didn't care. I was glad he got all the equipment back and I was relieved I didn't get charged. I apologized to him years later, and he was a gentleman about it, though I was still in the depths of my disease and it was just an email amends, I did make it. I was ashamed of those things, but I was able to write them off, or not think about them somehow. Rationalization.

The shame would continue to pile on though. After the summer of house arrest, I was back at my mom's house, and even had a car as I recall. It wasn't long before I was in trouble again. Henry Daniels had hooked up with the Mexican cartel, and was able to get weed for dirt cheap in pounds, or libras, as they called it. I was involved in a few of those drug runs, but by this time, my reputation was crap, and I was robbed several times of my weed, and thus my profits. Once at Independence, four big tall black guys asked me to sell them a quarter, and we all went for a walk. Ironically the school was right next to the church I grew up attending, and I took them to a little alleyway across from the school, right next to my church. Before we could get halfway there, they asked to see it and I showed it to them, and they just snatched it and calmly walked away as I stammered and yelled. One turned back and I realized it was four of them, and they were big, and only one of me and I was small. It was disheartening to say the least. I would see them all the time at school and they just laughed at me. I didn't tell anyone out of humiliation, but I deserved it, I was a stupid kid, trying to be a drug dealer.

Later on in that year I asked a girlfriend of mine, sweet Jennifer Garden, whom I was an asshole to constantly, and whom my mom loved, to give me a loan that I swore I would pay back, once I sold enough weed. She agreed and the first part went well, I got the weed. But Vijay Pashtel heard about it and set me up. It's comical to think about now, but at the time I was infuriated. I went up to the clubhouse to sell a quarter pound of it to a friend of Vijay's, Justin Ditka, and I met him in the parking lot a mile or so from my house. I had the foresight, or ridiculousness rather, to bring a large kitchen knife I took from my mom's drawer. So I'm sitting there waiting for Justin, probably listening to 311 or Bob Marley, thinking I'm cooler than school, and he comes and sits in the front seat. As soon as I pull the bag out, SNATCH, and he takes off running. So I get out and start running after him as fast as possible. Clear across the golf course and we're hauling ass, but he's a got a good 100 yards on me because I had to exit the car, and just from the shock of it all. As he darts into the woods I see a car I recognize as Doug White's, Justin's friend, parked and idling, and clearly the getaway car. I bolt into his car, pull the long kitchen knife I had hidden in my pocket, and put it to his throat. I'm 17 years old, and I'm threatening a kid I used to play baseball with in little league, with his very life. And he was scared. I mean it all happened pretty quickly. To this day I'm a shocked I was able to jump in the car, pull the knife out, and get it under his neck without him blocking me, or without one of us getting hurt. "Where's Justin," I yelled melodramatically, with the knife to his throat and his eyes as big as the moon. "I don't know, I don't know!" I knew he was lying, but I also knew I wasn't going to kill him. So just like those big black guys who walked away with my money laughing, I got out of Doug's car, and he drove away laughing I'm sure. It did make me feel better to hear later that Justin had to walk a few miles before he could reconnect with a ride. Small victories. The real victory is that nobody got hurt. I knew in my heart Vijay was behind it all, hell I'd heard him plan the same scenario on at least three other kids. I just let it go. I told my girlfriend I couldn't pay her back and I felt sorry for myself while I smoked the rest of my weed, which is all I'd really wanted anyway I think. Just to stay high.

It was around this time Jennifer Garden said something to me that stuck with me throughout my drinking and drugging career. I remember I'd gotten some acid and was tripping again, and smoking a ton of weed and listening to Bob Marley and she was there on my couch, in my mother's house. As I smoked she said, "Do you remember when weed would make you laugh so hard, and every time you smoked it you'd laugh and laugh and laugh." "Yeah I do remember that." "Well it's not funny anymore, is it?" For some reason that hit me like a pile of bricks. It wasn't funny anymore. I was only smoking it not to feel like shit. Just like with cigarettes. That was one of the first times I was really able to see that I was addicted to drugs. Maybe it was the acid, maybe it was just the way she put it, but she had a point. The weed had stopped making me laugh.

Kicked Out Again

Smoking weed in my mom's house didn't last too long and I remember coming home one morning after an all-nighter without calling her to find all my clothes in laundry bags. None of my CDs or books or anything, just two trash bags filled with clothes. I moved in with my on-again, off-again girlfriend Anne Marie, and signed up for my Social Security checks again. 750 bucks a month, big money to an arrogant little high schooler. I wasn't any good at stealing, was terrible at dealing drugs, but free money from the government was a good gig. I think I'd been at Anne Marie's house about a week or so before I broke up with Jennifer Garden. I think it was both her birthday, and Valentine's Day, because I was just that kind of gentleman. Yeah quite a fella, I'd stolen 500 bucks from her, and dumped her all in the same stretch of two weeks or so. I think I even was racist or anti-Semitic with her once or twice as well because she was Jewish, and I was, well, dickish. I wish I'd been a different person back then, but you can't shine a turd. I was an asshole.

Living at Anne Marie's house was easy. Her parents were laid back and as long as I didn't hit her, like her last boyfriend Kirk Reynolds had done, I was a good guy. Her parents took me in and continued to be there for me throughout my adult life. They are generous loving and caring, and I was manipulative, selfish and using, so it made for a great match. I remember that spring basically quitting high school, staying high all the time and hanging out with Faust Santino and his friends, or "family" as he called a lot of them. Faust had gotten his own apartment by then and I spent a lot of time with him and his then-girlfriend, Amanda. They introduced me to a guy that I only knew as "Hap". He was apparently wanted by the FBI or some such, so he would pay me a grand to deliver him a pound of weed every other week or so, on top of the money I was getting from social security, so I stayed pretty blitzed for most of that summer.

Driving up those back roads to Cumming where he lived, I would often times get lost, but it was an adventure and I loved it. I'd always be high, and nervous, but then I'd deliver the weed, get the money and be on top of the world. They were all hippies, and Dead heads, and I loved hanging out with them all.

That would have been the summer of 1995. We partied pretty heavily, staying drunk and high, and occasionally getting hallucinogens. That summer there was a drug called Black Pyramids -- mescaline, I was told. I only did them once, and Anne Marie's parents were out of town that weekend. I know this because we got in a fight, and somehow I pushed her through a wall in the makeshift apartment her parents had built for us in their basement. The 2x4's supporting the sheetrock were definitely not 16 inches apart as required by regulation, because when she went through that wall, it looked like something from a cartoon, with just the outline of her body breaking through the sheetrock. I felt terrible. I called my uncle and he was able to send a carpenter out to fix the wall before her parents got back, which was good, because if they'd kicked me out I'd have been homeless.

Road Trip, the Dead, and Billy Clubs

We made it to New Orleans a couple of times that summer and partied pretty hard on Bourbon Street, but the highlight of that summer, was when I decided to visit my friend Josh Daugherty whom had moved to Chicago. I took the little white Escort my parents had bought me and I cashed in a Social Security check, and I hit the road headed north. I didn't really have a plan, and was probably drunk when I set out on the mission. I'd visited Chicago once in the winter time, and maybe I just wanted to see Josh and see the Windy City with some sunshine instead of the icy chill I remembered from my first visit. Turns out that would be my only visit. A funny thing happened on the way up there.

Coming into Indianapolis I pulled out a joint and began to smoke it. After I was good and high, I realized that I was in a traffic jam at 4 AM, and I started cussing at the cars in front of me. Then I realized it was a VW bus. Then I looked around to see hundreds of VW buses, or so it seemed, and the car next to me, having seen me smoking on my joint, were all waving and laughing at me. I rolled down my window and asked why there was all this traffic. "It's a Dead show brother, have you ever been to a Dead show man?" I was like a kid at Christmas. I'd not only been to a few Dead shows, I fucking loved the Grateful Dead and all the drugs they stood for! Hell, I'd even put my hand through a window in a fit of rage, when denied this same opportunity a few years before, but not this time, not when I was free! I followed that car off of Interstate 75 and to a little cornfield in the middle of nowhere called Deer Creek, Indianapolis. I couldn't figure out why all these cars were parking so far away, because I found a parking lot right next to the stadium. The guy asked me if I was a Rainbow or not, and I said yes, and he let me pull in and park. I assure you mine was the only white Ford Escort in the lot. The rest were VW's, buses and some other vehicles, but none of them looked quite as ghetto glorious as a white Ford Escort and I felt like I stuck out like a sore thumb. Within a few minutes of being there though I took a nap. When I woke up, the parking lot was full and it looked like a carnival was going on. The cornfields I'd driven into in the early morning were filled with buses and tourists and hippies as far as the eye could see. It was amazing. There was a bonfire going in the middle of our parking lot, and fireworks were being shot off, and all kinds of things were being smoked around me when I stepped out of my car from my nap.

The car next to me was already celebrating, playing some music, and a few were playing some drums. A cute girl came up to me and asked me if I wanted to do a Jello shot. I'd never even heard of it before, but I noted it was 10 AM, and thought it sounded like an amazing idea! I started off one of the strangest days in my life with a Jello and vodka breakfast, and was fairly drunk before noon.

I started talking to another hippie pretty soon after that, that looked exactly like what I'd always imagined Jesus Christ to look like. He spoke in riddles too, never quite answering questions and pointing out vague observations. He told me things like, "I don't owe any taxes, because I don't work for the government." And "What do you know about Russia, you have never been there, you only know what they've told you?" He also gave me 20 hits of white blotter acid to sell. He told me to take a hit with the customer every time so I'd know they weren't a Fed. The very first customer I had wouldn't take the hit, and right when I was putting the shit back in my pocket, a couple of Feds swooped in behind me with walkie-talkies and mean looking faces. I put the acid back in my pocket before the deal could go down, though, and they disappeared in an instant. Once the Feds faded into the background, Jesus came back over and walked me to another van where they were playing a Dead song with the lyrics "Don't you let that deal go down." The synchronicity sent chills down my spine. We listened to the whole song and he looked at me proudly and said "Good work." The next customer ate the acid and

I ate some with him, right there in the middle of the crowd. I sold about 10 hits before I was tripping so hard I could barely speak.

I got lost several times walking up and down the lines and lines of VW buses, and throbbing crowds of dirty hippies, and redneck tourists puking all over the place. I opened the Porta-Potty at one point and saw a dead man, needle in his arm, sitting on the toilet, his eyes rolled back into his head. I walked away fast, leaving the door open. I stood there watching for a while as a pretty young girl ran up to see whoever it was dead and start screaming and crying. I watched morbidly grinning, high as a kite. The Jesus Hippie showed up again and said something like, "Life is good out here, but it's short." He led me away from the scene to show me the ways of the Rainbow Family. "When I'm thirsty I drink, and when I'm hungry I eat," he told me, and to show me this fact, he grabbed a half empty beer out of the trash can and chugged it down, then grabbed another. Some very beautiful young girl ran up to him and gave him a huge hug and a half a grilled cheese sandwich. He looked at me ogling the girl and asked me if I wanted her. I didn't know what to say, or if I could say words at this point, and then he asked me if maybe I liked boys better. I said "No thanks, I like girls." She shrugged and walked away beckoning me to follow her, but I liked the Jesus Hippie, and besides I was too fucked up to fool around with anyone. Hours passed like comets crash, fast, furious, and mostly unnoticed, but I was entranced. We walked all over the show's parking lot and he asked me a bunch of questions. I told him all about my dad dying, my mom being a bitch, my not wanting to go to school, I told him the life story of a spoiled little rich kid, and he knew it, but didn't say much about it then. This Jesus looking character took me to a crowded point on the verge of the amphitheater but about 50 yards away from the wall of the theatre. Someone's boom box was playing Dead and I could hear the music specifically and clearly singing "If I had my way, I would tear this whole building down!" He asked me if I had tickets and I said no. He said "Then stand right here, and when it's time, go inside." He grabbed another beer from the trash and disappeared. I stood there not knowing what was going on and tripping far too hard to follow any kind of orders. All I could do was observe.

A whistle blew and it seemed like every single innocent passerby instantly became a part of a coordinated hippie army. They rushed the wall quickly and with purpose and they built a human wall in an instant. I was fixated on the wall as the hippies arose shoulder upon shoulder to the very top and began ripping the vinyl siding that held the flimsy amphitheater together. It was fascinating.

They looked like ants, well trained insects, destroying the obstacle in their way. I was smiling from ear to ear. The wall came down and the Dead's music came blaring out of the concert louder than ever. The hippies completely tore out a section of wall and began flooding into the concert by the dozens if not hundreds. Someone told me to run in but I was frozen with a mixture of fear and fascination. I wasn't moving, I wasn't even thinking about moving, I was just watching and loving it like it was my own personal movie.

But it was real and the police arrived in force. With sirens blazing, cruisers going what seemed to be full speed, came barreling through the crowd of hippies. Right in front of me, a hippie I'd talked to earlier was hit by a police car and flipped over the roof. I would see him later with a knee that was badly damaged, but for now he disappeared as cop car after cop car formed a perimeter around the site of the breach. It was like the police were even better prepared than the hippies, it was like they'd expected it, and they must have, because they pulled out all the stops in what looked like formation, though clearly my sight was something less than 20/20. The police eventually stopped all the cars, exiting in full riot gear, gas masks and all, brandishing semi automatic tear gas launchers that looked like they were right out of the future, and began launching round after round of tear gas into the crowd. The perimeter of police cars was literally right in front of me, less than a few feet away. When they opened their car doors and got out, every last one of them looked exactly like Darth Vader! My trip instantly took a turn for the worse, I could even hear their evil heavy breathing in unison, through all the chaos. Then several more of them moved into the crowd portion that was surrounded and began beating the hell out of people, innocent or not, with billy clubs. I strikingly remember one girl that I'd talked to earlier being hit by three officers while she tried to block the blows with her arms. I knew what that was like and by this point I was horrified. When the billy clubs came out, the hippies on their flanks, behind the breach and to the backs of the cops, started throwing bottles, and rocks and you name it, a full out war had begun and somehow my dumb ass was stuck right in the middle. The cop cars just in front of me, and the crowd in the middle were dying down, getting beaten, or escaping into the concert. When the bottles from the hippies behind me began screaming past my face at those cops, I thought about running, but I was mesmerized. I watched for what seemed like an hour as the battle waged, but when the chopper swooped in just above our heads, my LSD drenched senses were overwhelmed, I looked up, and ran as fast as I could as far as I could.

I've since felt ashamed at running from that battle, but having had firsthand experience with LSD and billy clubs, I knew better than to stand and fight the police. I ran all the way back to my car. I watched from the half mile or so away as the chopper swooped down, hovered, then flew away to swoop back on the crowds again. The show played on for a while, and eventually died down, but my heart didn't slow down. I was nervous and scared for the rest of that night. When people I'd met started trickling back, they were mad at me for not getting into the show. They told me to launch fireworks, but I didn't want to do that either, I was afraid I'd blow my fingers off. I was filled with a fear that is hard to describe. Fear begets fear, though, and I began to really have some crazy conspiracy thoughts about these people, and about the police, the government, about God, you name it. It wasn't like your regular bad trip. From that point on I was scared to death. Helicopters flew over the crowds the whole night, and police walked all over the area, still in full riot gear, still looking like Darth Vader, with dogs barking at everything, all night long. It looked like Armageddon, and I wanted my trip to end, but it wouldn't. I spent the entire night, though, being judged by the hippies I was crashing with, in that parking lot. I came to find out I wasn't really welcomed in that lot, that it was for Rainbow Family, and that I wasn't one of them. They asked me to take some kids to Soldiers Field, Chicago, which was the next show, and I said no, and it just became a hostile environment for me the entire rest of that night. At some point they started playing the Beatles song with the lyrics "Get back, get back to where you once belonged." At the time I thought it was a Dead song and I really thought it was a sign that I should definitely go. I tried to relax, playing drums with the group as the night wore on, but the choppers and the dogs kept us all tense. Throughout the night, hippies would straggle back to the lot, bleeding, with stories of tragedy and demise. One guy said he was hit by a cop car, and I thought he could have been the guy I'd seen. His knee was split wide open and I thought he needed to go the hospital, but he refused. You could see the bone of his knee, and his entire leg was covered in blood. I wouldn't say I lost my patriotism that night, because I didn't, I'm still a patriot, but I was no longer innocent as to how we keep law and order in this country. We keep it by force. When people get out of line in the United States, it looks just like any other riot in any other part of the world. Cops beating up civilians. I'll never forget that day.

I couldn't sleep though, I was still fueled too heavily by the hallucinogens. My heart hurt also, at any moment I expected that heart attack my mom had always warned me about. I remember just mumbling about having a headache and someone gave me two pills.

71

I took it and the headache went away almost instantly. My heart slowed down as well. I imagine they were probably something strong. I couldn't wait for the lot to open so I could leave. I forgot why I was going to Chicago. I just wanted to go home. As soon as they opened the gate to our exclusive little parking lot, I hauled ass.

Dark Side Recruitment

I know I was on a lot of acid, and I know I was gathering meaning from things that were meaningless like that Beatles song, "Get Back", but I believe that car ride home is where my thinking took a sharp turn for the worse, and wouldn't subside until I began to get sober years down the road. I began to analyze the last 24 hours' events. Up until this point I'd completely disregarded my religious Methodist upbringing as nonsense, I was an atheist pure and simple. I had read the Bible through and through, several times and had long since decided that most of the stories were horseshit, that the text itself was created to keep the populations of civilizations calm, the opiates for the masses theory. When I began hanging out with hippies at Independence or Roberto Morena who had said he was "family," I'd discarded their theories as ridiculous and continued hanging out with them for the good drugs that all these people seemed to have. I remembered being invited to go to "gatherings" every full moon and solstice and what have you, and I'd always just said "no thanks" for the same reason I had politely told my mom "no thanks" for so many years as a teenager when invited to church. I regarded it all as superstitious bullshit for the weak. But for whatever reasons, and maybe they were psychotic in nature or at the base, I began to evaluate everything that had happened to me from a religious standpoint.

Coming down from LSD is a serious business, and not for the weak of heart, it can drive you mad, and you want it to be over with. The harder the trip, the longer it takes to come down, and I had tripped mighty heartily at this Dead show and was still going strong, but starting the massive analysis of thought that happens as it wears off. That, and I had roughly 12 hours to go before I got back to Atlanta. I began to believe the entire event had been ordained by some being. That my arriving in Indianapolis couldn't have been by accident. That perhaps God, or better yet, his opposite, the Devil, had made all this happen. I saw the Jesus like figure pointing me around the show, offering girls, boys, drugs, food, beer, the free show, all as bribes to get me to join him and the Rainbow Family. As I began plotting this all out in my head, I began to connect dots that may or may not have been there, but that suddenly became very real to me. Roberto Morena finding us in Little Five, giving us free weed, and the drug connections other kids dreamed of. All the free acid I got from Faust and Hap and his other hippie friends. I began to wonder if I wasn't being recruited to the Dark Side. Ah, how important it must have made me feel, that they would riot just to try to seduce me into this world of theirs. But I'd shown them! I'd escaped with my soul intact! AH HAH! That's what they wanted, my soul! Thoughts and theories began pouring into my head without warning or notice. I began seeing everyone on that road back to Atlanta as either with them, or against them, and I was chiefly undecided. No, I would await formal notification. If the Devil wanted my soul I'd need to review the contract. But subtle hints kept coming more and more, furious and fast. On that stretch of highway I saw more hippies driving luxury vehicles than I'd ever seen in my life. A huge truck with a cigarette boat attached by trailer, chock filled with hippies passed me first, all its long haired occupants staring me down. Then a BMW M3 with a Steal Your Face (Grateful Dead) sticker pulled up. The driver grinned at me, taunted me, and then took off. Psychically, I knew they wanted me to join them and this was their recruitment effort. To show me that they had people everywhere, that they were entrenched in society, that they had deep pockets! But it wouldn't work. Not with a few drive-by's anyway.

As I continued to drive back to Atlanta, retreating from the chaos, and the massive recruitment effort, I couldn't stop the onslaught of racing conspiracy thoughts, and plots to get me, and not only me, but society in general. I saw a phone company van with a Dead sticker on it, so they had people there too. I saw tons of VW buses and bugs, and hippies of every shape size and color. The other very strange thing that happened to me on that road, was that everywhere I stopped to get gas, the exact same course of events played out. In Deer Creek I pulled in to get gas and I paid, then I was walking out the attendant yelled "HEY, you didn't pay for your gas." I was tripping so hard, I didn't know what to say. I just looked at him, and then I saw two cops there as well staring me down. Scared, knowing I was guilty of something, and knowing these cops were probably wearing masks and beating up little girls the night before, I went ahead and paid the man a second time. I couldn't say much. But then it happened again somewhere in Kentucky where I got gas the second time. I paid cash, started to walk out and the clerk starts yelling at me, "You didn't pay for your gas, son!" I looked back, and cops walked in the front door this time, so once again I was in a precarious situation, so I ended up paying for a full tank of gas again. This kicked in all kinds of conspiracy theories, as well. They were organized. I wonder if this happened to any other underage, fucked up hippies leaving that show. Or were they just after me? I still don't know the answer to that question. I guess it is entirely possible, that I was just tripping so hard I walked up to the counter, thought I had paid, and didn't. But that would make too much sense. In my mind, they were definitely out to get me, and if not connected to the Rainbow Family, they were at least getting inside information from them. That was much more logical.

From that acid trip on, anything regarding the word "family" would take on a new meaning for me. I would never be able to pinpoint an exact organizational structure, but if you used the word "brother" you would, in the back of my mind, be a part of the vast left wing conspiracy out to crush the United States, steal my soul, and share everything you had like socialists. In fact, no wonder the Grateful Dead had dancing bears on so many stickers, wasn't that of Russian origin? Communist Russia in fact! Of course, communists lived in hippie "communes", these guys were good, but their plots weren't lost on me! They also generally just had much better drugs. Family acid for instance or Family ecstasy was always better than average. So though I would oppose the theology or their supposed ideals, I would eventually gravitate towards this imagined group, basically hippies, for their drugs and connections. It was on this road trip, escaping the riots and throngs of hippies that these thoughts would gain steam. The delusion was always so vague in my mind that people were inadvertently playing into it all of the time while I was drunk, stoned or generally high. "Yeah brother, we're family, Sin Brethren, rock on man, pass the joint," and such was so easily heard at any given moment, that though folks didn't realize, they would be helping me build a delusion that would last for years, albeit temporary, and really only when I was in that state of mind, smoked out or tripping, still it was persistent. When stone cold sober, I was never worried about a mafia of smelly hippies taking over the world, that's for damn sure. Problem was, I never spent much time sober.

Losing Time

I hit the road again and when I finally got to Georgia, I didn't get overcharged for gas. It was the 4th of July, and the rain was spotty. It would be pouring in one instant and the next it would stop. I remembered some hippie at the show talking about the government controlling the weather, and I remember thinking, it does always rain on the 4th of July, hmmm? I was tripping so hard I went by

Hap's before getting home to get some weed and unload about the adventure I'd been on. He handed me a bottle of Klonopin, probably sensing I could use the downtime from the nutty ass ramblings I was spouting off, and I went home, took a couple and slept for a long, long time.

I remember waking up, seeing the bottle of Klonopin and going to the ATM. I remember looking at my bank account balance, seeing that I had 700 dollars in there, and then I went to go get some beers somehow. I lost that entire week. I mean lost it, I couldn't tell you what I did that week to save my life. Alcohol, Klonopin, and whatever else I ran across in my rambling week after that Dead show, erased all memory from my mind of what took place that week. The only record I had of it was when I came back to consciousness and went to the ATM to find the balance was 0. I was so lost and confused by that I went through my car to look for evidence of what I'd done. All I found was about three Klonopins underneath my seat, so apparently, at some point, I'd thought it was a good idea to eat some while driving. Nice. Anne Marie, my girlfriend and roommate had been out of town for about two weeks now and she came home that day. She was a little concerned I'd blown through all my money already, but as always she forgave me and we went to go hang out at a friend's house.

We went over to Sean and Dianna's and it was there that Sean informed me I'd been drunk a good bit of that week, which I had pretty much surmised, but he looked a little pissed at me and that I wasn't comfortable with. "What happened to your table" I asked him, as I noticed their glass table was missing.

"You really don't remember?"

"Remember what?" but I didn't like where it was going.

"You came over here Wednesday, asked for a beer, took one sip and then passed out falling right though the table, shattering the glass and all. You didn't get a scratch on you."

"Really?" I was dumbfounded. But at the same time, it had been a rough few weeks, so I believed him.

When Diana nodded I took it as fact. It's hard to dispute things when you black out for weeks on end. At least Anne Marie was still a happy-go-lucky laid back kind of girl. She really didn't get pissed at me for any of this shit, though had it happened later in our relationship I'm sure she would have, at this point I guess we were all just kids. I guess in retrospect she helped enable me quite a bit, but at the time I just thought I was lucky as hell, and I still feel that way. We had a lot of fun together, and it still seemed like the drinking worked.

One day I was driving to see my uncle, maybe to pay him for sending the guy out to fix the sheetrock when I'd thrown her through the wall. I'd just finished smoking a huge joint in the car ride to go see him, and I turned too quickly in front of a woman, and even though I'd already made it into the parking lot, she panicked and turned into the parking lot to broadside the passenger side door, where Anne Marie was sitting. Once again it was a miracle that nobody was hurt. The car was a total loss, though, the engine would run but the entire side panel caved in making it undriveable. Shortly thereafter, Anne Marie and I broke up. This sucked pretty badly, since I lived with her. At some point all of my stuff was packed and put into that car, and it was a sad sight to behold. My beat up Escort with the scant possessions a 17-year-old owns, with nowhere to go. Homeless, not the first time already, but not the last either, and still just as frightening. I was still living there with her technically on the couch, but I had to begin looking for somewhere else to go, and my options were severely limited, having no job, being 17 and not to mention being a raging alcoholic drug addict, though I'd not even come close to considering this an issue at the time. I remember feeling pretty desperate.

Getting Pregnant

I remember also that Anne Marie talked a lot about having babies. She was a babysitter for Derrick and Barbara Rudolph, a nice, well-off couple down the road, and she had always romanticized being a mom. So when we got drunk one night and she eased my broken heart by making love to me, I remember thinking the logical thing to do would be to come inside her and make a baby, forcing us to be together. This was codependency at its finest, but I guess I figured it would end my homelessness, moving from the car in the driveway, or her couch depending on her moods, to her bedroom permanently, again, and of course fill the huge void I felt anytime I was single. It was me forcing my will onto the world, and I made the conscious decision to do so, though I was drunk, I still remember the decision, the ultimate "fuck it". She whispered "come in me" that night, and so I did. It was a magical night of romance and drinking and we were back together for the time being. I don't think it lasted very long, though, and was probably only fueled in the first place by our proximity to each other, being quasi-roommates, and of course by alcohol.

It was the beginning of our senior year at Independence, and wouldn't you know it, Anne Marie became pregnant. My plan had worked, all too well. And so I moved my stuff out of the Escort, back into the house. Things looked like they may work themselves out, and honestly even though the marriage ultimately didn't, I do believe her getting pregnant did save my life in many ways. I think we'd known for about a week before we had a talk about what to do. I remember it was a beautiful fall day, and in Georgia, a cool sunny fall day can be close to heavenly. We were walking outside while her parents were doing yard work and we sat down in the freshly cut grass. She was waiting for me to say something definitive.

"I think we should do it." I said, imagining us married, doing yard work together 20 years from now as her parents now were, on that corner lot near downtown Roswell.

She was instantly thrilled and our relationship had never been better. We were both very happy. I was under the impression it meant we would get married, but a few months down the road when I proposed to her with the first thing I'd ever financed in my life, and she said no, I realized I was sadly disillusioned. I immediately felt used and ashamed and regretting agreeing to having the baby, but it was too late in her mind, and she was dead set on having the child. I wanted to, provided I got my way, or rather, got her, but otherwise, I wasn't as excited.

I can tell you who else wasn't too excited either, and that was my mom. My poor mother, raised Southern Baptist, gone Methodist, and practically a youth minister at our church, Roswell United Methodist, was distraught. She had my uncle at the time, Eric Coleman, come to me privately and offer to pay Anne Marie money to have an abortion. "What would people think of her?" That's the way Eric had described it to me. I had already done my absolute best to convince Anne Marie to change her mind about the baby. Once I found out that her pregnancy didn't make Anne Marie instantly fall in love with me, and the possibility that I could end up single and having to pay child support became real, I had freaked out, and had begged her to change her mind but she was having none of it. In retrospect I thank God for that, but at the time I was already panicky. But even though I wanted the same result, when my mom had Eric come to me with this shady ass, backhanded, underground offer that she couldn't do herself, going against her own Christian preaching, which had been stuffed down my throat for years, I was absolutely outraged and disgusted. I told Eric to go to hell, and I told Anne Marie what had happened, and we stayed mad at my mom for years to come over that incident. It came down to her precious Roswell reputation. Her real estate agent image, I thought. She cared more about that than anything, the way things seemed to be, not the way they were. That is how it transpired, and though she is dead and not able to defend herself, it happened, and wasn't a proud moment for any of us.

It would get worse before it got better, though, unfortunately, on many fronts. My addictions continued to get worse, and though Anne Marie and I moved in together in a little house in Mountain Park, bordering Roswell and Cherokee County, I was still maintaining it mostly with social security checks from my father's death. As Anne Marie got bigger and bigger, I got more and more fucked up, and continued hanging out with my hippie friends and selling weed, acid and rolls, or ecstasy tabs as they're called. After my crazy thoughts from what I thought was my narrow escape from the Rainbow Family, I'd basically written off all of that spiritual experience to tripping too hard, and continued hanging out with the hippies that had the best drugs. Anytime something uncomfortable would come up, I would justify my company with the thoughts of atheism, that they were just as wrong as my Jesus freak mother who had turned out to be as big a hypocrite as any. And then something happened that made my skin crawl.

New Orleans and Computer City

We were on our way to the Jazz Festival in New Orleans that year, of course leaving my pregnant girlfriend at home, and we took my beat up old Toyota Corolla, me, this hippie Tyler, and a couple of other guys. We'd been going to out of state raves together unloading drugs and this was just another adventure, an excuse to get high. It was rumored Phish would play and before the trip was over we would watch them jam overlooking Bourbon Street. On the way down there Tyler said something about Jesus, and scoffed at the idea that Jesus was the son of God. And then he looked at me and said "You don't really believe Jesus was the son of God, do you?" Something in his tone, or his eyes, made my skin crawl. I shrugged, but I couldn't shake the feeling that he was after something spiritually, that he had an ulterior motive of some sort. We got to New Orleans and we stayed with the Hare Krishnas for free. He said it was simply because it was free, and I basically made fun of them, but there was something altogether sinister about the whole trip I felt. Perhaps it was just my perception of the events, but I couldn't help but falling back on the fears I'd established retreating from that Dead show that these people were after my soul. It may sound as ridiculous, as it feels typing it, but that's how I felt and I began to think about the entire affair, in more detail, drawing back on past delusions from the Deer Creek Dead show as well.

Around the same time I was working at Computer City, and doing a good job of it. In fact, they had hired a bunch of really technical, not so sales adept people to sell the computers, and I was a natural born salesman, though up until this point it had mostly been illegal products. I was the top sales guy there in what would have been my senior year had I attended. By this time, I had finished all my academic courses and was only working on electives, so what was the point I told myself? Besides, I was making 30k a year selling computers and enjoying it at the same time. At Computer City I ran into a very intense individual name Graham Flagg. He was extremely intelligent, and extremely spiritual, though not of the Baptist or Methodist type, and we immediately began debating the merits of the Bible, me of course arguing the lack thereof.

"Wouldn't you at least agree as a historical document it's an incredible source of old knowledge?" I remember him saying, and me responding, "Nope, it's a fucking fairy tale."

He told me he had three years clean and sober, to which I think I responded "Sorry," but it didn't make him blink, he continued to talk to me about how great his life was sober. I told him about my dad killing himself, and we connected right from the start. He was both intense and intelligent, but I still regarded him as somewhat of a whack job. We both smoked cigarettes though and we ended up talking quite a bit outside on our smoke breaks. Usually about God. One night the sun was setting across the mall at North Point where there are no trees to block the skyline and you can see a larger chunk of the sky than most places in tree-covered hilly Atlanta. I'll never forget him saying "The best artist in the world couldn't paint a better sunset. It took millions of years for all of this to come together so you and I could enjoy this sunset together." That has stuck with me since. I'm a better man for meeting Graham. I would be dead if it weren't for him, but he got me to thinking about God way back then, and perhaps that's why I was so uncomfortable when Tyler dropped that Jesus bomb on me on the way to New Orleans. Maybe it was all the Christian upbringing, my confirmation at 12, or the reading the Bible three times over, I don't really know, but Tyler gave me the heebie-jeebies that trip, no two ways about it.

When I returned from that trip from New Orleans, having drunk, smoked, tripped, rolled, and even spent hours curled up on Bourbon Street gripping nitrous balloons, I went back to work and things continued to get weird. Again, if analyzed it probably is easily all chalked up to THC induced paranoid schizophrenia or early psychosis, but damn if it didn't feel real. I think Graham could tell I was fucked up, and I think I'd probably called in sick a few days just to get the time to go to New Orleans, and I probably looked like hell, but he's not what I remember that day. After days of being trashed, and feeling icky about the Jesus comments, this weird guy from computer repair began asking me about my soul. "You don't believe in souls, do you Bryan?"

"Nope," I said, not sure where he was going with this. He continued, "Well then, could I buy yours for a dollar?" And he grinned eerily.

"Nope," I said, and then he stared at me some more and asked "Why not if you don't believe in souls?"

"Just in case, I guess," and I walked away from that whacko, avoiding the computer repair shop for the remainder of the day.

At that time there was a "spiffed" item at Computer City, and for those unlearnt in the lingo of sales, a spiff is like a commission except it's just a straight cash prize. Sell something and you get the commission, plus the spiff. The spiff was on an Apple clone from Power Computing. I'd been trying to sell the damn thing for months and nobody in the entire sales force had even come close. That day, right after that weird ass conversation about my soul, this very well-dressed gentleman came in looking like a lost puppy. So I showed him around, gave him the tour and ended up on the spiffed computer that would line my pockets with an additional 100 dollars. I was amped and I was eager to be the first to get the spiff. Now this is going to sound crazy, because guess what, it's likely I am, but I heard a voice in my head say, "For your soul, I'll give you this sale." I had to think about it, and then wrote it off as me just being crazy, and I said back to the voice in my head "Yes, you can have my soul for this sale." Then a really freaky thing happened. He bought the computer. Then he came back an hour later and bought another one. I immediately felt guilty. Guilty isn't the word for it. I felt like I was going to burn in hell for it. The incidents by themselves seemed irrelevant, but in my head it was as if the universe was plotting different people into my life all exploring the same values. Did I believe in the soul? Was I willing to sell it? The thoughts in my head raced, and I thought of little else compulsively. I was consumed at this time with Tyler asking me to deny Christ in New Orleans, the computer repair guy asking, however jokingly to buy my soul, and the voice in my head that offered the sale for my soul. It's hard to describe how an alcoholic's mind can focus on one thing and not much else. Usually the negative, but at that time I still had a solution that worked. That could quiet the mind and the incessant racing thoughts that were consuming my every moment. I went home and got drunk over it. As if I needed an excuse.

Drug Deal Gone Bad

I continued on my life of being a degenerate 18 year old father-to-be/drug dealer/computer salesman. The ridiculousness of this lifestyle came to a head one night, when I was offered a drug deal that seemed too damn good to be true. But I was young, I was tight on cash, and I needed a good deal, so I went along with it. My normal life, collided with my "thug" life, though, when I asked one of the guys I worked with, Jason, to come along with me. He smoked pot, so I didn't think he'd be shocked at a drug deal, and I needed to look stronger than just little old me by myself, so I invited this poor sucker along for the ride, and I didn't tell him I was going to buy a pound of weed. I also had my old drug dealer Bob's money to purchase the weed, which was supposed to be top notch. I had around a thousand dollars, which I'd hidden in my shoe. Jason and I were at my little house in Mountain Park, and we waited for Keith Finley and another guy named Jesse. Keith and Jesse came to pick us up and from there and we were supposed to go straight to the deal, but instead we went to a friend of theirs' house where Keith and Jesse took a few shots and began to get drunk. Well, this was strange and I was a little irritated, but thought nothing of it. Eventually, the phone call came for us to go meet the hook up, so we all piled into my car and began to head that direction. I was driving, poor Jason was in the front seat, and Jesse and Keith Finley were in the backseat. They both began to simultaneously close their eyes and doze off, remaining just conscious enough to lead me to the site where the deal was supposed to go down. I can't believe I didn't see it coming.

When they'd directed me to this parking lot, in an apartment complex off Roswell Road, I realized that the lot had one way in and one way out. As soon as I'd pulled in, one car pulled up behind me blocking my exit, and another car pulled in next to me. It was the perfect location for an ambush. A tall, rough-looking black guy jumped out, and came to my driver's side window. "Give me the cash and I'll go get the weed", he said. He failed to mention the amount of weed, show me a sample or anything else and I instantly knew I was fucked, but just how fucked I was, I didn't quite know yet.

"Let me see a sample." I said.

"I gotta go to a place nearby and get it" he said, but he really wasn't even trying to pitch it that hard, it was obvious they intended on ripping me off. I was instantly glad I'd stashed Bob's money in my shoe rather than in my wallet. I remember, looking in the backseat and seeing Keith and Jesse, pretending to be passed out. It all seemed a little too coincidental to me. Poor Jason just looked scared in the passenger seat. He certainly hadn't expected to be doing a drug deal in a shady part of Atlanta off Roswell Road, and getting blocked in had made us both nervous, to say the least.

I was a smartass: "Well my money is nearby, too. I gotta see a sample first and then I was going to go to an ATM."

About that time he pulled out a gun, hard and fast, I had a pistol up against my temple and he's screaming at me, "Give me the fucking money white boy, I know you got the money, give me your wallet!"

I was definitely scared, but for some reason, not panicky. I swore up and down I didn't have the money on me, and handed him my wallet which had like two or three bucks in it. The bulk was all safely in my shoe. Also it wasn't my money. I was thinking that if I give him the money, I'll just have a different gun against my head in a week. Might as well die right now. And I remember that thought giving me relief.

He pointed the gun at Jason and asked for his wallet, never once paying the two idiots in my back seat the least bit of attention, which was ultimately the giveaway for the two saps. Pocketing Jason's petty cash from his wallet the gun went back into my temple. I thought about hitting him, I thought about getting out of the car and trying to fight, and I thought about dying. Dying seemed to be the best answer, and I wished for it.

He screamed at me a few more times, and I said "Fuck you I don't have it." I wasn't about to give in to him. Out of pride, out of ego, out of suicidal tendencies, I choose to potentially die rather than give this guy Roberto Morena's money. Then he started a countdown. I
82

actually got excited. The feeling right before you go down on a roller coaster, the long ride up that first hill, the butterflies building up in your stomach until the wings are fluttering your tonsils. With a kid on the way, an addiction to everything on the planet I couldn't break, bills piling up, and my drug dealing career obviously on the skids with a gun to my head, I just remember thinking it will all be over soon and I'd rather die than give Bob's money up." 10...9...8...7..." He kept counting down, and I think he expected me to give him the money right up until he pulled the trigger. "3...2...1..." and then I heard the loudest click, metal on metal, you can ever hear on Earth. Before I could do a thing, he jumped in the car, and both vehicles peeled out quickly leaving the scene empty handed other than the few bucks from our wallets. I looked in the back seat and Keith and Jesse hadn't budged an inch, though I could have sworn Jesse had a smirk, and Keith looked a little worried. I was furious.

I drove out of the apartment complexes feeling angry, diminished and defeated. I couldn't even get shot properly, I'd thought for sure it was over the whole time. I drove Keith and Jesse back home, drove Jason back to his car, and went back to my little house in Mountain Park, a little relieved to be back alive, and with all of Bob's money, but still angry and certainly not victorious. I told Anne Marie what happened and she cried, and begged me to quit dealing drugs.

Payback

The next day I drove the money in my shoe back to Roberto Morena, and I told him the story. It took me explaining the whole situation to grasp how obvious it was Jesse and Keith had set the whole thing up. Bob said "There are no coincidences." That definitely stuck with me throughout my life from that moment forward, and I believe he was right then and in many instances later on down the road. But for all his bad, Roberto Morena offered me some good insight, asking me "Why'd I keep the money?" I said I really didn't know. He said it was because I didn't value my life. That life was worth a whole hell of a lot more than a thousand bucks, and I could have worked it off somehow. That I was basically stupid, fucked up, and had a lot of growing up to do. He also told me getting married was a mistake and I'd be divorced inside of five years if I were so lucky as to be wed. How right he would end up being. He also told me if I ever wanted to be able to deal for him again I had to set shit straight with these two guys that had set up the deal. That I'd never find the actual hoods that did the robbing, but that I needed to set things straight with Jesse and Keith. So I gave him his money back, went back to Mountain Park, bought a bottle of vodka, began to get real drunk, and asked a couple of friends to come over as backup.

Patrick Elliott, who had just gotten out of a two year rehab program in Idaho, and who'd just recently relapsed at my house, a bender that continues unabashed since that relapse, came over to back me up, and my poor friend Jason volunteered to come over as well. I don't think Anne Marie knew what I had planned, and to be honest, I wasn't quite sure what I was going to do, but I wanted to talk to them both, and of course I needed to be drunk to do it.

We had a very tiny kitchen in that little house in Mountain Park, and I had cleared off the marker board for the presentation I'd planned. One thing that pissed me off was how I didn't see it coming, how the ambush took place, and how intelligent they'd been in setting up a meeting place, to be able to completely block me in. So when Jesse and Keith got to my house I took them into the kitchen and I showed them the drawing of the meeting place, and I asked them how they could have known the spot, known the dealers we were supposed to meet and still not have known I was going to have a gun to my head? I was more than a little drunk, feeling ten feet tall, and I had Patrick, Jason, and my pregnant wife, all surrounding the kitchen as I drew out the obvious on this marker board. Jesse and Keith's faces, conscious this time, had the same emotions as when they were passed out in the car, Keith looked a little scared, and Jesse was smirking with a little evil grin, like he'd won something.

Now I honestly don't think I've ever won a fight because I was tough, or strong or tactical, but as James Brown says: I don't know karate, but I know crazy! My little 5' 6" ass kicked the ever living shit out of both of these two 6 foot plus clowns in my kitchen that day. This wasn't like when Vijay and Justin had run off with my quarter pound of schwag, though I'm sure that incident helped Jesse and Keith to conjure up this plan. No, this was different. They'd put a gun to my head and someone had pulled the trigger. I still don't know if it was empty, a malfunction, or a good old fashioned miracle. Every flavor of crazy unleashed on them in that kitchen, and I remember Anne Marie screaming and it all happening very quickly. Someone's head went through the stove glass, and I had Keith on the ground wailing into his face, and then Jesse reached down and tried to pull me off, and I punched him in the face again as he fell. I remember finally grabbing Keith, bloodied up as hell and screaming at the top of my lungs, and proud, "Get the fuck out of my house, get the fuck out of here!" We were all 18 years old and we were all stupid ass kids. But for that little while, I was proud. I also promised Anne Marie I would quit dealing drugs. She was a month or two away from giving birth, and even I could see how ridiculous the entire situation had been. But for that night, I was victorious, and Patrick, Jason and my pregnant girlfriend all sat around talking about how I'd beaten up two bigguys in my kitchen. An egomaniac with an inferiority complex in the making.

Alabama, Wiccans, God, and the Devil

That incident scared me straight for a month or so, until Tyler and the hippie crew again scooped me up one weekend and we all drove off to some rave in Alabama, and sold acid and booty rolls the whole night long, which is basically ecstasy, but with extra heroin in them. We still hadn't slept the next morning and this entire motley crew was at an art gallery in downtown Birmingham completely trashed and out of place as the sun rose. I was still awake when we drove home, and I'd made some cash as well, as I had five hits of acid and three rolls left. I remember waiting a few days before getting high again, long enough for the acid to work, and then with Anne Marie a week or two away from giving birth to my son, I took all the drugs I had and began what would in my head be a spiritual journey I wouldn't or couldn't soon forget.

At first I was having fun enjoying my trip and as it got late into the night and after Anne Marie fell asleep I remember exploring in my head the ability for me to know "all". I remember thinking I could remember past lives, that I knew how the universe worked, that I could recall a past life in Germany, vividly, pushing a cart out of a ditch, and being burly and hairy. Like it was yesterday. Then I remember controlling my heartbeat, or thinking I could, at least. Stopping it and starting it at whim, getting a rush the longer I kept it from beating. Right up until I couldn't get it to start beating again. I began to panic, trying to breathe and nothing would come out. I fell to the ground. I could see Anne Marie, pregnant and beautiful in our bed, but I couldn't move. I thought for sure I was dying.

Then I saw a vision that I wouldn't be able to shake for many years. I saw God, and I saw the Devil, right there in our bedroom in our little shack in Mountain Park. God was impassive, frowning, not looking happy, but not looking sad. In my vision, or what a doctor would later call my hallucination, God was the white-bearded character on the back of Tolkien's book Lord of the Rings, and the Devil, was Roberto Morena, Bob, my first and favorite drug dealer, who'd spent hours talking to me about "family" and Pagan ideas and philosophies, and he was grinning from ear to ear. He kept saying "Now or later, Bryan, now or later." I attributed the inevitability of that statement to my selling my soul already, in order to have sold that computer a month or so before. I thought I was going to hell, I thought I was dying right then and there. This time, unlike with the gun to my head months before, I was very, very scared of death. Back then, there'd been no God, but now, with there being a God, right in front of my face, and my so clearly having shamed him, I was going to hell. My mind and brain haunted me with the hours I'd spent with Faust Santino, a proud Wiccan, and his crew of Tyler, Hap, and others who'd invited me to every full moon event, or gathering in the woods for the last year or so, and I knew I'd been cavorting with evil. All this time I'd taken their free drugs, all the hook ups, the Dead shows in which I was treated like royalty. Even the lyrics of half the Dead songs jumbled up in my mind, convicting me of evil and sentencing me to death, and ultimately hell. I went from being an atheist to remembering every sin I'd committed in one bad trip and here were God and the Devil on my judgment day, and I was fucked.

Somehow I got to my knees and I begged God to be able to live, to be a good dad, and do the right thing. All the debating, all of the options I'd considered of running away, of leaving Anne Marie and going to follow Phish, or join the Rainbow Family or smuggle drugs through Mexico or any other escapist fantasy, all left me when I was suddenly able to breathe in again, and breathe deep, and my heart began to beat again, though painfully. It was thumping, and I was glad to be alive! It was a miracle! I was spared, and I was going to be the best father, husband, and good man I could be! The hallucination went away, and I went up to the kitchen to see if there was any milk to drink to get me down from this crazy ass high. My heart pounded, and again I feared for the fragile muscle and the inevitable heart attack my mom predicted. With the milk, it slowed and I began to feel better. Just like the last spiritual trip I'd had, it could all be explained scientifically, but inside I'd truly felt a miracle happen. Something within had changed, just enough, that I wanted to live, that I wanted to see what life had to offer, that I believed in God and he was good, that he'd spared me from death and hell. Perhaps my soul hadn't been mine to sell? Months later I would see a church sign stating exactly that and it would give me comfort, though lingering fears would remain in the backdrop for years.

I'd hoped to come down quickly but I'd taken a lot of ecstasy and acid and I was still feeling it the next day around five or six when

Tyler came over and asked how I was doing. I could tell Anne Marie was pissed so I went outside with him. I told him I'd had an amazing experience that I couldn't hang out with him anymore. He said there was heroin in the ecstasy I'd taken, and did I want some more? He could shoot me up and I'd feel great. We could leave from there, and never come back. I said hell no, and don't come back here. It felt like I'd stood at the crossroads and won, that I'd made the right decision. Anne Marie was glad that he was gone, still worried about me, but had faith in me, and I'm sure I made her a hundred promises that it was the last time I'd trip. I don't think I told her the extent of how high I was. I finally fell asleep that night, but not before what felt like another lifetime of analyzing, all-encompassing soul searching, like the experience of coming back from Deer Creek, where I Jedi Mind Fucked myself for hours on end, developing theories and rationalizing madness. Coming down from that trip was a trip in itself, and I thought for hours before finally falling asleep.

After Tyler, and the rest of the Wicca crew left, I began dissecting the year leading up to my meeting God and the Devil, and I came up with what I thought were some concrete assertions .

1. They were all Rainbow Family, Sin Brethren, and such, and they were mystical, magical, or maybe even demonic, they did want my soul, and I'd just barely escaped.

2. All my hanging out with them, using their drugs, going to their parties, and drinking their alcohol had been designed to attract me over to the dark side. The invitations of the last year to go to "Gatherings" were basically praying to "Mother Earth," they said, which clearly in retrospect as I contemplated it all, was to pray to the creations, and not the Creator.

They had told me they were Wiccans and I'd said I didn't care, that I was atheist, which was the ultimate defense. This allowed me to walk in the grey, neither good nor evil, but for that entire year since Deer Creek, I'd entertained, even if just subconsciously, the idea of going over to the dark side, as if it were an actual location, or an event that could take place. The ultimate escape in my mind, though, was running with the hippies, following the Dead, or Phish, or Widespread Panic, selling drugs, and giving society the ultimate finger. Consciously, every time I got high, I considered leaving Anne Marie, all my responsibilities, and joining this unspoken alternative to life. Thoughts are things, and while high, all year long, I'd debated the pros and cons of selling my soul, running with America's gypsies, and leaving her in Roswell to deal on her own with my coming son. I've still never seen that contract from the Devil, but man did it feel real.

All through my life I'd personalized songs, taken them into my mind as if they were written for me, and me alone, but that year, it had reached a new level of intensity, while this path to these crossroads peaked, I would hear songs on that radio that spoke to just me. Subconsciously edging me along down this road, I thought. Spacehog's "In The Meantime" became a theme song of this vast conspiracy, with its line "All in all we're just like you." It had played on the radio constantly and every time it did, it would kick-start my escapist thoughts. I mean, they were just like me, they were really no different, ya know?

Another one that would get me thinking was "Possum Kingdom" by the Toadies: "Make up your mind. Give it up to me. Do you wanna be my angel? Do you wanna die?" Crazy as that may sound, it was romantic to me, in a way. White Zombie's "Superhuman", "More human, than human!" raged in my head from time to time, hinting at the powers I'd be granted if I just came along for the ride. In my deluded stoned out mind, The Devil, darkness, the conspiracy, calling out to me, pleading with me to join, offering me nothing but what I'd conjured up with the help of other songs like the Grateful Dead classics "High Time" singing "We could have a high time, living the good life." And, of course, "Ripple," so ambiguous and vague, but to anyone who has ever been to a show, or for me at least, it's a call to escape, to run, to join and play in the Dens of Iniquity. That song was so powerful to me that year I'd probably listened to it a hundred times, debating on whether to stay or go, and I hummed it that night again as I lay there thinking, trying to come down from the long trip I'd been on:

Ripple

If my words did glow with the gold of sunshine,
And my tunes were played on the harp unstrung,
Would you hear my voice come through the music,
Would you hold it near, as it were your own.

It's a hand-me-down, the thoughts are broken,
Perhaps they're better left unsung.
I don't know, don't really care,
Let there be songs to fill the air.

Ripple in still water,
When there is no pebble tossed,
Nor wind to blow.

Reach out your hand if your cup be empty,
If your cup is full, may it be again.
Let it be known, there is a fountain,
That was not made by the hands of men.

There is a road, no simple highway.
Between the dawn and the dark of night.
And if you go, no one may follow.
That path is for your steps alone.

Ripple in still water,
When there is no pebble tossed,
Nor wind to blow.

You who choose to lead must follow.
But if you fall, you fall alone,
If you should stand, then who's to guide you?
If I knew the way, I would take you home.

- Grateful Dead

That beautiful poetry was such a call to arms for me, it promised such magic, such mysticism, I would listen to it repeatedly and add it to the escapist fantasies of that year leading up to that night, that crossroads. I'd recognized all my friends, the hippies, the Wiccans now, as co-conspirators, complicit in the attempted recruitment, along with, apparently, most of my favorite musicians. Having come to that crossroads, with Anne Marie about to give birth: stay and man up, or run away with Tyler and the hippies, the songs, the heroin and the like. I would, ultimately that night, choose to stay. I was scared for Anne Marie and me as I came down from the craziest, most spiritual trip I'd ever been on, but I was now proud I'd turned Tyler down on the offer to go to whatever hippie festival he'd asked me to go to, and that I'd narrowly escaped the hippies once again. I swore them all off, but unfortunately it wouldn't be the last time I gravitated towards that inept, delusional, drug-laced culture. Still, I truly believe that had I gone with Tyler that day, I would be dead, no two ways about it. I'm grateful I chose to man up and live up to my responsibilities. It would shape my destiny from that moment forward, whether real or imagined.

I analyzed that year of chaos, leading up to that trip for hours, but my last thought before finally sleeping and ending that ecstasy-laced acid trip was "Fit in the grid or die." The cynic in me has always been pretty loud and I guess that was the macro of the situation. To escape with the hippies ultimately meant death and to stay was to surrender and fit in the grid. "Fit in the grid or die," and I finally fell asleep after an exhausting two day hallucinogenic, mental masturbation cluster-fuck.

New Son and Going Almost Straight

When I woke up that morning, Anne Marie was going into labor. I still have the contractions time and date written in my journal. They started on May 22nd, 1996 at 6:18 AM. I felt great, I was no longer feeling the chest pains, or constant threat of death, my trip had finally worn off, and we got in the car and went to the hospital. Around lunchtime she still hadn't given birth and Faust Santino and a few other hippie friends came up to the hospital, and smoked a huge blunt with me in the parking lot of Northside Hospital, where coincidentally, I'd been born 18 years before and where my son was due to be born at any second. Pretty terrible behavior and choices as I could have easily been arrested and missed the birth of my child. But I wasn't, they left, and I went back in to see my son born, high as a kite.

It was the most miraculous, beautiful thing I'd ever seen. It sobered me up instantly. It's funny because I've watched the video since that moment, and it's just not the same thing I witnessed. To me, in that moment, it was the perfect unison of God, family, and peace. To watch your own child being born is beyond words. It changed my heart, and changed my life forever, instantly, and in many positive ways. All my doubt, all my lingering fear and paranoia left me for a few seconds as I held that crying baby boy in my arms, and I knew that God was good, and that this healthy baby boy needed a good man to be his father, and I swore I would be. I also swore I'd never abandon him like my dad had done to me.

Anne Marie's entire family was there at the hospital as well. Only my Uncle Jack and Aunt Gail came to visit us that next day. I kept waiting for my mom, but she didn't come. Neither did my brother or sister, and it hurt me deeply, though they were too young to have any say in the matter, I'm sure. I wish I'd been tougher than that, but I'd really thought we'd all pull together at the last instant, and we didn't. My mother's resentments and judgments would continue until the day she died. But overall, the next few days were harmonious. Anne Marie's family, as always, were enough for both of us, and were it not for Anne Marie's mom, poor little baby Jake's neck would have snapped several times over, but for her showing us how weak it was, and all the other nuances new parents, especially new young parents, simply don't know. We were truly happy for a while when all that came to be. My Aunt Betsy came to take pictures of baby Jake a few weeks after he was born, but my mom didn't so much as call.

So life was good, I'd sworn off hard drugs, and even pot by then, and was actually able to only drink once or twice a week, which I did for quite a while. I'd been fired from Computer City, and Anne Marie's boss gave me a number to call to work at TechMax to sell computers, citing my record sales numbers at Computer City, and my ability as a natural salesman, though I know he didn't really expect me to be successful. I almost didn't get in the door. The interview went well, and I got the offer, but like an idiot, failed the drug test. A 750 million dollar publicly traded organization had offered me an amazing job and I failed the stupid drug test. I called the VP of HR and begged, pleaded, and cried on the phone with him, swearing it was a mistake. He agreed to give me another test if I paid for it, and the miracle became official, I was offered the job and started in the summer of 1996.

When I walked into that office for the very first day, an amazing coincidence happened. In the AA program we like to say that coincidence is God working in anonymity, and this was certainly an example. One of the first people I saw was Graham Flagg. The AA guy who'd talked to me about God for so many hours outside of Computer City, me vehemently denying his existence and he so adamantly begging me to keep an open mind. And here I was, converted from an atheist to a Christian once again. Not a Bible-thumping holy roller or anything, but a believer nonetheless. It was good to see my friend and we instantly bonded and began having many lunches again, with him always talking about God, the Program of AA, his near death experiences, and mine. We talked of dreams, and of success, and of sales, and it was good to have a friend in the office right off the bat. I don't believe for an instant that God didn't put this man in my life at Computer City, and then again at TechMax. For though I ignored most of his words at the time about sobriety, when it came time, I found my mind was like a sponge, and that I recalled everything he'd said, especially one story in particular.

He told me his first job in sobriety was cleaning out Porta-Pottys after they'd been used all day long on construction sites. I remember I laughed at him and yet he had a solemn look of peace on his face even as I poked fun. "I was grateful to have that job," he said, with a Zen-like smile. I discarded it at the time but I would never forget it and I was happy to hear this strange bird's stories. It was just another small miracle at this point, first the job itself, and then this spiritual guru who I'd connected with so well at Computer City. I was grateful.

The summer of 1996 brought the Olympics to Atlanta. I didn't make it to a single Olympic event that year. I busted my ass at that job, I stayed drug free, or so I thought, only drinking on Friday nights, but God, did I look forward to that Friday. I spent 12-hour days at TechMax, I listened to hundreds of motivational sales tapes, and I drove in a 1984 Toyota Corolla that had absolutely no air conditioning and, worse, had to blow heat non-stop in order to keep the clunker from overheating. I listened to those tapes, which spoke of how things would get better, and how I needed to stay positive. I did stay positive, and I did begin to have success in sales at TechMax. I watched a Georgia Tech grad get hired and fired, and a UNC grad get hired and fired, and I continued to sell and grow my book of business, despite being a high school dropout. By the following year, at 19 years old, I was one of the top salesmen in the company, out of 100+ sales people. I was moved to West Coast Major Accounts, because I'd targeted and succeeded in penetrating some major accounts and was on track to make 75k that year. We had done the impossible. Everyone had told us we were making a mistake and despite the old vehicles, constantly being broke, and the struggle, we were defying the odds and not only surviving, but succeeding.

Getting Married

A strange thing happened around this time, my mom and Anne Marie began talking, and Anne Marie went from not wanting to get married to wanting to get married. I, on the other hand, was a little irritated by the fact she'd already said no while she was pregnant and only wanted to now, for the health insurance, and the new promise my mom made of finding us, and helping us purchase a house. By which she meant forfeiting her real estate commission. Plus, of course, to my paranoid mind, the ability for Anne Marie to get more money from me should she ultimately decide to leave me, which I was scared of constantly. Ultimately, though, after over a year of my mom refusing to see my son, because we weren't married, and were living in sin, I gave in and committed to marrying Anne Marie, using a ring that my grandmother had worn, that had supposedly been in our family for over 250 years, a miiners cut, pristine diamond. With the marriage on the table, my mom played nice, and met her grandson. When she was dying of cancer, with a few months to live, she still didn't apologize for this bullshit, but I bet she wished she'd seen the first year of her only grandchild's life. She was too proud to mention it, if she did. Or maybe she was just too scared. But we all chose to get married, and we did. We were both 19 years old, and it was just before Christmas of 1997.

It was Anne Marie, myself, and the Minister at the church on the corner of Holcomb Bridge and Mountain Park Road. Three people at a wedding is a pretty sad state of affairs, but I had a feeling it wasn't going to last and I didn't want to embarrass myself anymore than I was already certain would happen later on down the road, and Anne Marie went along with the small wedding as well.

When we came out of the church, some neighbors had put shaving cream all over the car and we had a little mini party in our truly humble abode in the woods of little old Mountain Park. Corey Black came over and brought some cocaine. I'd done it once or twice before, but never too much of it, and that night I think I did the most I'd done up until that point. As a result, I wasn't really interested in having sex with my new bride, though I never told her why. I remember feeling like shit for several days after, and I don't think I ever told her I got high on our wedding night.

The Money Machine

So now that we were married, and we were doing better, and things were looking up at work, I should have been less stressed and more carefree. Health insurance, car insurance, taxes, everything was cheaper married, and on top of that I was making more money. But I didn't feel better. I kept feeling scared. I was scared of a lot of things, to be honest. I was scared of Anne Marie leaving me, I was scared I wouldn't make any commission the next month, though my track record was strong, and I was scared that all of this was in vain and that no matter what I did I was going to hell. "Now or later" the devil had said to me in a hallucination, and I couldn't get rid of that thought. I mean it haunted my mind obsessively and compulsively.

That, and the simple word "pagan." Every blessing, every sale, and every positive thing that came to me I felt was coming because I'd sold my soul, to the imaginary voice in my head that had set up the verbal agreement in my mind when I was 17 at Computer City. I mean I just couldn't shake it. Day in and day out for years, I felt sick about the fact that it was all a sham, that it was all undeserved and that I was going to drop dead at 25 from my heart and it would all be worthless, that I was doomed to hell no matter what. One thing would relieve these racing, insane thoughts, and that was alcohol. I'd sworn off drugs, or so I'd told Anne Marie, and except for the wedding night excursion, that had been true. But in my head was this battle of thought, that I felt I was losing, and that had been going on for almost two years, and I'd never mentioned to anyone. Needless to say I just never felt at ease, even when everything on the outside was going so well, on the inside I was always uncomfortable.

That irrational fear, and those racing thoughts, quelled temporarily when I got drunk, came to a head, when TechMax introduced the Money Machine. The Money Machine, I think, was invented by a secret, closet communist, to defile and make mockery of the entire capitalistic system. That, or I was just an over-thinking, over-analytical, egomaniac with an inferiority complex. I instantly hated it and loved it at the same time. Basically, it worked like the "spiff" system, that I was certain I'd already lost my soul over. For every 100 US Robotics modems you sold, you would get to take a ride in the Money Machine. Well, they didn't really think their plan through though, because I had over 20 clients that would take a hundred pack of US Robotics modems, sell what they could, and then ship me back the rest, and US Robotics sure as hell wasn't going to get their money back on this deal. That is probably why they only ran the Money Machine event once or twice.

The Machine itself looked like a phone booth, with a fan at the bottom and a fan at the top. The three beautiful US Robotics representatives -- for some reason, they only hired the most gorgeous women on Earth -- were a redhead, a blonde and a brunette. They would empty a duffel bag of cash, thousands of dollars worth, into the Machine, and the winning sales person would get in the Machine, and grab as many wads of sweaty, disgusting, dirty, crumpled up cash as he could possibly fit in his hands, and hang on for dear life. It was exhilarating, and filthy all at the same time, usually leaving you with the feeling that you'd just pimped your grandmother for a buck. The entire company would watch you as you turned red and grasped wildly hoping to target the larger bills, turning red in the face, and looking as evil and greedy as you've ever thought yourself capable. But revolting as it was, and unhealthy as it felt, it was the most profitable spiff mechanism I'd ever seen. I mean to tell you I shipped more US Robotics in that day, than I'd shipped in the entire year previous. I had every mom and pop customer, as well as major accounts, prepped and ready to buy, with the promise that whatever they didn't sell, they could ship on back to me later. And everyone bought, as I'd promised them free shipping, lower prices for the next year, and maybe even my first born son. It was gang busters. I walked out of that spiff day with over $5,000.00 cash. I was 19 years old and King of the fucking world. This was on top of the big money I'd already begun making in regular commission, and I was already easily on track to make 100k that year.

Though I'd earned it legally, I felt like I was about to burst into flames, that hell would descend upon me in an instant, and that I'd lied, cheated, and stolen, and then gone into the Money Machine and desperately showed my true colors, scratching and clawing for every dollar like a possessed demon. Pagan, Pagan, Pagan, raced through my head, and "Now or Later" with even the Devil's Eyes grinning, shined on in my head like a movie that wouldn't turn off. On the outside, I was doing well, but I couldn't shake the guilt of my success, that I really hadn't earned it and that somehow later on down the road I'd pay for it. Maybe eternally.

So that when I came home to Anne Marie with that much cash, and Angie Hamilton just happened to be there. The redhead childhood friend of Anne Marie's. Well, we put on some booty rap music, and they both began dancing. Before I knew it I was putting that dirty cash into their bras and panties, and the next thing you knew, we were all naked, drunk of course, and kissing and groping each other. I don't think we had the full ménage a trois that very first experience, but before too long, this game had begun, and our marriage had become an open one.

Of course, though exciting and enthralling at first, like the cash machine, the next morning my head would be pounding and my mind would be racing with the thoughts of how evil and dirty I was, how I'd not earned that cash, PAGAN, PAGAN, PAGAN, "Now or Later" and eventually that incessant ringing in my ears, that feeling that I was not worthy of the success, drove me to a shrink. It was after Anne Marie and I had bought our first house, which at 19 years old was a pretty strong accomplishment. But surely I didn't deserve it, surely I was about to be condemned.

Now this shrink that I went to, was the same one I'd talked

to over and over about drugs while I had a quarter pound of weed in my book bag when I was in 9ᵗʰ grade. He was the same shrink, who in my eyes, had ultimately failed my father. Who goes to a shrink whose patients have a history of blowing their heads off, right? But I was desperate, I needed the relief. I didn't really have any friends I could talk to about the "voices in my head." And at that time, I wasn't close enough to Graham Flagg to share with him the insanity in my mind, though I wish I had then, and saved myself a lot of time. He would have understood better than anyone. But at that point in my life, the shrink made sense, because he couldn't go and babble to the world. So I finally made up my mind to spill the beans about my crazy thoughts, and quite honestly was half expecting him to lock me up for insanity on the spot. That's how an alcoholic's mind works, there is no middle ground.

I told him about the thoughts I was having and how I was pretty sure I'd sold my soul and was going to hell. He walked me through the hallucinations and asked me what God and the Devil looked like respectively. Intelligently and respectfully, he explained, without discrediting my spiritual experience, that what had happened, while I was on five hits of Family White Blotter LSD and heroin laced ecstasy pills, back before Jake was born, was simply a hallucination. Illustrating verbally that God clearly wasn't Gandoff from Lord of the Rings, but that I associated that picture with God subconsciously, and that I associated the Devil with my first drug dealer subconsciously, and that it was quite common to have uncontrolled thoughts. He explained that usually once you've talked them out and exposed their ludicrousness, those thoughts vanish into the abyss of where all thought comes from. From the moment he told me this, my fears of going to hell instantly subsided from a constant two-year roar, to a distant memory. Hard to imagine that I'd been that consumed for so long, by uncontrolled thinking, but it had happened, and I'd told no one and it had scared me half to death. Looking back, I think it was my first real brush with OCD. By sharing it with another man though, it dissipated into nothingness. I wished I'd done it sooner. The only relief up until then had been to drink.

Three's a Crowd

Having settled the incessant thoughts, I was able get on with my life and enjoy my accomplishments and probably possess a little more pride than was normal. I let everyone know I was proud as well. I was making great money by this time, and was one of the top five salespeople at TechMax. Well on my way to making 100k that year, I bought a leather couch, a bedroom suite for Anne Marie and me, an oak entertainment center, and even splurged on a Bose surround sound system that I loved. Almost as soon as we moved into the new house, our one time flirting and dancing with Angie Hamilton became a little more serious. Mainly, we began the sexual séance with dance, but got more and more into it, until eventually the three of us were sleeping together in a full on three-way. It felt great at first, but it wasn't long before it turned sour for us all.

It went from us getting a bottle of Vodka one Friday night with Angie, to every single weekend, for almost two months we had Angie over there, or another friend of ours, Lauren, and once or twice I got Patrick in on the action because I began to feel like Anne Marie was jealous that I was getting to sleep with her friends, but she wasn't getting to sleep with mine. It got messy real quick. Nothing on God's green earth is so over-exaggerated as a three-way. Nothing could have higher expectations and such lower enjoyment. After I was finished, I remember just wishing it were over already. But we continued to do it for months, with different girls, and all this while trying to be parents to a toddler and a normal married couple. Nothing could have been farther from the truth. It was affecting us heavily, and of course, revolved around the drinking of lots of liquor, usually vodka. Every weekend that Fall we moved into the new house, we would ship baby Jake off to the grandparents, send someone over 21 to the liquor store, and have sex parties at our house. All the while, I tried to justify it my head, that somehow it was OK, knowing damn well it wasn't.

It was shortly thereafter I remember mentioning to her that my company wanted me to go to Vegas, which in retrospect, was a complete and total lie anyway, but her response shocked me, though it shouldn't have. "Well if you go, you know you can cheat on me out there if you want, and it wouldn't bother me." In that instant I knew we'd destroyed any hope our marriage had ever had of succeeding through our sexual extravagances, I knew we'd never be the same. I told her we were done with the ménage a trois, no matter what, and we had to be faithful and loyal to each other no matter what from there on out. I don't think she was very thrilled about it, but on the other hand, I don't think she was very happy in the marriage at all, or she would have never let the adventures begin in the first place. It's hard to say, I felt like I'd instigated and started the sex, but had unleashed a monster I couldn't tame. I don't really know how she felt. I felt guilty again, though, and just wanted them to end so we could try and be a normal couple again. To control what I'd never had any control over.

Tahoe

Later on that winter, I decided to go to Lake Tahoe for snowboarding. Initially I invited my wife, but then after a fight, invited Vijay Pashtel instead, paying for the flight and the hotel, and telling Anne Marie she wouldn't enjoy snowboarding anyway. She agreed almost instantly and I remember thinking that it was odd, but that I had just negotiated it perfectly. I am good at giving myself undue credit, from time to time.

When Vijay and I were in Tahoe, I called home one night, and Lauren picked up the phone, handed it to Anne Marie, and I could hear Sean Morris in the background, one of our old friends, and someone I knew she'd fooled around with in the past. I was devastated. I was angry, and I was absolutely positive beyond a shadow of a doubt that she had had one of "our" parties without me. I didn't even snow board the last day I was out there, and instead got drunk that entire Sunday. It had been a good trip until that phone call, but from that point on, I was consumed with anger, suspicion, and of course, self righteousness, only briefly feeling that perhaps it was all my fault for opening Pandora's box in the first place.

When I came home, Anne Marie played it off like the phone call had never happened. When I accused her she denied it, and we had sex within moments of my being back home. Despite the fact I was sure she'd cheated on me, I made love to her and tried not to think of it. For the next two years, I tried not to think of it, and was as able to not think about her cheating, as much as I'd been able to not think of the word "Pagan" before. I was consumed by it. When I woke up, I wondered about it, and when I went to sleep I was thinking about it. I was paranoid about everything. Every song, every TV show, every word I heard from anything related to, had something to do with cheating. Unless I got drunk. I was able to forget about it while drunk, as I was with all my pain. But otherwise it was ever present. A few months later, Anne Marie went to the beach, and Angie Hamilton came over. I invited some friends, Henry Daniels, and Vijay Pashtel to come over, and they brought some cocaine. Probably only the third or fourth time in my life I'd tried it, but what the hell, revenge deserved some color. While we were waiting for the coke, Angie and I had a quickie in Anne Marie's bed, and I felt avenged. Tit for tat. I told Anne Marie about it. How stupid was I, pretty fucking dumb, but neither of us knew what we were doing. All I know is that none of it helped the marriage and we stayed pretty angry at each other for a long time, save for the moments we were drunk together, which came faster and faster since it was the only time either of us were happy together, period.

Partying with Hippies and Suspicion

A year or so went by, and one night Anne Marie and I went to a big party that was very strange from the get go. A beautiful redhead approached about 20 minutes after we arrived and assertively asked "Are you Bryan Smith?"

"Yes," I replied suspiciously, with Anne Marie leering at the woman the way only a wife who has survived infidelity may do. One who is still rightfully very suspicious.

"You owe me an apology," she said, and she seemed very sure of herself.

For my part, I was expecting the worst. In retrospect I should have trusted my gut.

"You were very rude to me on the phone today. Isn't your Uncle Jack Ball?"

"Yes," and it came back to me in a flood. I was rude on the phone while at work at TechMax when I'd called my Uncle Jack's business and his answering service had picked up. It was a heavy cold calling environment, a call pit or boiler room mentality where aggressiveness is rewarded, and I often carried it over into normal conversations, though mostly with my wife up until then, I thought.

"Oh right. I'm sorry, I just talk to a lot of people a day, and I'm so sorry." I was smirking as usual.

She did not forgive me. "Well you shouldn't be such an asshole to people, then." Then she walked away.

This redhead had recognized my voice in a busy party across the room, and stormed across the room in all her fury to demand an apology from me about a phone call that had happened hours before. I should have taken this as a warning, but later this redhead would play a very prominent role as I descended into hell again. The sultry redhead's name was Gwen Evere. Later I would learn there is a medieval fairy tale about a lady named similarly, who gets possessed by a demon, but as far as I can prove, these two are not the same. Robert Earl Keen plays a country tune eerily warning men of this modern day version of the spirit, but again, at the time I met her, I wasn't aware of either the fairy tale, or the song's warning. She was just a drop dead gorgeous redhead to me.

As fate would have it, the very day I ran into her at that party, I had called my Uncle Jack, who had an answering service. Gwen Evere's mom owned that answering service, and when Gwen answered the phone, I was apparently a dick to her. It's true that I had been a jerk to her, but what were the odds that I'd run into the girl I'd been mean to on the phone that day, at a crowded party, and that she would recognize my voice, and approach me? Crazy coincidence, and I didn't believe in that, I believed in fate.

Across the street from that party was where a young, good-looking hippie couple lived, and Anne Marie and I did a tour of their house that night. Another night a few months down the road, I found out she was at that same house, and I somehow knew she was cheating on me, intuitively and based on the previous two years of bullshit. I was pissed off, so I jumped in my car, leaving my son alone at home with my friend Josh Daugherty, and I drove to the hippie house to confront her and whoever she was cheating with. I probably would have done something awful had I gotten there and found out what they were doing. In retrospect I'm very grateful the police stopped me before I arrived, enraged. She was with the hippie couple, which consisted of a very pretty blonde, and a really weird, dumb guy, tall and thin. They had tons of birds in their house, and we'd met briefly at the earlier party. I was drunk as hell when I got in the car, and also just filled with venom. Justified anger.

The blue lights went on behind my car right when I turned off of Holcomb Bridge road. I made it to the hippie house, and got a DUI arrest right in front of the house where Anne Marie was. I was red with rage. Right inside this house, my wife was probably cheating on me, probably doing the same things we had done with her friends, but this time with different people, and here I was just outside being arrested. I screamed and yelled at that cop without even trying to claim sobriety. I was drunk and I knew it. I'd left my son with a friend, hauled ass to where my wife was, and I was angry beyond words. I cussed, spit, and cursed that policeman more than any other arrest in my life. I hadn't been to jail since being a dad, since being 17 even, since being an adult, since being a "responsible" man. Big Boy Jail, here I come.

I was humiliated. It wasn't like the times I'd gone to Juvenile. There was no romanticizing it, there was no blaming anyone else, I was just ashamed. I was being cuffed and imprisoned, while Anne Marie was having a blast fucking the tall blonde, and dirty bird hippie, and I was furious. Right up until I had to call her to get my dumb ass out of jail. I bit my tongue, begged her to get me out, and swore I wouldn't say a word about it, just please come pick me up. When I'd been in Juvenile I'd dropped to my knees and said some foxhole prayers for sure, but when I was in for that DUI, I promised God the moon and more. I promised to quit drinking, to quit smoking, to get our family back to living right, to put an end to the orgies, to stop disgracing God in all the vile ways I felt responsible for. Deep down, I still felt like even though Anne Marie was the one at that particular little sex party, I'd been the one to instigate it, I'd opened up Pandora's box.

By the time Anne Marie got me out of jail that night, we were both defeated, and humiliated. She knew that I knew, because Josh Daugherty told her, but she was more upset that I'd left Jake there with him than with my DUI. We were scared about my losing my license, or even my job. To have the job I had was a minor miracle, to have done so successfully at it, bought this house, defied the world and become the responsible, bill-paying couple and young parents we'd become, was now ALL on the line. If I lost my job we'd be sunk. Every month was hand to mouth really, it was a commission role, and if I lost my license, there would be no way we could come up with the $2500 a month it took to pay for her car, my car, the mortgage, and everything else we'd worked so hard to get. We were both mutually horrified with our behavior and how it was all now on the line because of this DUI.

Once again, God protects drunks and children. My work slapped me on the wrist, and even let me work from home while my license was suspended. That only allowed me to drink more, though, and I did. By this time, I'd built a network of PCs upstairs in our house, and I played Half-Life, Age of Empires, Command & Conquer, Total Annihilation, and any other PC game on a LAN through hours and hours of the night. I would have my two best friends, Patrick Elliott and James Price Watson come over, and we would sometimes play these ridiculous PC games 24 to 48 hours straight, drinking and smoking weed through the night, though I barely smoked herb while married, occasionally I would smoke with them. This also helped me escape my wife, my resentments towards her, and my all-around reality.

At 21 years old, our friend Corey Black took us to the Gold Club for our 21st birthday. My wife's birthday was the 18th, mine the 19th, and Corey's the 13th of October. He'd received a large trust fund when he turned 21 and was wasting no time blowing it as quickly and ridiculously as a 21-year-old can. I think he was given free reign over it for just a few months before his dad figured out just how much he'd wasted. He spared no expense at our 21st birthday, and we were at the Gold Club until it closed, in the VIP lounge, my wife and I both enjoying the dozens of girls he bought the large bottles of champagne for. I counted at least 10 of those 1000 dollar bottles of champagne. Bill and I rolled on ecstasy, and Anne Marie just got drunk. A limo took us there and back, and at the time it was a blast, but it shows how seriously Anne Marie and I were taking our marriage: not very.

When I got my license back and started driving back to work again, I immediately became jealous again. Conjuring up all those images that we're capable of holding onto: Anne Marie with the hippie couple, Anne Marie with Sean Morris, whose voice I'd heard while at Tahoe, Anne Marie doing it in the most slutty places in the world, ad infinitum. It was a nightmare. I stayed mad at her constantly and the thought of forgiveness was beyond me at this stage. Paranoia, however, was not beyond me. I'd had my phones tapped all through high school so I gave it a shot on my wife. I kept wondering why I would find spit in the sink all the time, and I'd never seen her hock a loogey in my life. Yet, the entire time we were married, I remember finding these in the bathroom, and they kept me in a constant, silent state of rage. So I tapped the phones, and I proved beyond a shadow of a doubt that she was still cheating on me. I accused her of it, I got drunk, and went to strip clubs without her, went out with Josh Daugherty and Corey, raging through the night, touching and staring at hundreds of tits, and then would come home enraged, indignant, drunk, and angry. On more than one occasion I would fly into rages, off the handle, tackle her, push her, and punch her in the stomach. Never in the face, but in the stomach, to insure it would be my word versus hers if she called the cops. She never did, but I would have deserved it if she had. I abhor who I was with her when I was in a jealous rage, and I'm sure it did nothing but fuel the fire, and build her disdain for me. I was a scumbag for ever laying a hand on her, and I've since made amends. It only happened a few times, but it was disgusting, and has to be brought up. Anger is better suited to those more capable of managing it than alcoholics. I am obviously incapable.

Things settled down for a while, after she admitted she'd

cheated on me again, and after she did I put the tapes away, far at the back end of the closet, and never admitted how I knew she'd cheated. We continued to drink all weekend long with a few nights during the week still getting out of hand, and I continued to be jealous and suspicious, but we weren't screaming at each other in the wee hours of the night anymore. I think I was spending much more dedicated time to the computer games upstairs, though, and things were by no means good. I loved her very much, but we were still pretty miserable together, though I really didn't know how bad, until we went to Hawaii together. I did very little with her, my son, and her family. I drank and stayed isolated in my computer room, with or without my gaming, drug, or drinking buddies. Still I thought I was a great dad, still I constantly thought I was the only one wronged. The victim defense.

Hawaii is a Bitch

It was the January after our 21st birthday, and I'd won two weeks in Hawaii, a full 14 days, from my job at TechMax. That fucking trip was from hell. To start, I got a speeding ticket on the way to the airport. Anne Marie found the tapes I'd secretly made of her on the phone, hours of them, from almost a year before, and she listened to them the entire flight from Atlanta to Hawaii. Needless to say, she was pissed. We landed in Hawaii, and from the moment we were there, until the moment we left, three days early, I had a splitting headache. I don't know if it was the allergies, or my racing mind's conspiracy theory of the military bases on that island, but my freaking head hurt like I'd been shot in the temple for the entire two weeks we were there. I went snorkeling and spear fishing, and they give you a bag to put the fish in once you've speared them. As I'm snorkeling, I saw a shark the size of a VW bus swim by me at lightning speed about 30 feet away, at which point I realized I had a chum bag attached to my hip. I swam as fast as I could to shore, almost in tears from the fear when I finally got out.

I tried to surf, and typical for an alcoholic, even though I had never surfed before in my life, my arrogance is only superseded by my ignorance, and I thought "I'll learn on the North Shore of Oahu!" There was a spot where you could drop in from a ledge to catch a wave rather than have to swim through the waves breaks, and it makes it much easier. It also makes it look easier. I almost caught a wave, but not really, as that wave was just toying with me. It picked me up, slammed me down, and then dragged me for what felt like a mile to the beach. The surfers who'd made fun of me even before I'd hit the ocean, must have enjoyed that spectacle quite a bit. Everything we did out there was difficult and painful. Mostly, though, we couldn't stand each other, we separated a lot during that trip. We began to really see that the only thing we really had in common with each other was our son. I wrote this poem while alone at the bar, away from her, miserable, feeling sorry for myself, and yet somehow righteous all at the same time:

Marriage

I've poured out righteousness, on simple destiny.
The tides of bleak, dark boredom rise, only dreams no liberty.
Chained to conscience dogma, freedom sacrificed.
Passive, quiet laziness, or evil deed's denied?
Apathy to nothingness, nothingness becomes depression.
A void with only helplessness, like bone grinding friction.
Yearnings to rant and rave and fight, battle the blacks of this fear.
Fire the guns of damned emotions, and watch the enemy tear.
But dogma slowly lifts it's head, and violently grabs the reigns.
Anger again subsides to thought, your blood starts to calm in your veins.
The links of the chain are just too strong, surrender to your load.
Unarm your cannons once again, and follow fate down death's road.
-JB Smith

We would keep struggling to keep it together. We both loved Jake very much and I don't think either of us could imagine sharing him. But for me the nightmares, jealousy and stress persisted. We depended on one another logistically though. I couldn't imagine running the house or cooking, and I don't think she could see how she would pay the bills. It kept us going for about a year, and then all hell broke loose. My drinking was still getting progressively worse.

Recruitment and Opportunity

Then, another funny thing happened that involved the AA program. Mike Rubin, VP of one of the top headhunting firms in Atlanta, called me out of the blue one day while I was at TechMax and began trying to recruit me to be a recruiter. I obliged both him and my ego, and went to interview with PMC Financial, which is now one of the largest contingency recruiting firm in Atlanta, though at the time they were number five or six. I would be leaving a sweet deal at TechMax, being 21, making 100k a year or so, with a book of business, but Mike Rubin did have something I wanted, I just didn't know what it was yet. Everett Monahan, the CEO, was a marvel as well. A Vietnam veteran, he'd had it all and lost it several times over, finally getting sober something like 20 years before, and he was an animated character. I loved him instantly. Chad Major was a manager over there, and he too seemed calm and serene beyond his years, and eventually it came out, that all three of them had years of sobriety through Alcoholics Anonymous. I was amazed for a few reasons. First, Graham Flagg up until this point was the only person I'd ever met who'd gotten sober, and I considered him somewhat of an oddity for several reasons, but these guys were all three sober, and also wildly successful, one them owning his own business. What's more, it was a business I saw took very little overhead to begin and to run successfully, or so I thought at the time. These men gave me a newfound respect for AA after having seen the fear in my father's eyes, and believing him when he said it didn't work, and then really disdaining AA once he died. Here before me was evidence to the contrary, that maybe there was hope. I didn't know what it entailed, though, and I guess I just hoped a little sobriety would rub off on me. Ah, if only it worked like that!

Regardless, I was moved by meeting these three guys, I knew eventually I would need AA, and I could tell my drinking was steadily getting worse. I remembered vividly my dad's progressive disease. Deep down, I knew one day I would need to get sober, and so we worked out a compensation package, and I left a very profitable book of business selling computers to come work for PMC Financial as a recruiter for Accounting and Finance. I was excited, I was scared, and I was very nervous. I'd been successful as a computer salesman, but I had no track record for reading resumes. Mike promised me though if I worked hard, I'd be just as successful, and in the back of my head, I knew if I could do it for PMC Financial, I could do it for myself and start my own business one day. I had it in my head that the only way to be happy was to be rich, and the only way to be rich was to run your own business. Ah, driven by such delusions, what could possibly go wrong?

Before I started at PMC Financial, I'd decided that while I was building up my new book of business, I wouldn't drink. With the start date quickly approaching and it being a Sunday, I changed that to: I would only drink on the weekends. By Wednesday of that week, with a knot the size of a bowling ball in my belly, nervousness piled upon anxiety, I changed that to: I wouldn't drink more than six beers on a weeknight. By the Thursday of my first week, I had abandoned that pledge as if it had never existed. It was the first time I can remember trying not to drink of my own volition, and I'd failed miserably. I wasn't really worried about it, though, I just remember attempting to slow down my drinking, making a conscious effort to do so, and then changing my mind about quitting or slowing down, and I was only 21 years old.

That first week at PMC Financial was hell. I remember thinking I was the biggest idiot in the world for leaving TechMax. The stock options I'd let go of that were under water at 7, jumped to 10 in the week I left, and nobody thought I was an all-star like they had at TechMax. I was just a nervous wreck. What I thought was bad, though, would get extremely worse as my personal life began to unravel at every delicate seam. Within one week of my starting at PMC Financial, Anne Marie and I split up.

Separation and Divorce

I remember that very first weekend of my new job, and I was trying to refinish one of the many rooms in our house. The week or two before I'd started at PMC Financial, Corey and I had gone to Florida, stayed drunk and tried unsuccessfully to fuck anything and everything walking, to no avail. Anne Marie left for Tennessee that weekend, and I guess it was only fitting, and only my own karma, that she was a little more successful in her endeavors. Of course, I was too self-righteous to think of that when she walked in that Sunday, after a weekend at her brother's college town, looking guilt-ridden and tired. I immediately said, "So who did you fuck?" She began crying and said she was sorry and didn't know why she'd done it, and I left that Sunday afternoon, got in my jeep, and hauled ass, self righteous as ever, filled with pride, jealousy, anger, and every other negative emotion I could conjure up. More justified anger, the most dangerous sort in my experience.

I drove to the church I'd grown up attending, Roswell United Methodist. I walked the grounds of the entire place finding nobody to talk to. I went to one of the pews and I opened up the Bible. I had looked for an answer to my marital problems in there hundreds of times, and I've since found that in the New Testament, three apostles say, "What God has joined, let man not separate." One apostle says the same, but adds "except when a wife has been adulterous." Every single time I'd looked for guidance in the Bible, I'd found the passage telling me to stick it out. But this time, I found the passage that said, excepting adultery. I remember feeling angry that nobody was there at the church. Angry that God was advising I get a divorce, and justified, in that if there was no help at the Roswell United Methodist, I might as well go to Taco Mac by the River, a bar. It was maybe my second or third time at Taco Mac, but this visit would start a trend that would last a long, long time, and the very first night's events should have indicated what kind of trend it would be.

When I got to Taco Mac, I began to get drunk, very drunk. The worst kind of angry, justified venomous drunk, out there. Vindictive drunk. I'd left my wife crying in shame and guilt, and I was completely a victim of this marriage in my deluded mind. Poor me, poor me, pour me another drink. If you think God has a sense of humor, just wait until you meet the Devil. Anne Marie's best friend growing up, and my good friend Lauren Hunt was up there that afternoon. She'd been involved in our ménage a trois, and was a good solid hard drinker like me. She felt very sorry for me, and we drank in lamentation of my failed and ever failing relationship. Within a half hour of Lauren and I drinking together, the very same tall blonde wife of the hippie bird house came in to Taco Mac, as if the Devil had winked. And before you know it we were all lamenting my failed marriage, and all feeling quite sorry for myself. We got more and more drunk. I called Anne Marie, indignantly, told her I couldn't live with her anymore and to get the fuck out of "my" house, manipulating her guilt to extinguish my lust, I made her leave, so I could bring the tall blonde hippie chick and Lauren Hunt to my house so I could screw them both, and pour out vengeance on my cheating wife. And I was justified in doing it, I thought.

Right up until I woke up the next morning. Then I felt awful. I was hung over, I'd kicked my wife out of my house, as well as my son. I had two dirty women in my home and I was running very late for work, with alcohol sweating out of every pore. I was a disaster. I was also an emotional basket case. The worst of it was that Anne Marie had left the house, and wasn't answering my calls. It soon became very evident that she was not only fine with leaving the house, but was very fine with us being separated. As I recall, she didn't want to get a divorce, but did want to stay separated. Within a week or two, she was celebrating her independence, and dating the antithesis of me, Trevor Rex, tattooed from head to toe, and grungy as it got. He had been a friend, or associate since I was both buying and selling weed from him at 15 years old, and it stung pretty bad. Worse, though, was the emptiness I now felt with her gone. I began to associate all my success with her and Jake living with me. Nothing mattered now. Without her I was useless, a wreck.

I began to be so depressed, I couldn't eat, and I couldn't sleep. I had a knot in my stomach at all times. I felt like I was dying. I hadn't realized how much I'd loved her until she'd left, and I missed my son beyond words. And I was angry. Defiant to the facts, I was indignant and believed she'd been the only one in the wrong, and I was a just an honorable man, who'd been a victim, manipulated, used, and was now about to be sucked dry. I expected the shoe to drop, the absolute worst from the coming divorce.

I didn't realize until it was too late how important she had been in my life. As I write this I'm 32 years old, have been through the rough first year of early sobriety, a year of painful interferon treatment, watched both my parents die, and a multitude of other major events in my life, but NOTHING was as emotionally painful as splitting up with Anne Marie, and losing my son. My entire identity was tied up in that marriage. We'd defied the world, and went from being poor to making over 100k a year despite everyone's predictions, and we'd done it together. We had a beautiful baby boy together, and we'd beat the universe. Now I felt like nothing. I spent more time crying those few months while she was dating Trevor Rex, than I ever have in my entire life. I was resentful and angry and would stay that way for years on end. I would drink in front of a mirror with a gun to my temple, cussing at myself, calling myself a worthless pussy, and crying and crying, too miserable to go out and drink at bars, and too scared to pull the trigger. I'll never forget those few pathetic months of my life. All my pride left me and I would beg her, over the phone mostly, pleading for her to come back to me, and she would say no, and I would cry and cry some more, looking into my eyes in the mirror, Glock to my face. Too scared to do anything but drink.

Let Me Tell You About Stress, Boy

I had only been at PMC Financial one week when all this drama hit and to say my work suffered would be an understatement. I couldn't sleep and I could barely eat, much less get on the phone in a new industry I didn't understand and sell -- cold-call no less. PMC Financial is ranked one of the best companies in Atlanta to work for by The Atlanta Business Chronicle, and they were nothing but patient those first few weeks as I was depressed and morose, but eventually my attitude came to a head. They moved me out of the pit and into a side room, giving me ample space and I was still accomplishing little, so wrapped up in my own self pity that Everett Monahan himself, the CEO, began to take notice. Everett Monahan is one of the most dynamic men I'd ever met, with a powerful magnetic presence that just exudes CEO, and a boisterous character to boot. He is not unlike Harvey Steiner, who had run TechMax. Passive and quiet he is not, but to this day I love to hear what he has to say, as it's always forceful, pertinent, and to the point. He came into that side room in which they were coddling me those first few weeks of my separation and he just said "So son, what's the matter?"

"I don't know, I'm just stressed, I can't sleep or eat, I'm just scared I'm going to lose my house, and my son, and..." I was meek, about to cry, pitiful.

"STRESSED?" He wasn't quite yelling at me, he is just one of the loudest human beings on earth when he gets amped up, which he was as he laid into me. "LET ME TELL YOU ABOUT STRESS, BOY!" Now he was yelling at what seemed like the top of his lungs and turning red in the face!

"On my second tour in Vietnam, I was there with my childhood buddy, my best friend, I knew his mother! Every time we left base camp, we got shot at by Charlie. That's stress, son! One day ..." and his face got redder and redder as the butterflies in my stomach became a swarm. "One day, we were walking through the jungle when Charlie just throws a grenade and runs away! Boom!" His eyes became teary. "Before I knew it, my best friend's splattered all over my uniform, son! That's stress, kid! I had to bring my friend's eyeball home in my pocket so his dear mother would have something to bury, son! Now that's stress! Now, get on that phone and make some calls or you'll be a whole lot more stressed without a job!" and he marched out of the room, while my VP Mike Rubin just grinned at me, having witnessed the entire scene. I wouldn't be paralyzed at work anymore, that's for sure. Everett told it like it was, and I needed to hear it, but I was still a wreck in my personal life. I would be OK at work from there on out, but with Anne Marie, I wanted closure and finality on the divorce so all my crazy fears wouldn't come true.

Ironically I forced divorce on her, I think to try to manipulate her back into my life, as ridiculous as that sounds. I know I didn't really want it, but I moved forward with it quickly, and seemingly without remorse. I was also very selfishly scared of losing my house, and her taking what little I had left. I was beginning to think she'd only married me to get the house, alimony, and child support. A plot, to attack me from all angles, aha! But it wasn't a plot, and she didn't want to get divorced, but upon my hiring a lawyer, and bringing her to a settlement hearing with a manipulative attorney, she signed the papers. Lo and behold we were divorced, within six months officially from the time she left.

Anne Marie is the patron saint of all ex-wives. She let me keep the house, only asked for child support, and when I stopped making as much money, she even lowered that voluntarily. And yet still, I was resentful, ungrateful, and angry as hell at her for taking my son. The reality of an alcoholic is a murky dark place. I can still become angry with her, over taking my son, though I know in my heart she had no choice. We have to carefully watch our resentments, but at this time, I was beyond self examination, and I resented her to the core.

Amsterdam

After a few months of begging and pleading to no success for Anne Marie to come back, I took the advice of some of the guys at work and got online to meet the next hostage, or victim. It is said around the rooms of Alcoholics Anonymous that we don't get into relationships, but rather, take hostages. I had a couple of disaster dates, and then I met Monica Taylor Staff. A beautiful brunette with an attitude, she was just what I thought I wanted. We were bickering online before we even technically met. Our dates were fueled with alcohol and we drank a few bottles of wine our very first night. We really did have fun, though, and she was smart and very pretty. After three or four dates, I drank a bottle of vodka and told her I loved her. She said she loved me too, and we were happily ever after... or not. Her parents went to Europe and we got to live in her big house in Alpharetta for a little while. Her parents loved me because I lied and said I went to North Point Community Church every Sunday. I'd maybe been once, but I knew all the right names to drop. They liked me because I had a house and a car, was 21, and a brilliant manipulator unbeknownst to them. It wouldn't last long.

Before her parents moved to London, she asked me if she should go to live there or stay in Atlanta, and I asked Monica to stay, and then we could visit London on vacation, maybe swing through Amsterdam, wink, wink. I paid for us to go to London and then a few days in Amsterdam, and thus I began smoking pot again regularly. I remember lying to myself and buying my first quarter bag, after many years of not smoking, and then just a year or two of smoking other people's randomly, that if I was going to Amsterdam, I needed to build up a tolerance, in order not to waste any while I was there.

So I began smoking weed again daily, in order to beef up for our Amsterdam trip. I did notice, that while smoking, I only had to drink 4-6 beers instead of the 12 or so every night, so I applauded myself even more for my amazing genius and incredible intellect for thinking of picking up weed again regularly once more. What a great liar I was to myself.

I thought England was a snobby, patronizing New York. It's a 2000 year old city, but we got drunk every night, and I judged it arrogantly as, well, not Amsterdam, where I really wanted to be. I wasn't enthralled, and I wanted to get to the drug culture of Amsterdam pronto so I gave London no fair chance. When we arrived in Amsterdam, we checked in and began walking the city. We went to a Rasta type bar first, and bought some hash. We smoked the hell out of it and then we went to Bulldogs, the most touristy of all the smoke shops in Amsterdam. The first night there, we just drank and got high. We found a bar called The Rockery, and it was mellow and relaxing. Everyone sat on mats, and the vibe was more natural than Bulldogs, and less artificial than the Rasta bar we'd been to, so we made it our home while we were there. The first night, we just drank beer, and smoked and relaxed. A beautiful redhead approached Monica and I and asked us, "Can I sleep with you tonight in your hotel?" She was Irish, with stunning green eyes, and perfect strawberry blonde red hair. If it had been Anne Marie, she would have been sleeping with us that night, but Monica either didn't hear her, or pretended not to, and I, being stoned instead of drunk, politely said no thanks, and she wandered off.

The next night, things got a little more intense, as they usually do with drugs. When I'd talked myself into smoking weed again regularly, I'd sworn to myself it would just be weed and beer and that was it, but sure enough things progressed. In Amsterdam, we found some shrooms. I tried to talk Monica out of it, remembering my heart, the chest pains, and the vision of God and the Devil. I was truly scared of tripping again, whether it was natural or not, but she wanted to badly, and eventually I gave in. We bought a quarter of shrooms, and ate the entire bag between the two of us. Now I'd done some shrooms at a few Dead shows, and once by myself at my house, and barely hallucinated. But shrooms from Amsterdam are an entirely different set of rules. I tripped my balls off. We went from where we bought the shrooms to the Rockery, and before we knew it, they were closing down. Walking out of that bar the world looked eerie and dark, all the signs written in a foreign language. I pulled out the map to figure out where we were, only to realize to my amazement that the map was moving as well. It was swimming, curling, trailing off the sides of the paper, all in Dutch, and I realized real quick we were lost as it would get, and worse, temporarily illiterate. I mean, I had no idea where we were in Amsterdam, where our hotel was, or how the fuck we were going to get there, but the bars were all closing down so the hotel was the only place to go. Monica said, "Where are we?" I laughed and said "I have no idea." She said "Well, look at the map!", and snatched it out of my hands. Within a few seconds we were both giggling madly, as she realized our predicament. We were both well beyond reading anything, much less a map in a different language, so we began walking. We walked up and down Amsterdam streets looking for anything familiar and finding nothing. She wasn't panicky, but I was getting there, as all my bad trips usually ended up with me in trouble, or in handcuffs. Before I could get too caught up in the panic, though, after hours of wandering around Amsterdam lost, I heard what I could have sworn was an Ice Cream truck pull up behind us. I turned around and it was the blue lights of a cop car, recognizable by the lights, anywhere in the world, whether on shrooms or not. I instantly knew we were going to jail. A foreign jail no less, and I looked around for somewhere to run, but the international predicament overwhelmed me. Even if I were to escape, they would get her and figure out where I was. We were doomed.

The policeman walked up to us talking to us gently in Dutch I assume, as he didn't speak much English. I soon realized he was trying to help us, and was offering to drive us around rather than just throw my head against the hood, grab my balls, or generally abuse me as I was accustomed to back home in the states. He was actually protecting and serving, not out to get us. We got in the car, Monica in the back and me in the front, and once again in my life, hopped up on hallucinogens, I felt like I was in a space ship. He hauled ass all over the streets of Amsterdam for what must have been an hour, but it didn't matter, on foot, or in a police escort, we still didn't have a fucking clue where we were. I did not care, though, we were in a space ship for God's sake! Eventually I grabbed my cigarettes, and asked him if I could smoke, thinking this cop is awesome, in the U.S., I'd have been beaten, and this guy is going to let me smoke! He nodded his head yes, and I went to grab my lighter but could only find the hotel matches I'd grabbed earlier in the day. The policeman saw the matches, and his eyes lit up, as he smiled and pointed to the clue! AHA! We were home free! Our lost wandering was over, we wouldn't spend the night in jail after all, which in the back of my head was where we'd end up if we didn't find the place soon, even though that cop was so nice, I think he'd have driven us around all night if need be.

112

So he took us back to the hotel and he indicated towards the front door, smiling. We were home free! I didn't want to leave our hotel again ever. I was afraid we'd turn the corner and get turned around, that all of the architecture in Amsterdam would change, in a plot to get us lost, and we'd be wandering the streets of Amsterdam eternally. After an hour in our hotel room, Monica talked me into leaving again. I begged and pleaded, but she wouldn't have any of it. We smoked some of our hash and went and sat on a bench. I had negotiated that the bench was in view of the hotel's front door. We watched the sunrise and the rush hour of Amsterdam bicycle traffic in a comical, surreal cartoon world of shrooms, hash, and burnt-out brain cells. We finally went to sleep around 9 AM, and slept the whole next day, missing the outing to the Anne Frank and Van Gogh museums while we were there. Her parents weren't exactly shocked, though. I flaunted my true colors that trip and what they saw was an alcoholic drug addict, because, hell, I was one.

When we left Amsterdam I smuggled some Cuban cigars back for my stepdad, and I left a ton of weed and hash in that hotel room. You can't possibly smoke everything you buy there in a week, but there was so much I had to try it all. It all made me stoned, though, and I kept on smoking. I swore I would quit after returning from Amsterdam. In fact, not only did I not quit, but Monica and I began flirting with some harder stuff as well.

Gay Bars Serve Drinks 24/7

When we returned from Amsterdam I decided to really focus on work at PMC Financial, which I did by quitting drinking and only smoking weed for about three months, and it actually worked out OK at first. I would later hear this referred to as the marijuana maintenance plan, and it worked ok for me, before too many of the long term side effects from weed kicked in. It stopped the heavy hangovers in the short term though, and I was able to buckle down on my desk for a while. I closed about 76k in deals with the treasury group at a major Financial Services client, and what was more, I had done it all with my candidates, and it was solely my client. So I definitely began to see how I could eventually turn this into my own business. For New Year's Eve that year though, I began drinking again, and Monica, Corey and I all went out for New Year's clubbing, doing coke, and taking ecstasy. We had a limo and it snowed that New Year's. Our limo driver was drunk on the way home at dawn, swerving all over 75/85, the main artery of Highway that runs through Atlanta, as we'd ended up staying out the entire night. But before the ride home we had ended up finishing it off at Backstreets. Backstreets was a gay bar in Atlanta, open 24/7 and had been around for something like 30 years. It was a drug addict's heaven, and if you went upstairs, you could get away from the sweating dancing men, where the strippers and other drunks and addicts all hung out once the other bars closed in Atlanta around 4 AM or so.

I had actually remembered my dad mentioning gay bars, in the telling of one of his stories when I was a kid. I remember asking why he went to gay bars, and he answered quite evenly that it was the only place still open once the bars closed, and they were still wanting to do some drinking. He was in a band, he explained, and after they were done working, they liked to let loose a little. So they would go to the only bars still open, the gay bars.

Another weekend, just a few past New Year's Eve, there I am with Monica, doing blow in the bathroom, playing blackjack with a transvestite at Backstreets. I ran out of money and quit playing cards, but Monica kept on winning hand after hand. I started to get bored and I asked why she wanted to win since it wasn't real money. It was a pain in the ass to go get drinks and come back, and I just wanted to sit at the bar. She pointed to the plaques on the wall dating back to 1975 of people that had won over a million in credits at blackjack, so I told her to keep on playing then, but I was going to the bar. I sat out on the back porch and sucked in whippits, small canisters of nitrous oxide, and drank beer. Every few minutes I would run to the bathroom for another line of cocaine. Eventually, she came and found me to tell me that she won, and I went to go look at her plaque, and there on the wall was a name close to my biological dad's name, M Smith, from 1976. My father's name was Morris Smith. That could have been my father. So, he too, could have just as easily been strung out and doing lines at a gay bar, a generation before me. He was gone, though, so I had no way to ask if it was him or not. Still, it was kind of eerie to think that it was, and here I was repeating the same sad cycle, headed to insanity and death, but I was too messed up to connect that many dots in a row. We left after we ran out of drugs, and took the long ass drive back to my house, with the sun coming up and the drugs gone. I remember the mornings coming harder and harder, with more and more pain, but still, not too many consequences. I sure did hate those morning birds, though, as most drunks and addicts do. They are the unflinching reality of the real world, and they made your delusion that everything is OK disappear instantly. You know you shouldn't hate songbirds, but you do, you just can't help it.

I was still doing the weekend dad thing pretty regularly with Anne Marie, but Monica didn't like little Jake, and that became a source of contention for both of us. We already fought a lot, but she told me flat out that she wished I didn't have a kid and that pissed me off. But every time we'd break up, I'd go right back to that codependent sniveling baby I'd been after I divorced and I'd promise her anything to get back together, and we would. I began running out of money, so I refinanced my house, pulling out 50k in equity from my home, and I was now 22 years old. I thought I was something else: 22, owned my own home, and had 50k in the bank. My ego was pretty solidly huge at this stage.

With the New Year and my new money from refinancing the house, I also booked a trip for Monica and me to go to Cancun, Mexico for spring break. I continued to work at PMC Financial, but my confidence in being able to start my own company was definitely growing, as the placements at the large Financial Services firm had made me one of the top sales guys in the company, or at least I was pretty sure I was number one, in my head at least.

Monica and I continued to fight off and on, breaking up, drinking, making up, and I think we were kind of on the rocks when we set out to make it to Cancun in the spring of 2001. Our brilliant plan was to bring 20 ecstasy rolls and sell them when we got there, taking one or two for free. As we were about to leave for the flight out of the U.S., my stepdad called with some news. "Your mom has a little bit of cancer, but it's really nothing to worry about, she'll start chemo and radiation in the next couple of months, but everything is going to be OK." I asked if I should postpone the trip to Cancun. "No, no, she won't even be in the hospital for a couple of weeks while they get everything ready, so you go and have fun, she'll be fine." I said all right and hung up the phone, and we went to Cancun anyway. I didn't even talk to my mom. I was so self involved, I didn't bother to ask her personally how she was, if she was scared, or anything. My first thoughts were simply that I hoped this didn't stop my trip somehow. It didn't. I was a grown man, and I made the decision to go regardless. I'm sure my brother and sister went to the house. I went to Mexico with 20 rolls of ecstasy under my ball sack.

Mexico

Mexico was everything I'd ever thought it would be. Dirty, dusty, and everything worked half-assed. I remember when we landed, we touched down so harshly that the emergency lights all went on, and all the oxygen masks fell out as if the plane would explode. Instead, I exploded into laughter. For some reason, I've always thought dying on an airplane would be a good way to go. It's hard to scare an alcoholic. We didn't die, but I did get a lot of scornful looks for my laughter from the other passengers and my girlfriend alike.

We successfully smuggled our drugs into Mexico, so my master plan was working! We got into our hotel and could scarcely wait for nightfall to pop our pills and begin our adventure. The very first club we went to in Cancun was a trip. I couldn't tell you much about it except that there were many different levels, and we began rolling shortly after we arrived. We danced the entire night, taking a pill every few hours, so I thought, until, magically, they had all disappeared. Towards the end of the night, in between our dancing, I remember seeing Pagan symbols in almost all the artwork hanging around the club. One of the pictures turned into an Aztec Pyramid, with a snake hissing around the entire base of it. I jumped away from it and grabbed Monica, but when I looked at her, her teeth were shaped like that of a vampires, and I once again, entered the Grand Delusion that this was all just a game, out for my soul, and here in this inebriated state I could taste and see the truth, it was the Devil and so was she! I know it sounds nutty, and it may well be, but in the midst of a high like that, it is hard to distinguish the true from the false. I never really trusted her because of that hallucination going forward. I even blamed her for this selfish trip, knowing full well my family was together consoling my mom as we rolled our brains out in Mexico.

At the end of the night I realized we'd been drinking the entire time, the club was shutting down, and all of our rolls were gone. We had eaten 10 rolls a piece. We walked home along the beach, as the sun came up destroying any semblance of a good buzz we'd had. They even have annoying songbirds in Mexico. Somehow we fell asleep that night, miserable. We woke up the next morning and went down to the spring break pool, and immediately began drinking. It wasn't long before we felt halfway decent about life again, drowning away our pity in Dos Equis, pissing in the pool at the poolside bar. Even we were a little amazed we'd eaten all ten of the rolls each. Good thing I had cashed in the equity in my house, I still had a lot of money left.

Many an alcoholic and drug addict has been in a faraway land, not knowing a soul, and had the Devil come up and ask them if they needed any fill-in-the-blank. Somehow, no matter what your favorite drug of the moment is, you will find it without too much effort, when you're in the midst of your disease. Such was the case with Monica and me in Mexico that second night after drinking all day in the pool, and jumping in a cab. "Cocaina" the driver said, after one look at the two of us drunk tourist spring breakers. "Yup!" Sounded good to us.

So we were off to the races again in no time. This time, unlike the discrete pills of ecstasy, we're doing that tacky-ass dance of sharing the bag of blow, and going to our respective bathrooms, at first every hour or so, then every thirty minutes until it's down to every ten or five minutes as the night goes on, and its potency wears off, or your body gets used to it. Also, the high starts to go away and you're just fighting that miserable, God-awful come down.

I was in the bathroom about halfway through the night when two Mexican security guards busted in the door. Bang, lots of yelling in Spanish, I'm up against a wall in a Mexican bathroom, about to go to a Mexican jail, when it occurs to me I have cash. I motion to my pockets, and the quasi-cop security guards grabbed all the cash in my pocket, about three hundred dollars, and left me standing over a toilet in Cancun, Mexico, all my money and drugs stolen. I walked out and Monica was just pissed that I lost the coke. So again, we walked home in shame, feeling disgusted with ourselves. This time, as in Europe, barely escaping jail in a foreign land, and feeling pretty stupid about ourselves.

We just nursed terrible coke and X hangovers the rest of the week with that God-awful Dos Equis beer that I hated even as an alcoholic, but it was the only beer we could get in our "all inclusive package." The only other significant thing I remember about Mexico was getting my hand caught in a closing elevator door. Apparently, it's only in the US that they open automatically when something's caught in them, because this Mexican elevator shut the door completely on my arm and began going up. I had a moment of panic before I finally ripped my arm free, feeling ridiculous. It wouldn't be the last time I felt like that in Mexico.

I was glad to be home. Monica and I broke up shortly thereafter. We'd been on again, off again for some time, and then I found her profile up on Matchmaker.com again, which is where we'd met 10 months before. I remember begging her not to go, citing the great times we'd had in Europe and Mexico, and her response was classic, "Everyone gets along on vacation." We would stay seperated. Still, I called her out to the bar one night and we got wasted again.

She came over, and we began to fight about something, and I don't even remember what. I do remember her hitting me over the head with a framed picture of my son, and me grabbing her roughly and throwing her on the bed. I don't remember hitting her, but then again, you don't remember blackouts. All I remember was throwing her on the bed, but when she left that next morning, it would be the last time I ever saw her.

A few weeks later, my mom asked me if I hit her, as apparently her father had called my mom and told her that I'd gotten violent with her. I told my mom I hadn't, but in all honesty, how can a drunk defend himself, when they are prone to blackouts, and not remembering all their behavior? To this day I don't recall hitting her, but who knows? I recall hitting Anne Marie, my ex-wife, in the stomach several times over, so how can I be sure I didn't hit Monica? I couldn't, and when I told my mom that, she teared up and just looked ashamed of me. I'm sure I just continued to get drunk in front of her, at her own lake house. She was thinking of me as an abusive drunk, and I was probably just worried about how much alcohol we had in the house. I denied it, and at the time that was good enough for me. I didn't think about it again until writing this, but if I did hit her, I am sorry, and I am sorry for what I do remember, which was throwing her on the bed by her wrists. Regardless of my state of mind, it is one more thing I haven't yet made amends for. They tell me this step is a work in progress, and I guess that's a good thing.

Meeting the Red Hurricane Again

I was still doing well at PMC Financial in the spring of 2001, and I'd yet to really cross the invisible alcoholic line as far as my professional life was concerned, and though I'm sure there were telltale signs of it, I was still putting numbers on the board and my work life was still going well. I had a roommate at the time, Andy Tulane, who I'd befriended in middle school. In 9th grade, I bought him and his brother tickets to see the Black Crowes. He was a musician, so he and his friends were drinking all the time at my house and by this time I was drinking almost nightly with them, as well as smoking bud whenever it was around. Things were still fun though, and somehow I was still holding down a job, though we managed to stay drunk and high with all his stoner musician friends, consistently.

He played at The Public House every Wednesday night, and Monica and I hadn't been split up for more than a week, when Andy and Jeff Janson, his band partner at the time, were jamming up at the Public House. They occasionally would let me play the drums with them, or a little conga drum anyway, and it was one night I was up there jamming with these two guys that Gwen Evere came into my life like a hurricane.

God was she beautiful. She still is I'm sure, but at the time, certainly a few beers into a buzz, a little pot smoke and jam band music in the blood, she looked like a princess. Better yet, a red-headed fiery Goddess! She was still a little mad at me for being rude to her on the phone all those years ago, and I was still blown away that she'd picked my voice out of a crowd to tell me that I was crass. I would later learn she had just known who I was through a mutual friend, but then and there, I believed it to be fate. I held onto to that illusion for a long time. I immediately began talking to her and she all but ignored me for the most part. I was pretty adamant, though, and the very next Wednesday, she was up there again, with all of us repeating the same cycle of drinks and going to smoke weed outside. She and I went to my Jeep, and I remember her being impressed by my having a Jeep with air conditioning. Or at least that's what she wanted me to think. We got high in there, listened to my custom tricked out stereo, and went back in to dance. I got her number and called her the next day.

When she answered, I said "Gwendolyn?," to which she was not at all pleased. To say Gwen Evere could be a cold-hearted bitch when she wants to is to dampen the ocean -- the woman can be as cold as ice in the darkest heart of space. She was not amused that I got her name wrong, but I recovered as quickly as possible. "Gwen, Gwen, that's right, I knew that. So, can we go out tomorrow night then?"

"First of all, don't ever mess up my name again, I hate it when people mess up my name. Second of all, fine you can take me out." I had already spent a few phone calls calling all her known girlfriends and begging them to talk me up, and at this time my reputation wasn't all that bad. I'd done alright by my ex-wife staying current on child support, and I even owned my own house, so I think my general rep wasn't too shabby...yet.

So we had our first date. I was a sucker for her the moment I'd seen her years ago at that party, and seeing her up at the Public House after just getting dumped, and being the codependent alcoholic that I was, I fell for her immediately. Of course, I did my best to not let her know. Fortunately, she was a drunk as well, so we hit it off almost instantly. I picked her up at her apartment, where before we went out, we both had a couple of beers and smoked some weed. Then we drove to Dave and Busters and we talked about our lives.

I told her that I had mad respect for her for having her own apartment, not relying on her parents, and having made it on her own. She was gainfully employed at a company called Netdial, and really did live independently, and not at her parents', like so many girls her age I knew. She had her own place and it looked like she lived life on her own terms, as I felt I had, having gotten out of my parents so young, and having made it as well. We talked about it still being tough, living hand to mouth, always worried about big bills, like dead automobile transmissions, and she was impressed I had my own house. I played it up as best as I could. Then we listened to my radio, an overly loud, expensive one, and she smiled like a schoolgirl when James Brown came on screeching "The Big Payback." She told me that in that song James yelled her name, and lo and behold, she was right. You have to listen hard but it's really in there.

We drove all the way to Dave and Busters high and a little tipsy, enjoying each other's company. When we got to Dave and Busters she told me her dad had killed himself when she was 12 or so, and I was blown away. I told her my dad had died, the exact same way, probably at the end of, or in the middle of a spree or a blackout with a .357 to his head, and for me the bond was sealed. We were meant to be together. The coincidences were too strong! I'd never met anyone whose parents had killed themselves, much less the most beautiful woman I'd ever known. We were both in shock really, as it was just surreal to meet someone that had been through the exact same kind of sufferings. And then the estrangement of the living parent, the way they looked at you from then on, the feeling separated from the rest of the family, it seemed like we were twins of the same soul. Soul mates, or at least that's what my illusion consisted of. I can't speak for her, but it really did seem cosmic that of all the people in the world the two of us would have this same chemistry and meet, and then, and only then find out that we shared this deep, vivid, and so unique of a scar.

I still remember the end of that night vividly. She wouldn't sleep with me right away, but we did fool around, and what I remember the most, was that when we began to fool around, the skies opened up and it poured down rain. Thunder and lightning excited the calm, as we listened to Otis Redding and James Brown, and held each other. At one point in that night, she stood up to go to

120

the bathroom, completely in the nude, and when she came back, the image of her perfect body, her red hair flowing and tangled, was so beautiful I thought that she must be an angel. That she must be God's gift to me personally. I was beyond moved by her, before... then... and forever. Early 20's, perfect body, redhead light complexion, just pure art in motion. The way she was in those moments is beyond words and will always stay with me, despite anything that happened later.

The next weekend or maybe two out from our first date, Gwen and I went to Charleston. It, too, was an alcoholic magically induced weekend. I remember I bought her a dress before we went, and she hated it. I don't think she ever wore it. I don't know what I was thinking, come to think of it, but I think I did buy the thing too big, never a wise move as judged by the female. Smooth. We had a good time, though, as we stayed drunk the entire time and I, of course, paid for every last thing.

Omens

I was glad that the trip solidified our relationship though as I was really falling for her bad. She moved from her little apartment to a little house out in the country in Alpharetta near the Cherokee and Fulton County line. While moving her, she showed me some of the books she'd read, and I remember her particularly pointing out <u>Women</u> by Charles Bukowski. I opened the book up and the dedication read, "Many a good man has jumped off of a bridge, due to a woman." I read her the quote and she cackled evilly, and I thought it a bad omen, but she was so beautiful, and so amazing in bed, I shrugged it off and we went on our merry way. I even remember praying about what to do with her a few months later, and thinking about that moment that I read her the quote, and the thought "Run!" came to my mind, as I recalled her evil laugh. But I wasn't really in tune with my intuition back then, and did I mention she was a beautiful redhead and great in bed? Just checking. Besides, you'd have to be crazy to jump off a bridge.

It mostly seemed magical those first few months of us being together in that summer of 2001, save a few foreboding moments. Aside from the Charles Bukowski <u>Women</u> quote, there was another series of events that made me worry quite a bit. There was a house for sale in Mountain Park and I took Gwen over there a few times, with the idea of putting into her head that I would buy it for us, and we could live happily ever after or something like that. We made love in that empty house a few times, drinking beer and smoking dope, it was a pretty chill spot to relax. I remember showing it to her the first time and she was smiling and happy, and then we got to the bedroom and she said, "Look there's even a window, so I can escape and slip out when I need to." Having just left a marriage where the woman had escaped whenever the hell she felt like, using the front door, this should have been another bad omen, but again, I was in love and stupid. I let it go, mostly, except you can't really let those kinds of things go completely. It was like the quote, lingering, as evidence my delusions of grandeur of the perfect love were fleeting and false. Still, she was a stunning woman, and it wasn't omen enough for me to turn and run. But then again, what would have been? A lot more would happen before we would end it, and on her terms, not mine.

Other than those two small things, I thought our relationship was amazing and I'd counter that evidence with our unprecedented love making, and the synchronicity of events of our lives. I mean, who else was I going to meet whose dad had killed themselves? When we eventually did begin making love constantly, it seemed like the sky would play along with us every single time, opening up and pouring down rain as if on cue. I began to notice red cardinals everywhere, whereas I'd never seen or noticed them before in my life, and they became a symbol for me of how much I loved this red-headed woman. A red cardinal for my redhead love. I couldn't help it, and I'd see them everywhere. And every time we made love the sky would open up rumbling, as thunder and lightning would arrive to add romance to the moments. And we were good together. We fit in bed. It all seemed so perfect, but it was always aided by weed and alcohol. At first.

We did drink too much together though. As Cher said about her and Sonny, "Two flowers, no gardner." I began constantly being late for work at PMC Financial. I also remember us being at Taco Mac by the River where a harmless old man kept flirting with her, calling her "freckles." Gwen didn't know how not to flirt, and when he followed us into the pool hall staring at her, my anger and jealousy built up and out of nowhere I just punched the older man in his face. He was smaller than even me, and probably 60 years old and grey. She would laugh, as would I, that night, but later she'd point out how evil I'd been, and she was right, and I did feel remorse. I would feel a lot of guilt about it later, but then and there, we were drunk, high on good weed all the time, and in love. It wouldn't phase me for a long time yet, and I made love to Gwen that night feeling proud and tough. In retrospect, it was weak and cowardly, but it's funny how a buzz can change your perspective. Poor little old man.

One Friday night, the day before I was supposed to get Jake, we did some blow. We were staying at her parents that night for some reason, and we both slept in until around 2 or 3 in the afternoon, of course. My cell kept ringing off the hook with Anne Marie calling, and when I did eventually answer it was my son Jake, who must have been 4 or 5 years old at the time. I told him I couldn't hang out today for some bullshit reason, and Gwen glared at me. It was the first time I'd ever stood my son up, and I remember it vividly and it was because of a coke hangover. It wouldn't be the last time, though, and I did immediately register how bad that was. I justified it to myself, though, and somehow, I became the victim, poor single dad, trying to manage relationships and fatherhood. "Don't beat yourself up, you're only human," I told myself. You don't get to undo those mistakes though, and kids remember them for life.

I didn't notice how many pills she took until much later, as I was just too lost in her body, too obsessed with what I thought was love. Plus, I was usually fearful of more ridiculous things, like whether or not she was trying to get pregnant, leave me, and make me pay for child support, because obviously that was all women's goal. Get knocked up by a drunk playboy who can barely hold a job, and then pray for the best! Regardless of the likelihood of the fear, I was worried about more ludicrous things than her pill consumption, and the fact that I was smoking and drinking more than I'd done since I was 18. I had a musician roommate and a party girlfriend, and life was all good. I truly thought I was in love, and I thought we were something special. Maybe we were, maybe I was delusional, but it wouldn't matter, because I would soon find a way to fuck it all up.

That summer my mom began going through radiation for "the little bit" of cancer she was dealing with, and my family got together quite a bit up at the lake house. Gwen would come and we'd drink and we were quietly pissing my mom off, I'm sure, but she was much more laid back after she'd gotten sick, or perhaps my being drunk all the time just made me think that. I told her one time at the lake, that I thought Gwen drank too much, and she laughed heartily. "She would have to, to hang out with you." I was oblivious.

One weekend at the lake, my brother and I went to run an errand together and had a strange conversation. "I'm the executor of the will Bryan. All told in real estate, stock and everything, she's probably worth 2-3 million dollars, and we'll be splitting that if, God forbid, her cancer gets worse." It's not that the thought hadn't crossed my mind or that I'd consciously obsess over that 2-3 million dollars we'd conjured up in that car ride, but I'd be lying if I said it didn't help me to say "Fuck it!" to some crucial decisions that laid directly in front of me. It's a lot of money to think about and it seemed pretty plausible that we'd be beneficiaries. Right from the beginning, the doctors seemed to be pretty pessimistic about her rare form of cancer. I'd instantly feel guilty for thinking about it, but think about it I did, and again with that in mind, made some very risky decisions in the coming months I may have otherwise shied away from.

Trusting the Taiwanese

Around this time, I was approached by a Taiwanese company, Teac Co, to become their Sales Manager of a branch in Atlanta. They were going to hire me and another gentleman, Jamie Lincoln, to both be VPs of Sales in the Atlanta office, and to grow the branch into something major. They were going to pay us 75k plus commissions, and they actually had a few references and connections that seemed viable. I joked about how we could both be called VPs and why didn't they just call me the Divisional Commander, but ultimately I took the job as a VP of Sales, leaving PMC Financial, and began commuting to this company in Norcross.

We were at that job a total of about two weeks before I knew we were fucked. They promised us a staff of sales guys and a warehouse guy, and some other things, but what arrived in the warehouse a week into our employment was a native Chinese man who couldn't speak a lick of English, but had a handwritten note, asking how to find Buford Highway, which, for anyone not from Atlanta, is where a lot of the freshest immigrants to the US go when they come to Atlanta. I wasn't very sure what he wanted, but did my best to give him directions. We got a call later that day stating he was our Branch Manager. I didn't know how that ranked above VP, but apparently it did, so Jamie and I were now being led by a guy who couldn't speak English, and most of our other contacts throughout the company, also spoke mostly Chinese. I got a couple of orders verbally and tried to ship them, but our internal contacts in Ohio didn't ship them. So we spent a lot of time getting high and dicking around on the Internet, still relatively happy that we were getting such high base salaries. A week or two went by, and the only development was that Kevin, the English-speaking Chinese guy who'd hired us, did a walkthrough of the company with several other Chinese guys, obviously showing off the fact that they had two white guys working for them, as most Chinese distributors had no

English-speaking employees at all. It was strange, but we just got high some more and went about diddling. And then Kevin, the man who'd hired us, came by the office a few days later and said to me in a very think Chinese accent, "I have a bad news for you. You fired, and you fire everybody else too!"

To which my jaw dropped and I laughed. I said "Fuck you, asshole, you go fire everybody else." So he walked in uncomfortably and fired Jamie as well. They even sent me my paycheck a week or two later. To the best of my knowledge, they used us to sell the company, so we were basically a part of a front, it seems. I really don't know, though, I was in a straight panic, unemployed, without a college degree, and now a job hopper, I was scared to death.

Starting a Company

I basically reacted, and within a day or two decided I would start my own recruiting business. I asked Gwen Evere her thoughts, and she said I should go for it. She said to just bust my ass, work really hard all day long, don't smoke any weed until 5 PM and pray, and you'll do fine. I believed her and I started my first real business. It didn't hurt that in the back of my mind I thought no matter what happens I'll be inheriting a substantial nut when my mom dies. My friend Corey Black told me his dad wouldn't mind if I used the name Fortune Staffing. Without a care in the world, or a bit of research, I started the company Fortune Staffing, and in August of 2001, at age 22 and only credit cards to finance it, I began calling Fortune 500 clients in Atlanta to market my recruiting services.

I bought a <u>Book of Lists</u>, and I literally made a desk out of an old door, used the phone of the kitchen wall, and began calling potential clients. I also began praying ritually every morning before I got to work. I waited to smoke my pot until 5 o'clock, like any good entrepreneur would do. Within a week, one of the top 10 private companies in Atlanta gave me a job order to recruit for a Senior Auditor. Within two weeks, I had a viable candidate, and by the third week, I'd made a placement. I placed a Senior Auditor with the client, but I still didn't know how long it would take to get paid. By a sheer miracle, the Director of Audit told me "We pay upon the start date", which was the fourth week of my newly shaped business. I was a genius! I wrote on the wall in big black magic marker, "Thank You God!", but I quickly forgot that note, and began reflecting on how awesome I was. Within a few weeks, my company had gone from 0 to $17,000 in revenues and I didn't even have an office! It's laughable to me now when I look back on it, but in my mind at that time, I had arrived, nothing and nobody could stop me now! I was going to be a rich man, just wait and see!

And so I began drinking more. Who wouldn't I thought? I began making big plans with the large amounts of money I was going to make. If I could average 17k every 3-4 weeks, I'd be rich in no time. I called my friend Josh Daugherty and told him to come on down from Chicago, I'd figured it out at last, our destiny only awaited us. My enthusiasm was so infectious Josh was down in Atlanta in no time. It helped that he'd been laid off and had some severance as well. So now Fortune Staffing, had two stoner employees, who started drinking and smoking at exactly 5 o'clock every day. But still, our run rate was pretty good with 17k our first month, and what could go wrong, right? I'd wanted my own company for years. Every motivational tape, every sales call, all my years of cold calling had prepared me for this moment, and it had finally arrived. I was running my own successful company. Never mind that we had two computers in my living room propped up on an old door I'd turned into a desk, hell, that's how all millionaires got their start, right? And we began living just as if the success had already happened. Josh and I began hitting up the Crescent Room, a trendy dance club in downtown Atlanta, every weekend, and it wasn't long before we hooked up with the coke connection in there, and were in the bathroom doing lines every chance we got.

This was mostly to my girlfriend Gwen Evere's dismay, as she'd much rather stay at home, drink a few bottles of wine, smoke some dope and dance for me. Which I loved, don't get me wrong, but it was more of a weeknight thing for me, I thought arrogantly. On the weekends, downtown Atlanta's lights and the music and the strangers at the Crescent Room beckoned. That was OK at first, Gwen didn't seem to mind. In retrospect, she probably enjoyed the freedom of those weekends herself doing God knows what.

It happened to pass that the Monday night before September 11th, 2001, I'd stayed the night with her. We had stayed up watching television and we'd made love in the evening, and woke up to make love again around 8:30 or so. 96 Rock, a local radio show, was talking about a plane going into the twin towers, and how they thought it was a practical joke. I turned on the television just in time to see the second plane crash into the twins. I get excited with bad news mostly, and couldn't wait to get home and turn on Fox News on the big screen, as Gwen only had the local news. I jumped in my Jeep and drove the back roads back to my house.

On that drive I remember hearing about the missing plane, and the attack on the Pentagon. It sounded like an all-out war. It sounded like Red Dawn. Growing up in the eighties and going to sleep afraid of communists, not terrorists, all I could think of was that it was China or Russia. I wondered if Atlanta would be hit next.

Josh was living at my house then and I woke him up to watch the towers burn with a morbid intense curiosity. We heard the reports of people jumping out of the buildings, we watched the chaos intensely, and I told Josh Daugherty about 20 minutes before they fell, that those two buildings were going to fall. He told me I was wrong, and 20 minutes later we stood in horror as the buildings crumbled into dust. We bought some beer, smoked a bowl, and began to wonder which country we would nuke first. If this could be the beginning of the end, if there were more attacks planned, and on and on we brainstormed, drunk and stoned, flipping the channels back and forth.

I remember the Scientologists getting their phone number up on the crises hotline, and I remember going to my computer to read anything and everything I could about Al-Qaeda. Talk about obsessions, I became obsessed with any news article regarding the war. The economy was already on the skids, but after 9/11 the Dow just continued to plummet. To me, in this crazy warped alcoholic's mind, 9/11 was all about me. It's insane to put into context, as so much of my life before sobriety was, and I couldn't or wouldn't have verbalized it like that even then. But somewhere deep down, I believed this world revolved around me, and 9/11 was God's personal way of bringing me back to humility. Or stealing my dream of being a millionaire out from under me. It was ridiculous but I felt it, God had it out for me personally. I liked to say that all my clients went on hiring freezes right then and there, and that's what put my business under. It isn't, though, for one thing I really only had one client. But wow, what a scapegoat I had in 9/11. I used it from there on out to explain why my business had gone under. Before it even had.

New York City After 9/11

Within a few days of the strikes in New York and DC, the news got worse and worse. Giuliani said, "If you really want to help New York City, come to New York City, spend money, that's what we need." So, in a Patriotic fury, I decided right then and there that it would be my duty to go to New York City and spend some money.

I decided that Gwen would go with me as well, and I booked us two plane tickets and a hotel room before I'd even asked her if she wanted to, or if she could even get the time off from work. When she said she couldn't, just to give you an idea of how arrogant and self righteous I was capable of being back then, I called her boss directly, bribed him with Falcon's Tickets, and he accepted. She called me back infuriated, as was her right, but I was flabbergasted, unable to understand why she would be upset. "You got the time off, right?" That, apparently, was not the point. I was a perfect example of self-will run riot. I couldn't fathom as to why that had bothered her, hadn't I made it happen?

But she did get the time off and the first day planes were flying out of Atlanta's Hartsfield International, Gwen and I were on our way to New York City, drinking the whole plane ride up like a couple of deranged tourists, headed to a war zone with Champagne bottles and confetti. It was a vacation to us, and I was trying to do a patriotic thing, as well as just be an observer to history, but I didn't know what I was in store for, and I couldn't figure out why nobody understood why we were going. Gwen's mom especially gave us the third degree about it. "Why are you going, isn't that a little bit morbid?"

"To witness history," I said, "I would have gone to Pearl Harbor too. If I enlist, I want to see firsthand what they have done."

Other than to write about it, and see it for myself, I don't really know why I went. It was all so unbelievable, as well as just such a shock to my plan of being a millionaire. When those Towers fell, in my head, so did my ideas of successfully starting a recruiting company. I don't know why I used it as an excuse to quit, but I did, and I suppose I wanted to see this man-made force with my own eyes. Or maybe just to gawk, or maybe I just followed the wind like a feather, I couldn't really tell you to this day. When we flew into New York, about nine days after the Towers fell, it was like a different world. Deep down, I've always wanted to be a writer and I told Gwen to bring her camera so she could take pictures and I could write about it, but when you've never really written anything, I guess it's hard to tell people you are going just to write.

The airport was filled with soldiers carrying automatic rifles and looking mean and surly. This was definitely not the JFK I'd last seen when I was 12 and had come to see the Broadway plays. I'd even stood at the top of the Twin Towers and seen the New York skyline back then. It was a hell of a coincidence, I thought.

We checked into the hotel that night and Gwen and I went to a nice restaurant, ordered a few bottles of wine, came back and went to bed drunk, of course. We awoke and began searching for the ruins of the World Trade Center. Before we hailed a cab for that direction, an artist in Times Square made a rendition of Gwen's face. I thought it was a beautiful job, but I was a sucker for the woman, so what did I know?

Before we found anything of any significance, I asked Gwen to take a picture of what I thought were accessories to bulldozing equipment for the emergency workers. Some local New Yorkers kindly pointed out that they were for pushing snow out of the way, adding, "You fucking morons!" Which we certainly felt like at this point. Snowplows. Oddly enough, it's one of the only pictures that ended up coming out in the end.

What I hadn't expected to see were all the survivors of the dead, still, nine days later, looking for their lost loved ones, not giving up hope. Pictures of the dead smothered every available inch of wall space for blocks leading up to the wreckage. And wandering relatives, most of whom were out of tears, not afraid to ask any stranger if they had perhaps seen the person whose picture they were holding. They all looked hungry, tired, lost, and sad. Some bawling in tears still, "Have you seen so and so?" and then on to the next person. Nine days later. It was moving and it was surreal. And that was before we even got to the wreckage.

Turning a corner and seeing that wreckage, is a sight that will never leave my memory. A smoldering pile of debris, so high that it dwarfed the other buildings surrounding it. Smoke was still pouring out of the top, and close up, you could see twisted metal and black and brown outlines of a building, crumpled, piled higher than any other building around it. Beyond words. Gwen took a slew of pictures, and we left after touring the perimeter of what they would allow us to see. It was awful, and it was gloomy, and I wondered why the hell I'd wanted to come see it. I don't know what I had expected, but it was just plain horrible, and it tore my heart out, and made me feel utterly helpless and useless.

Hogs & Heifers

We got in a cab and left, both of us moved beyond expectations. Gwen asked the taxi driver where the closest bar was, and then she said "Hogs & Heifers! Take us to Hogs & Heifers!" I didn't really know what it was, but Gwen said it was the bar that

Coyote Ugly, the movie, was written about, and I wasn't much for arguing, a bar sounded just about right. She said it was supposed to be a biker bar, but I didn't give a shit, I just wanted a drink after leaving that war zone.

We got to Hogs & Heifers, and the place was packed. Most of the bikers were standing in a line outside, and somehow Gwen in her sexy-ass outfit got us into the bar. It was packed, but you could tell it wasn't the usual crowd. There were firemen and iron workers from all over the New York area in there and they were all getting wasted. It was the perfect place for Gwen and me to go. I started buying shots for folks, and asking questions as Gwen flirted with every gawker in the place. They were commiserating lost friends, and were tired as could be. Most were just off the job site, deconstructing the rubble, and a few told me they'd been up for days on amphetamines the government had given them in order to keep them awake to work through the nights, desperately trying to find survivors -- of which they told us there were none. They were angry, but also drunken and jovial as we all got wasted and drowned our sorrows and fueled our rage at the bar. Eventually I got Gwen to dance on the bar. I should say, Gwen got on the bar and danced for everyone, as I really didn't have a say in the matter, but a couple of the firemen and ironworkers bought me shots for me being so nice as to let my girlfriend get on the bar and dance for them all. Like I had a choice, but I soaked it up, drank their shots, and shouted and yelled for her to keep on dancing. Hogs & Heifers was famous for girls taking off their bras, famous girls apparently, and so Gwen was honored to strip down to her bra, take it off, and throw it on the wall behind the bar. I laughed and we partied in that bar like nothing tragic had happened just a few blocks away.

At some point some bikers who'd made it in were apparently pissed that Gwen was stealing the limelight from their surly girlfriends on the bar dancing topless with Gwen. They grabbed me, and before I could even react, which I'm sure would have only been a poor decision, the firemen and ironworkers had grabbed the bikers, carried them to the front door and thrown them out. It was one of the craziest bars I'd ever been in, and the mood in there was electric. With a big-tittied redhead, loose and dancing on the bar for everyone to see, I was treated like a king in that joint. We had a blast that night and partied late into the morning, feeling like we'd accomplished something, and in some respects I still feel like we did. I bought a lot of drinks for good people who were tired and sad, and we'd talked war and how we would invade Afghanistan and rip out Bin Laden's throat. There is nothing like an angry justifiable drunk, and we came, saw, and conquered on that note.

Not a Good Business Plan

The next day we packed it up and went home. Returning to the home office, Josh Daugherty's strategy and mine continued to be: wait to see what happens. While we were waiting we were getting drunk every night, watching the news, playing Sudden Strike, a World War II military strategy game played on the computer, and smoking mass amounts of weed. In retrospect, this was not the best of all business strategies we could have implemented, but, hey, I was 23, a drug-addicted alcoholic, and had a faith of some sort that it was all going to work out. I'd worked out a plan to refinance my house with one of my former wife's cousins, who worked for her Uncle Carl, who owned a mortgage company. Seeing as I'd easily secured the last 50k, I thought it would be a breeze. I'd already blown through the imaginary 50k equity in my house, and of course I still had about 10k in the bank from the deal I'd closed, so I was able to tell myself I was doing OK. We smoked weed all day long, played video games constantly, and absorbed as much of the news as possible regarding the new War on Terror. The Patriot Act seemed to come about mighty quickly and we devoured the conspiracy theories surrounding it. We read every news article we could find on the Internet, and watched a ton of CNN and Fox News, as the anthrax scare, the plane falling out of the sky in NYC a few days after 9/11, and the seemingly endless train de-railings that weren't being considered terrorist attacks, seemed to pile on top of each other. And the stock market continued to fall. Again, I couldn't help feeling like this was all God's plan to destroy my idea of running my own business. Ultimately, though, the only thing destroying my business was me. To run a business on your own, it helps to actually work, I've learned.

After visiting ground zero, my anger swelled at the obvious target, Al-Qaeda. I went to a Marine Corps recruiting office and tried to sign up. I'd tried once when I was 18 and they said no because of my juvenile record and my heart murmur. But, hell, we were at war! I was certain I'd be eligible now! I didn't even get into the juvenile incidents or my medical history before that Marine Corp Sergeant laughed me out of his office. He said just a quick look at my background showed I had too many traffic tickets. It pissed me off, but I figured I'd just begin toting my Glock around in my Jeep instead. What did the Marine Corps know? So much for juvenile records really being sealed, one more freedom bragged about this country doesn't actually honor. More lip service.

Roswell's Finest Yet Again

That October, I was getting wasted every single night. A few musician friends of mine and I headed out to make a night of it. I had bought a bunch of Valium to help me cope with the cocaine hangovers from the Crescent room, and it was Halloween night, 2001 as we went out on the town. There's nothing like a drink-fueled Valium night on the town to make you swerve a little more than usual. We left from a bar near my house, and were headed to the Derby, intending to buy some blow, when the blue lights went on. I knew instantly that I was fucked. James Price Watson's dad was my attorney, and he had said if you want to get out of a DUI, just refuse to get out of the car. I'm sure there was more to the legality of this strategy, but due to my drunken state, I could only register that first part, which in retrospect, is probably not as effective as the entire strategy. Come to think of it, it probably only works if you're actually sober, which I of course was not.

"Please step out of the car Mr. Smith."

"Uhh...No." Dripping with all my wit.

"Step out of the car right now Mr. Smith or I'll pull you out."

"No, my lawyer has advised me against it. Go get a warrant." Man you've never seen cops this pissed off. Roswell is famous for having asshole cops. I've heard that the reason is that Roswell is the first place they serve after getting out of the police academy, so they are go-by-the-book, hard-nose, don't let anything slide, pricks. They did not like me this night, and it wasn't about to get any better.

Andy and Matthew were saying, "Get out, dude" but I was in no hurry to go to jail. The funny thing is that this strategy of not getting out, did actually hold them at bay for about an hour, but ultimately more cops arrived, car by car, and eventually it looked like I'd robbed a bank by the time the police came to my door for the last time that evening.

"Mr. Smith, we've talked to Judge Hilliard, and if he has to come down here to give us a warrant, he can promise you 90 days in jail no matter what. Now do you want to step out of the vehicle, or would you like to serve 90 days." I don't know if it was a bluff or not, but he sounded pretty sure of himself.

132

"All right, all right." I was so drunk I had to pee by this point, so I eventually gave in, but I'd forgotten about a couple of things. Number one, in my patriotic furor, on top of going and spending a lot of money in New York City, I'd also put my Glock 23 in my car, and not in the legal place, but right next to my seat, with one round chambered. You know, in case I ran across any terrorists. In the console was a bag of weed and a bowl. Not a good combo, apparently, but I wouldn't learn about that until later that night.

"We got a gun!" The cops screamed and we were all manhandled out of the car, slammed onto the ground, and cuffed as if we ourselves were the terrorists.

"One in the chamber, this guy was going to shoot me!" No I wasn't, I was too high to remember it was there, but whatever. They were certain I was out for blood.

"We also have marijuana, oh yeah, these guys are going to jail. Don't you know drugs help the terrorists, you fucking traitors." That was actually said. We would have laughed but the cuffs were terribly tight, as these cops had not appreciated my keeping them at bay as long as I did.

We were all going to jail that night. My bail turned out to be $77,000 because of the combination of pot and the firearm. The DUI was secondary to this combination of a weed that grows out of the earth, and a gun that our constitution guarantees our rights to. But the combo together apparently was enough to make my bail more expensive than a rapist's. Whatever, I've ceased fighting.

All my friends were pissed at me obviously, but ironically I was the first one out of jail. My mom had to put up a mortgage on a property she owned to get me out. I really appreciated that, and was very surprised, but went home and tried to sleep it off. Over the next week or so, I took all the Valium I'd gotten. Because of that, the excessive drinking, the now-pending charges, I'm a little fuzzy on the timeline of the next several events. But they were staggering nonetheless, and they would shape my future for some time to come.

I ditched Gwen's birthday so Josh and I could go to Crescent Room and get high on blow. I really did love her but I was deep in the downward spiral by now, losing control. I played it off like I'd just gotten the day wrong, and that didn't go over so well. She broke up with me, and I tail spinned into a depression like I'd never felt before. I was running out of money, the imminent refinance I was hoping would bail me out fell through, when the fraudulent documents I provided the mortgage broker didn't work (go figure) so I was headed for insolvency, couldn't stop smoking weed, snorting coke, and drinking every day, now had lost my license and things were just getting worse and worse. And now the only thing I really loved, Gwen Evere, had left me. By this time I wasn't visiting my sick mother, and I wasn't getting my son on the weekends anymore. So all I had in my feeble little disillusioned mind was Gwen Evere, and she'd had enough.

The Devil's Playground

It was around this time, not long after the DUI, and not long after we'd returned from New York City, that I went to a bar one fateful day at around 11:30 in the morning. Dwayne, a hippie friend of Gwen's I'd bonded with, and I sat at that bar all day long, and I began drinking in the morning, and drank clear through the entire fucking day, leaving the barstool to piss every once in a while. Needless to say I was tanked. I was lamenting Gwen Evere the whole time, and eventually Dwayne and I got into a discussion of philosophy.

"This is the Devil's Playground, you know that right?" Dwayne eyeballed me mysteriously.

"What do you mean?" I asked.

"The Devil runs this place, man, I swear it, he can do whatever he wants in here, you know. And you come to play all the time," and he chuckled with his little gypsy laugh.

Then he got up and walked to the pool room as I stared into my drink, feeling sorry for myself. A few minutes went by and I heard a scuffle. I looked over to see Dwayne at a table near the pool room getting beer poured on top of his head, and at that point I lost my mind temporarily.

I redded out, which is different than a blackout, in that I actually remember everything going red, my being angry, and then poof, it's all a mystery what happened next. I now know what happened next, from the numerous people who've told me what happened, but from that moment until the time the bouncer was sitting on my ribs, I had no idea what had happened. In fact, they put us in different cop cars to take us downtown and when I got

134

to Rice Street, covered in blood, my shirt drenched, with the entire group of people in the cell avoiding me like the plague, I still didn't know what had happened fully. I didn't know if I'd killed someone, or if I myself was wounded, when I first came to. It was a terrible awakening with unknown blood all over me and no real memory of what happened to me. I didn't know if I'd be in prison for life, or let out in a few hours. I was terrified and began pacing...paranoid.

Dwayne was in the cell with me though and filled me in quick. He said I attacked a man, hitting him endlessly until he was down and then I was kicking him in the face with my boots. I don't recall a bit of the violence, and I certainly wouldn't think that I'd be capable of hitting a man while he was down. But I did remember coming to with the bouncer on my chest. I remember handing my Rolex to Gene Gibbons, another hippie I'd gone to high school with but barely knew at the time, and asking him to hold it. When I saw the man I'd attacked, I remember asking someone, "What happened to him?" I really had no clue. His face was grotesque, mangled, cuts and gashes everywhere, and swollen.

It was eerie. I was beyond scared, I felt like I was even capable of murder if I could do that and have no recollection. Even eerier was that Dwayne had just told me that Taco Mac was the Devil's Playground, that he could do whatever he wanted to in there. That statement was not lost on me, and I began to play it through in my head over and over. Was I the conduit of the Devil himself, however briefly? Ridiculous, I told myself.

When I got out of jail that next morning, for the first time in years, I called Graham Flagg, my sober friend, and I told him what had happened. I really felt awful about it. I couldn't believe I'd attacked an innocent man like that, for spilling beer on my friend. I told Graham the story, but I sure as hell didn't go into the extent of my problems, I just told him this one particular instance. His advice was good and sound. To go find the guy I'd attacked, and apologize, and let the cards fall where they may. If he were to kick my ass, then I deserved it, and to take it like a man. He was right, and I did just that. They wouldn't let me into Taco Mac, but I waited outside while he came out.

His face had what looked like over a hundred stitches in it. He was a perfect random stranger. He was getting married in a few months, and his fiancé wanted him to kill me. I said I was sorry, and that he could kick my ass right here and now, and that I really didn't know what had happened to me. That I felt terrible and would take it back if I could. He wasn't a big guy, but he wasn't small either, and I stand at 5' 6" on my toes. I fully expected to collect a deserved ass-beating right then and there, but God protects drunks and children, and the guy told me he forgave me. I walked away without a scratch, and he even said he wouldn't press charges. He was more than a gentleman, and though I felt better, I was still pretty appalled at what a scumbag I'd been. His face all fucked up for his wedding pictures, I mean what the hell had I been thinking? And he turned out to be a nice guy. I felt like an ass, and of course I was one. Taco Mac banned me for a year, and I wouldn't answer to those charges for another 4 years, as Atlanta's justice system moves as slow as molasses. He may have dropped the charges, but the state never would.

I remember talking to Graham Flagg about it after the guy had forgiven me, without beating me up, and my alarm bells weren't ringing quite as bad. He asked how I felt about myself, and I said I didn't know, but that waking up in jail covered in blood was one of the scariest things I'd ever experienced. All the other times I'd been in jail at least I knew why I was there. He said, memorably, "Yeah, who knows what you did. Did you fuck a pig?"

"No", I said, thinking it ridiculous.

"How do you know?" I made up some excuse and got off the phone with him.

Now after being locked up twice since 9/11, my initial anger towards Al-Qaeda would soon refocus inwardly on the U.S. Government for allowing 9/11 to happen. Silver bracelets can make resentments fast. Those too were tough times for anyone predisposed to paranoia, as a pothead drug addict can be. Hell, I'd read all about Carnivore, and how the CIA used it to literally record every keystroke on the Internet, every click, and how every phone conversation was stored, scanned for keywords, and played back, overseas. I knew full well how powerful Carnivore was, and reading the Patriot Act, well hot damn, it was obviously all a conspiracy! The Patriot Act allowed Carnivore powers internally, or inside the United States borders. Hell, Bush could have easily allowed the attacks to happen for just that reason! Bin Laden could easily be a spy, hell we all knew he was a CIA connection in the 80's when Afghanistan was at war with the Soviets. That snowflake, and the Internet, would become an avalanche of conspiracy theories in no time, but then and there, I thought I was the only kook thinking that stuff. I would drink, smoke weed, read the news and grow more and more delusional. In fact, maybe the end was nearer than I thought.

Deserving the Binge

The punches were coming pretty relentlessly in December of 2001. Gwen was gone, Josh Daugherty, my roommate, was gone, sensing the ship was sinking, and I didn't blame him. I was running out of money fast and I didn't know what to do. I felt like I was under attack. I felt completely justified in letting it all go. I'd worked hard from ages 18 to 23, and I needed a break. I lied to myself, and truly believed it was 9/11's fault, it was Washington's fault for not blocking the terrorist attack, for bailing out the airline industry and giving emergency loans to business big enough, but letting little guys like me go bankrupt. It was everybody's fault in the world but mine. And every weekend, I went to Crescent Room and blew a little bit more of the money I had left, up my nose in a crowded bathroom, hovering over a disgusting, pissed-on toilet. Followed by days and days of Xanax and Valium and weed. Everyone was against me, I had no friends. The guys I'd let hang out in my house, Patrick and James Price, never came by anymore now that I'd turned the game room into an office, and now that I was broke. They had probably sensed the insanity coming on for months, and they avoided me like the plague.

I had a few last cards I was going to try to pull out of my sleeve, though, that justified my continued bender, as if a miracle would stop the ship from sinking in one fell swoop. One was the refinancing of my house. About mid-December, the falling through of the refinance was final, and there was no hope of a refinancing mortgage miracle to bail me out. The only person that would hang out with me in those dark days was my one friend Corey Brown. I would screw him over eventually, too, but for that dark time he was there. Not only did he come over to hang out, but he would buy the beer almost nightly, and we'd get drunk and sing songs downloaded from Kazaa.com, and wish we were rich. We dreamed and plotted grandiose strategies to do so, but mostly we got drunk and burned wood in the fireplace. At some point he told me "Don't worry, I'll never let you be homeless. Worse comes to worst, I'll let you live in my basement." I think I clung to that statement and continued the downward spiral unabated because of it. Enabling I think it's called now, but who knows, I'd have probably lost it all regardless.

In my head, though, I'd chosen this path. I'd decided to go broke, as if I had the right. As if, I knew I would only be able to do this one more time, so enjoy the hell out of it, and go down slow. It didn't occur to me that I was insane at this point, not once. I was making the conscious decision to sink the ship, and I was determined to get as fucked up as possible for as long as I could. Throwing away the good credit score I'd built since I was 17, tossing aside the house I'd put hours upon hours into, and fought so hard in the divorce to keep, hell, had forced the divorce in order to keep. I remember justifying, "Well I've done it once, I can do it again." It was easy, people as smart as me can afford to trash their lives, because they are talented enough to rebuild them, smart enough to start again. So I'd enjoy the burning of my life, as if it wasn't precious, and not only that but I would arrogantly figure out a way to become proud of it.

Later when it was completely all and entirely gone, washed away in a waste of sloth, and drinking and drug use, when I'd blown all 50k of the equity, all my savings, and the 17k my company had earned, I would say, well, my father blew his head off when he went broke, but I survived it. I can survive anything. At that time I thought my father had killed himself because he couldn't handle being broke. It wouldn't be until much later, when the drinking and drugging quit working. When the shadows on the wall themselves could speak, and the voices in my head ranged from five to twenty five, that I would realize, my dad didn't kill himself because of money. He killed himself because he'd lost his mind. Because of his alcoholism. But back in 2001, I thought I'd mastered my father's demons. That by throwing it all away, or losing it because of the government and 9/11 and any other thing I could blame it on, I was simply challenging myself to overcome what had killed my father. I had many reasons for throwing it away at the time. The real reason was simply this: I didn't want to work, I preferred being fucked up, and during this process, I stayed fucked up for longer than I'd been able to do since my son was born -- hell, since I'd been alive. It was a luxury, I told myself. Enjoy it. All the other bullshit, all the other justifications and blame were lies. Lies that I believed, but were false. I just wanted to be drunk, and just couldn't see it, the forest through the trees.

Trying to Get Back on Track

So January rolled around eventually, and I began dating Maria Espinoza, a Georgia Tech graduate who I'd met on Matchmaker. com again. Guess I was real slick behind a keyboard. I'd gotten it in my head that love didn't really exist. That all I really needed was any woman on earth, and I may as well find a programmer so they could help me with my plans for a website I was working on. That's literally what I thought when we began dating. She was cute, she was smart and self-reliant, a little nerdy, sure, but that was perfect, she was everything Gwen wasn't. The Gwen break up had hurt along with all the other failures preceding 9/11, but I still hadn't shaken it, and I was hoping a new woman would fix it. Codependency at its finest. I put the full court press on Maria, with what resources I had left, and we went out to dinner, got drunk a lot, until a week or so into it I dramatically declared my love for her, and just like that I had a new girlfriend.

The lights were still on at my house when we met, the Internet was still running, and the big television still had DirectTV. I bet if she'd met me a month later, the warning signs would have been too blatant to ignore, and she would have run for the hills, but I met her at the tail end of my successes. As Stewart Black, Corey's father, would later tell me, fortune and business are like a huge train. They are hard to get going, hard as hell, but once they're moving, it almost takes force to slow them down. I found out that with good credit, and longstanding relationships with all my utilities, mortgage, and other bills, when I quit paying for everything in December of 2001, nothing really got turned off until February of 2002. Had I known there was that much flexibility, I wonder if I'd have been as stressed all the time. It was interesting to learn that, but it probably wouldn't have changed anything. I would have still seized the moment to drink myself into oblivion, and blame 9/11. The hammer did take longer to fall than I'd believed it would, though. I guess a lot of the pressure of the preceding years had been an illusion. Like most of my fears, only in my head.

A couple of really strange things happened to me around this time that I believe now would indicate how capable of insanity I would later become. I say they happened, but more accurately put is that I perceived them to happen, and then began using them as points of reference for the existence of magic and the unknown. Somehow amongst all the chaos, the drinking, and the drugging, I still managed to meditate every once in a while.

One night as I was going to bed, I sat on my bed and began to meditate. Tensing my muscles, starting with my toes and feet, and working my way up my body to my neck and back, and timing my breathing as I'd been taught to do years ago by my English teacher at Paideia, I mixed in the thoughts of my soul leaving my body, traveling above my house, above my city, my nation, my Earth, the moon, Mars, Saturn, Jupiter. I'd found this to be relaxing for several years, but usually not much more than relaxing. This time, and to this day I can only explain what I saw, and what I felt, but a tiny ball of light entered the candlelit room, and I began negotiating it across the room, keeping it between the palms of my hand, feeling high, feeling powerful, capable of moving this light, this floating little sun right there in my room, it was remarkable, and it felt good. And then, it went directly above my forehead, and it felt as though it was giving me information, as if it was feeding me thoughts directly into my brain, or my chakras, or whatever the hell you want to call it, but I could feel it communicating with me through the forehead area, and I lost the ability to control the light. It said to me plainly "You're mother is going to die of cancer in a few years, be there for her, and let her know that it will be OK." And then it rose away through the ceiling in my bedroom, and disappeared. It didn't leave me feeling scared, or shocked, but rather awed, and comfortable. I remember trying to tell Josh Daugherty about it, and he dismissed it, as have most of the people I've ever told about it, but it happened to me, or it happened to my consciousness, it appeared to happen, and it seemed spiritual. All in all, it left me feeling good, but anytime I shared it I felt stupid, so I tried not to mention it too often. It would also fit as a symptom of paranoid schizophrenia... but I digress.

It did remind me, though, that through the perceived losing of my business, the loss of Gwen, the DUI, the assault charges, the drinking, the drugging, and the pain, that through all of this my mom had cancer, and was going through her own hell. Somehow in all of my tragedy, I'd truly not paid much attention. But, instead of going to ask her how her world was, I went and asked her for some money. I felt like I deserved it. I'd saved them all kinds of money by not going to college, and by God, my dad had left my mom 750k and she owed me a little bit of help. Plus, 9/11 put me out of business, so I felt completely justified in asking for a loan, to get back on my feet. I had a job lined up to go sell mortgages, through Spencer Jackson, a friend I'd met while at PMC Financial, and I felt confident things were going to be fine. I'd let this go far enough, I would get this loan, and I would get back on track. It would be the first failed attempt to get the train back on the track wholeheartedly. I'd never asked my parents for anything I thought, so this was the least they could do, and then I'd turn this ship around.

I asked for a loan of 5k, and though my mom looked like she may give it to me, my stepdad was adamantly against it. It took a few days of discussions, but eventually I went over to my mom's house in early 2002 and she wrote me a check for 5k, that I would never get the chance to pay her back. Hell, I honestly couldn't tell you what happened to it.

As soon as I had the 5k mini bailout, I went home to make phone calls. The first call I made was to American Express. They asked for a $900 dollar payment and they told me that would reactivate my card, so I made the payment thinking it would open up my credit line again, and then maybe I could up the limit and all my other problems would be solved. They took the payment and two days later I got a cancellation notice on my card, and my resentments went through the roof. How dare American Express take my money only to close my account? I was livid, just as I was after Gwen and I broke up, just as I was when the Towers fell, so I did the same thing I'd always done when angry, and that was drink. Before I knew it, I was headed downtown, doing the same song and dance, running to the one club I knew to get coke, and realizing that I hadn't been there for a month or so, because I'd been poor. I planned on spending a couple of hundred bucks that night, and I remember the drive, and I was thrilled, like a kid before Christmas. The drive downtown that night, when I got to Buckhead, heading south on 400, the butterflies in my stomach kicked in. The anticipation when I got off at Sidney Marcus Blvd was incredible, and when I turned that bend to see the Atlanta skyline I could taste the cocaine in my throat, and my nose began to drip. I swore I would only spend a couple of hundred bucks. How amazingly powerful an addiction to cause physical side effects by the mere thought of the drug itself, so it goes with cocaine. One hell of a drug.

Two days later I woke up back at my house, littered with beer bottles, straws, and dried up old pizza boxes, and I looked in my wallet to find it empty. I drove to the ATM thinking I must have some more money in there, and it was all gone. I'd spent four thousand dollars in a weekend, and I didn't have shit to show for it. I thought I'd been robbed. I tried to think back over the weekend of how I could have spent all that money, my bailout, my last ditch effort to save my house, and become a human being again, and I couldn't recall a thing. The entire weekend, from the first bag of blow at Crescent Room to my coming to in my shithole, drunkenly devastated abode, was a black, sad empty void in my mind, and here I was broke, and right back where I started, except for worse, now I'd borrowed money from my dying mother, and blown it all. Now she would never leave me any money, and yes, that's what I thought of -- how this would affect the two million dollar inheritance that my brother had said we were in line to get if she were to die. I was honestly scared this time, because unlike the lie of me throwing it all away because I could, I had really tried to salvage my life with this money, and I'd been completely unable to manage it, had completely failed, and was utterly frightened of my powerlessness, though I didn't have a clue as to what to do about it.

Uncle Owen's Visit

A few days later, my uncle from my dad's side, who I hadn't seen since my father's funeral, called my house and said he was on a cross country trip and was going to stop by. The power was still on, and the internet was still working at this time, but my mind was certainly shot out. I believed the Mark of the Devil was the internet, and every time I touched my Microsoft mouse, a pitchfork red light would flash up on the wall. The Bible said the Mark of the Devil was on your palm or forehead, and that everyone on Earth would need to have it to conduct business. Well, holding that mouse, and aligning the internet with my forehead, I pieced together I was staring right at it! The Internet was it, and I was the only one who knew! The headline news was still terrible, and the Patriot Act had been passed, which recorded every keystroke, and every phone conversation, and I'd begun to sink into maladjustment not unlike the come downs of all those bad trips, but without all the LSD, which was scary, when Uncle Owen called me out of the blue to tell me he'd be there in the morning. Paranoia was already running rampant when I got this call from my father's brother, and even regardless of my growing insanities, this was a strange occurrence. Owen and Gavin Wright had left my life after my father died, and my mom never talked about these two, other than to say they were in a weird cult. I'd forgotten that fact for the most part, but immediately began piecing these two into my delusions of the Rainbow Family trying to recruit me and ultimately steal my soul. In my journal notes of the phone call informing me of the visit, I wrote fairly sanely about the upcoming visit and then followed up with a cryptic PS: "Paranoia feels a deadhead connection. Owen said that Gavin wears Deadhead neckties...Interesting." Needless to say before Owen even walked into the mess that was my house, I'd already begun piecing together delusions of grandeur and conspiracies.

His visit was interesting from the outset. I was lost, but still adamant in my Christianity, mainly out of superstition and fear of hell, but it turned out OK because he'd recently been converted, too. The story went something like this. Owen and Gavin had followed Maharishi in the 70's, and then throughout the 80's and 90's, followed another guru who had eventually died. Owen felt like he'd wasted a whole lot of time, and Gavin still clung to the idea that this guy had real powers. That was interesting to me, because I too, felt like I'd been lured in by mysticism before, with Roberto Morena, who'd also conveniently doubled as my pot dealer. Nonetheless, I had believed in those subtle powers, and I'd believed he had even showed me some of them, leaving me awed and confused. Also, all the Wiccans and hippies had believed in mysterious, vague spiritual laws so I wasn't unfamiliar at all, I'd just already come up with a theory for all of them, very black and white. They were evil. It may have been obtuse of me, but it helped me stay out of the confusion. Gavin went as far as to believe in levitation and magical powers. I told Owen of my story of all things outside the realm of proven science, and how I now believed the rest, the mysticism, was just designed to confuse us, and ultimately lead us away from God, that the Devil or darkness, whatever name you want to give it, worked in many ways to lead us off course, but that there was only one way to God. With the intelligent, one of the ways to distract us was to show us powers, and things that seemed like magic. He agreed, and we communed about philosophy and politics, and of course my father. He told me of my dad's last days in Ormond Beach, Florida, where they'd had him committed for three days (the Florida maximum for involuntary committals) to try to dry him out.

He told a particular story about Owen interrupting one of my father's alcoholic moments. It sounded as though he'd been mad, and that fit, as I'd known my dad in his last year of drinking, but was interested in hearing more about his last few weeks. The story went that he was watching a color television, but had turned the color off. He'd drawn all the shades and curtains closed, had turned off all the lights in the house, and was watching, in black and white, a TV movie that he could have viewed in color. Owen told me that he walked in on my father with a bottle of vodka in front of him, spellbound by a B movie, "Date With An Angel". At this precise moment in the movie, the angel's repaired wing had been restored and the angel had spread her wings in full glory. When Owen came in unannounced, it seemed to shatter my father's mad little black and white world, and my dad had attacked him, uselessly drunk, and was quickly subdued, by my sober, martial artist uncle. A day later, they had him committed, and a few days after they let him out, he left Ormond Beach to go back to Atlanta and ultimately to kill himself. He walked into a bank and got a 25k loan on good looks and charm, drank himself into oblivion, and blew his head off. The story of the TV moment was strange, but it would later make sense to me, when I got to that point of despair, confusion, and deranged delusion.

Owen and I talked about my grandfather as well. He was a Colonel in the United States Air Force, and I told him I remembered playing with miniature die-cast metal toys, of tanks, airplanes, and even one particularly awesome toy in my childhood memory, a replica of a Nuclear ICBM missile. I told him of the story I'd remembered of my grandfather coming to play toys with me, and me asking him what war was like, and I remember saying it must have been fun. I must have been 7 or 8 at the time. He looked at me and said "War is not fun. One time we called a bombing strike on a base in Europe, and the Marines had already been there. Hundreds of our own men died. War is anything but fun." I remember being spellbound, and Owen was impressed with the story. He said that Jack, my granddad, had never told them any war stories at all. He told me it was possible that he'd been in the OSS at the time (the Army's Office of Strategic Services, the precursor to the CIA), and that as he hadn't left the service, he could have pursued that path and gone into the CIA after the war, while officially staying in the Air Force. Well, that may have been just a planted seed, but I would later let that small seed grow into a Great Red Oak as my imagination towards the end of my drinking ran wild. I could never get that idea out of my head, regardless of the secondhand nature of the comment, and the entire lack of proof, it seemed almost implausible to think anything else from then on. It would later help to explain the mysteries in my life.

I'd also always had dreams of my dad still being alive since he died. I wanted to believe he died for a purpose, and though I couldn't quite come up with a story in my head good enough for his death at the time, this CIA delusion would later grow larger, and play a prominent role in my explanations for everything unsuitable to me in my life, from my father's death, to my mom's cancer, to you name it, it was an easy delusional scapegoat. But then, I was just letting the embers glow for a later date. More fuel would be needed. We talked of my dad traveling to and from Colombia smuggling drugs, which apparently had actually happened. A plot he'd gotten himself into was to bring the drugs back into the states and be busted with them, supposedly then being released by a crooked DEA agent, which he never went through with. He told me the details of my father being drafted to go to Vietnam, shooting dope and being discarded as 4F. We talked about his alcoholism, and his suicide, and we bonded over being disgruntled with Uncle Sam, with the Patriot Act, and going to war on emotion as we'd done so easily after 9/11. Regardless of my being sad, depressed, and losing it all, it was good to see my uncle, and it warmed my heart. I'd not thought of committing suicide at all through all of this, as I'd explored my bravery with that notion after my divorce, and found it wanting. I simply couldn't do to Jake, what my dad had done to me, but I get the feeling my mom was worried about me and had sent Owen as a last ditch effort. It wasn't needed to prevent my suicide at that time, but it was much appreciated, none the less and I'm glad I reconnected with him.

144

Owen also told me he was looking into an old family story that we were descended from Daniel Webster, a name I hate to admit I hadn't even known at the time. I believed it, though, when I Googled him and found he was one of the first and only congressman to pull out his pecker in Congress and wave it around. It sounded just like something I would have done if I was drunk and in Congress. And so we talked of reincarnation. In my uncle's words, "Completely fascinating, but utterly useless." I agreed, and we discussed the possibility that I had been Daniel Webster back then, getting drunk and flashing my cock for the distinguished gentleman of the United States Senate. Sounded plausible to me. And then there was something spooky. The story of "The Devil and Daniel Webster", in which Daniel Webster was the lawyer who represented a man who sold his soul to the Devil, and who argues with the Devil interminably, until the Devil relents and gave the man his soul back! This sounded just like my mental struggle from years past! Funny coincidence, or perhaps I was the man in a past life, I'd thought grandiosely. It didn't matter, it was fun to get drunk and debate the ridiculous. Eventually Owen proved that we actually weren't related at all to him, but it was fun to imagine, and it also gave me a sense of undeserved importance, probably one that I needed after losing it all in those last few months.

We called Gavin in Paris, the first and only time I've talked to him since my father's funeral. We debated socialism and capitalism, and he ranted on about Enron, and how it would take the Bush administration down. I called him out on his witnessing levitation, and I don't think he appreciated being basically called ridiculous by his nephew, but he was nice enough, and it was good to know he was alive, well, and blood to me. He would later send me a copy of his book about his experiences with his guru that Owen had left, but that he still held in high regard. Regardless of their views, or their being gone from my life for as long as they'd been, it felt really good to be reconnected, and I could care less why my mom had banned them from our lives. My gut told me it probably had to do with money, which Owen verified. Later, I would tie it into my delusions, as they must be undercover CIA agents, but later, hell, who wasn't. Even the cashier at the grocery store would be suspect later on!

I may not yet have been full blown schizophrenic delusional psychotic yet, but I certainly was working on my quirks. I didn't believe invisible people were chasing me quite yet in the winter of 2002, but I did believe, around the last day that Owen was there, and only briefly, those last few hours we were together, that we were able to communicate telepathically. I could hear his thoughts in my head, or at least I thought I could, and he could hear mine. This, I believed, explained the awkward moments of silence in our everyday conversation. Because we were communicating on a deeper level. I really believed it, and that last day, I was so excited by it that my heart was pounding really fast the last few hours he was there. In retrospect I believe this was another precursor to full blown DT's when this kind of thinking pervades every thought, but this was just a taste. I remember giving him a hug goodbye, and running over to Maria Espinoza's house, and telling her all about it, when she promptly told me I was crazy. So I didn't really tell that to anyone else. Not even Owen, I think that would have shattered the illusion and besides, even I knew it wasn't an exact science, it was merely a fact that I choose to believe. I couldn't sleep that night a wink, I was so electrified by his visit, and the telepathy, the two long-lost uncles I'd been reunited with, the CIA connection, and Daniel Webster for God's sake, I was practically American royalty! There was something there, something beyond reality, something magic, I couldn't quite put my finger on, but it was good and it was invigorating. Being broke didn't matter for a little while. And I continued to drink, with a newfound superiority, however based in fantasy it may have been. And the paranoia and telepathy subsided a bit, as the alcohol soothed my fears as always.

Losing it All

Personal Journal, February 6th, 2002:

I don't know if it's ever been quite this bad, but my gut says no. Downward spiral has cost me in this order a) Gwen Evere, either the best at concealing faults or more likely the best all out woman who has ever loved me. Tried a last ditch effort to salvage us today, and she said I was scaring her off and if I stopped by her house again she would have to take "drastic measures". Never mind up until now she's encouraged me to grovel her back, oh well, a woman's infamous switch, you never know till it's a week too late. Fuck. I was going to propose to her. b) monetary, I'm now roughly 12k+5k+6k+1K = 24k in the hole, no sign of making money and in serious danger of losing my house. c) Mental state, I'm jaded on love, American Freedom, money, drugs, and life in general... Suicidal thoughts aren't uncommon though I brush them aside with force. I would never do that, I would never leave Jake alone in this world. So what have we learned from all this? Inactivity doesn't work, women even tolerant women, have a threshold before they flick their switch, and yes, even soulmates lose interest. Debts can accumulate frighteningly fast. And it's hard to attract good women when you're broke, facing numerous charges, and your phone, electric, water, and gas are all shut off, your only companion a stray cat, and your only entertainment the wildly licking flames in the fireplace. I should have gotten a job months ago, but I just kept fucking up. How did this all happen so fast, 3 months ago, everything was fine. Man, that's scary, a New York Minute and it's all gone. I saw it coming, or didn't I create it? I think the latter is closer to the truth, and that's even worse. How will I stop it from happening again?

- JB Smith

So I'd lost it all. The house, the utilities were now off, there were rats in the kitchen, and I could see my breath in the cold living room, as I sat next to the fire, drinking and smoking cigarettes. Somehow, I'd managed to never go without alcohol and cigarettes though the rest had gone to shit. I was in debt to the tune of 25k, the creditors didn't have a phone to call, and I'd done it all to myself, and I knew it. I was dating Maria, but I still couldn't get Gwen out of my head, so much for the any woman would do theory. I was miserable.

I finally had gotten a job selling mortgages through my friend Spencer, and I began a long-ass commute to Norcross every day. I would drive and listen to country music, sad, depressing, missing lost love country music. I couldn't get Gwen out of my head. I should have taken heed when she said if I stopped by her house again she'd take "drastic measures", but I simply couldn't get it through my thick egocentric skull that she could have moved on. I'd done everything I knew how to do to get her back and she just wasn't coming. For some reason, all of my problems didn't mean shit to me, but this one. It's as if I condensed all my misery, and loss into one problem of losing her and I began obsessing over it. I also was engrossed with the thought that she was missing me just as much. I'd tried desperately in a last ditch effort to give her a wedding ring, the ring that had been in my family's name for 250 years or so, and she'd laughed at me horribly. The only reason she'd let me come over I think was to gloat about the new guy she was dating that worked at a Major Entertainment Conglomerate, which she obviously enjoyed rubbing in my face. We hung out a few hours, her teasing me with the weight she'd supposedly lost, her tight ass clothes, and her unabashed flirtation, but she just wouldn't let me get close, and when the phone rang, she literally dragged me to the front door and pushed me out. It made me livid. I'm sure I went over to Corey's and got drunk.

Corey and I began getting drunk all the time together. He was a good friend through all of this, but it wouldn't stop me from manipulating him and treating him like shit. I'd continue to use him for many years to come, but right now, he was just buying drinking tabs, and bringing beer to my powerless house.

Eventually I broke down and asked my parents if I could move back in with them, chucking my pride out of the window. So, at 24, I moved back in with my parents. I promised all kinds of things, like doing chores, going to church, and such, but I didn't live up to any of it, and Corey and I went out and got drunk almost every night as my career in the mortgage industry went absolutely nowhere. The mortgage company I went to work for gave me one advance for 1k, and when I quit, a month or two later, they threatened to sue me to get that money back. I laughed and told them to get in line, I owed around 30k by now. I felt fucked.

Killing Car and Telephone Pole

Not too long after I moved in with my parents, I drove up to my brother's in Chattanooga, Tennessee. I was there a few hours and he was throwing a party at his house, with a keg and the whole nine. Beautiful country, his house backed up to a hill that overlooked this valley he was in and the little street he lived on. I don't even think it was night fall before Carson and I began arguing about our real father.

"Dad was just sick, Carson." Repeating the age-old argument, but drunk and belligerent.

"Dan Jones is my father, Morris was just a pussy that left us all." Carson rebutted, both of us set in our opinions.

"He was a good man, Carson, he was just sick. He felt that suicide was the best answer for everybody, and he couldn't see how bad it would be for us. He didn't think he could stop drinking and rather than go on hurting us, he killed himself, leaving Mom some money. I've thought the same thing, maybe killing myself is the best thing for everybody."

"He was a selfish bastard, and I don't have any forgiveness for him at all."

"Well maybe I just understand it because I can see how suicide would make sense," and I stormed off. That is roughly how I remember that argument going in what was probably the first conversation my brother and I had had in several years. It infuriated me that Carson couldn't have compassion for our dad. I felt like he didn't know him before he'd gone crazy, and that he didn't love him at all. I ran to my car in tears, angry, pathetic, and drunk. I revved up the Jeep Grand Cherokee, gave it some gas and promptly nailed the telephone pole in his neighbor's yard, completely trashing the Jeep, whose insurance I'd let lapse, of course, along with every other bill on the planet. The telephone pole fell, shooting off sparks and making God-awful noises, bringing out Carson's neighbors and setting me off in a panic. I jumped out of the car and hauled ass across the party through Carson's back yard, wasted, with adrenaline pumping, and hid in the hills overlooking the house, and the wreck and the small fire I'd started in the neighbor's yard. A symphony of chaos ensued, the police and fire department all equally pissed and wanting to get their hands on the fugitive, searched Carson's house and yard, negotiated with my brother for what must have been an hour or so. Despite my cussing him out, bringing up nasty family business in front of his college friends, and completely embarrassing him and myself, my brother held his ground, stood up for me, and somehow got those cops to leave without arresting a soul. I would later go back to court and have the entire thing dismissed. The car, on the other hand, was a total waste. The $3500 dollar ridiculous stereo I'd installed, completely stolen. The car itself, undriveable, and the insurance had been completely ignored, so it was uncovered. I was once again fucked. Once again I'd done it to myself. I remember telling Corey this story when I got back and it was one of the first times I said to myself maybe I just need to quit drinking. Corey said, "No man, you just need to quit doing stupid things when you're drinking." That sounded good, and I'd ride that theory a while longer before even attempting.

Obsessing About Gwen

My mom and stepdad, though, were not quite as thrilled. My mom was in tears, and asked "Why did you tell Carson you would kill yourself?"

"I didn't say it like that, Mom, it was a hypothetical for the

149

sake of the argument."

My stepdad said, "You should know better than to have a hypothetical argument with your brother, he's not going to see the finer points of an argument. And let me tell you something, your mother has to love you, but I don't. And I'm about sick of this shit." This from the guy who'd given me $500 bucks to run away at 15, I thought to myself, rationalizing my ignoring him. I blocked it all out, and followed Corey's advice. I'd just make better decisions when drinking from now on. Like not hang out with my brother, that made more sense.

I did spend a lot more time with Corey though. He was very forgiving of my atrocious behavior, as well as picked up a lot of bar tabs, using his mom's credit card, so our friendship really blossomed. We drank and drank and spent a lot of time in bars commiserating over why the women in our lives had wronged us, and how women were just greedy gold diggers and the like. We spent a lot of time drunk, and almost every time I'd get drunk, I'd get to thinking about Gwen, and I'd call her, pretty much nightly. Mainly to get voicemails, lots and lots of voicemails, but I was beyond taking a hint. I was in love... I thought.

Somehow I groveled and got my old job back at PMC Financial. I probably told them I would get sober, or that I at least wasn't doing hard drugs, and I think when I'd moved back in with my parents I'd vowed not to touch hard drugs ever again, blaming drugs, not alcohol, for losing my house -- as well as, of course, 9/11, which I continued to tell whoever would listen. I got my job back at PMC Financial, and continued recruiting. Mostly, though, I continued to compulsively print out news stories of our impending attack on Iraq, and the War on Terror on the PMC Financial printers, irritating my bosses to no end. I recruited while researching the war, I told myself, I was smart enough to do both. I also continued to obsess over Gwen, and while dating Maria, tried to also date as many redheads as possible, trying maybe to replace Gwen Evere with another redhead, but that didn't seem to work either. I dreamed about her almost every single night.

I kept seeing Gwen's face everywhere I'd go. I'd be driving in midtown, and lo and behold, I'd see her in her jeep. As it turned out, she'd moved in with her new boyfriend, who just happened to live right down the street from Maria Espinoza's house, so I actually was just randomly seeing her from a far from time to time. Then I'd see cardinals all the time, and just assume it was fate, that we were meant to be together, that it was destiny of some sort. And when wasted, and Maria wasn't around, I'd call her. Always to get that cold hearted voice mail. But she still loved me, I could feel it, damn it! Occasionally I'd think we must be thinking of each other at the same time, across time and space... usually while high... which again was consistently.

One night, Corey and I went to Brandy House, and there she was. She, of course, thought I'd followed her. I went up to her in front of her boyfriend and everyone she was with, and told her that I'd gotten my job back at PMC Financial. I was drunk, and I guess I didn't know what else to say. Her response was, "Quit following me!" That pissed me off, the nerve of suggesting that I would follow a woman around. I mean stopping by the house once or twice and banging on her door was one thing, calling her every other night for several months was another, and I mean, long drawn out emails, hell, everyone does that -- but follow her? The nerve of that bitch, I thought to myself. "I didn't follow you, Gwen, you just happened to be at the same bar as me, you're not that special," I emailed her along with another few pages of sentimental drivel that I'm sure she deleted. But, damn, did that piss me off. I'd let it stew for a while before I reacted, though, thinking of her constantly and taking every red cardinal I saw as a sign from God we were destined through it all to reunite.

Home Again, Kicked Out Again

The foreclosure proceedings continued on my house and an interesting coincidence took place. I'd worked out a deal with my next door neighbor, to sell the house to him, minus what I owed on the 50k refinance, for the price of about a 5k Toyota Camry. I'd left my Jeep in wreckage in Tennessee, was about to lose the house anyway, so it seemed like a good strategy. One day after we signed the papers and I got the car, I closed a deal with my old client, that would have never happened without my sales skills, and without my candidate. I mean to tell you, they had made the decision to use another candidate, and I sold the VP of Audit of a multi-billion dollar corporation, on the attitude and good heartedness of my candidate, over a more qualified CPA and extra year of experience the opposing candidate had to offer. My client had changed his mind mid-offer and given my candidate the job, which is unheard of. On a 15k fee or so, which had I kept the faith and kept my company going, I would have collected 100% of, but because I'd gone back to PMC Financial and the account was now somebody else's, all in all I'd get about $2500. So basically if I'd kept the faith, I would have had exactly what I needed to save my house from foreclosure and get back on my feet with my own company all in one fell swoop, not to mention what other deals I may have closed had I given it two cents of effort. But I hadn't. I'd drunk and drugged it away and I'd crawled back to PMC Financial on my hands and knees.

To me, though, it was God showing me to keep the faith, and never give up. The next time I'd start a business I would not soon forget that. Had I not chosen to give it all away, I would have been just fine, not even bringing into account all the self-prescribed tragedy my drinking had brought, if I'd just kept trying, I would have been fine. It took from January to July or so to foreclose on that house. That was something else, I didn't know how much effort it took to throw everything away. I thought it'd be gone in a New York minute. Everything happens for a reason. The deal I closed with my client would have saved it all, but now I worked for PMC Financial so it only paid me a fraction.

I remember when I closed that deal I felt pretty proud of myself regardless of whether it was $2500 or 15k that I would eventually get. Shane Oleander came over that afternoon and we began drinking early. Summer of 2002, I was chasing after Emma Lott, and Shane Oleander was my ace in the hole on this one, for as Emma only seemed halfway interested in me, her friend Mary seemed to be in love with Shane. So I begged him to come over and hang out and that way Emma and Mary would come over as well. My parents were in Spain, my mom in a break from her chemo and radiation, and I was taking full advantage of the house while she was gone. In my head I'd have it all cleaned up by the time she got back.

First Shane and I went down to Little Five to score an eight ball, down at the Samson Lofts. We played indoor baseball, got coked up and numb for a while. Then we came back to Roswell, bought a bunch of beer, rum, and wine and called the girls over. I had done a lot of coke in the last year, but mostly in grams, and this was the first time I'd remembered buying an eight ball. It was the first time I really ever did coke with Shane other than a few times we'd run into each other at bars out and about. Shane Oleander laid out that eight ball like he had a million dollars. Usually I could make a gram last a few hours, but this guy was putting down lines that make my stomach queasy just writing about. As long, and thick as a cigarette, we got high, high, high. And then the girls came over.

We were so fucking high, I can't believe they wanted anything to do with us, but we got them drunk, and hid our doing coke the entire miserable night, as the thrill and high from earlier playing baseball was just replaced with the inevitability of just trying not to come down. We eventually wound up back at my house, after making the rounds of their favorite bars, and I was glad, to get back behind closed doors, so Shane and I could continue our coke binge. Suddenly around 2 or 3 AM, the coke was gone. My heart was beating so fucking fast I thought I was going to die. I didn't have any Xanax, any pills at all, and I was utterly miserable. It was unlike any other coke bender I remembered, because I couldn't drink it away. My heart pounded as if bombs were exploding in my ears. Emma wanted to fool around, and I couldn't even pretend to be interested, but was so freaked out by my chest pain and the booming in my ears, I couldn't even be embarrassed by my impotence. Somehow I think I talked her into the shower, hoping it would help my head, my heart, and maybe if I was lucky my dick, but it was a lost cause. My pecker just wasn't working under these conditions. I'd never done that much coke in my life. We'd killed an eight ball in a few hours, and the real thought of dying became a reality. We got the girls to leave that night eventually and I spent a good hour or so on my knees begging for my life. Eventually I fell asleep, leaving my mom's house a complete disaster.

I remember waking up the next morning to my mom screaming and yelling, but I had no idea the magnitude of what my response to her was until a few weeks later, when my sister told me. I simply was in a blackout, I guess, as in my mind it had just never happened. She told me I yelled to my dying mother, "Fuck you, you God damn bitch, you fucking insane bitch, leave me alone!" As I slept in on a weekday while she was supposed to be in Europe. I didn't then and don't now remember saying it, but Carrie informed me several weeks afterwards that I'd done it, after they had rightfully kicked their 24 year old, ungrateful little shit out of the house. The journal entry I wrote a few months after this, puts my arrogance into perspective, I think:

Personal Journal, October 28, 2002:

... **"Apparently I was living lavishly and comfortably at my parents house, and in their eyes selfishly. I had a misunderstanding with my mom regarding work, and in a morning blackout I cussed her out. I didn't know I had done this for several weeks later when my sister told me. I was very sorry and told my mom, but actions speak louder than**

words, and hence ever since then I have done much more wrong."

I love that I called it a misunderstanding. Yeah, a misunderstanding, like she didn't understand why her house looked like a coke binge had been thrown in it, why there were more than three dozen cases worth of empty expensive beer bottles all over the backyard, and why the hell I wasn't at work on a weekday. She probably also didn't understand how a child could cuss out his dying mother. Misunderstanding. I had a lot of those with the world, in fact, I dare say, I was misunderstood. Ridiculous.

So I'd been forced out of the luxurious Brookfield West home of my mother, who probably needed a little peace while she dealt with her cancer, and was probably a little hard-pressed to get that with her first born gallivanting into the bars every single night, coming home wasted at all hours. In retrospect, it's understandable, but at the time, just another resentment, another misunderstanding. In my deluded feeble little mind I was now forced into moving in with Maria Espinoza, who up until now, I had simply dated and kept at arm's length. Suddenly I needed a place to live, and just like that, our relationship got more serious.

Key West and In With Jen

Before manipulating my way into my next hostage's house, I connived a trip to Miami and Key West, all on her dime. It was a great trip and we had a blast. The turquoise rainbow of mahi-mahi streaking towards my hook off of Key West is something I'll not soon forget, but it's funny how my best memory of the trip is when I'd left my girlfriend in the hotel room. I was a selfish prick, but I justified it in all kinds of delusion. If I had the money, I'd be paying, so what's the difference? The vacation went well enough, so we decided to move in together, as I'd been pressing for, and probably because of that, I had been on my best behavior. In the words of Monica Staff, one of the previous girls, "Everybody gets along on vacation." I must have used our vacation time with her in Amsterdam and Cancun to justify our staying together towards the end. I still think that's a great quote.

She was right, when Maria and I got back to Atlanta, I moved in and we fought like cats and dogs. Within a week or so of living together she'd read through my entire journal and found that I still had feelings for Gwen, that I'd called her some pretty ugly names more than once, and that I was a manipulative lying son of a bitch.
154

So I finagled and lied my way out of the hot seat, and we were back in good graces, so long as I was pouring out my unconditional love for her at all times, whether I was feeling it or not. So I was lying. When I told my friend Spencer this, he said I was a bitch, and it stung. We lived in the Old Cotton Mill Lofts in downtown Atlanta, and though I fell in love with the area, and the view from the rooftop, that place itself does not give a very homey feeling. Stone floors, long hallways, it felt like the place was haunted most days. We could also hear our upstairs neighbor piss every morning at 7 AM, and then promptly flush the toilet. Also it was one big room and she was crowding me I felt. Really, I was miserable. I told her I didn't like the two cats we had. A week later, the cats had been released into the cemetery across the street. This should have been a warning sign, but it wasn't. I continued living there with her, and as Spencer said, being a bitch.

Around this time an editorial I'd written about the one year anniversary of 9/11 came to be published. I'd written a small piece for MSNBC, while I was supposed to be recruiting at PMC Financial, and submitted it to them via the Internet. They had picked me and a few other writers to publish, and this being my first published work of all time, it immediately went in my head from editorial to article. The irony, too, is that the few paragraphs I'd written were all about not giving up, not letting the terrorists win, not letting us be paralyzed by fear, but rising above the challenge, and meeting it head on. Meanwhile, in real life, I'd frozen up in fear, quit working, given up on life and begun the long slow steady process of destroying everything meaningful in my life. But still, it was MSNBC.com and it was being published, so I was pretty damn proud. I'd laid off the phone calls to Gwen, and even the occasional errant email for the week or so we'd been in Miami, so I figured she'd be completely cool with speaking again. Lo and behold, she wasn't. She, for the wackiest reason, didn't want to speak to me at all. All I wanted were the photographs she'd taken in New York. She emailed me back and said she didn't want to speak to me, no matter what it was about. That being the case, I contrived a way that she would want to call me back, and then I could explain and clear up the matter. I told her I'd written a short story about her, and that it was going to be published in Stuff Magazine and I needed to talk to her about something. Well she did call me back, and she said something to the effect of "Back off, you psychopath." She was so silly.

"Gwen, listen I really just need to get the photographs from New York, you know the trip I paid for, that you took the pictures for, come on, it's really important." I pleaded innocently I thought.

She seemed venomous, livid, like she could kill me right at that instant. I felt pretty lucky and lighthearted about being published, but something in her voice made me nervous. "OK, Bryan. What is your address, and I'll send you the pictures." She had almost growled it, but I'm a sucker for a beautiful woman.

"Well, good," I thought, she was finally seeing the error of her ways, and putting the pictures in the mail. My complicated, threatening plan had worked, and once again I'd manipulated and lied my way into getting what I wanted. I gave her the address and hung up the phone feeling pretty good about myself, being a published author and all. Hell, Gwen was probably just jealous that I was about to become a famous writer. And I entertained that fantasy for a few hours, if not the entire day and night.

The next day, I had just finished smoking a bowl of weed at our loft at Maria Espinoza's when a loud heavy knock interrupted my buzz. I jumped up out of the carefree zone it had put me in and ran to the front door. Peeping through the hole, I saw a policeman. I begged Maria to go talk to the policeman, and she did such a good job of telling that policeman I wasn't there, that I began wondering about what else she was lying about. I mean she was smooth. The cop left, and she wanted to know why Gwen Evere was pressing charges against me. Holy shit!

In the morning I went to work as if it never happened and the police delivered a subpoena to me at work and I was shocked. In front of everybody in the office, no less, and worse, I was at a lunch meeting that I was called away from to respond to the subpoena, as it was their second attempt to deliver it. I left the lunch and I got to the office seething. This woman had not only sued me, but gotten all of her friends to sign up as witnesses to the -- get this -- STALKING charges! I was outraged and indignant, and never in my life had I been so insulted. The very nerve of accusing me of stalking via email and voice messages, I mean it was trumped up to all Hell and back, and even worse, people I'd thought were my friends had filled out most of the statements against me. Melissa Gilbreath, Tina Kimba, people I'd known for years and had gone to school with, really did just blatantly lie against me in order to press these charges and to make them stick, saying they witnessed things, that (a) never happened, and (b) they couldn't have been there to see if they had happened. Man, I was furious. How dare she? I would never speak to that unholy bitch of all bitches again as long as I walked this planet. I would repeat that mantra again and again, never committing to it seriously, similar to my pledge to quit drinking, always true in the moment, but always reversible at the first hint of discomfort.

It turned out there weren't any actual charges, it was just a harassment suit, and all her Legal Aid attorney wanted was a restraining order. I walked into that courtroom 30 days later, and took one look at her and her boyfriend, who looked scared, and I wanted to leave immediately. I found her attorney, told her I'd sign whatever, and she said I needed to stick around until the judge got there, but I didn't care. "Give me the paperwork to sign," I was familiar with courtrooms and proceedings, I'd sign it and then I'd go. The woman looked at me confused, as if I was going to fight it, as if my reaction didn't line up with the description Gwen had given her. She went away and came back with the restraining order for six months, which I signed, and left. I would later learn that because my last name was Smith, near the end of the alphabet, Gwen had to sit in that courtroom all day long before the judge would verify the terms. I didn't give a damn, I had to get out of there. I signed the restraining order, grimaced at the additional mark on my permanent record, like I would ever run for Congress, and got the hell out of Dodge. I was beyond livid. Now, though, looking back, it had been months since I'd banged on her door, still, I can see how she'd let the fear build up and up until she had no other choice. But at the time, I was nothing but justified in my anger and resentment towards her. Obviously it didn't help with matters at home either. Maria was less than amused that her live-in boyfriend had been served a restraining order by his ex-girlfriend.

Now also, living with Maria at Cotton Mill, I was much closer to my favorite club, the Crescent Room. I continued Friday night partying, though never blowing as much money as I'd done in the past, but still getting a few grams from time to time. I noticed somehow, almost on cue, whenever I'd do coke, I'd get some news about my mom's cancer getting worse. I'd visit her in the hospital about once a week, never more for more an hour, as I wrote in my journal:

"Seeing her in pain about kills me every time. I can't do anything about it. Nothing, and I just feel scorn from my family the whole time. All the respect gone, from the moment I went broke."

As if my family was thinking about me, while my mom lay dying of cancer in hospital beds around Atlanta. I would stay for no more than an hour, and never more than once a week. My sister, on the other hand, was a soldier. She was there all the time, and she

157

was going to Georgia State full time, and working full time at Lenox Mall. I was just a pussy. A selfish, self involved addict, bitch.

Maria and I were fighting everyday and unless we were drunk together, we never got along that great. I tried to get her drunk as much as possible but, unfortunately for me, she wasn't that big of a lush. One weekend around my birthday, I told her while drunk that Adam Archer and I were going to the Braves game. I think she asked for the rent money or something, and I, of course, had spent it on better things, mainly myself. It got heated and she grabbed me and at some point in the ensuing struggle, and drunk, I punch her in the stomach. I left and we went to the Braves game anyway, and wouldn't you know it, she asked me to leave the next day. Another strange thing happened that night as well. On the roof smoking weed again, some guy and I began talking and he said men should never hit women. Although he didn't know me, and I didn't know him, it felt like a warning from a stranger. We had been talking about something completely different and yet it came out in conversation. He wasn't threatening or malevolent at all, but just said it as a fact. My mind would briefly fall back on the family delusion, that somehow it was all connected and this was a message, but only for a second. Rather, I considered it a moment of clarity, and I felt awful for what I'd done, again. Briefly. Up until that moment I think I'd forgotten about it. It is an example to me now, of God speaking to me through other people. I moved out a few days later into the Samson lofts down the street from Maria near Little Five, to make a new beginning once again.

Samson Lofts

I had moved in with Adam Archer and Henry Daniels, friends from my high school days, into the Samson Lofts near Little Five, and I had all kinds of deja vu's moving into that place. I painted over the yellow in the bathroom, still resentful of my mom painting my room yellow as an adolescent, and I moved all my stuff out of Corey's basement, which I'd used as storage while living at my parents, to really try to make a home. I still had my job at PMC Financial and things were going well, so I had high hopes. I shouldn't have pegged them there. The lofts I moved into were filled with drug dealers, hippies, ravers, skaters, and you name it, all peddling drugs from the distribution level to retail. I was right smack in the middle of it all, but I was planning on moderation. How funny that sounds in retrospect. Vaguely, I felt as though I'd moved right into the middle of the Rainbow Family, but I was only flirting with this delusion at this stage, for the most part I'd written it off. But when very high, stoned, or drunk, I could let the thoughts mingle.

Within a few weeks of living at the lofts, things were slowly but steadily going downhill. My roommate Henry was and still is a highly respected MC in the small but committed world of Drum and Bass music, and it made for a good night life at the time. More importantly, it made for mostly free covers, and free drinks. One night driving home on a weeknight, I ran through a stop sign with a good eight or nine beer buzz, and saw a cop in the rearview mirror blow up his blue lights almost a half mile away, and come hauling ass after me. I pulled into the lofts, took the sharp right along the ledge of the backend of those lofts, turned off the car and the lights, pulled up the emergency brakes, ducked my head and thought to myself what a great criminal I was. Right up until I heard the tap, tap, tap, of the policeman standing over me as I crouched in the fetal position on my front seat. Shit. I got out and begged the policeman to let me go, telling him I lived right here. I put it all out there, my divorce, my two DUIs, my son -- hell, I even think I told this policeman about my dad being an alcoholic. He didn't believe that I lived there, and from the outside, it certainly doesn't look like residential homes. I walked him to the front door, and he let me in and better yet, let me go. My roommates, all of whom had mass quantities of weed, were not very amused with me. It wouldn't be the last time. I was always bringing trouble around. I got away with that DUI, the cop was a miracle. I was driving without a license, and without insurance, but somehow he let me go. I think he was looking for crack offenders down there, and I was just a drunk. God protects children and drunks, for though I was acting like a child, I was a grown ass man.

Christmas and New Years went by uneventfully and, though we partied hard on snorted up, crushed OxyContins on New Year's Eve, I wouldn't really go down that opiate path for some time. My job continued to plug along, and, though I wasn't hitting any home runs, I still wasn't fucking up too terribly badly. However, one thing did go down, that would make me an enemy for years to come to certain professionals I worked with in the recruiting industry. I was approached by Brian Huff, a recruiter at PMC Financial who was knocking the ball out of the ball park, closing deals left and right, to help him start up a new recruiting firm. It would be him, Chad Major, and Christopher Stanley all going to start this company, and though they didn't want to bring me on as a partner, they certainly would like to have me as a recruiter. I was instantly pissed they hadn't asked me to be a partner. Hell, leaving PMC Financial and starting your own company had been MY idea, I just got fucked over by 9/11,

159

and now you're going to copy my best plans, and leave me out to dry, but you'd like my recruiting efforts to join your team? "Well, gooooo fuck yourself," was about how my thoughts went along.

I didn't at first tell Brian this, though, giving him ample time to make me a partner in said venture. Which he still did not. So spitefully, but I believed justifiably, because of the manner in which they were doing it, I went to Everett Monahan, the CEO of PMC Financial and told him the plan, but begged him to keep me anonymous in those proceedings. In fact, I advised him just to keep track of Brian's personal emails, so he could therefore keep me out of the loop entirely. This he did not do, but instead, picked up the phone and forced the issue by bringing all the involved parties together, and creating a huge cluster-fuck of denials, finger-pointings, and general hatred towards myself, which rightfully, I deserved. In my deluded mind I was only telling Everett this, because they were doing it in the wrong manner, setting up the company while working still at PMC Financial. Most importantly, the manner in which they were setting up one deal in particular, with a huge telecommunications client, did seem to me to be embezzlement, and I thought by telling Everett this I would be in his good graces forever. I thought I was doing the right thing, in a bad situation, for the right reasons, I thought I was doing good. This is what I told myself, and the stuff that was borderline embezzlement was not something I wanted my name attached to at all. But when I'm truly honest with myself, I did this out of resentment, out of anger, and out of bruised pride that they didn't offer me a partnership. Though, in retrospect, who offers a partnership to an active drunk?

I've made amends to all those involved in that matter, but it did happen. Those gentleman wanted to start their own company, and wanted me to go along, and trusted me, but because of my injured pride, I went to the one man they were trying to keep it a secret from, and told on them. I felt like a rat. Everett even called me out on it when I went into the office.

"So basically they didn't make you a partner, so you're telling me?" Everett had me figured out.

"No, I'm telling you because of the potential illegal nature of what they are doing," I defended myself, but that good man had seen right through me. Even my roommates at the time called me out on that one. I really messed up people's lives with that blunder, but again, I was able to write these things off with ease, as the mind of an alcoholic is set up to defend itself from attack, as it has been attacked by logic for years and years to no avail. I went along as if nothing happened, and I even thought that since I'd thwarted the all-out mutiny of his top four billers, Everett would hold me in the highest regard. But that would turn out not to be the case.

Ice and Sage

The club scene with my roommates continued on unabated. There were some random women in between the benders, as every night was a different party, but nobody serious again until I met Sage. My roommate Henry had already begun doing ice all the time -- premium crystal methamphetamine. I wasn't far behind him in usage, as unlike coke, a little baggie of ice could last you a week or so. And then I met Sage. Sage was beyond any shadow of a doubt a meth head. Her teeth were stained from bulimia, but other than that she was a pretty, petite natural blonde. Had my sister not pointed it out when she met her, I'd have never noticed the teeth or known about bulimia. I followed Sage into the depths of hell of ice usage over the next few months, and how I didn't lose my job immediately is beyond me, other than I suppose it kept me artificially focused and productive at work. We'd go three, four, or five days without sleeping, and eating rice and corn forcefully, so that our body had the nutrition to keep going. With ice, I always felt like I was on the verge of some great discovery, something huge was about to happen, but it never did. Almost instantaneously I was an everyday user. Also, I could drink all day and all night on ice which is what really appealed to me. We had several different dealers, but one in particular sticks out in my mind.

He came over to the lofts one night that early spring. He had a name, but when I met him, I instantly called him "Doublewide," and it stuck like glue. Within a week, everyone in Atlanta called this guy Doublewide. We were all playing basketball, and he laid down some lines. They were so fucking big, I thought they must be coke. They were not, they were ice, and at first I was pissed, because instead of the smooth numbing of your face you get from coke, ice feels as if battery acid and sinus medicine have just been fire-hosed into your nasal cavity. It hurts like hell, but then you're taken over by the high, and you feel a little bit better, albeit weird, to say the least. Wired doesn't begin to describe.

This night we were all began playing basketball on the shit, and at some point he showed us how he could grab his heart. He literally reached into his chest, which he said had been cracked due to heart surgery, and gripped around his pounding heart, as we could see it beating through the skin. It was creepy. That time alone, one of the first stretches, I stayed awake from a Saturday to the next Wednesday. It was too much, but Sage and I got closer and closer due to the drugs, and the addiction. Eventually we began smoking it through light bulbs, tinfoil, whatever, but I preferred to snort it all up, and chase it down with a ton of beer. She always wanted to tweak out and stay at home, but I loved taking it and going out to clubs. Smoking it gave it away, though, at work. I came in one day, and my boss Mike Rubin, said "His knuckles are black, I know what that's from, and you only get that to happen by smoking crack! Bryan's smoking crack!"

I was so offended about being once again falsely accused. I was smoking ice, by God, get it straight, but I just denied it all and went back to making tons of calls. If it hadn't affected my productivity so positively, I'm sure they would have fired me right then and there, but at his stage it was still making me produce.

Sage and I were together a few months, tweaked the hell out, and pretty paranoid, but still nothing compared to what would come. I was still visiting my mom once or twice a week, and she was still sick, bald from the cancer, and every time I saw her I could just feel the disappointment in her eyes. I felt so guilty looking at her while I was high, and the looks I would get from my sister made my shame ignite. I would have to leave, literally running from the lobby of the hospital to get to my car, and snort a line of ice. We got it almost free, driving old Doublewide around on errands, and God knows what else Sage did for the guy when I was at work, holding down my 9 to 5. It was strange though, because it seemed like everyone at the lofts was doing ice, except for maybe Adam Archer, who never let any drug get out of control. Henry and I, though, were off the chain on ice for several months that year. I started to slow down once I began having out-of-body experiences in my sleep on a regular basis. I mean I would fall asleep, and dream extremely vividly that I'd left my body and was floating around the house like a ghost, almost always trapped within the confines of that loft, and those dreams became more and more regular. Things would get worse before they got better.

One weekend, I'd gotten some rolls and Sage and I went to Piedmont Park. I completely blacked out and came to while she was driving the car. I couldn't figure out how to stop the car, because I didn't have the pedals in front of me, so the most logical thing for me to do was jump out of the car. She said I just came to, freaked out, opened the door and jumped out of the car, though I don't remember jumping. Luckily, we were right near my house, and going slow, not 75 miles an hour down the freeway. Luck saved my ass more than once.

If it comes back to you it's yours...

I was still dreaming of and writing about Gwen Evere in my journal, but I'd kept good on my promise never to email or call her again since she'd sued me back in October. That didn't mean obsession wasn't still a friend of mine. Sage and I had been together for just a few months when I got that fateful call from Gwen, a good solid month before the restraining order was up.

"JB?" I'd recognize her voice anywhere, as she'd recognized mine all those years before.

All the anger, all the resentment, all the justifiable rage, went out the window with those two small syllables. The blonde next to me stared at me with suspicion and dismay when I answered. It was 7 am and I hadn't even got out of bed yet.

"Hey, are you OK?" I asked her in my most loving voice, completely incapable of being hard with her.

"No, I'm not OK, I need your help," and she started crying. My heart melted and I wanted to see her right then and there, that instant.

"Can you meet me today for lunch?" I asked her.

"Yes, I can do that." Soft, vulnerable.

"Good KB", and I was relieved.

"Ok, I'll call you at 11. Bye JB."

That morning Sage was the best girlfriend I'd ever had. We made love, she cooked me breakfast, she begged me not to go to work. "Under my thumb," by the Rolling Stones came on and I sang it in on the way into work, remembering how much begging and pleading I'd done to get with Sage, and how it had turned around just a few months later, with the threat of losing me to Gwen. Women are funny. I had sung that song a lot when Anne Marie was pregnant, and she'd gone from cold and indifferent, to begging me not to leave the house. I guess it's just human nature. So Sage had treated me

163

well that morning, and yet all the feelings, all the emotions of love for Gwen had been brought to the surface, and all the anger and rage had disappeared in that one phone call, yet I was still conflicted. Gwen called me that morning and asked me to meet her for lunch somewhere near my office, and I just remember feeling nervous and paranoid about the whole thing. The most obvious fear was that it was a setup. It was only five months or so into the restraining order, and given the cold calculated way in which she'd served me the papers, at my girlfriend's house, I felt I had every reason to be cautious. But my love for her overcame the fear, and I met her for lunch that day.

She was as beautiful as ever, except that all her confidence, and her self reliance, and all the things that had attracted me to her in the first place were gone. She was a wounded bird, her wing still torn, and she told me an awful sob story about her new beau wronging her, and her going crazy. Ultimately she'd been checked into rehab, suicidal and depressed, the beau had left her, but gotten her an apartment, once again, coincidentally just a few blocks from my lofts downtown. She was sad and broken, and I was eager to put her back together, and to apologize for all my wrong-doings, my forgetting her birthday, my harassing her, though I still deny actually stalking her, I was able to put it in the past and we hugged and kissed, and set forth in motion the chaos that would be that spring of 2003, for both of us.

The downward spiral would once again gain steam as ice and weed, and, of course, the ever present booze, along with the Bohemian lifestyle of the lofts all combined to accelerate the self-destruction, so rampant in my life. I juggled Sage, Gwen, Maria and whoever else was attracted to the mess. Anytime drugs would get bad, the "Family" delusions would pick up, and now I was beyond a doubt one of them, in my head. I was dancing with the Devil in the darkness, and it would afford his advantages, though I'd never admit it, claiming all the time I was a Christian, and even saying the Lord's prayer, almost superstitiously, every morning no matter how terrible or hung-over I felt. From time to time, though, "Devil's Luck" would be so obvious it would be hard to deny. Once after doing coke all night, I'd said how nice it would be to have some Percocets, heavy painkillers, when a neighbor walked into the lofts, and right then and there, offered us all some Percocets. We laughed and laughed and said we were magic. It was surreal and even creepy for us then, but it felt real, and while going down slow, that Devil's Luck would never be too far out of reach, keeping us high constantly, and out of jail. Most of the time anyway.

164

And "Family", hah! I'm sure more than one person was confused when I'd drunk their last beer or smoked up their weed, saying "Man, it's all good, we're family!" I guess it just feels good to be a part of a bigger movement. That drinking and drugging bonded us together against society, and we were working towards a common goal, by somehow rebelling and always staying fucked up. Hell, in my mind, we were practically revolutionaries, and so long as nobody asked me to sell my soul, or denounce Jesus Christ, I'd smoke the free weed and drink people's beer all day long. I wouldn't talk about "Family" much, as details were sketchy to everyone. In fact, whenever I explained I was family to anyone at all they just looked at me funny, either accepting it, or denouncing it, or just writing it off as crazy Bryan, which I undoubtedly was. Neither Gwen or Sage knew what the hell I was talking about, whereas Corey Black accepted that I was family and that he was not, and therefore didn't come to the lofts that much. Adam Archer and Henry, I think just took it as our inside joke, never really realizing the extent my paranoid, over-tripped mind had taken it to. When I was high, we were a loosely bound confederacy of dope smokers, and borderline socialist revolutionaries, working in the grid, awaiting the inevitable call to arms against society as a whole! I think a lot of people live in this drug induced delusion, and music and media help to propagate it, but it really amplifies it to stay stoned most of the time.

So I was still with Sage when Gwen and I began hooking up again, and I was still smoking ice before going into work. Mind you again, PMC Financial is one of the most prestigious accounting and financial recruiting firms in Atlanta, requiring a full-on suit and tie, and I was walking in cracked out on ice, with alcohol coming out of every pore. They knew, but I was still showing up, and I was still putting numbers on the board. It wouldn't last forever, but it was still going strong around this time.

Gwen wouldn't commit to me again, so like the selfish prick that I was, I kept Sage, Maria, and a new girl named Catherine that bartended at American Pie all in a codependent holding pattern, so that I'd never have to be alone. But I was fully in love with Gwen this whole time, and anytime she called, I rushed to be by her side. Mostly, though, she just strung me along.

Eventually Sage followed me to American Pie, where she saw me talking to Catherine. She confronted me there boldly, and I ushered her to come talk to me outside around the back of American Pie and I got Adam to hold the back door so I could rush back inside and leave her crazy ass outside, planning then to give the bouncer

20 bucks to not let her back in. Sage, not to be outdone, kicked in the backdoor of American Pie and came at me with claws! She was held back, but found a beer bottle and threw it at me, missing me but hitting some other poor drunken slob in the back of the head. We were all kicked out, and Sage broke up with me.

Then Catherine called and told me I was only the second person she'd ever slept with and I'd given her chlamydia. Whoops! She was a beautiful, albeit naïve, young girl, but once I'd given her an STD, it's amazing how quickly her adoration for me fizzled into the atmosphere. She had been a ballerina and was very flexible, and I'd spent quite a bit of time bragging about that to my friends. She spent no time at all in changing her phone number. I went to the doctor and took some antibiotics, and wasn't in the least bit bothered by contracting and then giving chlamydia to another woman. I'm pretty sure I blamed Doublewide, who I suspected was screwing Sage for free drugs.

Maria and I were still seeing each other from time to time, lucky her, though mostly when I was broke and wanted her to buy my drinks. That all came to an end when Gwen walked in on us a block or two from our house in the Highlands, got some money from me while Maria waited for her to leave, and then threw her drink into my eye. Yes sir, I was a charmer. Fortunately for Maria, we'd always been safe in bed, so I didn't bother telling her about the chlamydia.

Gwen and Fireworks

So eventually I was left with just Gwen, which was some seriously shaky ground, as she just wouldn't commit to me. In my codependent alcoholic mind, I knew that I had thrown it all away back in 2001, but really it was 9/11's fault, and what I needed was a good woman to motivate me, as my former wife Anne Marie had done. Once I found this soul-mate, I would recover all my financial losses, pay off my debts, and be an upstanding citizen again. So I kept on searching for that perfect girl. And this time, I wouldn't give her chlamydia. Gwen kept washing out, proving not to be the best hope for that, but there were still some magical moments that I held on to, in between the chaos.

One moment in particular was when she got back from California where she was visiting her cousin. We were on the roof, smoking some weed and watching the skyline. When we kissed, and right at the moment we kissed, fireworks began to go off. "Fireworks,"

166

she said softly, "I missed you." Just a simple moment like that could keep me going for months, if not years, with this woman. I would cling to it in the times she was accusing me of anything from rape to infidelity in the relationship she wouldn't agree to. It was crazy, but I just couldn't stop loving her. In that spring of 2003, so many other moments of chaos came to pass.

One day, and I'm anything but proud of this, she asked me to go to Cheesecake Factory, and bring her one slice of everything. Of everything. Which I did, like a bitch, bring them to her apartment that she barely ever left. I got there, and she looked over all the slices and started screaming at me at the top of her lungs about not bringing ice cream. I bolted, as I often did whenever she would get violently angry and I went to, where else, the closest bar, off Ponce De Leon, The Local. I drank about five whiskeys and began my walk home, which, between Ponce and Little Five, happens to go through one of the last bastions of the mini ghetto Atlanta still has near Boulevard.

I remember looking down at the writing etched into a sidewalk and seeing the inscription 666 Devil Magic, when a hoopty Cadillac pulled up to the side of where I was walking. The black woman driver gave me the eye and grinned from ear to ear. I was drunk, angry, and full of the devil. I said, "Hey darlin', why don't you give me a ride home." She asked for twenty bucks and I said, "Sure." Next thing you know, this woman was giving me head on my bed inside my loft. I never heard or saw Gwen come up those steps or open that door, but I heard someone run down the steps, cry, and slam the door madly! I didn't climax, and the whole scene made me disgusted at the reality check of someone else witnessing this awful scene of sin, and I asked the woman to leave, which she did. But then I sat there, certain that Gwen had walked in on me getting blown by some ugly ass skank, wondering how the hell had I gotten here so fast? Anger and drunkenness were never a good combo for me.

Another bender Gwen and I suffered through began on a Friday night by visiting every club we knew about. On Saturday, we bought a bottle of vodka and went out to paint the town red. Come Sunday, rather than being hung over, we asked Corey Black, our favorite enabler with a credit card, to come down to Atlanta and we'd all go up to Front Page News, a New Orleans style Cajun brunch spot. We drank up there all day long, starting off with Bloody Marys and, of course, hitting the whiskey later on in the afternoon. Around five or six, we went back to Gwen's apartment and, completely wasted, we fucked in the kitchen while Corey sat in the living room with absolutely nothing preventing his view from the whole drunken, sloppy, albeit brief, mess. We passed out in the kitchen afterwards, and when we woke up around 1 or 2 in the morning, both Gwen and I were feeling like shit. She kicked me out in a rage. It was always my fault. I went home and, looking back, I think this may have been the first time I really began to detox, as I felt like I was tripping on acid all of a sudden back in that apartment all by myself. I wrote in my journal, mean damning things about Gwen, almost two pages worth, and then a few minutes later, she called. "JB, I'm scared, will you come back over?"

"Of course, baby girl, I'll be there in a second." I then wrote an equal number of pages in my journal about how much I loved her, and how I'd straighten up and get us put back together again. I went back to her little studio, and we stayed awake feeling like spiders were crawling all over us for the first time in both our adult lives. We both called in sick that Monday, I'm sure for the 99th time, and finally got to sleep around 8 AM that morning. I remember simply blaming it on the Front Page News waiter for putting shrooms in my drink. That seemed plausible. In my mind, we'd definitely been dosed, and by that afternoon I'd even called Front Page News and complained about it, but ultimately, in retrospect -- and now having been through a full alcohol detox -- I think what we experienced was our first detox from alcohol after a long two-day bender. She blamed me, though, and we didn't talk for a while after that.

Losing Another Job

The beginning of the end began at PMC Financial around this time. I'd already been accused of smoking crack, and the black knuckles were damning and all, but I think my sales numbers were still OK when that happened. But as will happen, my productivity began to slide with the prolonged drug and alcohol abuse, and things just weren't getting any better on any front at all. My mom's cancer was worse and worse, and inevitably I always received the bad news the day after a long-ass drug bender. I began to suspect it was God's way of punishing me. More than likely, though, that was just when my family was able to get a hold of me. Addicts get that selfish, that my mom's cancer was about me, but those are the thoughts that were going through my head. I still couldn't visit her for very long at a time and I was growing more and more ashamed by the weekend. I think I knew I'd blown the chance for any inheritance by now, but still, it was painful beyond words to visit, and I could only bring myself to do it once or twice a week, briefly, and inevitably followed by an outrageous, justified alcohol and drug spree. I think my mom dying also helped to keep my job secure at PMC Financial, as the leadership there were such gracious and charitable Christians, but even they would have their limits, as I would soon find out.

Everett Monahan, the President at PMC Financial had been on a waiting list to visit the Pope for some time. Before he went and prior to Mother's Day, I'd given Everett, after he kindly asked me for something, a Methodist Crucifix, to be blessed by the Pope in hopes that it would help my dying mother. She had literally been given six months to live at this time. Her cancer had spread to her lungs, they'd removed chunks of both lungs, leaving her looking weaker than I'd ever seen her. She was still alive, but according to the doctors, had about six more months left. I remember hearing that news, and throwing a beer bottle up against the loft's brick walls, spraying glass all over the upstairs and shrapnel raining down into the living room. I remember Henry saying, "Fucking great." My roommates, too, were running out of patience with my antics.

So Everett had gone to Rome, Italy and gotten a Methodist crucifix blessed, with the flame decoration and all. A minor miracle in itself as he was none too thrilled that it was Methodist, but he said that he would try. By this time, PMC Financial had moved my desk into one of the tiny interview rooms, about the size of a broom closet, but I wasn't taking the hint. In fact, I'd taken the opportunity for privacy to spread a big ol' sub sandwich across my desk which Everett discovered when he came back from Rome and delivered the cross to me. I knew that Everett had been gone that entire week before, and I'd taken it upon myself to do a bunch of morphine, OxyContin, and even a little speed, which I'd sworn off again when Sage and I broke up officially while he was out of town. I think I'd been in the office two days out of the five while he was in Rome. He gave me the crucifix kindly, took one glance at the uneaten sub on my desk, in the makeshift office of this interview room, and he left my closet-like workspace in disgust. I left the office boldly, with a childlike faith for someone on such thin ice at work, and I delivered that crucifix to my mother, telling her it had been blessed by the Pope in Rome, and gave it to her as a Mother's Day gift.

I got back to the office that afternoon, and Everett, Mike, and Chad were appalled with my behavior. Where had I been all last week, why was I perspiring out of every orifice, and did they look stupid? They did not, and I was sweating out all kinds of opiates, amphetamines, and the like, and my Brooks Brothers suit wasn't covering up the junkie one bit. I begged, pleaded, and bargained for one more chance. I think I even cried. I blamed Sage, and said that she was gone for good. I promised to go to their sacred AA meetings, get a sponsor, whatever they wanted me to do, and I played them like a violin, manipulating their 12 step obligations to my ultimate advantage, as I knew their sobriety and overall graciousness made them have pity on me. I probably meant every word I said at the moment, but forgot it the second the flame came off my ass. I was on a tight wire, yes, but I'd saved my job for the moment.

About the same time, I met a girl named Colleen on Myspace, probably while at work. This was an interesting set of circumstances, filled with synchronicities, warnings, and even one prophetic warning from my still-dying mother. I was still only visiting her once or twice a week, because you know, my life was so busy. I still had Gwen on the side, but she had moved from Atlanta to Alpharetta, so some of the chaos had died down a bit. Sage, Maria, and Catherine had all been effectively removed, so I began afresh with this new woman. Her dad had drunk himself to death. Not the all-or-nothing .357 headshot my dad had done, but he drank himself to death "Leaving Las Vegas" style in their suburban middle-class home in Roswell. Still, though not as dramatic, the effect was just the same. Plus, this girl Colleen was a redhead, to boot. So we hooked up on a date after a few hours of Myspace drivel and chat, and it immediately proved that we were compatible. We both drank like fish. I'd sworn off the hard stuff, and what do you know, so had she, so we drank and drank and drank.

We ended up going back to her house that night, and despite this being only a few weeks after my stern talking to from the CEO, VP, and direct Manager at PMC Financial, I decided to take a weekday off, in order to once again nurse a hangover. The reality is I had once again, drunk more than I'd planned, and needed a Tuesday to recover. When I woke up in her duplex, I looked out the window and saw that it was off Armand Street near Lindbergh. I remembered, vaguely, that when we'd come home to her place the night before, I noticed she lived in one my Nana's (step-grandmother) rental units. Jesus Christ, my car was out front, and I was definitely going to hear it from my Nana! In fact, right about that time I checked my phone and saw that my mom and stepdad had called several times. This wasn't good. By coincidence I'd had a one night stand that ended up at this duplex, next door to my almost 70 year old Nana's house, who was going to be none too happy that two unmarried sinners were fornicating in her own rental property!

Colleen had actually managed to suck it up and go to work,

but I was a puss and had stayed at her place. About the time I realized the drama I was in, I heard the front door open and sweet little old Nana say "Bryan." Ah hell, I didn't know what to do, but I was butt ass naked in her tenant's bed. I busted into the closet, closed the door, and prayed my Nana didn't come in to inspecting the bedroom. She took the house as empty and left me alone, naked, 25 years old, and hidden in a woman's closet, in, by sheer coincidence and God's unlimited sense of humor, my grandmother's rental unit. I got dressed, hauled ass to my car, and went home, dodging my Nana completely, but glad to be far from the scene of the crime! Never mind that I'd missed work yet again, never mind that I was having unprotected sex with one night stands, I'd escaped my sweet Nana. I cursed my luck and God, the cosmic galactic jokester, who was probably soaking it up right about now.

I never softened the blows for my mom, but always told her the brutal, honest truth. When I was joking with her about this strange set of circumstances, out on her front lawn, she said, "You'd better be careful, you're liable to get hepatitis C. Jesus, Bryan, when are you going to grow up?" I laughed her off, but something about that statement stuck with me, and it would eventually turn out to be prophetic. How she knew I never found out, but she'd called it years before it would become my reality. She would be gone from Earth two years before I'd even be diagnosed.

For whatever reason, probably begging and pleading again, I wasn't fired from PMC Financial that time either. Two weeks later, though, Colleen and I went to a club and didn't get home until 4 AM or so. I rolled into work around 11 AM, certainly smelling like a drunk, as always, and I was fired. It should have happened months earlier, but they had been more than gracious, and had given me every opportunity to change. I just wasn't ready yet, I guess. I cried like a baby when I knew it was final, but it didn't help. I walked out of PMC Financial ashamed, sad, and pathetic. I think I went and got drunk.

Gwen called not too long after I was fired, and literally begged me to drive to Alpharetta to bring her cigarettes and a bowl of weed. I drove all the way up there, and when I knocked on the door she said she'd call the police. "Go away, you psychopath!" she screamed at me. I drove all the way home and vowed -- again -- to never talk to her again.

All the while fatherhood beckons...

Mind you, during all this time, I'm still justifying my terrible sporadic parenting by lying to myself and claiming that no matter what I was still doing better than my father had done. No matter what, I wouldn't kill myself, beat my son, or ever ignore him totally. The things my Dad didn't do for me, I would do for my boy, and I did love him very much, albeit when it was convenient and didn't require too much sacrifice from my drinking and drugging. I was consistent on a few things though. I always paid my child support, even if I'd get a month or two behind occasionally and I'd always make his baseball games. Also, when I was with him, I paid attention to him, which was more than I felt my Dad ever did. I played board games with him, took him to kids movies he wanted to see, and though again, I was anything but consistent, I tried my best and always fell back on the "better than my dad loophole". Still, I could have been much more positive, and I'll never get those years back. My mom noticed my behavior and wrote me about it. My arrogant response says so much about my state of mind at the time, it would be impossible to give an honest appraisal of myself to the world without including it.

Personal Emails between Mom and I (circa 2003):

Dear JB,

I am very disappointed in your responsibility to Jake. You are after all his father. You know in your heart what a little boy needs. There is only a little more time left when he will love you the most. Then the world becomes more important. If you haven't given him the courage and GOD knowledge he will not be able to stand strong against evil. I try hard not to comment on any choices that you have made for you are an adult, and I taught you all I could. However I worry, I worry about Jake, I worry about the relationships you find yourself in. I worry that you haven't picked the right friends. That the people you've picked aren't Christians that they are game players and that you don't have the skills to understand that. Mothers always worry it is the nature of the job. Yet I can't anymore. I have to watch my health, worry and stress are not good for me. I owe it to my family to let you go. Yet I feel like you are in the dark. Everything is always someone else's fault. Never mind that you frequently were not at your office when you should have been. I have failed. I failed to teach you honesty, integrity and the simple joy of a job well done. I

172

failed to teach you that when you are committed to a job you follow that commitment through even if you don't like what is happening in your job and plan to quit. If you have a job then you have the integrity to follow through with your responsibilities, not lower yourself to the positions of those you scorn. I failed to teach you commitment to family. To your child, to your parents, to your brother and sisters to your grand parents. I am sorry that I failed to teach you that commitment. My family is the most important part of my life. I am sorry it's not for you. I failed to teach you to love and respect your body, to eat healthy foods, get proper and regular exercise and to get the right amount of sleep. I worry that soon your health will begin to deteriorate. I worry I have failed to teach you how to be successful at love and in relationships. Destructive relationships will ruin your chance for happiness and success. Seek out friends who are positive and successful people who bring you to a higher level. I want for you what Dan and I have.... unconditional, caring, TRUSTING, supportive Love. It's not always easy. Sometimes we disagree, sometimes we fight, but underneath it all there is love and respect that will endure all. I am sorry I have failed to teach you that you deserve a relationship like that. I failed to teach you to love and worship GOD. Not just when you are hurting but when you are happy for everything is GODS. I failed to teach you that you get what you want from life through hard work and organizing your life, with GOD as the main focus. I love you very much, I am sorry I failed you in so many ways. Forgive me! Try to overcome my failures. But it pains me to see your suffering, because of my failures. I can do no more I pray for you daily. You are not a mistake GOD made you for a reason. Don't let yourself and Jake down. Don't fail; Jake. It's a pain that you can't live with trust me.

Love always.
Mom

My Immediate Reply Email:

Dear Mom,

I love you but you worry too much. Jake is constantly surrounded by love, and he knows his father loves him very much as does God. You didn't fail me, you never have,

I just think at a different level mom, and I wouldn't expect you to understand it or accept it, just that it is...different. Not necessarily good or evil, smart or stupid, just different. Because money isn't everything to me, does not make me a failure, quite the contrary, I think the stress you bring upon yourself, scrapping and selling crap that people don't want or need is the root of a social system that the world is proving is broken and needs fixing. I'm not thinking about things in the small individual manner that you worry about, but the much larger picture of humanities march towards self destruction, and the possible options that could keep her going for a while longer. So, yes, I failed at PMC Financial, but I honestly don't care, other than for the financial hole it has put me in, I feel great. I didn't like the job in the first place, and I will get another or start my own firm up again, depending upon several factors. To say I failed my family however, whom you speak of unconditional love about, would be an ironic twist, as how could I fail them if I still love them all, and have unconditional love for all of them. It would seem the conditions are only on one side of the fence mom, as I love my son, parents, sisters and brothers, and grandparents without judgment, unconditionally, period, the end. Because I'm not a good social butterfly with them, or feel things too intensely sometimes to be around them sometimes, does not make me a worse person, though I'm certain it does make it easier to talk about me, and assume whatever latest rumor you may have heard, and come up with new things to worry about.

Honestly, I know where I am in life, in this world, and in this universe. I love God and my family, and even my enemies, or those I think live their lives differently from me. I do need to spend more time with Jake, and that's one of the biggest reasons I'm moving back to Roswell, when I really don't want to. I'm also going to get into some therapy as it has helped Gwen Evere a lot and Corey Black seems to be doing better as well. I don't have any money though, so I'm going to bill it directly to you, and I'm sure you won't mind as you've asked me to do this several times, and you're right, I definitely have issues I need to work out, and maybe some good legal drugs, instead of all this self medication. It's working for Corey and Gwen, so it can't hurt to try.

Please don't think you failed me mom as I don't

believe I'm a failure. I have to explore philosophically and socially, as I question everything. Someone once said, "I believe the sole purpose in openings one mind is like that of the mouth, to open it only to close it again on something of sustenance". Everything I have been through or will go through will only make me stronger, and regardless of how you want to define failure or success, I have my own definitions as well, and so long as I'm here on planet earth, I have not failed my son, nor will I.

I love you more than you know, and thank God everyday for the miracle I believe he granted you, arresting your cancer. Please stop worrying, everything is fine. Peace, love and blessings....

Respectfully,

JB Smith

Wow, as I've heard it said, "You can always tell a drunk, but you can't tell them much." What arrogance, pure, clean, uncut pompousness. I state my thinking is at such a higher level, I can't be bothered with my mother's petty worries. What a jack ass.

Not long after this brilliant email exchange with my worrying mother, she would show me, rather than tell me, since I was obviously incapable of listening, the meaning of family and commitment. While battling cancer, recovering from lung surgery, and on chemotherapy, she would show up to my son's ballgame, shaking, shivering, and still cheering him on. She was a fighter, and she never gave up on me, or life in general, never surrendered, though I couldn't see it at the time, she was one tough ass woman. I wish I'd been sober then, because I didn't recognize it until much, much later.

Spree on Corey's Mom's Credit Card

I was broke, owed two month's rent at the lofts, and my roommates were sick of me getting shit-faced drunk, breaking bottles, mooching their Sunday beer, and, oh yeah, not paying rent. I called on Corey, who'd promised, and I'd not forgotten, that I would never be homeless, that I could always go live in his basement. What a lifesaver. Still, I wouldn't move into Corey's until I'd completely exhausted my leeching ability at the lofts. I partied for a while longer, out of a job and out of money, but somehow always able to get fucked up.

Fourth of July 2003, and we bought a few bottles of Crown Royal and broke out the OxyContin, someone in the "Family" had brought over for free. I barely remember the day, blacking out mostly but I vaguely remembering blasting off my 40 caliber Glock 23 on the back porch of the lofts, and even getting in someone's face with it, who was kindly asking me to stop unloading it into the air. I screamed and yelled at the total stranger, right in his face, waving a loaded gun. Thank God I didn't shoot him, though I could have just as easily, in that mind state and never thought twice, and now be serving life. He eventually walked away, intelligently. A little later, another kid named Jeremy Payton who lived in the lofts brought his whiskey and a four wheeler over, which is always a great combo. I remember snorting a line of Oxy, drinking some Crown, smoking a bowl, and going to jump on his four wheeler. The rest of that day was mostly a blur, though I was told we wrecked it, flipped it, ran over each other, and caused all kinds of drunken rampage wreckage that day.

Later that night I crashed out on Adam's couch, in the little mini living room/cave, underneath his bedroom at the lofts. I woke Adam up about 4 in the morning and told him that some spirit was trying to come through my body to grab the muddy bottle of Crown Royal sitting on the table right in front of where I slept. I was really freaked out by it. I vividly remember the dreams I had that entire night, and it felt like a soul was trying to reach through me in the dream to take a pull off that sludge covered, four wheeler dirtied, nasty bottle. The same recurring dream, all night long. I even woke up to tell Adam about it, then went back to sleep to have the same nightmare.

That morning, one of our neighbors came over to tell us that, late the night before, Jeremy Payton had driven into the back of a tractor trailer on his motorcycle, going over 100 MPH, and had died instantly. I still believe that drunk came back to where his last drink was, trying for one last sip. It was eerie as hell, and I'd told Adam about it, so we were both moved by the event. We even went to the funeral. We protected that bottle from being drunk for about a year, but eventually we killed even that bottle.

Things kept getting worse at the lofts, and emotionally I was a wreck over Gwen as always. But coupled with being broke, out of a job, and even my roommates having turned against me, I was feeling pretty awful. Quitting drinking had still not crossed my

176

mind, though a new thought had. Perhaps I was just far too gone to be saved. It wasn't a good surrender, but it certainly justified the next few months of wanton waste and spree drinking Corey and I did on dear old mom's credit card.

I moved into Corey's mom's basement eventually, and the first weekend she was out of town, we got to partying. We got an eight ball of blow every time she'd go out of town, and more than once, I found myself on my knees begging God for another chance. Like PMC Financial, I felt he was losing patience with these false promises, and even I realized the futility of my mindset, as I wrote in my journal:

Personal Journal, July 14th 2003:

"I'm a piece of dogshit. Not even manshit. Everyone thinks so, my life is ass, I'm evil and I rampage through life fucking over anyone unfortunate enough to come into my path. I'm subconsciously diabolically evil, because though I never intend harm, be damn sure, harm will be the result. I'm like an evil sin lusting demon. If it's bad, all good, I want in."

Personal Journal, July 23rd 2003:

"Forgot my (dying) mom's birthday. Drugs are a big distraction, as is Gwen. God I miss her."

The only good news around this time was that my mom's cancer had gone into complete and utter remission, to the total surprise and astonishment of the doctors and my family in general. I obviously felt responsible, having given her the crucifix that the Pope had blessed, regardless of our being Methodist -- surely it had helped. It was, in fact, a near miracle, though, and I didn't seek any praise for getting her the crucifix. We were just all happy she was better. That was a private sentiment I kept to myself, not really certain if it was miracle or coincidence. I checked on these facts once I sobered up as well, and it did all happen in that order. She received the Pope blessed crucifix, went to the docs a week later, and would remain cancer free for about six months, which was a nice reprieve, regardless of how it came to be. It's almost enough to make me want to go Catholic...almost.

My behavior got worse and worse, though, as alcoholism is a progressive disease. I was late on child support, as always, and barely saw my son. The one weekend in forever that he came over, I told Corey nothing, left Jake in my bedroom, and left to go downtown to the lofts to party. I fully intended on being back by morning. I hooked up with some folks doing ice and stayed out the entire night, not making it back to Corey's until 1 or 2 the next day. Anne Marie had called, Corey had blown my phone up, and somehow I wasn't disgusted with myself. I think I felt beyond help at this point. I knew it was wrong, but I just didn't care anymore, and worse, I didn't know how to stop it. The temporary solution to that was to not get Jake anymore at Corey's house. I still made the fall ball and spring baseball games through all of it, but that is the only fatherly thing I did consistently through my addictions. In my mind I'd always fall back on "Well, I'm better than my dad was."

Colleen broke up with me when I decided to not hang out with her one weekend in order to wait on a call from Gwen that never came. It was OK, I wasn't in love with her anyway, and she had ugly feet I told myself, but once again, I was lonely and waiting on Gwen, at her beck and call. I got a job selling computers again, but it only lasted a couple of weeks until they figured out I was a lazy, irresponsible drunk, and fired me. Things were going great.

I got a job waiting tables, and did you know to make ends meet in that business, you have to work 12 to 13 hour days, and NOT drink up all your earnings at the end of every shift? It's insane. I was fired within a month, but not before meeting two more floozies at the job and dating them, then getting dumped by both for cheating on them, with the other. Smooth. One of the last days I called in sick, which was about the third time in that first month of employment. I'd been drinking tequila all day instead of going to work and decided to go meet Adam at the lofts. I got on 85 south and headed on my happy-go-lucky, drunk-ass way. I remember it was still light out, but I was pretty tanked already, so when I went to take that left at North Druid Hills, I went right into incoming traffic. Being as quick and lightening fast as I am, when I recognized the traffic as oncoming, I hopped the double curbed median, and got back on track, headed the right direction on North Druid Hills, applauding my amazing reaction skills. Never mind I was so wasted I'd turned into 3 lanes of traffic in the first place! Right then, the blue lights went on again. I went right into the shopping center at Briarcliff and North Druid Hills and my self-praise was all but gone, and the foxhole prayers had begun. Somehow, once again, I received a warning. The cop was new, or just plain dumb, as I kept my tequila breath pointed the other direction and thanked her for the warning, claiming that I was tired from working too many hours, or some such nonsense. It probably helped that it was early in the day still. I left the car there, paranoid that it was some kind of elaborate setup, and Adam came to get me. I stayed at the lofts the next day, calling in sick, and that's when I was fired. I was just plain unemployable.

Not only was I unemployable, but I was blind. So what did I do when I came so ever close to getting my third DUI, probably jail time, and definitely the loss of my license? Well, I sold my car. The last little bit of profit from selling my house to the neighbor, I sold for something like 2k. My justification was that Corey had a car, and I'd buy office supplies and start up Fortune Staffing again, and let Corey be my chauffeur. Seemed logical to me. Society wouldn't "let" me drive drunk, well, I'd show them. So I sold the car and set up an office downstairs, quite proud of my entrepreneurial spirit. Really, it was out of necessity and my inability to hold down a real job. I wouldn't start right away, though, we'd drink and party through the holidays, and start fresh in the new year, allowing for plenty of benders and bar hopping. We'd quit with the blow and I'd sworn off ice forever, but we were still drinking like madmen. I remember being proud of myself for quitting the hard stuff -- coke and ice were out. One too many out-of-body experiences, and leaving Jake with Corey had struck me as well. I'd sworn it off, and of course, felt noble in doing so.

I think that's why when my mom showed up outside Corey's house, being escorted by my stepdad, obviously as drunk as, if not drunker than me that particular night, I was so easily able to brush off her offer of help. It was done in such a pitiful way, too, that I just didn't know how to react, but I guess it was her way of trying. They called the house, and asked me to come out to the car, which wasn't even in the driveway, as my mom didn't like Margaret Black, Corey's mom. I got into the car and she said, "So what do we have to do, pay for you to go into rehab or something?" It didn't come out as drunken slurs, as my mom would talk slowly and methodically when drunk, but you could always tell. "No, Mom, I don't want to quit drinking." I remember thinking, "I just gave up blow and ice, drinking is all I have."

"Then what, this is your plan, live with Corey Black for the rest of your life?" she said with all the disdain she could muster. I felt awful, I felt guilty and irritated by her visit, but I shelved it all, and said, "Thanks but no thanks, Mom, I'm not ready." And then I got out of the car and walked into Corey's house, and Corey promptly made me feel better about the whole thing. We were great drinking buddies, always able to write off the major reasons in our lives to quit. He'd had my back for a long time, and this wasn't an exception.

179

I brushed off my mom's visit, and continued our daily and nightly drinking, feeling good about quitting the hard drugs. Almost saintly in fact.

Gwen's Hospital Plan

By this time too, Gwen began calling me during work hours and making me take her to hospitals all over north Atlanta to get shots of morphine, Dilaudid, or whatever she could scam. Her delivery was weak, but it worked quite a few times. She would complain of an oncoming migraine, advise that her doctor had suggested she come to the emergency room for a shot of Dilaudid -- featured in the movie "Drugstore Cowboy," and similar to morphine or heroin. In those first few visits, it worked every time. I didn't mind taking her because I got to spend time with her, take care of her, and ultimately, once she'd gotten the shot, we'd go home and have a good time, usually stopping by the liquor store beforehand. She was very amicable after those shots, so I didn't mind one bit, at first. Eventually, though, the hospitals would catch on, and it quit being quite as much fun. But by then, our addictions had advanced beyond a bi-weekly hospital trip anyway. I said "our" addiction; me to her, her to opiates...at first. Thus began the slow downward progression of opiate addiction for me. Though the first dozen or so hospital trips I was just along for the ride, I would soon start diving into her pills. Once, I even took advantage of the gullibility of hospitals.

Over those holidays as we waited for the perfect time to re-launch Fortune Staffing from Corey's mom's basement, Corey and I were spending a lot of time at Taco Mac by the river, as we always had. One night there, in a brash, daring, and oh-so-charming manner, I walked by a group of ladies and stole one of their chicken wings right off a woman's plate. I have no idea why I stole her chicken wing, I was wasted. I did not see the boyfriends all sitting one table over, and the manning up, showing off, and wanting to kick my ass in Taco Mac started out once again -- but this time, I deserved it. Somehow, we avoided a major altercation, but when Corey and I were leaving the bar, three guys followed us out, and right as I was opening the car door, I was hit from behind with a hard fist to the cheek and then tackled. The struggle that ensued was chaotic, not to be helped, of course, by my drunken state. When I got up off my feet, I punched the closest guy next to me, who just happened to by my only friend in the parking lot, Corey Black. Immediately we were attacked from behind again, and I got wailed on three or four times, rising from the concrete parking lot, and again punching the first blur I could find. Which, again, was Corey Black.

"Hey, asshole it's me, they're leaving! Quit!" Corey yelled at me.

They had hit me a few times, but mostly in the back of the head and on my jaw. By the time I got my senses back together, though, they had gone back into the Taco Mac, and Corey and I were leaving. We laughed about my hitting him, and I remember going back to the house, and calling up the "Family" to go help take care of this situation, and hopefully take out some revenge. I got Layle on the phone who said, "Man, we ain't in the mafia, call the police or something," since they'd hit me from behind. I was shit-faced, so I did it. They said they'd look into it, and did I need medical attention, should they send an ambulance? And then it hit me, what better time to visit a hospital and get that famous Gwen Evere package than right after getting your ass kicked in the parking lot of a bar? So I said "Sure, please call the ambulance." And they did.

The ambulance brought out all the neighbors at 2 AM in the country club community of Brookfield West. I got on the stretcher, and used the Gwen Evere script to a T, getting them to shoot me with morphine in the ambulance, which I said wasn't working. When we got to the hospital, I told the oh-so-trusting doctor the same sob story, and even gave him the dosage and exact medicine Gwen usually requested. It worked like a charm. The Dilaudid was injected into my veins, and I remember telling the nurse, drunk and still belligerent though already numb with morphine, "It isn't working, you didn't give me enough, why are you standing on the ceiling?" And then I blacked out.

I woke up the next day around four in the afternoon strapped to a bed in the hallway of the hospital, not able to move. I guess I'd been a pain in the ass, but I didn't ask anyone. Once I finally got a nurse's attention, I bolted from the hospital, not signing a damn thing. Who knows what kind of antics I caused in that hospital, but once conscious and unstrapped, I wasn't sticking around to find out. I called Corey, and he came and picked me up. We got a twelve-pack, and I told him all I could remember about the adventure. We had a good laugh, and I apologized for punching him. He forgave me, and we chuckled about our fun and harmless chaos, though I still couldn't tell you what I did to get strapped down. I didn't want to know. I was pretty appalled at myself for resorting to Gwen tactics, but I told myself it was a one-time target of opportunity and I wouldn't do it again.

As fate would have it, or with the addict's dumb luck, or Devil's luck, I ran into a guy at Taco Mac a few weeks later whose dad was dying and had extra high-grade morphine pills, that he would sell to me super cheap. For all the hell Gwen put me through, I thought it was worth making a little scratch off her, as an addict can justify just about anything. He was selling them to me for $20 and I was selling them to her for $100. By this time, she was on medical leave of absence from Netdial, and had taken out a 15k student loan that she was spending on dope. I think we were in a fight when I negotiated it, because I'd never had a markup like that before, but she was a dope fiend and the hospitals had run out of patience with her. Neither of us were yet at the booting heroin stage of our addictions, so I raped her on profit margin, and felt justified in doing so, since, besides, it wasn't her money, it was her student loan money. I'd gone broke years before, exhausting all my credit lines, so it was her turn, I told myself. Nice guy.

I'd started up Fortune Staffing again, and was making some phone calls, but it was slow progress, as Corey and I were still getting wasted every night. It's hard to cold-call hung over, and therefore I wasn't doing much of it. But I was spending more time getting high with Gwen Evere, crushing up Oxy's and Morphine and snorting them. I never had as much as her, though, because she'd hoard most of it, but when ever I brought her drugs, we had a functional relationship. Otherwise, it was rare for her to call me.

One of those rare times, she came over unannounced, and Corey let her in upstairs, sensing a massive cluster-fuck of excitement and drama. Lori, a girl I must have met in a black out, because neither of us have any recollection of our meeting, but we continued staying in touch from around 2001 on, had come over sick, and had fallen asleep on the couch in my bedroom. Gwen came in, jumped in bed with me, obviously drunk, and we made love passionately, all the while I kept one eyeball on Lori, praying to God she wouldn't wake up. Gwen and I finished and lay smoking a cigarette, relaxed and comfortable, and right at that moment, Lori snored. Drama queen that she was, first Gwen laughed, but I knew it wouldn't last, and then she got her stuff on, yelled a bit, and stormed out. I defended my position as she was the one that didn't want a relationship, but it was just chaos, all around mayhem, and she would add that additional incident to her arsenal of justification and reasons for hating me moving forward.

A few days later, I brought her some more pills and we would make up. It was Valentine's Day, 2004. We went to a porn shop off Cheshire Bridge in Atlanta, and bought some cheesy toys, a mini vibrator, and some edible underwear. We hit the liquor store and made it back to her apartment in Alpharetta. We broke up a few morphine pills and she snorted about three times what I did, as she wouldn't allow me anymore, and we made love for about ten minutes. Then she went into convulsions for a little while, which didn't freak me out, being as high as I was. When she stopped convulsing, she was still breathing, so I said a little prayer, laid her out in the living room, and spent Valentine's Day night checking every 20 minutes or so to see if air was coming of her mouth, while I flipped through the channels and drank up all the liquor. She didn't move the entire night, and I watched her naked, crimson-laced face with an obsession. I'd conquered her, I remember thinking, after a restraining order, and all the times she'd rejected me, here I was the man of the house, making sure she got her drugs, and was still breathing. In a weird way, I felt like her man, even though she'd never call me that out loud, or God forbid in public. Her dog maybe. And so I watched her sleep for hours on end, naked, sprawled out on the floor of her own apartment, God only knows how close to death. I wasn't worried, I'd check her breath every once in a while, like a gentleman.

And then another bomb fell on my surreal little life. My mom's cancer had come back, and this time it was serious, she and everyone else said. Margaret Black is the one who told me. I'd been watching the movie "Man on the Moon," and I mentioned to my mom how the main character reminded me of her, funny and able to laugh in the face of adversity. But that's not how my mom took it.

"Didn't he die of cancer?" She said accusatorially.

"Yes." I said innocently as I could muster.

"Thanks." Heavy on the sarcasm with a topping of guilt, and boy would the latter leave an aftertaste.

I gave her a hug and went back to Corey's. I felt awful, I knew I was sliding down the slope fast, and I knew I was losing my mother, but I didn't know how to stop either of those things from happening, so I just kept on drinking and drugging. I wasn't doing morphine regularly yet, but it was progressing already, just like every other drug had and I was damn sure drinking every night with Corey, and not much was getting done on the Fortune Staffing front.

Getting Funding

Then an idea formed in my head that may have been under the surface for years, but I felt brilliant when I came up with it. Corey's dad, a millionaire many times over, Stewart Black, had granted us the right to use the name Fortune Staffing back in 2001, and I believed that favor should help us to start the company up again. I thought this was a phenomenal idea, and I hoped he'd go for it, to give his son something to do. I asked Corey to approach him, and at first he said no, which was probably the wisest thing Corey had ever said to me. But I wouldn't listen, and I begged him night after drunken night, until he finally agreed to talk to his dad about investing in our company. I told Corey we could get some kick-ass office space, and we'd meet all kinds of women who would be impressed that we owned our own businesses, and that our offices were in Tower Place, and he finally went along with the plan. Impressing women with our office space never really worked, incidentally, but hell, at the time it seemed like a great idea, and it sure as hell beat working out of Corey's basement.

Stewart Black signed on, and came to meet with us. We agreed to work very hard and diligently, and to have sales meetings with him via teleconference every Friday, and Corey and I set out to find our office space. We got a good deal in Tower Place, in the heart of Buckhead, where I'd set my sights, and we moved in pretty quickly. We even had a good showing of early success, placing Tyrell Andrews at a Fortune 100 client in downtown Atlanta, within our first 30 days of working with Stewart. I think he may have even been proud of us. He would have been even more proud if we hadn't celebrated that 15k deal as if it were a 15 million dollar deal, and immediately began drinking at lunch and partying like rock stars, who'd banked their first million.

And so it began that one day Corey didn't want to go to work, and he let me drive his prized white Ford Cobra, a magnificent vehicle. We drank every single night, but when we worked, I expected him to make phone calls. After the first month or so, he accomplished one thing, and that was getting the business cards. To his credit, the business cards were phenomenal, but in the cutthroat world of recruiting, you've got to be a phone hound, and phone hound, Corey was not. It was going to be a long partnership, and I was immediately disgruntled with both his and my performance. But being the fool that I am, found it much easier to blame his performance, the speck in his eye, if you will, ignoring the plank in my own.

After a few months of not very diligent work, and now

having an investor to lighten the burden, I found a hash connection, and became very laid back about our Fortune Staffing adventure. I made a lot of friends with that connection, though, and one adventure would lead me down a strange but entertaining set of circumstances. Smoking some hash with Stefan Agassi, a friend from Roswell High, who for some reason, ate up all my "Family" talk while I was wasted introduced me to a fellow drunk who wanted to go hang out at Piedmont Park. Then this new buddy wanted to go meet with his friends he'd grown up with, who were playing a show at The Tabernacle. He said the group was death metal, but that it would be fun since we would get to go backstage. We got to the Tabernacle, and I basically thought this guy was full of shit, but we walked up to the front and they gave us backstage passes to Slipknot, who, up until this point, I'd never heard of.

I went right to the bar upstairs, and met the distributor for Jägermeister, and with my backstage passes, was promptly bought several Jäger shots to add to the two-day bender I was already working on. The rest is really a blur. I remember being backstage and I remember someone asking if they could smoke some of my hash, and I made fun of him for wearing a mask, and then he took it off, and I let him smoke some. Then there were a bunch of guys and a few girls smoking my hash, and I just remember thinking I was going to be out of hash tomorrow. As it turned out, these guys were the band, and I was backstage at their show, so I continued to let them smoke it. Eventually, they gave me a full unlimited backstage pass, and I went outside to try to get one of the groupie chicks to come back and see the band. Either I was completely trashed and looked scary, or it just isn't like the movies, because I struck out with every halfway decent girl lined up outside to try to get autographs from the band. It was all very blurry, so more than likely I just looked too wasted to be an official anything or even remotely believable as I said I was "with the band", but I remember being irritated, and eventually I lost all memory of the adventure as the night wore on. I don't have any recollection of how I left, or even got home. Seeing as it's the only backstage passes I'd ever gotten in my life, it would have been nice to remember meeting the band and the rest of the adventure, but drunks can't be too regretful over such trivial consequences as total and complete memory loss.

Cat Food Connoisseur

Two days later, back in the office at Tower Place, trying to pretend I was a good businessman, I get a phone call from a girl who says she met me at Slipknot, and I said, "Who?"

"Backstage, at the show." She said, in a soft, cryptic voice.

"Oh yeah, sure, how are you doing?" not having a clue who she was.

"I'm good, I wanted to see if I could come over and bring you some beer tonight?"

Well hot damn! This woman knew me well.

"Sure, come on over." I said.

And thus, a relationship began.

Cindy came over that night, and she wasn't petite but she wasn't huge. She had an ass that made you think she was huge, but a skinny cute face, with dark hair, dark eyes, and a pretty little southern accent. She was a strange bird, though. For one thing, she initiated the relationship just like that. The first night she came over, we slept together, and she didn't say much, but when she spoke, rest assured it would be something weird.

She was there in Corey's basement about five minutes before she said, "Do you want to have sex?"

Well hell yes, this woman could read my mind. She was the perfect alcoholic's girlfriend, but she didn't come without her eccentricities.

"I like blood," she told me that first night.

"OK." Well, thanks for the beer and sex, I thought, "Are you going to bring some beer over tomorrow night?"

"Maybe Thursday or something." She'd say in a deep southern accent. She was a trip, very simple, but that's probably about all I could handle at that point anyway. Gwen had disappeared, but I wasn't worrying about it too much. I'd later find out she had met my morphine connection and was pissed at me for charging her so much. We'd been off and on for a couple of years now, and I was getting used to the pain. Having Cindy, the hash, and Corey's nightly vodka would somehow get me by.

Cindy and I barely talked about anything but beer and sex. I knew I'd settled, but it was easy and Gwen was gone, and hell, I

186

thought, I had no standards at all. That is until one day she would lower the bar when I'd thought we were already at sea level. One day she brought over some beer and we headed off to my cave in Corey's dank basement, passing the table that held the cat food for Corey's mom's two huge cats. The food was always scattered across the table and was usually a couple of days old at least. Cindy looked at the table and then scooped up a huge handful of cat food and put it into her mouth, chewing and smiling as if she'd just walked into a Thanksgiving dinner. Even my drunk-ass standards didn't go that low.

"You eat cat food?" I was disgusted. I kissed that mouth.

"Yeah, it's good." She looked at me, like I was the oddball for asking.

"Get the fuck out of here, weirdo!" I'd finally hit my quota for strange.

She had no remorse and thankfully left me the beer. I called my other friend who I believed had standards that low, and, sure enough, Jason began sleeping with her within the week. Alcoholic relationships were easy come, easy go, and the cat food connoisseur was just too much for even me. Besides, I missed Gwen, as always.

Gwen didn't stay mad for long, though, but eventually her work made her go back to Netdial, so her hardcore opiate benders slowly came to an end for a while, with the assistance of much Xanax, and massive amounts of muscle relaxers. I was there to drive her around for that and keep her company at her house, treated much the same as her little rat terrier, except for I wasn't allowed on the couch like he was, I had to sit on the floor. I didn't care, I loved her, I thought.

Besides, she was so convincing regarding her back pain, I didn't know whether to believe her or not. I went between skepticism and empathy constantly with her, never knowing if she really was treating a real back and neck pain problem, or if she was just completely addicted to drugs and the pain was psychosomatic. To this day I don't know how much of her pain was real or imagined.

I visited my mom at Saint Joseph's weekly, and we continued to try our best at Fortune Staffing. After having a heart-to-heart with Stewart Black about our productivity, or lack thereof, Corey and I swore: no more lunchtime drinking. That left us the weekend, though, and I would disappear for the two days of the weekend, to hang out with Stefan Agassi and that crew, or most often with Adam Archer, Henry, and the Samson Lofts "family." I was still doing my best to stay clear of the hard drugs, after our stern talking-to with Stewart Black , and the threat of his leaving our little Fortune Staffing project, which was the only damn thing keeping it alive. So from nine to five, we were recruiters, but outside of that, we were usually raging drunk. Corey, mostly at his house and at the Taco Mac by the river, and me anywhere, all over Atlanta, wandering aimlessly, looking for that next good time. In my mind, we were just enjoying life, or at least, that was the justification I kept giving myself.

Broken Ankle

A month or so went by without Gwen and me speaking. The night I broke my ankle, I was thinking that if I got hurt, I'd get all kinds of meds, and then Gwen and I would get back together. Adam Archer and I had gone to a little art gallery party, and I'd only had about four or five beers, and Adam had even made a comment about my drinking less.

We got back to the Samson lofts, and Phoenix and his crew, all professional skateboarders, were trying to ollie -- to jump off the back dock at Samson lofts, about a three or four foot drop. It would have been tough for me to pull off when I was 16, at the pinnacle of my skating career, and I use the term pinnacle as lightly as humanly possible. But for whatever reasons, whether it was subconsciously an attempt to get drugs and reconcile with Gwen, or whether I was just trying to be the big shot as drunks so often have to do, I began trying to jump off the back dock on a skateboard at about three or four in the morning, with just a light beer buzz.

The first attempt was close but no cigar, so I thought I'd give it all I had, and stick the landing this time. I rolled from the front door of our lofts out to the ledge on this skateboard at 26 years old, and did my absolute best to land that ollie. I came down hard, and I instantly knew I was fucked. You could hear the bone crush inside the skin. My right foot was at a 90 degree angle to my leg, and it wasn't moving an inch. I immediately went into shock looking at it.

"Get me a cigarette and a beer!" Three skaters, Adam, and Henry laughed when I said that, but it wasn't meant to be a joke. I wasn't crying yet, due to shock, but I would be before the night was over.

They got me the requested items, as I stared at my foot, bones

188

and blood coming out the right side of my ankle, the pain starting to build up. Phoenix took command of the situation and a few of his friends grabbed me and threw me in the back of Adam's car. Not before they took a picture of the grotesque injury, that supposedly made it to the front page of the Thrasher magazine website. I never saw that picture, though, and it could be hearsay, but it would have been worthy.

We got to Grady Memorial Hospital, and Phoenix screamed and yelled to get a doctor, which put us in front of about 50 people in that waiting room. I thought for sure that, at Grady, we would be in the waiting room for hours, but Phoenix made it happen, and within five minutes, I was in a hospital bed, and they were giving me some bad news.

"We're going to have to reset it." The doctors were telling me.

"No, give me some morphine first!" I screamed through the tears, pain searing up my leg.

"We can't..." I didn't get to hear the explanation, because by this time, I was screaming at the top of my lungs, tears pouring down my face, as the pain was excruciating, and they were grabbing my foot, positioning their hands to reset the break.

I heard the noise, the bone grinding friction, and felt pain so intense that it blacked me out. Thank God for that, it was a hellacious few minutes once that shock wore off. I woke up in a hospital bed, in pain, but nothing like the night before. Apparently, I had meds in me. They told me to go home, keep taking meds, let the swelling go down, and come back in a few weeks, so they could operate. They gave me all kinds of prescriptions for pain. I went home and set up shop in Adam's basement, being fed and taking pain pills every few hours. Adam told me I could spend the next few months there in his basement, and damn it, I wish I had. But something cleverly retarded, deep inside my soul, knew better than to do the right thing. I called Gwen, and told her I'd broken my ankle, shattering it, requiring all kinds of surgery, and I had some meds. Wouldn't you know it? That woman was down there within an hour and half, all the way from Alpharetta. She hadn't talked to me or returned my calls in a month or so, but now, she suddenly had a renewed interest. She even offered for me to live with her while I waited for the surgery, since, Corey's house had a long flight of steps, and I'd be on crutches for months to come. Oh, and by the way, could she have a few Percocets? Her back hurt as always. I was too blind to see it, though, and was just glad she'd met me at Johnny's Pizza for a few beers, and we got drunk and were seemingly happy. I'd move in with her that day, and she immediately begin raiding my pills, claiming it was for her ever-constant neck pain.

That neck injury is a sore subject with me, because every doctor she's seen has given her a different reason for her pain. I'd shot Lidocaine directly into her back for months with a hypodermic needle, and we'd been chasing pain meds around for years, and for the first time, I began to doubt its validity. Pain in another person is a hard thing to judge. Especially in an addict, so adept at manipulation and acting. I still don't really know if she believed her pain to be real, or if all along it's been her sly rationale. She's that good, really it's not her fault, we are all professional liars and actors through years of practice.

And so we'd have our arguments about the pain meds, but ultimately I'd lose. It was easier for me to become skilled at manipulating and scoring multiple doctors, than it was for me to argue with her, because our arguments began getting more and more intense. They would often lead to violence at this stage, and with my not able to stand on my own two feet, quite literally, it was better to argue with docs than with her. And so I became an expert. I'd be willing to bet, for every scrip written, I'd have three or four more times the amount advised by the doctors, using various ploys and scams. But I had to, she'd eat all my meds whenever I wasn't looking, and by then, my own habit was becoming a monster in itself. Though I had real pain, I was certainly still an addict. I called Grady hospital all the time, and I set up other docs, and although we had three or four different sources of pain meds between both of us, it seemed we were always running out of meds. But at least we were still in love, I'd lie to myself.

And so I was living with her, and we were both hopelessly addicted to pain meds, anything with opiates really, and our tolerances were well above the Percosets, and the hydrocodones that the docs kept wanting to give us. So, of course, we had to do more. Eventually the surgery rolled around, and though my whole family knew about it, they were all just disgusted with me. My mom laughed that even the cat had health insurance, and she was appalled that Grady would be doing the surgery. Quite honestly, I resented the fact that they didn't offer to help me, but I was too disgusted with myself to ever mention it. I didn't have a leg to stand on, and I knew it. I deserved the free care at Grady, hell, I was lucky

Atlanta had a free health care system period. I'm still grateful.

For Mother's Day 2004, Gwen drove me to my mom's house, after we'd taken some pills and drunk a few tequilas at T.G.I. Fridays. I can't recall the context of the arguments or the conversations leading up to it, but I remember Gwen slapping me as hard as she could right before I went in to tell my dying mother, Happy Mother's Day. I hugged my mom and kissed her, but didn't stay long, as Gwen was in the car waiting. We drove back to her house, and I did my absolute best to ignore her, letting her take her place on her coveted red Ikea couch with the spoiled rat terrier, and I went to see who was on Instant Messenger.

"Thewildasses" is the screen name of a timid dressmaker I'd met a while back, and the name had remained on my friends list. When she popped up to chat, with the sound still on and the beepity beep signature of jealousy, Gwen took one peek at the name, grabbed a wine bottle, and did her absolute best to break the bottle over my head. Being drunk and weak, she was only able to make it bounce, but still, that shit hurt. Moreover, it was scary being hit over the head from behind like that. Thus ensued our first real extended physical dramatic episode, to be followed by many more afterwards.

I couldn't get her away from me at first, having my foot still wrapped, and still waiting for the swelling to go down. The crutches from the surgery were on the other side of the room, so a comical stand-off erupted. I kept pushing her away as best I could, but she was on foot with me on my ass, and I was at a distinct disadvantage. Then I had the keen idea to sweep her feet out from under her, and holy shit, did it work. It worked so well, due to her natural state of drunken imbalance, that she hit her ass hard and it made the entire apartment building shake. I broke into laughter, pissing her off even more. She got up, looked at me in shock, and rushed me again, at which time I stuck with the strategy that was working, and swept her ankles up once again! I saw the cripple karate move work twice as well, her big clumsy ass hitting the floor like an atom bomb, and again I laughed my ass off. A third time, to the same results, and then she threw the phone at me from across the room, then went into her bedroom with her cell phone to call the police. Super.

"Shit!" I said to myself, and I moved as fast as a one-legged drunk man on crutches could move. Through the woods to avoid the potential police, four miles on crutches, on a side street to the closest bar, where I would hook up with any number of random strangers, with a fictitious sob story about returning from Iraq and wanting to get wasted which always got me a few drinks with such an obvious injury and the crutches. Even then I was ashamed of that, but no amount of shame could slow my psyche from getting the next drink. That set of events happened no less than ten times while living at those apartments. I was so afraid of the police coming and throwing me in jail, I just hauled ass at the very mention. I usually had drugs on me, but I always traveled light, and I was so used to vanishing that sometimes I'd start a fight just to get out of the house and go on a justified adventure. I had pills to trade, and Gwen would always let me back in when she sobered up, precisely because I had the pills, so the entire time I lived there with her in that Alpharetta apartment, a week didn't go by that a major knock-down, drag-out fight would take place and I'd run like hell. I never hit Gwen, though. She hit me a few times, but for whatever reason, maybe because I was on the floor, I never lost it enough to hit her like I had before with other women. Maybe I was afraid she would kill me in my sleep.

Ankle Surgery

The day I was supposed to have the surgery done at Grady, I was expecting to be picked up by my stepdad, who didn't show, and who I had to call that morning. He sent his secretary to give me a ride to Grady Hospital. My feelings were hurt, but what could I say, it was better than being entirely written off. At least someone was coming. My sister told me she'd be at the hospital and wait for me to come to, so I was OK. My dad's secretary didn't talk much, and I'm sure my foot was ripe as hell smelling and swollen in the temporary cast, that I'd marched all over kingdom come with, in the relationship debacles Gwen and I were battling. I rested the swollen, sweaty, nasty, useless limb on her dashboard, and she looked none too happy about the assignment her boss, my stepdad, had given her that morning. She almost drove me to the hospital without getting us into a car accident, but not quite. Right when we were merging onto 75/85 from 400, she rear-ended the truck in front of us, sending my very tender foot directly into the windshield. Not cracking it, but just hard enough to make it feel as though lightening had shot from my foot to my brain. She was sorry she said. So was I, as my entire leg throbbed the rest of the way to the hospital. I was happy to get there and happier to be knocked out for the surgery.

I wouldn't have been if I'd have known the kind of pain I would be in when I awoke. I mean to tell you from the injury itself, to the resetting, to the mangled thing going into the windshield, all together and multiplied by ten wouldn't describe the agony I woke up to with all that newly installed metal in my foot. Tears streaming down my face, I asked for my sister, but the nurses told me that she wasn't there, and so I cried. I cried for the pain, and I cried feeling sorry for myself. I cried that I'd so alienated myself from my family that I was there in Grady Hospital , surrounded by strangers, and the docs wouldn't give me enough pain medication, and I wailed like a newborn child, because it hurt so freaking bad. I'd had four screws and a metal plate put into my ankle, and I could feel the metal in the bones. I begged, screamed, and pleaded for more drugs, and they kept shooting me up with morphine, and it just kept hurting. I told them I had a high threshold for pain meds, I lied and said it was a medical condition, and I needed Dilaudid. They didn't give Dilaudid to non-insured patients, but they could give me a prescription for that, and morphine and some OxyContins, and whatever other pills I wanted. I begged the docs for as many scrips as I could get, and eventually the morphine they'd shot in me, at least five times, began to take effect.

I called my sister, who didn't answer the phone. I called Gwen, and she left work to come get me, knowing damn well I'd have scrips to go get us some more meds. She squeezed every bit of guilt she could from that incident, though, as she was fired a week or two later, and it was, of course, all my fault, and the fact that she had to come pick me up from Grady. Never mind that I'd taken her to the hospital at least two dozen times in the middle of the day, not a few months before. She did come, though, and I eventually got out of there, and we went and filled the scrips. I laid on her floor at the foot of her couch for two days in pain, unable to move, trying desperately to get at the stitches deep within my cast that itched like hell, as they mutually healed and begged my opiate buzz to scratch them.

Within a couple of days, Gwen had stolen, and I had consumed, all the pain medication again, and Grady was reluctant to give me any more. I ended up getting some more later that day, but for a few hours, just a few days after the surgery, I'd been out, and it had hurt badly. I would recall that helpless feeling later on, but not because of my own pain.

Mom, the Dealer

Not too long after the surgery, I was visiting at my mom's, and I was telling her my woes about running out of pain medications. Before I could even get to where I was headed with the story, she offered to give me some of her morphine. 80 milligrams, the good shit, no time release, that only the dying of cancer can get, and it was on from there on out. I instantly felt like shit while she was giving them to me, though she offered, this was something I'd sworn I would never do, and I was doing it. Gwen had been asking me to do this on and off for almost a year, and I had resisted. But the surgery pain was real, the addiction even more acute, and the likelihood of us mysteriously running out again was a constant. I needed to take while the taking was good.

And as I left her room with the machines, and her feeble little bald head, and the dozens of pill bottles at her bedside, for the first time, I wasn't feeling sorry for myself. In fact, for the first time I was excited to see my mom again soon, to get some more drugs. I immediately began thinking "she's doing this so she can see me more often. She knows if she gives me these drugs, I'll be back for more." And instantly I began visiting every two days, instead of every week, and I knew it, and I knew why, and I hated myself for it instantly. She was a smart lady, though, and she'd see her son more in her last few months, than in the whole time she'd been sick. Or maybe she was just being kind. Maybe she was just so out of her mind on morphine that she didn't even remember it. I don't know, but I know it was something I swore I'd never do, and there I was doing it. But it would get worse.

That summer and Fortune Staffing are a blur for a while after that surgery. Stewart Black said, "Well at least you didn't break your mouth, you can still sell." I agreed with him for the most part, though my mind was steadily going. I lived at Gwen's mostly with the drama and the fights and the pills, and that miserable little yappy dog, and somehow I kept going to work, and kept making the phone calls.

At some point over the course of that summer, I was back at Corey's house, probably because of the fights Gwen and I were having. He'd been meeting girls on Match.com and a few had been over, and this one in particular had eyeballed me the whole time she was there getting drunk with Corey and me. The next time she came over, I was downstairs smoking some hash, alone in my room, and she just popped her head in and said "What are you doing?"

"Nothing," I said, and she literally got down on her knees, zipped down my pants, grabbed my dick and started blowing me. She'd been doing it maybe 10 seconds, long enough for me to have said stop, which I didn't, and Corey walked down and saw the whole thing. It all happened just that fast.

194

"Get the fuck out, both of you." Corey was rightfully enraged, though I thought it was a little dramatic, her just being a Match.com girl and all. Still Corey was pissed, and would never really forgive me. We, too, had been fighting like cats and dogs. I was making friends everywhere I went.

So I was kicked out of Corey's officially, and this little tiny 1980's Ford Escort, with all kinds of furniture and kid's shit, pulled up to pick us up, and drive the two of us to wherever this girl lived, which apparently was with her two kids, in her parent's house, somewhere in Cobb County. Gwen wasn't answering her phone, so I was along for the ride. All of this drama with a huge cast on my leg and the crutches to match. I got drunk when I got there, amazed with the rapidity of the situation, and then I slept with the girl. We fell asleep and I woke up to her crippled toddler waking me up saying, "Are you my new daddy?" I mean to tell you I ran far, and I ran fast. Or rather crutched. One foot or not. I felt awful. I spent what little money I had to get a cab once I'd gotten to a gas station, and I ended up sleeping at the Tower Place offices, broke, ashamed, now homeless, again, feeling like I didn't have a friend in the world. It wouldn't be the last time, and it sure as hell wasn't the first. Self-inflicted drama.

Corey and I would fight verbally over the phone for the next few days, and he told me that Phil, his mom's boyfriend who was also a PhD and someone I had a lot of respect for, had called me a "small time con artist." I was offended by the notion that I was small time, since I was a legend in my own mind. As I've heard said since then, "I may not be much, but I'm all I think about." I was pissed he called me small time, when I should have just been bothered I'd been referred to as a con artist. My thinking was completely backwards, ego-driven, proud, and wrong. Stewart Black had put it in more concise terms, that I was simply a thief. I think that was closer to the truth, I was just completely incapable of seeing my part in any of these actions, I was always the victim, I thought, in the whirlwind of chaos that seemingly always left me homeless and broke.

Despite the dispute Corey and I agreed to continue working together, as it was his and my only gig. It solidified my living with Gwen again, permanently, and I think about a week after that was permanent, Gwen lost her job. Things were going splendidly. My mom's cancer was getting worse, she had months to live, they told us, and Corey and I hadn't closed any deals in a while. It must have been early August around this time, and Gwen and I were going to have to move from the Alpharetta apartments. The only place I knew to go that would tolerate my sporadic income was in Little Five Points, living near "Family" again, I thought.

We moved under a Jerry Lennon roof, the same guy who owned the hippy inhabited Samson Lofts of my previous address. He was an obvious ex-hippie as well and a sort of leader of the confederacy of "Family" in my deluded mind. We moved in after I begged, borrowed, or stole an advance from our patient investor, Stewart Black depending on how you look at it. Gwen and my strung out ass moved all of our shit that couldn't get along in a one bedroom apartment in Alpharetta, to an even smaller studio apartment in the heart of drug darkness, Little Five Points, Atlanta. The Haight-Ashbury of Atlanta, if you will, where drugs are on every corner, and your neighbors are happy to keep you high. Brilliant plan.

Ah, but the brilliance didn't end there. When Gwen asked me to get a mohawk haircut, I obliged, shaving my head to look punk rock for her, so out of my mind, high on opiates I couldn't have cared less. I was visiting my mom every two or three days, and by this time she'd begun giving me her Fentanyl patches, which, for the uninitiated, are eighty times more powerful than morphine. You could slap a patch on your back, or arm, or ass, and it would keep you rolling on a powerful morphine buzz for up to five days, or less if you wore it in the sun and soaked it up quicker. Those patches kept us going for a while. With those potent Fentanyl patches, I was able to work more consistently than I'd been able to with the pills, which were more sporadic. Corey was still coming to work, but in all my wisdom, I'd finally talked his father into letting me fire him, his own son, and bring on Gwen full time, because she'd lost her job and had convinced me it was my fault. I'm sure this didn't piss Corey off at all. I didn't care, I was high as a kite, thought I was on the verge of making my first million, and I knew best how to handle the situation. Except for when my mom suddenly slipped into a coma-like state, only half conscious and delirious for a few days in a row, making it impossible to ask her for drugs as I'd been doing.

Thief in the Night

It was right before my brother's wedding, which she'd told us all she was going to live to see. All of a sudden, my opiate connection, my dying mother, was not available. I went into my office to try to get some work done, and I crutched into Tower Place, feeling noticeably more sweaty that day. By about ten o'clock that morning, I was curled up in the fetal position, sweating out of every pore, cramped, and in pain from the physical withdrawals from opiates, wondering how I could possibly get some more meds. I called Grady a few times, to no avail, I'd gone by St. Joseph's Hospital the night before, to be met by my disapproving stepfather guarding the door, taking care of my dying comatose mother. I was fucked, out of drugs, out of money after the move, and was going through the first major physical withdrawals I'd suffered due to the opiates. It was close to hell, but not quite there. Hell would come later. It was the sickest I'd ever been physically, though, shaking, sweating and occasionally crying underneath my desk there at Tower Place, pretending to be a businessman. Eventually, after several not very successful attempts at taking liquid shits to settle my stomach, I bought some Pepto-Bismol, and gathered enough strength to go to Saint Joseph's, to ask my mom for some medications, ya know, for my ankle, knowing damn well she was in a coma like state. I was lying to myself, I had more sinister plans.

When I got there, the addict part of my brain was happy, because my stepdad wasn't there guarding the door. My soul was sick, screaming don't do it. I went into that hospital room, and heard her muttering to herself as she did in those days, halfway between a coma and consciousness. I saw her purse and reached my hand into it, relieved to find the huge pill bottle of 100 milligram morphines. Her dosage had gone up. I had a brief moment of my soul saying don't do it, quickly forced out by thinking of how good I would feel, and better, how happy Gwen would be, and I grabbed the bottle, and poured out about 20 pills, more than she'd ever given me at once, and I slipped out of her hospital room, like a thief in the night, ashamed deep down, but for the time being happy. I remember when I told my friend Spencer about this, I completely blamed Gwen, and yeah, it's true she'd suggested it more than once, but I'd done this all on my own account. But he told me straight "Man, that's fuck up." And this was a guy who had cosigned my bullshit for years. I would feel guilty over it for years to come, as I should have. It hurt then, but I was able to cloud it out, to not think about it. It would hurt much worse later on.

Within a week Gwen and I had done all 20 of those pills, and whatever bliss we'd experienced was gone. The scar my soul would bare would linger much longer. We had a pretty steady supply of Xanax and other pills to tide us over, but I felt awful as hell. I felt even worse, when I found out that my mom had run out of pain medications, and her doctor had been out of town, and she was unable to refill her prescription because she was so many shy of where she should have been. They questioned why'd she taken so many, and it took her a full 24 hours before she was able to re-up her supply. I'm sure the cantaloupe-sized tumor in her hip felt ten times worse than when Gwen had left me without Percocet's after my surgery. They said that she could have died from the shock of that pain, that it was beyond belief, and secretly I knew it was all my fault. I didn't think I'd ever be able to tell anybody that story. I was directly responsible for that pain, and worse, had gone through that exact turmoil of suffering through pain because of theft, and I'd condemned it, only to do it ten times worse to my dying, frail mother. I was scum and I knew it.

Brother's Wedding

My stealing morphine and Gwen starting to shoot heroin really scared the shit out of me. I called my stepdad and asked for rehab. He blew me off, I'd asked too late, and certainly he had enough on his plate, but still I felt rejected and indignant that I was offering to get sober, and nobody cared. I sensed for the first time that I'd be alone when mom died. It was a painful realization, that absolutely nothing good was to come of this, that I'd written myself off, and that nobody cared. I knew I wasn't worthy of the inheritance my brother had mentioned years before, but still I had hope that maybe that would come through, and I could get into rehab, pay off my debts, and rebuild a life. And I felt guilty for those thoughts, as well. I hoped there would at least be money for rehab, that perhaps my mom would stipulate could only be used for rehab or the like, I fantasized.

Moving into Little Five, Gwen had fucked our next door neighbor the very first night of our being there. Simply addict behavior. We were miserable together, and all the pain and the culmination of hatred over the months wasn't even fixed by the drugs. Even the week we had the morphine from my mom, and the patches from before, we were at each other's throats in that small hellish little studio apartment. Everything was dark, everything was sour.

My brother's wedding approached and I didn't plan for it all, meaning I didn't have a supply of drugs for it ready. Though I'm sure I'd known about it for a year or longer, when the day came to me to meet up with my sister to drive up there, I had no money to get anything, and I had banked on being able to ask my mom for some pain meds. But nothing was to come of that, as I was too ashamed after stealing, and I was going to suffer through that event with the

198

moderated drinks at the reception and rehearsal dinners. It was painful, but at least there was alcohol, I told myself. I remember praying that I wouldn't get blackout drunk and embarrass myself or go too badly into physical withdrawals. I bit my lip all weekend.

My mom was a sight to see. She was pitifully brave to be there. The story went that she'd been told by her doctor that she couldn't go. Entirely incapable of not getting her way, she wrote the nurse a check for 50k to quit her job and take her to the wedding. That's the story I heard anyway. Everyone was shocked, as she'd been in a semi-coma for the weeks leading up to it. Somehow, the Thursday before the wedding, she came to and was able to convince a nurse to escort her to the wedding, almost illegally. That was my mom. You just didn't tell her no, and if you did, prepare for war. Thank God all eyes were on her, because I was quite the wreck myself, sweating and withdrawing, I looked almost as much of death as my dying mother with a port in her chest and bald head from the chemo. Worse, the night before we all left, I'd asked Adam Archer to shave off the remainder of my ridiculous mohawk, and he'd done a half way decent job of it, right up until he nicked the top of my head with the shaver, leaving a line in my head that made me look like Dr. Evil had an epileptic barber. I was a mess. That is the image of me, preserved infamously in my brother's wedding albums, as I was graciously still allowed to be in the pictures. Me, withdrawing from opiates, with a bad haircut, and a line cut into the top of my hairline, almost signed "Dumbass". I felt like one, that's for damn sure.

My brother had fully taken on the Golden Boy status of our family with this wedding, I thought, resentfully. Informally, he'd been mom's favorite since I'd rebelled and left the house, and he went on to be a state champion award winning wrestler, but this wedding, wow, in my mind, it made it official. My mom wouldn't even talk to my ex-wife, and here we were at the rehearsal dinner on top of Lookout Mountain, overlooking Tennessee and Georgia, on top of the world, and though I knew it wasn't about me, it wasn't hard for me to think that the whole event was thrown in my face to gloat about how well my life could have gone. It was difficult not to get resentful, as I knew I'd done it all to myself. So I got drunk as soon as they starting pouring wine at that rehearsal dinner, and I promised myself I wouldn't talk too much. I was an embarrassment to myself, the less I said the better, and I think it was the best strategy I've ever employed while drunk. I didn't embarrass myself, and, thankfully, the night really wasn't about me. I was able to hide out in the shadows, and I was able to stay shut up for the most part.

When I tried to spend time with my mom that night, in that beautiful clubhouse on top of Lookout Mountain in Tennessee, she would literally snub me. She was high on the meds, and she only had enough energy to spend a couple of hours at that reception, but the few times I would try to speak to her, she would turn away from me. Had she been sober it would have been subtle, but high as she was on opiates, it was an obvious exaggerated disdain that hurt like hell. She would look at me with plain, blurry, disgust, and then turn her head away. It was as if she knew I'd stolen the morphine from her, but more so, it was if she just detested me. It was the scorn of leaving her when I was a teenager, multiplied by making her a grandmother so young, simply intensified and amplified, by my stealing her morphine. I was so ashamed I could barely speak that whole night. Eventually, she was wheeled out to the car, and I waited as she was being loaded into the car. Once she was in, I put my head in, and she saw me and turned away. But I said anyway, "Tonight, you were the most beautiful woman in the world," and that melted away her scorn. She smiled and said, "Thank you, baby boy, I love you." I closed the door, her nurse got in the car, and they drove away. I went to the side of the building and cried just like a baby boy. I felt terrible.

The next day was more hell. I'd barely slept, and debated the entire night about breaking into her room and getting some more meds. But I didn't, already too ashamed of myself to even leave the suite that my family had rented me -- because, of course, had they not driven and housed me, I wouldn't have been able to attend. We took the wedding photos, and I tried to hide my shaking hands and sweat, and the pictures went by slowly but surely. I hung out with my brother in the back as we prepared for the wedding moment, and right before the wedding began, he asked me to sit in the row behind the family, not quite with them. I didn't blame him, but still felt bad for myself. It was over soon enough, and I drank to oblivion again the night of his wedding, wishing I was anywhere else in the world. Feeling less than human, wanting to die myself, while my mom so vividly and bravely clung to every ounce of life she could get. I was pathetic and I knew it.

Little Five and Going Downhill

Returning to Atlanta, the studio apartment, and the hell that was our temperamental on-again, off-again relationship, the only escape was drugs for both Gwen and me. I spent many nights up until morning waiting for her to come home, which reminded me of all the discomfort and agony of my failed marriage, rehashing insecurities and reliving forgotten pain almost nightly. We only got along when high, so I'd get us as many pain meds as possible, mixing it occasionally with some Special K (Ketamine, or Horse Tranquillizers) one weekend, some Ecstasy the next, but it got more and more miserable, regardless. Having slept with the neighbor on night one, every time I saw the guy, which was daily, I wanted to murder both her and him, and in that order, along with her yippy little mutt. We had one TV channel and eventually my patience just ran out, and I moved a few miles down the road to one of Lennon's even shabbier rental units. But it was away from her, at least, I thought.

Within a week Gwen, was living with a heroin addict junkie named Asia, another redhead as fate would have it. Fine by me I thought. I could only assume she was shooting up by this point, but I had no idea and she wasn't divulging any information. Lennon had put me up in a rat-infested, hell-hole off Ponce De Leon, across from Krispy Kreme doughnuts, where the roof leaked and the front door didn't even lock. I tried to get sober, and actually did OK staying off the hard shit for a couple of days, but staying pretty consistently drunk and stoned. Once again, I was attempting to control my drinking and drugging.

After I had fired Corey and hired Gwen, an incredible executive decision that I'm surprised Fortune Magazine didn't give me accolades for, we soon after moved offices to Midtown Atlanta in the Proscenium. I'd worn a mohawk for the first week or two of our being there, and had even managed to get in a shouting match with the Canadian Ambassador over the elevators. I'd ended that by crank calling her later, saying I was a reporter with the Atlanta Journal & Constitution and would be writing an article about her awful behavior in the lobby. The poor woman panicked, which made even me feel a little guilty for the call. We were just making friends wherever we went. Gwen had been fired and was collecting unemployment and had maybe worked four hours total, but once her hippie friend moved in with her and I moved out to the dump on Ponce, she was gone completely and I was actually able to get some work done for a few weeks in the office by myself. I also felt a little more professional minus the mohawk, which had not fit in at all in this A1 office space in midtown, and I'd cut for the wedding by then.

Occasionally, I'd leave the office and go down to Fuego where I met Kristen, and we became instant friends -- mainly because she knew and hated Gwen. We got stoned a few times, she was a sociology major and very intelligent. I'd shaven my mohawk for the wedding, so she didn't think me completely loony. Yet.

So I was living in the creepy old apartment, smaller and leakier than the studio in Little Five that I was still paying for, that Gwen was now sharing with a junkie, and I was doing my best to close some deals, and having some moderate success. I closed a deal with a major energy client, bringing a candidate from NYC down to Atlanta using Craigslist, which was more luck than skill. But still, it was enough to keep Stewart Black on my team, and without Gwen, things were just beginning to settle down. She called me every once in a while to tell me life was horrible and she was going to kill herself, but when I told Stewart this, he told me it was emotional blackmail, and if I really believed it were true, I should call the police. I didn't do anything at first. Gwen was just pressing my hot buttons, knowing how my dad had died, knowing what my last words had been to him, so I did my best to ignore her, but I wasn't sleeping very well because of it and all the other chaos and of course opiate withdrawal yet again. I thought quite a bit of her and my mom dying, and the irony that one clung to life with all her will, while the other wanted nothing to do with life at all.

My mom was back at home again, and though I'd kicked the morphine for the most part, I went to go visit one day, bringing her a dozen yellow flowers in a vase. I told myself I had no intention of scoring any drugs having withdrawn for the most part, I intended fully on just seeing her now that she was out of the coma. I had been paid a little of the commissions owed me and I wanted to show my mom I cared and that I loved her, and all the things I should have said to her over the many hours I should have spent with her, but I couldn't. I got there, gave her the flowers, and she literally begged me to take the rest of her Fentanyl patches. It was so surreal to have the woman who'd fought against any and all of my drug use for so many years, pleading with me, to in fact take the last of her drugs, and it was the last thing in the world I'd expected. I tried to say no, but it was just so easy, and I was only partially through detoxing, I just couldn't resist... My aunt Betsy walked in on my mom giving them to me, and I was almost in tears, but for some reason, my mom really wanted me to have those patches that time. Tears in my eyes, I took them and went home. I put one on and went back into a state of bliss for as long as I could. Without Gwen there to hijack the meds, I was able to make them last a lot longer. My sister painted my mom a portrait of those yellow flowers the next day, and gave her the painting. On the back of that painting, it says:

The Vase

If I could buy you flowers every day, I would,
but until then,
these will have to do!
Love,
Carrie

Carrie later gave me that painting, and it's my favorite piece in the whole world. We were all hurting, but Carrie stayed strong that entire time. While I was losing my wits, and while my brother had moved to Tennessee to marry his long time girlfriend, Carrie stayed by my mom's side like a trooper and spent more time, and spent more strength and energy with her than anyone else on the planet, except my stepdad who lived with her. Carrie was my angel then, and she always will be. She never gave up hope on my mom, and she's always been there to tell me like it is. That painting symbolized to me how unimportant those flowers I got mom really were. That I couldn't buy off the lack of time I'd spent with her, the stealing drugs, the letting her down. It hangs on my wall and reminds me every day to be the man I should be, not the man I was. Still, I'd tried with those flowers, and when I left, I went into another tailspin.

Hurricanes Ivan and Gwen

The remnants of Hurricane Ivan struck Atlanta on September 16th, 2004. Gwen called me that morning in a panic like I'd never heard her before. I mean, she was a wreck. She was screaming about a tree falling on her, and when I left my little apartment on Ponce to go see her, I was so confused by the phone call, I'd thought she'd been in the Jeep when an oak tree had fallen on her. That wasn't the case, and when I arrived, it was such a sight that all I could do was laugh. I'm always laughing at inappropriate times. This 150 year old oak tree, that had stood unfettered through the Civil War, through the Great Wars, through the Civil Rights movement, through it all, had fallen due to the winds of the night before, and only managed to smash -- and I mean demolish -- exactly one car on all of Euclid Avenue. It had somehow navigated its way directly on top of, and into, Gwen Evere's prized Jeep. She was in tears. The news crew had been there earlier and she'd done her makeup in order to be on television, where she promptly cried and went into hysterics. I don't think they used her footage, though I think they showed the wrecked Jeep. All I could think of was that it was a sign from God, and I told her so. "This is what you get when you shoot heroin, you dumbass."

She begged me to kick the junkie she was living with out of her place, and I took the girl on a long walk, made it clear that I paid the rent, and that she had to go. Then Gwen and I had makeup sex, and like an idiot in love, I agreed to move back in. She agreed to quit smoking weed, and quit doing heroin, and morphine. I didn't tell her I had a patch on at first, but she figured it out. She put her car in the shop, got a rental, and we were lovebirds for a few days, while she negotiated my moving back in. We got some Special K one of those nights -- horse tranquilizers -- and I remember us doing lines of that shit, and screaming at the top of our lungs that we were the King and Queen of China, running through the hallways of the old apartment naked, loud, and obnoxious until about 5 AM that next morning. Our neighbors, even hippie "Family" neighbors, were none too thrilled with us that evening.

One of the things my sponsor tells me now is "Avoid the female superior position," and this was no exception. Right up until the moment I'd moved everything, maybe a box worth of shit, into her rental car, Gwen had sucked up to me and kissed my ass. The very moment I'd committed to moving back in, basically when I'd given the landlord the key to the second unit, and loaded up the car to go back over to the Little Five apartment, Gwen instantly became a bitch. It was instantaneous, and I remember thinking, "What have I done?" It would only go downhill. Hell, where else could it have gone?

She began coming back to work with me, and instead of working, she was spending a great deal of time on Myspace.com. I jealously installed a key logger on her PC so I could record all the passwords to her email, and all the communications back and forth on IM that made her giggle so much, and made me furious while I was trying to work. More than once at the old apartment, I'd walked in on her in her underwear, flirting wildly on the webcam, furious that I'd interrupted her, and I was eager to find out once and for all, how harmless this all was. I quickly found out that she was plotting to leave Atlanta and move to San Diego, on a haphazard mission to move in with a guy she'd been talking to for almost six months. At first I was furious, but we weren't fighting quite as much, and I needed the rides, as living on my own, crutching around Atlanta still, had worn me out those two weeks. I figured I had to take the good with the bad. These were desperate times, so I said nothing, and bided my time.

Hospice

My mom was put into a hospice in late September. I went to visit her one night shit-faced drunk, and she was awake and lively. This was the first and only time I'd ever visited her drunk, and it was a mistake, but there I was, and she had demands.

"Bryan, oh thank God you're here! Please help me, get me out of here, let me die outside! Nobody will let me die outside, take me home Bryan, let me die outside, please!" as tears streamed down her face. She was just about as scared as any human being facing death can be, as scared as my dad when he couldn't stop drinking, and maybe worse, having abandoned all hope. It was the opposite of peaceful, my poor mother held onto life with all her heart and soul.

Like the drunk idiot I was, I passionately got involved in this moving her outside cause. Letting her die outside seemed noble, and it seemed like the least I could do. "She just wanted to see the stars," I thought, "wouldn't I?" The nurses and doctors, however, were none too excited about it, and even less so when I began berating and belittling them, crying as my mother was, and they asked me to leave, to which I vaguely remember telling them to fuck off. I went back in my mom's hospice room, and said I didn't know what to do. I called my stepdad and he told me to leave the premises. He said they were calling the police if I didn't leave. I kissed my mom, and when I walked outside, the police were there. They were kind enough to call me a cab, and I had to leave my car there at the hospice. Once again, I probably evaded another DUI, but I'd made yet another drunken spectacle of myself.

The next day, my brother called me in a rage. "What the fuck were you doing?" And we fought, we were all angry. Angry at each other, angry at the world, angry with God, the situation just sucked. Carson said to me, "Dan Jones is a good man," to which I replied, "Yeah great guy, gives his stepson 500 bucks to run away at 15 and you call him a good guy, mom just wants to die at home, her home, why can't we force him to let her." Dan Jones had every reason, he'd been advised by all the doctors and nurses, but still, I wanted my mom's last request to be filled, and it made him an easy target. "Fuck Dan Jones, let mom die in her own home."

"Bryan, chill out and don't go up there drunk anymore. I don't believe that Dan ever gave you money to run away, and you're just a fuck up, leave him and her alone." My brother was as mad as I have ever known him to be.

And so I drank, and I drank, resentful, drowning in self pity. I told Gwen about my woes. I told her all kinds of crazy stories to vilify Dan Jones and I don't even know why I did it. I told her I'd buried bodies for the guy, that he was the Devil incarnate. She would later cite that story as the reason she would leave me, though it was bullshit, she'd made her plans way before then, she would refute that what I rambled about burying bodies, that I'd made up on an imaginative lying whim, was the deciding factor for her escaping Atlanta. Delusional crap, she was leaving anyway, I had proof. I'd read all her correspondence to her upcoming Myspace.com victim. It didn't matter, I'd have left me too at this stage. I punched a wall through the plaster at those apartments, which the super, Winston, later told me he'd frame as the only hole punch that ever penetrated the wall in the place. Towards the end lots of things got punched, walls, doors, cars, people, it didn't help, I was still enraged, lost, ashamed, and utterly powerless in my drunken state to accomplish anything at all to ease my mother's last dying days on earth. Save quitting drinking, and God knows that was off the table.

A couple of days later my brother called and said that Dan had admitted to giving me the money to run away. I hadn't made it up, and he was sorry. That was impressive and it probably began the recovery of the relationship between my brother and me as well as with Dan. I'd expected him to deny it. My mom had done a very good job of vilifying me over the years, and that was the first morsel of evidence for my side I think my brother had ever digested.

It was in the middle of these benders, as my mom lay dying in a hospice, as my family officially shunned me, not outspokenly, and not just under the rug, that Gwen and I went to go get some heroin. I remember thinking, fuck it. I'd run out of the Fentanyl patches, and Gwen had finally talked me into it. As my mom laid fighting for every breath of her life, I was doing my absolute best to end mine.

It was a dirty, nasty apartment complex where we went to score the dope, and we went to CVS in the Highlands to get the needles. What I remember of that night was nothing like the movies. Similar to threesomes, great in theory, overrated in practice I thought. I remember spilling my fucking spoon, not shooting enough, not shooting into a vein, not getting high, getting so high I'd forget the needle was in my arm and walk around. But it wasn't glamorous, and it was more of a pain in the ass than I'd ever thought it would be. Hell, I didn't take the time to remove seeds and stems from my weed, this heroin business was more work than surgery. Getting the drugs on the spoon, adding just enough water, heating them up perfectly, probably with not the steadiest of hands, then tying off your arm to find a vein, to be quite honest, it was all just more of an aggravation than I'd ever imagined. And the high wasn't as clean as Fentanyl. I was somewhat relieved the next day when I didn't want to do the entire process all over again. To be addicted to that cycle, has got to be the most time consuming, irritating business on Earth. Shit, Gwen and I even fought half the night over some bullshit, so I know it wasn't that great a high. We laid in bed for a long time, but for the most part, I hated it, thought it was stupid, and I wanted nothing more to do with it the next day. I'd stick to black out drinking, thank you very much. I guess I'd expected a religious experience, and maybe it was just bad shit, or maybe it was a miracle I didn't get high, but I truly didn't enjoy the experience, and vowed to just smoke pot and drink from there on out. I don't remember sharing needles with her that night, but then, I don't remember a lot of things about that night, the days leading up to it, or the days following. I would later find out, though, that we had probably shared needles. Tracing a virus back isn't an exact science, but that was probably the night.

Mom's Funeral

A few days later, Uncle Jack told me my mom probably didn't have much time left and that if I wanted to see her, I should go now and say goodbye, soberly if possible. Her last words to my brother were "Keep running son, nobody wants a fat husband." Her last words to me were, "You have to quit drinking, baby boy, it's going to kill you if you don't." I cried, gave her a hug, and she died that night, October 12, 2004.

When somebody takes as long as my mom did to die, and was in as much pain, you feel a momentary release. But I also felt guilty for wondering what the will was going to say, though I didn't have much hope for it, I was more moved by my guilt of even thinking of it than I actually was by any real expectations. Gwen's hopes were high though. The funeral would be in a couple of days, and I began withdrawing from all the opiates, heroin included, in the days leading up to her death. My sister asked me if I wanted to speak at the funeral and I said yes, I would read a poem, and I knew that I would write something when moved, most likely right before the funeral. My Uncle Owen said he wanted to come down from Boston, when I told him about her dying, and I even tried, uselessly, to get my contacts at the Major Multimedia Client of mine who owned the local paper, to devote a page on the front of their living section to my mom, to no avail. My contact and VP of Audit there was a gentleman about it, but once again my best efforts were futile. My stepdad wrote a good obituary though.

In the few days between her death and the funeral, I felt some relief that I'd finally be able to kick the opiates, though I hadn't given up trying. Grady Hospital had long since stopped giving me pain medications like they were, only allowing me one bottle of Hydrocodones a week, which Gwen and I would kill in a night. We were just drinking and doing sedatives, trying not to feel the full effects of the withdrawals. The morning of her funeral, I wrote the poem I would read at her funeral, and I, of course, an egomaniac with an inferiority complex, thought it was a masterpiece.

At the viewing, dressed in a black suit, walking with a cane, looking like Dr. Evil with my shaved head, I remember asking Lauren Hunt's mom, who had just been in a motorcycle accident, if I could have some of her pain medication. She said no, and I felt stupid for asking. I kissed my mother's cold corpse, and I felt alone. We said our thank you's and shook lots of hands, and we went back to Little Five to get shit-faced once again.

We took a bunch of Xanax the morning of the funeral and headed to Roswell United Methodist Church for the actual funeral ceremonies. We went into the backroom, where my brother was practicing his speech, and where several other friends of the family were looking at Gwen and me with a look of menace, as I perceived it. They probably weren't thinking much about us at all. A lot of it all is still a blur. I remember at some point my stepdad was angry with me for inviting Uncle Owen. It made me feel ashamed all over again, but I couldn't quite a put a finger on why.

When it was my turn to speak at the funeral, I got up to the podium at Roswell United Methodist Church, looked out at the hundreds of people crowded into that room, and I read my poem rapidly, as if it was a confession, as if it was a race. I wasn't as good at public speaking as I'd imagined. I don't think anyone understood a word I said. My brother got up there and sounded like a magnificent statesman. He spoke like the champion he is. He was proud and strong, and spoke about how hard life can be and how all we can do is live it and be strong. He was a much better son than me, I thought. He was definitely a better public speaker, and it made me feel a little more worse than I'd felt. And then I felt shame for not being proud of him, but instead jealous. Had anyone been able to understand my poem at the breakneck anxious pace I read it, this is what they would have heard:

Fare Thee Well Eternally

Definition of dignity,
Purity, blended with passion.
Fighter and solder, defeat not an option,
Values are truths, never fashion.
Your battles waged, sad pain endured.
Challenges, fought with a grin,
Release, pinnacle of a comet's trail,
Escape this Earth for a spin.
Race along with the speed of light,
Smile upon us generously and constant,
Shine on in grace, burn bright.
Rage on strong spirit, enjoy the ride,
As many tears prove you are sorely missed,
Our hearts know you're by our side.

-JB Smith
October 15th, 2004

Then my Aunt Jenny got up and read a very long speech, in which she mentioned every single family member at least one time, except not once did she mention me or my son, who was sitting by my side. Of course my self centered ass noticed that and I dwelled on it. Woe is me. And my resentment towards my entire family grew. Right or wrong, I was filled with boiling anger by the time the actual service was over.

We drove into the huge cemetery, and I looked up to see a hawk following our caravan, seemingly right above our vehicle, and it gave me some assurance, that my mom was up there looking down. The burial went by quickly, and the Minister told a story of a man whose life was still invigorating in him, but his shell or body was giving in to Father Time. At the end of his story, the wind blew hard and almost toppled the makeshift tent they'd put up around the burial plot, and out loud I tried to make a joke about this "shell" giving in to the wind. Nobody laughed. Burials are a hard place to experiment with comedy, I decided. Inappropriate I guess.

Anticipating the Inheritance

We all went back to what was originally my biological father's house, that was then my mother's, that was now my stepdad's, and I couldn't help but hope that the Will would rectify this situation, someway, somehow. Gwen and I began to drink pretty heavily, as always, lest we begin shaking like the epileptics we resembled with the sedatives wearing off, and we gravitated towards my Uncle Owen, who probably also felt alienated at this funeral after-party. I don't remember much about the party, except for that someone asked me to print out the poem, so that I gave it a cheesy title, and printed out 50 copies. I bounced back in forth in my head as to whether it was a masterpiece, or a piece of shit, and I shrieked inside every time anyone said anything about it, appalled with myself that I would take this event to boast of my writing. There was another moment I remember clearly, of Gwen, Owen, and me sitting by the pool my father had bought the house for back in 1988, and we were laughing hard at something, and a few people all looked down at us at once. As the hours went by, and we became more drunk, our laughter grew more and more inappropriate, until I rounded Gwen up and we left again for Little Five Points, where we could be obnoxious with less judgment.

And so we went back to Little Five, to drink with our "Family." Gwen was sure I would get some kind of inheritance, as was Adam Archer, whose father had just past and left him something. Henry was a little less sure as I recall, and I really didn't know, but couldn't quite imagine getting absolutely nothing. I mean, hell, it had only been a few years before that my brother had told me we would inherit millions, and I still somewhere back in the recesses of my mind wanted to believe that that was possible. I wanted to believe I'd thrown it all away back in 2001 because I knew this day was coming. That a ball of light had told me my mom would die, and well, hell, I was entitled to that money. Everybody had an opinion.

We finally got the call from my stepdad, and little Shelly Dover, our past next door neighbor and friend of the family, guided me to a little room in an accounting office in Roswell, and asked me to sign some papers, stating I wouldn't sue for anything. I was just still in so much shock, and my stepdad said it wasn't that big of a deal, and, hell, there wasn't any money left over anyway as he put it, that I just signed those papers. I felt so guilty about my life in general, the last thing I wanted was to be a leach. Honestly, I felt relieved to sign it, so that I could mourn without the conflicting feelings of anticipation for money. I could just feel sorry for myself.

I signed the paperwork, and then afterwards I talked to my brother and sister who told me that they too would just sign the papers. The last thing I wanted was to be any more of an asshole than I'd already been. I decided that no matter what, I didn't have a right to do anything other than what my siblings wanted.

I did, however, go check the Will out in public records the very next day, limping, casted with crutches still in hand, to inspect just when the Will had been changed. It noted that it had been changed years back. Right after I'd lost it all in 2001, to be exact. So my brother may have been right about it when he told me about the will, but my behavior after 9/11, my obvious losing of my mind and every asset on earth, had changed my mother's mind. My stepdad was an easy target for anger though, and my resentment towards him percolated.

Gwen was shocked that I didn't get a penny. I was in shock, and totally alone now, able to comprehend her death in its entirety for the first time. For the first time not clouded by the hidden guilt of anticipation of money, of freedom from my sales career, of all the trite things we humans dream of when great fortune is around the bend. It was just a lonely void, an emptiness, she was gone. We would never speak again, she had left us penniless and alone. Our father had died in 1989 and our mother in 2004. Sometime right after the funeral, my brother, sister, and I went to go see the movie Lemony Snicket's "A Series of Unfortunate Events". It was surreal, as if it had happened to us. We were all three in shock, I believe. We hadn't a clue what that movie was about, but it turned out to be about orphans, having their inheritance stolen. It amplified what we were all feeling, I thought.

Wedding in Florida

Shortly after that, through a strange set of circumstances, Gwen and I begged, borrowed, and stole our way into some money to get down to Melissa Gilbreath's wedding in Homosassa, Florida. We didn't have a spare dime to do it, but somehow managed to make it happen. Gwen was having pills Fed ex'ed to us down there, and had all kinds of crazy scenarios to try to keep us high. But we were quickly running out of money and drugs, and even rent. We got to that weird wedding of a high school friend who'd lived in Turkey with this man and were back in the states to get married, and it was a mix of white American punks, and Turkish family members, most of whom didn't speak a lick of English. It would have been a painful,

211

boring event had an evil miracle or the ol' Devil's luck not happened the Friday night we arrived.

Gwen had been trying to get pills Fed Ex'ed to us through a crazy set of schemes that I knew would never work, and she was more than a bit flustered about the whole scenario. The place we were staying in Homosassa was a dressed-up trailer park, surrounding a river that led into the Gulf of Mexico, but was several miles inland. The cheaper trailers were split in two right down the middle, turning each trailer into two units, with a paper-thin wall divider between. We were in our half of one of these for about 20 minutes when a Harley biker gang showed up to stay in the place next to us. Within 30 minutes of that, Gwen is screaming at the top of her pretty little lungs at the bikers to not park in the pebbled sidewalk, which both units shared, to get to the bar.

So she came in to tell me how rude these bikers were, and wasn't I going to do anything about it? I had to set forth to negotiate the murky waters of asking the bikers to move their hogs -- politely enough not to be killed, but forcefully enough to make it happen, and not be killed by her. I engaged this adventure, only to find that the bikers had actually moved the bikes already, and what's more, had left a huge bottle, a freaking gargantuan prescription bottle, not unlike the one I'd robbed my mother a few pills from, sitting there helplessly in the sidewalk. I grabbed the bottle and walked back into the trailer.

The prescription bottle didn't say what it was, but it looked like Oxys with the time release coating scraped off of each individual pill, and there were over 100 of them, at least. We crushed them up and started snorting. Briefly, I regretted that I would once again have to wean myself off of opiates. Albeit briefly, I remember the thought clearly, that they were almost out of my system, and yet I still couldn't bring that previous pain to consciousness with enough force to stop myself from breaking up these stolen opiates, and snorting several of them up as soon as humanly possible. Then Gwen and I made love, as drugs had always improved our romance.

Then through the paper-thin walls, we heard those bikers begin to go ape shit. They screamed and yelled at each other, they tossed their entire half unit trailer. They drove off, drove back, eventually knocked on our door, where a much more pleasant, even sweet, Gwen Evere told them we didn't know what they were talking about. "Sorry." And then they overturned everything in their unit next to us again, all while Gwen and I tried our best not to laugh out loud, high as kites. Eventually after about two hours of them searching, and making a huge racket, the bikers left, and we had our wedding weekend, complete with plenty of opiates, in total peace. A couple of dope feigns, withdrawing, finding a bottle of high dosage scrips is the closest thing to heaven that can happen to a junkie, so we lived it up a few days, the wedding went a whole lot smoother, and we even made it home OK, before we ran out and all hell would break loose.

10K by December 10th

I arrived back in my offices to find my investor was livid, and where the hell had I been since my mom died? I'd been anywhere and everywhere but the office, the landlord was also calling, and Gwen needed $2500 in cash to get her now-repaired car out of the shop. The walls of Babylon were collapsing on every front. I had about 3k left, and 0 income after that for the foreseeable future.

My investor had patiently been teaching me the details of Think and Grow Rich, by Napoleon Hill, and I'd been practicing, but barely, as I'd mostly been high or drunk. Now he came on with it in a fury. He explained that there was nothing I could do about my mom's inheritance, and there was nothing I could about Gwen's drug addictions, suicide attempts, or drinking, but that all I could do was close 10k by December 10th or he was through with me. He told me I had to be dead certain of this fact, and to have the belief that I could do this, or as he put it, "Be as certain as if a gun was pointed to your son's head over it." This was motivating, though I judged him for it at first. Then I began to implement the Think and Grow Rich plan. The plan consists of many parts, but all I was able to grasp, and all Stewart Black was forcing me to do at this stage, was to repeat my Definite Statement of Purpose, before I went to bed at night, when I woke up in the morning, and several times during the day. I'd done this before when starting Fortune Staffing in 2001, and it had worked but thus far in this business venture I'd been too discombobulated to even attempt it. Now, with the heavy hand of my investor prodding me along, I began to do it again, with a new level of thinking and faith, because if it didn't happen, I was going to be broke. My statement, which I repeated, dozens of times a day, read "I will close 10k in deals by December 10th, 2004, by being the best recruiter I can possibly be." I read it over and over again, dozens of times, and made hundreds of cold calls throughout November. Now, with no inheritance, with no job offers, no other options, I had to make it work, so I followed my investor's advice, and I repeated that statement and read <u>Think and Grow Rich</u> every day , as well as <u>The Richest Man in Babylon</u>, and I focused.

Meanwhile, Gwen plotted. I knew it was coming, I'd been reading her emails back and forth to some unlucky fellow in San Diego, and though it broke my heart, I knew I was fucked if she stayed with me. We just kept screwing up, kept getting pain meds, and weren't getting any better together. She wasn't helping me accomplish my 10k by December 10th, which was all I cared about now. Her leaving probably saved my life. I knew when I paid the $2500 cash to get her car out, she wasn't going to drive me around as she'd promised, but I didn't care, I just wanted her gone. I paid the money, and the next day she told me some bullshit story about her leaving to stay with her grandmother, and then she disappeared. I was happy at first, then sad. Then utterly alone and depressed. If it hadn't been for the mission, the closing 10k by December 10th, I'd have probably lost my mind when she left, even though I knew of it and prepared for it, it hurt like hell.

When I told my ex-wife about her leaving, who stayed a good friend through even this latest debacle, she said bluntly "Good, I just don't think you realize how low she took you down." Anne Marie always had a way of putting things and though I couldn't blame it all on Gwen Evere, we'd definitely fueled each others self-destruction as low as either of us had ever been. Her leaving had been inevitable for both of us in that state of mind. Otherwise we would be both be dead.

But I was torn between the most depressed and alone I'd ever been, and the mission of closing 10k by December 10th. I would do my absolute best, nine to five, to focus on the mission, but every other waking hour was spent trying to forget the pain of her, my mom, and life in general. Yet I was wallowing in it, commiserating with it, whining to anyone who would listen at Elmyr, the closest bar to my apartment, and crying myself to sleep half the time. I tried at first not to drink as much after Gwen left, and within a day or two, I would be right back to getting wasted. But the opiates I swore off, detoxing finally with drink and mild sedatives like Xanax, weed, or whatever else I could scrounge up for a while.

I even made it to my first AA Meeting, after briefly and drunkenly talking to Chad Major, my old manager at PMC Financial, and I remember I walked to it, in downtown Atlanta, and it turned out to be a very urban, all black meeting. I could barely understand anything they were saying with their thick southern urban accents and slang, so I simply judged the whole scene, and left the meeting feeling helpless, and ultimately hopeless.

So I just kept on drinking, angry at Gwen, angry at God, angry at my mom now for leaving me nothing, and with my real dad for leaving her money thinking that would be a solution, and angry with my stepdad for stealing my inheritance. But most of my anger concentrated on Gwen, as I wrote in my journal in late November:

Personal Journal, November 26th 2004;

Gwen, how dare you? I'm nothing now. My mom died a month ago and you found it able to plan an escape, the whole time dragging me down. Making me suffer. You met a man online and drove across country to escape and then had the nerve to call me back and ask me for a job reference. $2500 for your car and that ridiculous wedding, and you bail the moment you can, lying to me even about your destination. You suck...

It goes on and on, pouring out and ranting negatively, proving my hatred and rage to the woman, to the world, to life in general. And yet I was still able to show up at my company, riding MARTA, hopping along on crutches, still in pain, to cold-call accountants, nine to five, ever repeating the mantra "I will close 10k by December 10th." Lo and behold, Napoleon Hill, the man who studied Edison, Carnegie, and Ford, must have been onto something, because despite all my drinking, my rage, my self-pity, my one-legged transportation, my withdrawal from opiates, and my budget issues, I somehow closed 11k on December 10th 2004, by placing Melanie Allbright at a Fortune 500 downtown, proving to me that Think and Grow Rich's philosophy worked, and that all I needed to do was implement that strategy from here on out. Sobering up would help, I thought, but, hell, so far I'd made it work.

On the back of that closing and Gwen's swift Atlanta evacuation, I would drink and write and lament. Dozens of poems, a few of them even remain legible, having been written on Elmyr napkins.

Escape

Your wasted brilliance in tragedy,
Anger of mine only pity.
Migraine of sorrow, your negativity,

Point the finger of blame, to him or me,
The all time great, capitalistic society.
Yet every chance was offered to you,
Every one kindness bestowed.
You spit in the face of graciousness,
Laugh at gratitude showed.
As if to kill yourself quite slow,
On your deathbed, the quickness is fury,
Your death will bring judgment in a hurry.
Still connected to you, addicted to your madness,
My body aches to suffer more,
But the fires subsided to sadness.
I watched you chase darkness in its every realm.
The grin in your eye for any sin.
Then talk about purity, to make it worse.
Your cravings for death a joke,
You scared weak little girl.
I watched my mom fight and pray,
For what you nonchalantly piss away.
It hurts more than you know to say farewell.
But the path you lead me down has only one destination, hell.
And I won't go. I choose life.

-JB Smith

Funny how the things I accuse her of most passionately, were exactly the most blaring defects of character in myself. It was always anyone else's fault, and though I was capable of observing her wrongs, I was pure as the driven snow, faultless, incapable, as it were, of being honest with myself.

Goodbye to Opiates and Acting

The good news of Gwen's departure, though, would be that I could once and for all, for the fifth or sixth time, but more importantly, for the final time, withdraw from opiates. It would be painful and it would take weeks, but with her gone, and my mom dead, I would drink myself out of that dependency, taking the occasional Xanax or Valium to help. After it was done, I would pat myself on the back, thinking "I couldn't have that addictive of a personality, hell, I'd weaned myself off cocaine, ice, and now even morphine, heroin, and opiates. Alcoholics and drug addicts lie to themselves amazingly well.

Right before Gwen left, she made me bring her to an audition for a play, "Miracle on 34th Street." They wanted her for a small part, and then, quite accidentally, wanted me for the part of the lawyer, which was a much larger role. I'd only been there for her, and had only read lines at her insistence. I then took the part at her insistence, and then she had left, and they still wanted me in the play. They'd finally taken my cast off and I could barely ride the new bike I'd bought. Shit, I did my best to show up, riding my new bicycle onto MARTA, and showing up to rehearsals, once or twice in the freezing rain, for about three weeks, before a bender got the best of me and I told the Director I was done. I'd felt terrible, but I told myself I was a writer, not an actor. Really, I was just a quitter, and I had no control of the benders. I told myself I was doing them a favor, but I felt awful all the same for ditching out on that commitment. They begged me to come back, but I just couldn't commit to a play that way, not knowing when the next bender would hit.

Stewart Black came to Atlanta a few days after I closed the 11k deal and strongly suggested that I move out of the office complex at HQ Global, and into a home office -- my little studio apartment -- and that he would use the profits from 2004 to cut me a check for 3k every month while I closed 10k a month, utilizing the strategy I'd made work, and had proven was plausible and effective, over the last month or so. It all sounded like a great idea, and I moved offices for the fourth time in 2004, into my studio apartment, and I awaited my first check for 3k.

On the family front, Thanksgiving had been full of suspicion and irritation with my stepdad having a profile on Match.com less than a month after my mom had died. Christmas was no better. Dan Jones tried to introduce us to a woman named Tracy, and Carrie and Carson were enraged beyond belief. I just got drunk, came home, and wrote about what an asshole he was and what a fool my mom had been for marrying him, and spending, then leaving all of our inheritance to him. And I drank. Dan Jones is a good man and stuck with my mom through her entire ordeal, he was just lonely too, but at the time, resentments raging, he made himself an easy target, and the whole family struggled with some of his actions.

I dated another redhead, Courtney Ellington, though really

we didn't date as much as just randomly hook up when we were both shit-faced. She had a boyfriend who called her one morning while she was in my bed, from his onsite filming of a documentary in Afghanistan, and I laughed and mocked him, as I'd thought the boyfriend in Afghanistan was a bullshit line. Apparently it wasn't, but Courtney and I still hooked up from time to time. She was supposed to meet him in Indonesia to visit, and the week before the tsunami hit, we stayed out all night getting hammered and smoking weed, and she missed work and got fired, which then negated her trip to the South Pacific -- which ultimately saved her life. I took credit for that, as obviously I'd had a subconscious feeling there was going to be a tsunami that would kill hundreds of thousands of people, and getting drunk with me was the solution! How grandiose! It had been the solution for a long, long time, it was nice to finally give drinking a little credit where credit was due.

The Marie family, my ex-wife's parents, let me have an old Buick so I didn't freeze to death, limping around Atlanta that winter. It was ancient, had a huge crack in the windshield, and was ugly as sin, but it was a car, and once again my ex-wife's family showed what a kind and caring family they were. Unlike mine, who I thought were cruel and punishing. All my inheritance gone, and the Marie's, broke as they were, were more giving than anyone in my own blood family. Never mind that I'd wrecked many cars from my family before, or that I had no real picture of my mom's financial situation after her being sick for so long, the resentments just piled high, real or not, it didn't matter.

January 2005 rolled around and though I had the best of intentions in implementing the Think and Grow Rich business plan, my investor had taught me, I couldn't get past the fact that 3k a month kept me pretty drunk, all day, everyday, in Little Five, and I just wasn't as motivated as I had been. I barely made a phone call for Fortune Staffing, but I limped up to Elmyr quite a bit, drinking at lunch, and stretching it through well into the night, always finding someone to smoke some herb with, and of course, proud of myself for quitting all the hard stuff.

Still I knew I needed to quit drinking, and I begin to actually talk about it, albeit still doing nothing. My Uncle Jack suggested I read A Million Little Pieces by James Fry. I bought the book and read through it in a few easy days. For one thing, one of the first stories was about having his teeth taken out without pain medication. My dad used to brag about doing that all the time, and my mom would roll her eyes. I didn't believe my dad and I didn't believe James Fry,

218

I think it's some kind of urban legend every addict thinks makes themselves out to be a badass, but no dentist worth his salt would actually perform. He was off to a bad start with me in that book, but then it got worse. The major thing that pissed me off was that he was in one of the top rehab facilities on Earth, Hazelden, and yet felt so damn sorry for himself. In my mind, my mom and dad were dead, my stepdad had already said no to rehab, I was self employed with no health insurance, and if Grady Memorial's rehab was anything like their ankle surgery, I felt doomed. I was broke but this author's in rehab, all paid for, and he was whining about it. And then the author meeting a Federal Judge and then a Mafia boss were just too convenient.

I called bullshit on the book, and told my Uncle Jack the same. The main reason, though, wasn't all those obvious red flags, to me it was his pride. He talked too boastfully of how he'd done it. Every truly sober person I knew, Graham Flagg, Chad Major, Everett Monahan, and Mike Rubin, were all the picture of humility when it came to their sobriety. No matter what religion they were, as they mostly differed, they were humble about their sobriety, not proud, as Fry was, all the way through that entire book. Later, it would all come to light that a lot of his book was pure fiction. Even in my state of mind, I called that one out, but probably just because I was an alcoholic. I can easily see how Earth people (non-alcoholics) would buy into that book. It was well-written and a romantic idea, and it was intriguing. I just knew it was too proud. I told my Uncle it was crap and he said maybe, but would remember it when the news broke that the book was fraudulent. Meanwhile, I still didn't quit drinking, and it hadn't helped me at all.

I Remember When I Lost My Mind.com

In late January of 2005, Gwen called and said she wanted to come "home." Since the day she'd left, I'd had nightmares of both her and my mom returning, banging on my door. I told Gwen no, followed by regretting it every moment since. She was only that vulnerable for a momentary lapse of time, and only out of circumstance. Apparently she'd been in jail over the holidays. Having arrived in San Diego, her relationship with the gentleman she'd moved in with had been rocky from the very start. Within a couple of weeks, she'd gotten drunk and hit the man, and unlike myself, who was always deathly afraid of the police, and would always just leave within moments of the violence, this guy had called the police. She'd spent several weeks of the holidays in jail, and having been released, was homeless or lived in a shelter, and worse, now wanted to come home. I tracked the guy down who she'd lived with and got the story from him, as well, laughing at her plight, making jokes at her expense, and telling him I owed him one for taking Hurricane Gwen off my hands. He told me I should have warned him, eventually I told him to go fuck himself and hung up the phone, but ultimately the call made me reminisce, and for many months thereafter, I wrote in my journal about how much I loved and missed her, feeling alone, and wanting her back. As for that initial phone call, my pride wouldn't have anything to do with it. I would continue partying in Atlanta.

I chased a lot of women around at this time and slept with quite a few while drunk, but one that I never was able to coerce was Kristen, the blonde bartender from Fuego. She was great looking, very smart, and very fun to be around though, so we hung out a few times, usually starting by drinking at her bar, Fuego, and then heading out around midtown. One night, though, she came to my cramped little studio, where we smoked a little herb and went out to Elmyr, my favorite bar, and coincidentally, the closest dive bar in Little Five. Four or five beers into this particular buzz at Elmyr, I began brainstorming loudly about creating a website, a blog of sorts, called "I remember when I lost my mind.com" where random people would all tell their story of the last sane things they remembered, or literally the moments leading up to their insanity, as if the whole world was crazy and not just me. Both Kristen and the Elmyr bartender thought it was a fantastic idea, and we ranted about it for hours. I'm glad I had witnesses who remembered it as well because one year later, as my real insanity would be picking up steam, that Gnarls Barkley song with the line "I remember when I lost my mind" would play on the radio every 15 minutes. Coincidence, I suppose, but we had carried on about it in that bar, a full year before it would ever be heard on the radio, and it would later feed my neurotic paranoia.

And so the chaos continued unabated, me staying relatively off the hard shit save a few instances, and somehow, even closing a huge deal with my energy client for 18k, that I'd really set in motion six months before. I couldn't have started the deal in the shape I was in, but I was able to finish it, and Stewart Black took the opportunity to exit gracefully from our partnership, in which I had in every way, let him down. I'd fired his son, had not been able to work but 30 days of our entire agreement to his liking, and I was completely ashamed for blowing the opportunity to work for such a prolific businessman, only to have failed miserably. He would send me a check for 13k or so, my portion, and we could cut ties. I knew

I was sunk. I couldn't run a business like this, like a drunk. I waited for the check, and in the meantime, went to work construction for my uncle for two weeks, awaiting my money.

I even managed to not drink those two weeks, as I didn't want to let my uncle down, and be late to work. I couldn't even hold that shitty acting role due to my drinking and I just didn't want to do the same with my Uncle Jack. I did manage to stay sober for two weeks, but I was absolutely miserable. Every day of those two weeks, it felt like pins and needles were escaping out every pore. It's beyond words. I hoped I was cured, though, and when the check came in, I took a twelve-pack to the parking lot behind Little Five Points, in the apartment grass adjacent, and I drank those beers. I thought if sobriety sucks that bad, I guess I'm just going to die an alcoholic. I wonder how many souls have thought exactly that.

Returning back to my house drunk that afternoon, I emailed Gwen and asked if I could come visit her. She asked if I would buy her some clothes, and I said sure, thinking that was just her ego trying to justify my visit, and I booked a flight to San Diego that afternoon, to leave in the next few days.

Leaving from the Atlanta airport, I ran into the director of the play I'd bailed on. She was cordial, but I could tell she was still upset. I didn't have much of an excuse, but it was nice to see her. She was on her way to Harvard to direct plays somewhere important. Made me wonder what other opportunities I'd blown from being drunk. Hell, all of them. So I got drunk on the plane ride out there of course.

I rented a car and went to find my hotel. Gwen called me back the first night, but stood me up, instead asking me to meet her at her doctor's appointment the next day, a Friday. Waiting in the parking lot of the doctor's office, everything felt the exact same. Waiting on Gwen, waiting to go to the doctor. She got there and we hugged, and I went into the office with her and waited in the lobby. Then we went out to dinner. She drank one drink and said her drinking had been much better since she got there. I drank one, and was miserable until she left to go home, and I was able to get back to the hotel and get tanked.

The next morning she wanted me to pick her up to take her clothes shopping, which I did. I spent over $500 dollars on her at an outlet mall that reminded me of Atlanta. America, every town has an Applebee's and an outlet mall. It's all the same shit, I told myself, and seeing Gwen didn't make me happy. Fishing in the Pacific didn't make me happy. I found out, and finally officially recognized on that trip, that I was just miserable if I wasn't getting and staying drunk. Gwen came back to my hotel, and we fooled around, but she wouldn't let me go as far as I wanted, or anywhere really. So we laid there, and she took some pills and fell asleep. I laid there, staring at the ceiling, pissed at myself. Feeling used, abused, manipulated, and now robbed once again, this woman had gotten me to fly all the way from Atlanta, after everything she'd done the previous fall, taking $2500 from me, leaving me rentless, carless, and lonely, and here I was staring at the ceiling while she slept in my arms, nevermind in reality it had been my idea to come to San Diego in the first place. For a brief instant, I was happy at simply having her in my arms, but then the resentments, the anger, and this new assault on my ego of buying her all these clothes, and getting no loving for it, affronted my pride. I snuck out of her grip, and went down to the bar to assuage my anger. I drank six or seven vodka and orange juices and when I went back upstairs, hoping to sneak, unnoticed back into her arms, but Gwen was storming the room like an angry girlfriend. We fought for a split second and she asked for a ride home. I called her a cab, gave her a hundred bucks and kicked her out of my hotel room. I passed out and woke up the next morning still seething.

I promptly jumped in the rental car, and went to a liquor store, bought a bottle of SKYY Vodka, and began heading my way to Tijuana, where I'd find a whore, a bar, oblivion, and if I was lucky, maybe just die. I wasn't that lucky. Parking my car at the border, I walked over and got a cab, which took me to a strip club inside Tijuana, with some of the ugliest women on Earth. I mean worse than the women we'd glanced at while in Amsterdam, these women were scary. After some tequila, though, and then one of them got me some coke, I was off to the races. I spent the night in that hellhole, I suppose in a dump room above the club, but I can barely remember.

I vaguely recall waking up, going straight to the strip club downstairs, and finding it completely empty. I remember paying for whiskey, and I remember fucking a whore in the VIP room, but most of the two days I was down there are a complete blackout. I remember being escorted to the ATM by a police officer or soldier. Draining my accounts until the ATM quit working, and then I remember being escorted back to the border by Mexican police with M-16's, but I couldn't tell you what for, and I couldn't tell you what happened. I know I spent a few thousand while in Mexico those two days, but I don't really know what happened to get me kicked out of the country. I remember thinking the US wouldn't let me back in, and then being relieved when they were happy to let my drunk ass in. I was ecstatic to get a double cheeseburger at McDonalds, right inside the US line. I was thrilled to find my car, and I was very happy to get back to my hotel room, walk to the liquor store, and continue my bender unabated. I was glad I hadn't gone to jail, but I didn't know what the fuck had happened, and being scared, decided to spend the rest of my holiday, safe and secure inside the Holiday Inn. If I was brave, maybe I'd venture down to the adjoining Applebee's, and that's exactly what I did. That, and drunk dial every single person I knew, including Gwen, threatening to kick her roommates' asses, my stepdad, saying God knows what, and of course the regulars, my poor friends Adam, Henry, and Corey. Of all those drunk dials, I remember my stepdad being more than kind for some reason. I was lost, and I think I was talking about suicide. I stayed drunk in that hotel room for about three days straight.

Appeasing the Boss by Going to AA

Eventually, I made it back to Atlanta. No job, about 8k less than when I'd left for San Diego, and as God has done for me my whole life, a miracle presented itself. Brian Huff and Christopher Stanley, who I'd fucked over while at PMC Financial, offered to give me a job recruiting for their small company, CV Confidential. Having zero other prospects, I took the job, and, within a week of starting, began being late to work every day. I was miserable, though. I wanted to quit drinking, but couldn't. I tried another AA meeting to no avail and I wrote about my state of mind.

Personal Journal, July 22nd, 2005;

Bombs in London, I dreamt of my mom again. She was beautiful, and it made me cry in my dream. She was with Jenny and Becca (her sisters) and said "Bryan, did you forget someone?" I had to pray in my dream to Christ that I had given Jake to Jenna, his grandma, and that I hadn't gotten drunk and forgotten him somewhere. She said he was turning out great despite having an alcoholic for a father, and that it turned out, having a drunk for a brother was a good thing. Vivid, I had a girlfriend and a truck she couldn't drive for shit, as we rode it around aimlessly.

I continued along at CV Confidential, though I still hadn't closed much, and I was not getting any better on the drinking front. Every weekend, I'd promise Brian and Christopher that this week would be better, but things just kept getting uglier. A month later, I wrote again in my journal:

Personal Journal, August 23rd, 2005;

... "I just lost my gas, so no shower tomorrow morning. I haven't cooked for myself in ages. I'm a raging drunk, but I can't stand those damn meetings. I should just force myself to go, I'm so tired of being in debt, and being a drunk, or as I've been hearing more lately, a dork. Guess I'm not as funny as I think I am when I'm drunk. I just wish I wasn't so miserable when I was sober. Went to a shrink and he all but gave up on me once he "discovered" I was an alcoholic. Big revelation genius. I've known that for years. I want to stop, it's pure sin for me, and I'm fat and ugly because of it. Not to mention broke again. I burn through cash as soon as I get it, on whores, drink then drugs, then sometimes if I'm lucky, violence, but never productivity, never serving others, always just thinking of myself. Pure selfishness. I wish God would come to me and tell me how to quit. I went 13 days and that's the longest in 5 years. 5 fucking years. I'm a social stigma to my brother and sister, my dying mother wouldn't look at me as she was dying, and I couldn't let her die outside because I was too drunk to convince my family it was the best thing. The only reason I'm not killing a bottle right now is that I'm dirt poor and luckily had a Xanax. I hate it, but I can't stop it. I miss my mom. I miss my dad. I miss Jakebird (my son), and Anne Marie's unwavering love and that of her family's is the only reason I haven't killed myself. That and the fear of hell. I have to quit drinking, failure is not an option. Whatever it takes, if I have to walk to Argentina, do it, but get this God damn shit over with."

It would be another year before I'd really try to quit. The shrink had asked me a few questions the same day I wrote this, and, basically, when he found out I was a drunk, he had turned his brain off. He told me to go to AA, that they were the experts in quitting drinking, and that he couldn't help an alcoholic at all. Their mental twists were too intense to even assist, if they were still drinking. He suggested I go to 8111 on Roswell Road. I suggested he prescribe me some Adderall to assist me during the days at work, and Xanax to slow my drinking down at night, and he laughed in my face. Seemed like a good idea at the time, but he wasn't buying it. I also asked him if being obsessive compulsive had any relation to drinking and he said he didn't think so, but to come back and discuss it if I ever decided to get sober. It would be a while before there was enough pain for something that drastic.

Still I would manage to write at least, allowing my conscious the bare minimum of defenses as a struggling artist, misunderstood, dejected:

Spiral

The spiral picks up pace towards the end.
No amount of pills or prayers,
This pain doesn't pass like the wind.
A tragedy of free will and choice,
I've decided to kill myself slow.
Ironically in the pursuit of life,
Addiction to the world only kills.
Look to the sky for pleasure,
The quick ways all have their price.
You'll pay for eternity according to God.
What a bitch, I hope that's bullshit.
For if it's not, I'll burn in hell,
For selfishly drinking and doing drugs,
Since I knew they were there.
Such is life, such is death.
At the end of the day,
There's simply too much inequity,
My soul should ignite in the next breath.
I am sorry, I wish I was better.
I'm just not. I'm an addict of everything,
Cigarettes, beer, opium, coke, I'm fucked.
Do better than me son. Say no.

-JB Smith

To appease Brian Huff and Christopher Stanley, though, I moved away from Little Five Points, into an abandoned home that Anne Marie's uncle owned in Roswell. It had been all but condemned, not even possessing a mailbox, and was over a hundred years old, but it could be fixed up, was free to stay in, and would get me out of Little Five Points, which I was sure was the root of all my problems. Except, starting over again, I found, I stayed just as drunk in Roswell, as I'd been in Little Five. Wherever I went, there I was. Son of a bitch.

I closed a couple of deals at CV Confidential, one with Catrina Huffington on the day Hurricane Katrina hit New Orleans, placing her at a Fortune 100 downtown, and then a couple of weeks later, I identified a candidate escaping New Orleans, and placed her at a multimedia conglomerate located at Perimeter, so I thought I had some leeway with work, but probably not as much as I took. The week of my birthday, I basically disappeared from CV Confidential, while Melissa Gilbreath and her husband Cem Yilmaz were in town, and spent a lot of time wasted with them, right back to my old stomping grounds of Little Five Points. Brian Huff, my boss, blew my phone up with messages, and I turned the phone off. I spent all my paycheck, and all the trust Brian had had in me, and it even got to the point of my brother being called and him tracking me down, to tell me what a fuck up I was being. I remember telling my brother I had Brian just where I wanted him and not to worry about it. After about a week of missing work, I called Brian, and he told me I was fired. He told me I was super fast racing boat, dragging three tons of anchors. Ultimately, he told me to go to AA.

I didn't want to, but I figured I'd do it to appease him, keep my job, and then things would get back to normal, whatever the fuck that was. I'd join the gym, too, it would be a self improvement kick. I didn't really need AA, I thought, but I'd give it a shot and not drink, and keep my job. Obviously, I wouldn't quit everything, I would smoke weed everyday, and that would be just fine. I didn't want to give up my entire life, I mean c'mon, it hadn't been that bad. Right?!

So in late October, early November of 2005, I pull up to my first AA meeting at 8111, right off of Roswell Road, in Sandy Springs, Georgia. As soon as I arrived, and opened my car door, a strange thing happened. I got out of the vehicle and a Bic lighter fell from my pocket, bounced off the car door, hit the pavement, and exploded into a million little pieces. I'd never seen a lighter do that in all my years of smoking, and it left an impression on me. Because of that Bic explosion, I wouldn't forget the first time I pulled into 8111, the Sandy Springs AA Clubhouse.

I walked into that meeting and heard all the reasons I wasn't an alcoholic. For one thing, I could quit drinking, I just didn't like to. These people sounded like they couldn't stop, period. Also, in general, they all looked old. Also, most of them were ugly, and most of them were crazy. I did find, though, that it made it easier those first few days and weeks, not to drink, but that, I couldn't wait to get home and smoke my few hits on a joint, that I'd allocated to myself, for being such a model employee. I didn't follow any suggestions from within AA, and I didn't decide to do the suggested 90 meetings in 90 days, I didn't get a sponsor I could work with, I got one who would suffice, and who if need be, my boss could call and would appease him. I went to the meetings, but I wasn't yet teachable.

I went home the very first night, and smoked two hits off a joint, and was just fine. It was going to be easy to quit drinking, I told myself. You could have made a flowchart for addiction with how unwell my marijuana maintenance program went. The second night, I smoked half a joint, the third a whole joint, and by the end of the second week, I was waking up, smoking a joint, and was cranky and irritable all day long until I made it home, after my meeting, to smoke yet another joint. All the characteristics of my failed marijuana maintenances from high school began popping up as well. Sleeping through the alarm, being slow and forgetful, leaving my keys, cell phone and wallet everywhere. Forgetting everybody's name, a crucial piece of being a recruiter. Remembering people's names, sounds basic, but introduce yourself to a stoner... a few times, see what I mean.

After about three weeks, I realized I was smoking too much weed, and was still craving a drink, but I figured I'd give it 30 days, and by then my drinking could go on like normal people's did. But the graph by which I began smoking more and more, was ever there in my mind, and for one of the very first times, I remember thinking, "What if I just can't quit drinking and doing drugs at all? Then I'm doomed." For the very first time, I was very scared about my addictions. Up until that point, I had really just lied to myself repeatedly, that I was only drinking because I wanted to. That I drank for the same reason a dog licked his balls, because he could. For the first time, I really was frightened that I might just be fucked. I think deep down I'd always suspected it, but I'd always been able to navigate the troubled waters, or maybe the addiction just wasn't as bad, but this go around, a sense of doom shadowed me that I may be destined to die an alcoholic death, just like my father, and that it was closer now than it had ever been.

Probation Violation

I was still clinging to the marijuana maintenance program, not working the steps, and I was now dating an AA chick, Caroline Gerard, who I'd noticed drinking from airplane bottles of vodka during the meetings. Two weeks into my first stint in AA, I got pulled over after dropping Caroline off at her parents' house. The officer told me I was violating probation. I'd already answered to the assault and battery charges from 2001, and I'd been put on probation a year before, around the time my mom had died. I'd even bribed the probation officer with Falcon's tickets to have him write off my community service hours, as I'd found him sweating at his desk over a bottle of Oxycontins, and I knew instantly he was crooked, and probably even "Family". A year before, he'd accepted those tickets and said my probation was over. When I moved from Little Five Points, I didn't leave a forwarding address, I thought that shit dating back to a bar fight in 2001 was all over.

When the officer ran my license, he came back and told me I had warrants. Just like that, I was arrested. Being in Cobb County, I was transferred to their jail system to await transport to Atlanta's infamous Rice Street jail. I would wait 12 hours for a Fulton County Marshall to show up to deliver me to Rice Street. I knew it was a probation violation, but I wouldn't really know how it all came down for days, I was just pissed and resentful that here I was trying to get sober (well, mostly), and two weeks into it, the law was still fucking with me. I called my boss, Brian Huff, once I got to Rice Street and told him my status. He worked his ass off to get me out of there, but the level of incompetence in Rice Street is unprecedented. They've had Federal scrutiny over them for years now, it's so bad.

The first night in Rice Street I was in a room with 25 black men and myself. I didn't sleep a wink. Sometime during the night, the guards delivered a frail old black man, who'd been beaten by the police, and was having trouble breathing. His pacemaker had been ripped out of his chest, and the guards refused to listen to his pleas for help or my pleas to take him to the hospital. He went into convulsions in that jail cell, and died in the middle of the room. He was in there 30 minutes before the guards moved him out. That place is a hellhole.

I called Brian Huff again the next morning, surprised he hadn't gotten me out immediately, and he told me he was shocked I wasn't already out. He said my probation officer faxed the release form to the jail the day before. I pleaded with the guards who were either malicious or incompetent, but they would just respond, each and every time with some variation of "Shut up, white boy, fax is broken," or "Shut the fuck up, cracker, we lost your paperwork," and went about ignoring me completely for the next three days and nights. It was a nightmare not knowing when I would get out. Living in Little Five points I'd heard rumors of people being locked up in Atlanta or Dekalb for months because of reverse racism, sheer incompetence, or who knows why. Anytime I'd ask about anything, no matter how politely, the response was "Boy, you'd better shut your mouth or we'll lose your paperwork for good." That was scary and beyond frustrating.

I blamed the system the whole time I was in there. Never did I look at my own part in being there, just the unconstitutionality of my detention over a bar fight from 2001 for which the victim didn't even press charges. But the state had done so unfairly, and probably for no other reason than to incur revenue and work for this inept, corrupt probation system. Job creation. Maddening bureaucracy, and abuse. Never mind that I'd given some random stranger over a hundred stitches. This was just plain unfair bullshit in my mind.

Every night, 20 or more black men and me would fight over floor space, and I would barely sleep, miserable and scared that if I did sleep, I'd get raped. Eventually, 4 days later, they found my paperwork, and that caused me and a few others slated for release to wait in a cell as they finalized our papers. I was relieved and exhausted. They marched about ten of us into a smaller holding cell supposedly near the exit, and about 20 minutes after they put us in that cell, alarms and lights went off and the entire Rice Street jail went on lockdown because of an escape. I had been so close. This room was even worse: it had no ventilation, and the water in the sink or the toilet didn't work. Eight excruciatingly painful hours later, a guard came by to tell us the lockdown was over. It would be another full hour before they let us out.

I was so tired and relieved to be free that I didn't even complain to the news cameras outside covering the escape. I walked straight to the liquor store. I thought about buying a drink but instead just bought cigarettes and called my boss, Brian. He gave me a ride home and my car was already there waiting as my sweet former wife Anne Marie had met the policeman there as I was handcuffed in the back seat and led to Cobb County all those nights before, when the whole ordeal began. Two weeks, partially sober, with no alcohol, at least, yet the wreckage of my past was right there behind me, breathing down my neck, waiting.

Caroline laughed when I told her I'd been in jail for four days. She said "That sounds about right." She was the perfect girlfriend for an alcoholic. When I reported to probation the next day after getting out of Rice Street, I walked into the lobby and sat down right next to my old probation officer.

"What the fuck?" I said confused he was in the lobby instead of behind the locked door, behind a desk like usual.

"Oh, man, I got busted taking bribes." He stated, matter-of-factly.

I rolled my eyes...just my luck.

"Not mine, right?" I hoped.

"Nah man, we're cool." He whispered.

"Man!" I was both pissed and relieved.

"Mr. Smith?" At that moment, I looked up to see a no-nonsense female probation officer this time. She apologized for the broken fax machine at Rice Street, though I still thought that was bullshit. She said I hadn't paid any of my fines or done my community service. It had been a year and I didn't have any filed receipts, that's for damn sure. I also didn't have any legitimate community service hours. I had a month to come up with them both. It was bullshit, I'd paid all my fines and forged my community service hours, and they'd both been signed off on, but the asshole who'd signed off on them was now waiting in the lobby, suffering the same shit as me. I didn't have much of an argument.

I learned my lesson though. I wouldn't bribe the probation officer, I'd bribe the community service center instead. And that's exactly what I did. I paid the fines again, and presented false hours, and walked away scot free. Well, minus the double fines and the four days in Rice Street. Alcoholics will always find the shortcuts, or think they have, at least. That's the high cost of low living.

The New Girl

But things were looking up at work at least. I had something like five deals, all SEC Reporting roles, in their final phases of interviews, and I had to believe that it was God's way of rewarding me for getting sober, or making the attempt. I'd also been in the gym every day of those initial 28 days, and even though I'd stayed stoned, I hadn't missed any work. I'd been slow, and I'd been late, but my productivity was at least better than when I had been hungover. I was mildly proud of myself, and thought there may be something to this sober stuff after all. Especially if it was going to make me rich, right?

The step work seemed a bit overboard though. I'd sworn to myself to never under any circumstances share that I'd stolen morphine from my dying mother, because it was just so damn ugly. Nobody ever needed to know that, so being completely honest about a fourth step was ruled out by me early on. I wasn't telling some stranger sponsor how sick I'd once been, forget about it.

Another one of the things they tell you when you come into AA is to not get in a serious relationship until you've got a year sober. This was one of my biggest objections, as I'd been in back-to-back relationships since I kissed Adrian Whitehead in the fourth grade. If I wasn't in one, I was looking for one, and I'd admitted my codependency to myself long before I'd admitted to myself about my alcoholism. So, of course, I met a girl. These idiots in AA didn't know anything anyway, I thought, and besides, we were perfect for each other. She was sober and miserable, and so was I.

We fooled around a little bit, both of us sober and awkward and discontent, and for whatever reason the magic just hadn't happened yet. I didn't know how to make a move sober, and apparently neither did she, or at least she didn't want to. I know we went to one meeting together on a Friday, and it was my 28th day "sober." The entire meeting focused around not getting in relationships until you'd worked the twelve steps. Bah, humbug. Roger Henderson, the man leading the meeting didn't know shit about being single, he'd been sober since the Earth had cooled, and married since dinosaurs quit hunting humans. I knew better than this old goober. I would notice later that, even though I hated most of what that man said, I could remember almost every word of it. At the time though, in my mind, he didn't know what the hell he was talking about. I had 28 days "sober," a beautiful girl at my side, and was even about to close 30k worth of deals at work. I'd be just fine, cupcake, lead your meeting about something else. I resented being the focal point of that meeting. It's always about me upstairs.

We went to a comedy show that night, and afterwards we laughed about how the old timer had picked on us during the meeting, and how those ancestors didn't know shit about life, and we'd stay sober just fine. The Comedy Club we went to must have gotten an email from Roger Henderson about us, because the comedian's entire show was devoted to AA. He told AA jokes I'd never heard, that I would later hear an infinite number of times, but it was spooky, and I guess, as would be said now, was one of our first God shots. Synchronicity, coincidence revolving around the program of AA. To leave an AA meeting to go on one of our first dates, and hear nothing but AA jokes was pretty coincidental. He told such classics as "I'm allergic to alcohol, every time I drink I break out in handcuffs," and then threw in how it would be funny to put LSD in the coffee pots at an AA meeting and watch everybody sharing about trails and colors. We laughed, but it was ominous, for sure.

We went back to my rat shack that night, and began to watch TV, both of us obsessively thinking about drinking. I said, "Well, we could just drink tonight, and just drink once every 28 days, and it would still be better than being sober for life, right?" She agreed wholeheartedly without pause, and we went to the liquor store and bought a twelve-pack. We drank six beers apiece, and had sex easily together for the first time in our dating. It was phenomenal, and we swore we would just drink that night, but we agreed that maybe it was just the social lubricant we needed to break through the ice, and it was a good thing. We told each other sweet lies, and I slept easily for the first time in my 28 days of partial sobriety.

The next day we starting drinking around noon, and from there on we were off to the races. We had lied ourselves right into a relationship, and right back into drinking. But, hell, I told myself, if I quit for 28 days, I can quit anytime. And I didn't regret it one bit. At first, I was just a little superstitious, that maybe to drink was to die for me, but having drunk and lived, it was on. Back to the races.

Ironically, the weekend after I drank, all five deals I had in the pipeline fell apart almost instantaneously, and I was negative in my draw at work, which in sales is the worst place you can be. It was like I was being punished for not quitting drinking. If nothing else I was beginning to think that maybe drinking was plain old fashioned bad luck for me. As if those deals were gifts from God in the first place, and then had been taken from me as a slap in the face from God to me for not quitting. Well, I'd fix that, I'd just work twice as hard, I'd make it happen on my terms, and I didn't need his help.

I'd been working on a solution for hangovers for a while in my head, and it was time to implement the plan. Caroline, my new

AA girlfriend, had mentioned I should get on Adderall.

The Adderall Cure

In anticipation of the massive hangovers and the lack of productivity, I went to Adam Archer's family doctor, dropped his name, told him I'd been diagnosed with ADHD several times over, which was true and I needed Adderall, for which he prescribed 90 milligrams a day. I had found the solution to my drinking. I could drink as much as I wanted, wake up, pop two pills and jam like I hadn't skipped a beat, all day every day, working like a recruiting Terminator, talking a million miles a minute, making an ungodly number of phone calls and placing more online ads, nationwide, in a week, than I'd done the entire previous year. I was on fire. I was cured. Adderall was God's gift to alcoholics! I would be rich now. Nothing would stop me I thought.

When I'd gotten the Adderall prescription, they also found that all my liver functions were off the chart. I had an ultrasound and the nurse told me everything was OK. Rather than follow up with the doctor like I was supposed to, I just assumed everything was fine and went right along drinking. Briefly, I had the thought of Chad Major, my boss at PMC Financial, mentioning his sponsor had had hepatitis C, "the bad kind," and was very sick from it. But again, I was able to compartmentalize that ominous quote, and go right on drinking and using like nothing had happened. Hell, I'd found the miracle drug for alcoholics. Who cares that my piss was a darker shade of brown every single day?

I'd even found the miracle girlfriend for alcoholics, another alcoholic. As long as I fed her alcohol, she was great. Sex whenever I wanted, never bitched about my drinking, and a tight little body, that probably wasn't eating healthily, but sure wasn't fat. So what if she passed out every single night? That was perfect timing for me to smoke weed and play video games. One night, after I got off the computer from slaying geeks online in Battlefield 2, I turned on the TV and looked at her passed out. "Well, at least she doesn't eat cat food," I thought to myself. My standards weren't that low. Just about then, she opened her eyes and looked at the door to the bathroom, then she looked at me. She grinned, closed her eyes, and pissed herself right then and there on my leather couch, barely conscious, but grinning the whole time. So much for standards. "Meh, at least the couch was leather," I thought, perfectly stoned out. I took off her pants and threw them in the dryer, and dragged her into bed. "Oh well," I'd justify it, "You gotta take the good with the bad." It was still better than eating cat food. We crashed and still woke up on time for work. We were functional alcoholics, I lied to myself constantly.

Still, I proved my productivity was way up to Brian and Christopher, and I set a goal of closing 200k in 2006. I read Think and Grow Rich every single night, drunk or sober, and I stated my mantra daily beginning in January of 2006, and right on through May. We placed a couple of candidates through this timeframe, keeping me just above my draw, but I wouldn't see major success until May of that year. Meanwhile, I was talking a million miles a minute, day in and day out, was drunk every single night, but was making so much progress at work that they kept me on, and put up with my antics a little while longer.

We signed contracts with 3 major corporations, all Fortune 50's and several others, and we had a ton of business in the hopper, but I was slowly and steadily losing my mind, more so than I'd ever done before in my life. Nothing is written in my journal from the time I took Adderall on, but enough long drawn out emails exist that I'll never be able to run for politics. Despite my increased productivity, I was still managing to piss my bosses off incredibly well.

With the new work ethic came a new ego, came the realization that, with this new drug, Adderall, I could easily run my own company again. Somewhere in the back of my mind, I thought it would even be a good idea to get a company name and website, and actually tell my bosses about it, stating it was simply to have a duplicate name, a way to creatively recruit out of Big 4 and appeal to them, since CV Confidential was such a crappy name, my ego thought. I adamantly told my bosses my new strategies and they watched me with a growing concern and suspicion for my motivations. In all my jacked up brilliance and militaristic creativity, still obsessed with reading every news article I could get my hands on about Iraq and Afghanistan, I came up with the name Seek And Employ, Inc. and had the website designed while I was still working with CV Confidential.

Caroline and I were drinking every single night now, unabated, almost always twelve beers or more, and it still didn't faze me, due to God's gift to drunks, Adderall, or as it says on the prescription bottles, amphetamines. I didn't care, it did amazing things for my self confidence, for my productivity, and ultimately, for my ego. I even began writing a book about recruiting, Seek And Employ, An Ethical Guide to Modern Headhunting. I mean who better to write it, I'd successfully run two recruiting companies into the ground, and had been doing this recruiting gig since 2000. I should write a book! And so I did, as I'm doing now, minus the Adderall, and God willing, with a lot more humility.

During those first few months of 2006, I must have made a million phone calls. I was staying late at night, I was placing tons of ads, and I was even working through severe chest pain I would occasionally get from eating so many amphetamines, and having a heart condition. "Fuck it," I told myself, if I die trying to accomplish my dreams, who cares? I wanted to close 200k, I wanted to bank 100k, and I wanted to launch Seek And Employ, Inc. to become a millionaire, and that's all I wanted, and I was going to make it happen no matter what! I continued on with my mantra, "I will close 200k by being the best recruiter I can possibly be by December 31st, 2006." I would religiously chant this, and I believed it with all my heart and soul. I also believed this combination of drinking and amphetamines would go hand and hand together indefinitely without harmful side effects, but unfortunately, my beliefs really weren't founded in reality. I'd ignored the test results on my liver, but when I started pissing almost black instead of the brown from the last year or so constantly, and painfully, I don't know why alarm bells didn't start ringing. Somehow, though, I'd write it off, I'd make 200k and that's all that mattered.

Secret Commission from the CIA

Around April of 2006, I also began seeing connections where they didn't exist, and coincidences too strong not to mean something cohesive in my mind. One of the first real examples I remember is when I began to suspect that a major chemical company's search for Arabic-speaking, American-born auditors, was actually an undercover way for me to find CIA and NSA candidates, without them letting me know. I mean Arabic-speaking auditors, that had to be born in the US, and the major chemical client reaching out to me to find them? Yes, I'd called every single one of their Internal Auditors, through a roster I'd purchased from a friend, but certainly they had simply recognized my superior talents as a recruiter, done their research, and realized that there was no one better to assist the CIA than J. Bryan Smith. With ego as expanded as it had ever been, having just written a book for God's sake, and with 200k in deals just waiting to fall into place, certainly this had to be the case, right?

I was already obsessed with any and all news regarding the

war on terrorism since 2001, and hadn't slowed down obsessing over it whatsoever. So perhaps, just maybe this was finally my shot at helping the nation I so dearly loved. Surely someone high up had researched my name, seen that I was capable of keeping a secret, given my experiences with drugs and the law back in my high school days, that my family had military ties, my grandfather being a Colonel in the Air Force, and for all I knew was in the OSS -- I mean, it wasn't impossible to imagine.

And so I was honored to search out Arabic-speaking auditors for this international chemical company, wink, wink. The irony there is that in placing ads for Arabic-speaking auditors, I ended up making a placement of a candidate at one of my local clients, but never actually did place one with the international chemical company. Still, I was involved in national security, I thought, but I wouldn't tell anyone anything, because, you know, I was on a need-to-know basis, and right then, I didn't need to know. I would keep it to myself while I closed these deals, and somehow, it would all work itself out.

The international chemical client's search for Arabic-speaking auditors hadn't started out as a grandiose undercover spy operation, but just a normal job search. It was my own imagination, and moreover, my gloating about the search to anyone who would listen, that allowed it to grow in my mind to such a national security priority. I remember telling Greg Gerard, Caroline's father, about the search once or twice, implying I suspected its intelligence gathering potential, before even I would swallow the lie. But the more I relayed my suspicions, the more it would become cold hard fact in my head, until eventually it was just a matter of course. I was recruiting for the CIA, under the cloak of recruiting for this international chemical client. Come to think of it, it was about damn time someone high up had recognized my superior recruiting skills. And so the lies would grow, and the dots, universes apart, fueled by Adderall and drinking, would become connected in my deluded, grandiose little mind.

Fired Again

I had begun Seek And Employ, Inc. initially to just be a front company for CV Confidential, but I would soon need it, as the house of cards at CV Confidential was about to topple. Probably, starting a company and developing a website and an obvious exit strategy, all while telling the managing partners all about it, didn't help to get the trigger pulled on me, either. Another development of that spring had been bringing in Shane Oleander, one of my best friends, to train and become an accounting and financial recruiter. He had been in jail, due to numerous drinking and drugging offenses, but I told Brian Huff he would be amazing at the job, would work super cheap in order to get out of jail, and could sell ice cream to eskimos, all of which was true. They paid him ten bucks an hour, with the promise that after 90 days if he proved himself, they would bring him up to a decent draw, and give him health insurance and the whole nine yards. It never occurred to me that I was training my replacement, because, you know, I was doing national intelligence work as well. But I should have seen it coming. I trained Shane well, even wrote my book so he could use it to train, though I don't believe he actually read it. But still, he listened and learned, and in all my years and half a dozen of potential recruiters I'd tried to train, Shane Oleander picked it up the fastest, and implemented it with the most results. It probably didn't hurt that he inherited my entire book of business, once I was fired, but I believe he'd have done well regardless. You see, he was sober. Whereas I was losing my mind, some days quickly, and some days slowly, but it was going.

Around May of 2006, Brian pulled me into a side room on a Monday and said I was fired. I told him, he couldn't fire me, I was about to close five deals, and he actually gave me until the end of that week to prove it. By this time, though, a tough thing was beginning to take place. Around 5 PM every day, I absolutely had to have a drink. 30 milligrams of Adderall in the morning, followed by 30 milligrams at lunch, definitely left me parched. I mean I would start getting crazy around four or so, and so at five on the dot, I'd hit the road. I couldn't even make it all the way home, I had to pull into a nearby bar, and simply had to have a drink. It just couldn't wait and that was a first even for me. I wasn't worried about that, though, and I wasn't worried about them trying to fire me. I had two deals at a major financial services firm almost done, one at my best multimedia client, and a Manager at a major fortune 100 downtown, all within days of closing and then it would be smooth sailing. In the back of my mind I must have been debating quitting anyway, because Brian and I were arguing every day, but I was so drunk, almost all the time by this stage, I can't quite remember the transition perfectly.

I closed every single deal I thought I was going to close, roughly 100k in billings, and thinking that I'd just proven to Brian and the world how amazing I was, and I was going to the next phase of life, success, and happiness -- when lo and behold, Brian and Christopher fired me and I was instantly jobless. Within a few phone calls I had found out real fast that nobody was interested in my drunk, high-on-amphetamines, 100% attitude, ass. I was pissed off to no extent. All the anger I'd ever felt in my life condensed into those moments after CV Confidential fired me. I could think about it for a while and begin seeing red. I would stay lividly angry for weeks and months to come, and not only that anger would build up, but all the resentments I'd built up of my family, the government, you name it, and that anger would drive me mad. Literally.

They fired me, told me they would only pay the commissions after all the guarantee periods were up, which is to say in six months or so, basically leaving me penniless. They handed all of my accounts over to my best friend, Shane Oleander, who wouldn't give me any information, and who wouldn't even bring me my files, for fear of losing his job that he needed. They'd let him bring me a box with maybe 25% of the shit I'd left on and around my desk, and it took every bit of prayer, clear thinking, advise from my Uncle Jack, Stewart Black, and everyone else that would listen to my crazy ass, that I didn't have a legal recourse, that I was penniless and powerless, and that I needed to move on, because they would win any court case. I was doomed, and completely and utterly at their mercy. I panicked, not believing for a second that they would pay me after the guarantee periods, and while drunk, angry and impatient, settled for 10k of the roughly 50k or so that they owed me, as well as the right to continue working the deals I'd been working with my new company, Seek And Employ, that I'd conveniently already built a website for. They agreed and we went our separate ways, but this paragraph doesn't do justice to the amount of cussing, screaming, and yelling that Brian Huff and I did with each other to reach that point. I hated him, I felt plotted against, conspired against, used and abused, and I felt it was all his fault. I spent weeks seething and angry, and ultimately powerless over the entire process. At one point Brian actually asked me to meet him to fight, and like a pussy, I left my house, drove to Little Five and got drunk at Elmyr. I was certain it was a setup, that he'd have me arrested.

I was so enraged, though, at the entire world, that I couldn't see the forest through the trees. Everybody on Earth was conspiring against me. Brian Huff and Christopher Stanley had conspired to fire me and keep all my commissions, my stepdad had abandoned me and stolen all of my inheritance. I was certain my brother and sister had helped conspire against me as well. I was sure that my mom had left money to Anne Marie to help her and her new husband with a new house, and once again leaving me in the lurch, and I was sure that none of them wanted anything to do with me. I was mad at God, for taking my mom and dad, for taking my money from CV Confidential right before it was due to me, and I was mad at the universe in general, for allowing God to be such an asshole. I began thinking about the Devil a considerable amount of time, and I began thinking perverse thoughts, such as perhaps Jesus himself was the Devil, fooling everyone that we could be forgiven our sins, when in fact we were all just worshipping the Devil, lost in his deceit, lost in general. And the chaos and the paranoia continued unabated.

I was also certain, that in our high stakes business, Brian was tapping my phones, and checking all my emails. He actually had been reading my emails while I was working for him, as I'd tested it by sending an email to myself about him, that he read, and I was able to tell by how pissed he was the following day. But even after I'd been fired and was a few weeks removed from CV Confidential, I was certain he'd hacked my computers and was reading every keystroke I typed. I began changing my Yahoo passwords daily, and I increasingly would see connections where connections didn't exist. Some days I would change my passwords three or more times, and once I bought a new keyboard, just in case.

Seek and Employ

With paranoia and delusions growing, I settled for the 10k and I began Seek and Employ, Inc. in earnest. Unfortunately I also began my drinking and Adderall usage in earnest as well. Up until this point I'd at least been able to not drink until 5, but with Brian Huff off my back, and my business to run in my own way, fuck it, I'd begin drinking when I damn well wanted to begin drinking. It worked fine for a while, but that paranoia and delusional thinking continued to get the best of me. Drinking from noon on would exacerbate things...quickly.

I began posting ads internationally for Arabic-speaking auditors, and I began receiving resumes from all over the world. I began dropping hints to everyone that would listen that I was recruiting for the CIA, and even though deep down I knew it was bullshit, it became exciting and I began to live it, and love the adventure of it. The possibility that Al-Qaeda could someday come looking for me, and that I'd have to kill some Islamic terrorists, began to consume me. I began pacing my house, waiting for them to come, and ultimately I really began to scare Caroline, who up until this point had really just gone along for the ride.

I closed a couple of deals at a privately-held Buckhead-based

239

software company, staying afloat by the skin of my ass, as deals would close and I'd collect in just the nick of time to continue my drinking and drugging rampage. I drank clear through June and into early July, and the unconnected dots began presenting themselves clearly. I really was working for the CIA.

Still obsessively reading every news article ever printed on the web, through Drudge Report, Jane's Weekly, CNN, Fox News, and anywhere else I could get the news, I read about a thwarted attempt in London, where they'd arrested several suspected terrorists who'd attempted to travel to the states through Heathrow. In my mind, the names looked identical to several of the candidates that had sent their resumes to me via Craigslist for the Arabic-speaking auditor jobs I was continuing to post all over the world for free, as Craigslist will allow any delusional jackass to do. The names in fact matched the resumes I had. I don't remember researching the names all that thoroughly, but I they were close to the names I'd received from Egypt, Italy, and Britain, close enough for me to believe, anyway, and I was at first, mighty proud of myself. And then in the following days, arrests were actually made in connection with the bombing attempts, in Italy and Egypt, and my pride once ballooned, now turned into fear. Crazy, paranoid delusional, fear.

That fear would spark into a psychosis unlike anything I'd ever experienced or ever wish on my worst enemy. I ran to my blinds and began peeking out them immediately. At any moment Al-Qaeda could rush my door. And certainly, the CIA, NSA, and FBI, were all keeping tabs on me in order to ambush the terrorists. I'd been set up! I was a pawn in this huge espionage game, and though we'd saved a 747 full of hapless citizens, I told myself magnanimously, they were watching me and waiting for the terrorists to show up.

As if to reinforce my beliefs or maybe I was just being tested, I went to buy beer and using my passport, the Arabic guy behind the counter said "Oh, American passport, worth a lot of money nowadays." My eyes got real big and I thought about jumping over the counter and strangling him to death in the name of patriotism, but it probably would have slowed down how quickly I could drink the beer I needed so badly.

I got home and called Homeland Security on his terrorist ass. They had to know I was an undercover operative anyway, so they could take care of that obvious suspect from here on out. I'd just sit back and enjoy my beer from the house, until we got bored and antsy and went out on the town, feeling heroic. That night, everywhere Caroline and I went, I was convinced there were agents, watching our backs, protecting us.

I didn't leave my house for a few days after that. I built a lamp out of an American flag that I cut up, which I thought at the time was patriotic, plus an Air Force flag, a bicycle tire, several trips to Home Depot, and liquid nails. I thought it was a masterpiece, my girlfriend thought I was a nut. She was closer to the truth than I was, I just thought I was being resourceful. It took several days to build the lamp, but it was beautiful in my mind. My girlfriend disagreed, and so did my neighbor, who I brought over to share this with.

I also got him to give me a ride to the liquor store a few times, in which I broke my cover to him, and told him I was undercover with the CIA, and he was so unsurprised, I immediately recognized his involvement. Of course, that's why that Winnebago had been parked there for so long! He was in on the plot! All the agents were inside, watching my house. When I went to inspect the Winnebago in the dead of night, finding it completely empty, I realized the level this conspiracy had risen to. They were in a different dimension, making them completely and utterly invisible. Anything is plausible in that state of mind: different dimensions, time travel, and even aliens would all become handy explanations as I fell deeper into the rabbit hole of insanity. Why not, it's the perfect strategy? As soon as we shared the Atom bomb with the world, people began copying our inventions. Surely now, when we create new and incredible technologies, we didn't share it with the world, but kept it silent, deadly, and secret. I would run back to my house, enlightened.

I was part of a vast network of spies, and I was being watched by invisible agents. It all made perfect sense. I was also out of amphetamines, so I would need to get more of those as well, but I'd do that when the bottle was almost empty. For now, I must make Arabic-speaking auditor job postings online, and once finished, go to the North River Tavern, the old Taco Mac by the River, and await my next orders. If I'd received one set through the international chemical client, surely my next orders were coming down the pipeline any day.

I would finger the bolts and screws poking from my ankle as I worked, posting Arabic-speaking Auditor Ads all over Craigslist, internationally, and nationally, and I would find the x-ray of the 5 long screws in my bones, the clear markings of serial numbers, and I would build a new and terrifying delusion, as if I hadn't created enough. The entire injury, was a CIA ruse, a plot to get serial numbers, and probably micro-chips into my ankles! It would be ok at first, who cares, I'm one of them, I didn't mind if they kept a close eye on me. But surely I had a government tracking device in my ankle, I mean, I hadn't paid a dime for all that ankle surgery at Grady, obviously they had installed some espionage related equipment. It was ok, it meant they were keeping a close eye on my back, they would know the second I was in trouble, and they would be there to help me out. Hell, I was practically invincible! I thought about carving it out with a knife that first night I'd brainstormed this new offshoot theory, but when I put the knife to skin, fortunately I thought of a softer, easier way. Putting my foot in water. That would temporarily stop the satellite tracking. So if ever I wanted to, ya know, go off the reservation as it were, I need only stick my foot in a bathtub or a bucket of water. Good to know. The very first night I thought this up, I would drink the night away, my right foot submerged in the bathtub for a while. That would throw the sensors off.

The Colonel and Tracking Muslims

And so again I was at North River Tavern babbling about my respect for the military, and my involvement in covert things I couldn't speak of, but was unable not to, when someone told me I should meet Stephen McPherson. I shook his hand, and we hit it off immediately. He was a Colonel in the Marine Corps he said, though he looked just like Freddy Krueger, or maybe like the Devil, and we began talking for hours that night. I asked him to come home and see some of the missions I was working on. He came over to my house, saw the Air Force flag lamp, the Arabic-speaking auditor job postings, and the resumes of the fugitive terrorists on the wall, who I'd convinced him, I had stopped from bombing a 747. We put Platoon in the DVD player and watched the whole movie, drinking and smoking, and me dreaming about killing Arabs personally in Afghanistan. I told him I'd do anything to get overseas, and he told me he'd see what he could do. He stayed the night the first night that I met him, and he was just as convinced as I was at how bloodthirsty I was to kill terrorists. I remember him saying to me, "You know the reason I was interested in speaking to you, Bryan? Because you were so open?" From the moment I met him, until the last time I saw him, I thought it was more than possible that he was the Devil himself.

My friend Spencer Jackson, a very intelligent, educated black man I'd befriended from my days at PMC Financial, came by to visit me after having not seen me for a year or so. We went to hang out with his friend Jamal, who he'd told me was Louis Farrakhan's son. Now I'd met Jamal before and thought nothing of it, but when I'd met him before, I wasn't working undercover for the CIA. Now it was clear, I'd been unknowingly surveilling these two Muslims the whole time! It all made sense to me now! We drank at The Tavern at Phipps for a while and then Spencer drove me home to pick up Caroline at my house and drive us up to the liquor store. At some point on the ride back from the liquor run, Spencer driving, Caroline in the front seat, he looked at me through the rearview mirror and I snapped, lunging towards the driver's side seat, and began choking him as he drove 50 miles an hour down Coleman Road in Roswell, a mile from the rat shack. A few seconds of choking him and yelling, I opened the door and jumped out of the moving car, rolled across a lane that thankfully didn't have any oncoming traffic, and landed in the bushes, having escaped the Muslim bastard! Later he would tell me he looked at Caroline and said "He's really crazy! I mean he's lost his mind!"

"Yup, that's Bryan...crazy," Caroline said very nonchalantly, used to the circus.

He dropped her and her beer and liquor off at the rat shack and left. When I returned, Caroline didn't even mention it, she was so used to my insanity and antics. Leaping from a speeding vehicle at 50 miles an hour hadn't even fazed her, or better yet, me. I was completely unharmed, and we got back to the business of staying fucked up.

Gnarls Barkley and My Lyric

So the closing of the software company deals would temporarily lighten me up on the resentments towards my ex-bosses. I was still pissed at the world that conspired against me, but it was ok, I was going to survive, I thought. Right around that time, a song that would become the theme song to my insane summer came out by Gnarls Barkley, wherein they sang the line, "I remember when I lost my mind." The first time I heard it I immediately called Kristen who'd been there when we brainstormed this idea loudly at Elmyr. She laughed "I knew you'd call me about it, I know it's crazy!" She didn't know crazy, but that song amplified my problems tenfold. I felt robbed at first. I remembered the band Mastodon being at Elmyr all the time and I imagined they'd heard my brainstorm and relayed it to Big Boi at the studio, or some such plot. Hell it wasn't impossible, Dangermouse and Mastodon all recorded in Atlanta for sure, right? I mean I knew I had nothing to do with the amazing musical talent of these two geniuses, but seeing as I'd never been recognized for anything I'd ever written other than a brief MSNBC editorial, it felt like a punch in the gut, even though it was just one little lyric, and I had no real evidence at all. Still they played that damn song 100 times a day on the radio, and every time I would get a mix of resentment for the lyric getting copied and then adversely, pride that my brainstorm had been worth copying. I even verified it with the bartender at Elmyr, making sure I hadn't imagined the whole thing, but she as well as Kristen verified I'd had the exact same line written for my website idea a year before. Only one line of the song was copied, I thought, but the entire song was eerie to me, given my state of mind. The entire lyrics themselves were a trip, and played right into my state of mind. The chaos and delusions reigned, and the song was a soundtrack to madness for me.

Crazy

I remember when, I remember
I remember when I lost my mind
There was something so pleasant about that place
Even your emotions had an echo in so much space

And when you're out there without a care
Yeah I was out of touch
But it wasn't because I didn't know enough
I just knew too much

Does that make me crazy?
Does that make me crazy?
Does that make me crazy?
Possibly

And I hope that you are
Having the time of your life
But think twice
That's my only advice

Come on now, who do you
Who do you, who do you, who do you think you are?
Ha ha ha, bless your soul
You really think you're in control?

Well I think you're crazy
I think you're crazy
I think you're crazy
Just like me

My heroes had the heart
To lose their lives out on a limb
And all I remember
Is thinking, I want to be like them

Ever since I was little
Ever since I was little
It looked like fun
And it's no coincidence I've come
And I can die when I'm done.

But maybe I'm crazy
Maybe you're crazy
Maybe we're crazy
Probably.

-Gnarls Barkley

Wow! It was a message to me, I thought! It was cool, though, it was like a subtle nod in my direction that it was all good, and maybe, just maybe, "Family" had heard it, and incorporated it. Sure, why not? Seemed plausible to me. Like my CIA missions though, it went from probable, to "That's the lyric they stole from me!" within just a couple of days. Regardless of the fact it was just one small line, and the music itself was obviously completely original, I felt robbed, and almost mocked when I heard the song, which played every 15 minutes that summer. Every time it would kick the conspiracy machine in my head into high gear. Coincidence and synchronicity mixed with a touch of resentment, real or delusional, would haunt me constantly and vividly. There had to be a deeper meaning I was missing and I would analyze and drink, and wonder why my life wasn't fair, while at the same time feel a bit of delusional ego that I'd played a part in such a popular song.

Night at the Ritz

And my delusions grew more and more grandiose. I'd closed the Software Company deals, drunk and high as I was able to be, and my ego hadn't suffered one bit because of it. Caroline and I went to Nordstrom's July 3rd, and though I think she was looking to get out of the relationship, I was still a pretty easy way for her to stay drunk and away from her parents, so she was still around. I was probably also still pretty entertaining to be around, albeit nuts. I remember before we left my house that day to go to the Phipps Plaza, I picked up a rock from my front yard, that I was certain was an ancient Indian arrowhead. I would need this, I told myself, one eye probably cocked thinking of the potential Arab attacks I may have to contend with. On the way to Nordstrom's, "Crazy" blared over the radio and Caroline rolled her eyes as I sang along "I remember when I lost my mind!"

"I don't want to hear another word about Bigbounzyballz.biz!" she would scream at me at the top of her lungs. She gone along for the ride on the CIA and the Arabic-speaking auditor ads, but for some reason, this concept website I would tell anyone willing to listen, drove her up a wall. It was just a brainstorming website, an idea, I'd come up with, madly, on the way back from her grandfather's funeral. Bigbounzyballz.biz would be a website where people would converge to brainstorm even the most far flung, off the rocker theories of how to break man of the burning fossil fuels habit, and yet still enjoy the freedom of movement that we did. Now even in my deluded state, I didn't really believe we as a species could make millions of huge, big bouncy balls, that men or women could enter, and then be catapulted from their backyard, or say a neighborhood catapult, to their place of work, but I did go into detail, whenever given the chance, to explain every aspect of the mad scientist project. It drove poor Caroline up a wall, more so than any other insane delusion I had, but I mean I'd put so much thought into, I just had to tell everyone about it. You see a bouncy ball, launched by catapult, would use only kinetic energy, or so I believed, and would not burn any fossil fuels, therefore be better than cars. The bouncy ball would have enough space to enter, be filled with gel or some sort of shock absorber, so as not to turn the human inside into spaghettios, and then be launched, again via modern catapult, with precise military, and space age precision in the general, or hopefully specific direction of one's destination. Once it arrived at said destination, it would then hit an approximate funnel type apparatus that would of course need to be installed on the top of every single office building in every single major metropolitan in the world, and that funnel would have a huge, toilet bowl or sink like target for which the huge bouncy ball would be launched, then caught, slowed down via the funnel system, circling around and around, slowing the velocity of the bouncy ball. Not unlike the way you drop a coin in those funnels at a Mexican restaurant, and it loops around and around until dropping into a big pile of coins. Except for rather than being a big pile of coins, the ball would drop you into a big pool of little, smaller balls, called a ball pit or a ball crawl, most commonly seen at Chucky Cheese. Thus, you could travel to and from work, quickly, without getting hurt, and without burning gasoline. And also, when you looked up in the sky, you would be living in Dr. Seuss's universe. I would go into intricate detail of how each individual's bouncy ball would be programmed, to adjust for wind, humidity, the rotation of the earth, and the like, as well as the safety advantage, of accidents, when two bouncy balls collide, they would just, ya know, bounce away from each other. It all made perfect sense in my head, and if I was drinking and you were around, I was going to tell you about it. Caroline, who'd heard the plan more than once, would beg me to shut up. But I mean, to me, even if it was a crazy idea, the site was only going to be a site, for people to submit their crazy ideas of how to attain such travel. Whether it be vaccume tube, as seen at banks, or on "Futurama", solar powered skateboards or what not, but I guess, as drunk and jacked up as I was all the freaking time, I would occasionally come off as if I really believed big bouncy balls would soon replace cars, which in retrospect, I agree, is a little looney.

"Roger, roger, we have clearance for Clarence!" I would talk a million miles a minute and I was crazy, but it was still fun. I had all kinds of movie quotes stuck in my head. We arrived at Nordstrom's, bought a shirt, and I bought her a pink, "Life is Good" hat. I was on my way to becoming a millionaire. I was still reading <u>Think And Grow Rich</u>, and through all the chaos, I'd started Seek And Employ, put some money in the bank, and though I could only tell a select few like the Colonel, I'd saved a 747 for civilization because that was just the kind of guy I was. We ended up getting drunk and laughing and loving life over at The Tavern inside Phipps Plaza, that July 3rd.

After about six drinks or so though, the paranoia crept in. I didn't want to drive home, for fear of being followed, so Caroline and I walked over to the Ritz Carlton and booked a room on the top floor. She was pissed, she didn't want to stay the night for some reason, something about work, but I had them wheel in a huge brass bowl, filled to the brim with Bud Light and ice and she was able to keep her complaining to a minimum, though at first, she'd been adamant about leaving.

A few beers into our buzzed celebration at the Ritz Carlton, I began to get restless. We had to go meet Mooney, I told her, a hippie I'd known since my Little Five days, who'd fronted me drugs numerous times, and who I thought was "Family," and who did actively and consciously acknowledge that he and I were both "Family". He was from the Rainbow Family, and somehow, that was all connected to my espionage, though I couldn't have explained how, and besides, I wouldn't have, as it was all need-to-know. On the cab ride down, I made a scene about us being followed. Every van, every extra antenna, every time the radio would fuzz in and out, I'd reference our being followed, though I couldn't exactly tell Caroline how or why we were being followed. Her amusement was running out, while I thought it was all extremely entertaining. I freaked the cab driver out so bad that he dumped us out in Little Five, and when we met up with Mooney. We had to get a new cab driver to drive us back to the Ritz. I got Mooney to bring the weed, some mushrooms, and an unknown substance that we took in liquid form, though I still couldn't tell you what it was.

We got back to the hotel, and began the madness. For whatever reason, Mooney believed me and my delusions and ate it up about all my madness, my undercover work, becoming a millionaire, and whatever else I was ranting about. We thought of all kinds of new websites we'd create and make a million dollars on: deeznutz.biz, bigbounzyballz.biz, and z3.com, which would all somehow save China's economy and even more! All the while, Caroline got more and more irritated into the night. Mooney and I talked politics, and business, and the wars, and how Russia was the real leader of the world, working behind in the shadows, waiting to pounce and lead, as aliens had given them the powers to rule the Earth. Made sense to me. We ate some of the shrooms, and then I asked Mooney to leave while Caroline and I got shit-faced through the night, and she listened to me babble on and on about the CIA, Family, Gnarls Barkley, aliens, and whatever other crazy conspiracy theories would come to mind.

Around 3 AM, her cell phone rang and she went to grab it. But I was quicker than she was. I took out the Indian arrowhead, and smashed her phone into a million little pieces, "Who could possibly be calling you? It's either your contact, or a new boyfriend." Either way, it was a threat, and I destroyed the threat, and then told her the rest of the evening what a force I was to reckon with, not the least bit concerned for her feelings, or whether the phone had been a gift from her parents. I was psychic, I told her. Psycho is more like it, she said, and I'd smash up the phone a little more. For the first time, she looked a little scared, as I obviously wasn't getting any saner.

We slept for about two hours before we were awakened by the loud beating of a helicopter rotor, and it sounded like it was coming from right outside our window. I jumped up and opened the blinds, and sure enough, there right in front of my eyes, was a huge, hovering, black helicopter. When I opened the shades, both the pilot and co-pilot looked over at me, butt ass naked, with what must have been shock. Holy shit, I was freaked out, and I think maybe at that moment, the last little bit of control I had over my delusions left me, as I panicked and went into full fledged conspiracy fear and rambling voices in my head.

"Run!" one voice would tell me. The other would scream "Stay." They had different tones, different objectives, and seeing as I'd discovered the invisible technologies already, this must be their way of training me. The CIA was also psychic and they were testing me to see if I could hear. In fact, all of this had been a test, and so far I was doing great. Why else would they have placed me here on the top floor of the Ritz Carlton on the day of the 4th of July, except to help protect all these citizens from a potential bomb? It was all connected, and I was right in the center! Why else would I have gotten such a great room, and why else would there have been a helicopter right outside my window? "Leave and get rid of the shrooms," I heard in my head, clear as day. So we packed it all up and began the trek back to the car, a few blocks through the Peachtree Road Race foot traffic, back to the parking lot at Nordstrom's. Along the way, I found a Porta-Potty and threw away the quarter bag worth of shrooms I'd been fronted. It was all part of the mission.

We got back to the car and navigated our way out through the Peachtree Road Race crowds. By this time, even Caroline was starting to buy parts of the story, as the helicopter right outside our hotel room had really existed, and was scary. With my salesmanship and loud mouth, even she was starting to buy into the delusions. We got home and slept for what felt like three days. When we awoke, it was only 6 pm, and we were both flabbergasted by how it was still only the 4th of July. I screamed, "Oh no, I left my Rolex and my family wedding ring at the Ritz!" Then a few minutes later, as she was looking for a Family Guy episode to watch, she pulled out a plastic bag with my Rolex and the wedding ring in it. She was convinced as well -- something or someone had put that there, and something or someone had gotten her to look for it. In fact for them to have placed those items there, the CIA must have time traveled, into the future, returning to the past to place them back in our room. Of course the CIA could time travel, it all made sense! What better defensive posture, than owning time?

Assignment at Mountain Park

Things were getting spookier and spookier. I told her about the invisible agents and for just that day, I had her bought into the whole of the delusions. We must have time traveled as we slept, because what else would explain it? And the watch and the ring being left at the Ritz only to be replaced back at home where she then just happened to look, c'mon! The universe and even God himself might be involved.

Then the voices, my psychic connection to Langley, told me to get Caroline, and call the limo driver we'd been using extensively, a Nigerian cabbie named Winston, who was now a part of the plot, and who played right along with all my delusions. He came and picked us up. We were to go to Mountain Park to watch the fireworks, and I was to look for suspicious behavior. Excluding, of course, our own. Caroline got scared and said the cabbie's eyes were changing colors, and I said, "Of course they are." Everything fit together at this point, no matter how obscure, and didn't require anything close to fact to substantiate the plot. It all made sense. It was all a stream of consciousness, and it all was coming together, of course his eyes changed colors, of course they did.

We picked up a twelve pack and had Winston drop us off at Mountain Park, near the show. We'd brought the beer, and I had a knife, and, of course, my Indian arrowhead. We watched the fireworks and we got tanked, and almost immediately I began to get super paranoid, even beyond what I'd been before. I don't even remember how the conversation started but I remember Caroline saying something I thought was cold, and instantly, I saw her for what she was: a robot. She was the ultimate spy. I'd had this thought before with pets, thinking that they had cameras in their eyes, but never with a human being, but the voices told me it was the truth. And then the voices told me, since she was a robot I could kill her, she was a part of the plot, one of them, not one of us. It would be OK, I thought. Another voice negotiated "Don't hurt anyone, just run!"

I ran like a madman away from her, leaving poor Caroline in the middle of Mountain Park, and hauling ass to several people's houses I'd known in Mountain Park years before when I'd lived there. I began talking about the CIA, and the plots, and I realized very quickly that I'd said too much. Brett and Lonnie Underwood, who'd I'd known for years, looked at me like I'd lost my mind. I ran two houses down and heard a man talking to himself on the front porch of his house. I walked closer to see my Elementary School baseball coach, who I told all about my mission, and how I was training to be in the CIA. He didn't judge me, and he didn't look at me like I was crazy, he just said something to me that I couldn't get out of my head for weeks and months later. "Don't get yourself into anything you can't get yourself out of." Jesus, he was in on it too, and if I joined the CIA, I'd be in it for life, I'd never get out, it would be like the Mafia, and I'd always have these voices in my head. "AHH!" So I kept running.

Alone, scared, drunk plus high on amphetamines of course, and mushrooms coursing through my blood, I ran back across Mountain Park to see if I could find Caroline, to see where she'd gone after I left her all alone in a strange place. If she'd escaped successfully, it would prove she was a double agent. Sure enough, she was gone. The voices were going crazy, and I wanted them to stop. I wanted to stop being tracked by the government, and then a voice came through "Carve the microchip out of your ankle!" It was so obvious, when I'd broken my ankle years back, they must have installed a microchip! If I could carve that son of a bitch out I'd be OK, my sanity would come back, and the voices would stop. I got out my knife and went to cut out the titanium alloy that Grady Hospital had so successfully installed, and that I'd nursed back to health, and I just couldn't justify it to myself, even in my insanity. Just like with the killing of the robot, the idea of carving out my microchip began the mental negotiating "Don't cut into your ankle, just put it in water." Eyes cocked, that made some sense. In fact hadn't that worked just a few nights before? Maybe if I just put my ankle in water, they would stop tracking me. That was it! Water was the perfect answer! Thankfully, I put my knife away. In retrospect, it's as if my brain was creatively trying asinine ways to hurt, kill or maim me. My own mind had completely turned against me.

I hauled ass to the creek that feeds the lake in Mountain Park, probably a mile from where I'd left Caroline, and I jumped into the creek, up to my ankles, and awaited orders. "Ok, now follow the creek, you're doing great." The killing of the robot and the carving out the microchip had just been a test to make sure I could follow the orders from the CIA clearly. It all made sense now, and I marched through mud, several miles up that creek, dodging all signs of human life, through the golf course of Brookfield West that I'd grown up in, ever keeping my foot submerged, going under tunnels in the golf course, and whatever other obstacles stood in my path. Orders were to keep the foot submerged, and I did just that, until I got to the end of the creek along the waterfall in Brookfield West, and I awaited new orders.

"Walk to the Taco Mac, get a cab, and go home, then the mission will have been a success." So I walked through the woods, abandoning the creek, but OK with the new, more mellow orders, and hiked with purpose all the way until I got to the Taco Mac on 92, whereupon I went inside, ordered a beer, and called a cab. Funny how so many of my orders from there on out would end me up at a bar.

Ordered to Chattanooga

The next morning, July 5th, I awoke with the voices screaming. "Get out of Atlanta, head north to Chattanooga, more orders to follow." I wasn't scared. In fact, I felt important. Walking out to get in my car, I looked down at the spot I'd found the Indian arrowhead I'd been carrying around for a week or two, and I clearly saw two additional rocks that looked important in my mania. I grabbed them both, and in my mind they were quite clearly a moon rock, and a space rock, or meteorite, and it was obvious that they were meant for me. Among the regular gravel, I'd found three rocks, all with some sort of power from the Earth, moon, and space, and they all looked symmetrical and perfect while I was in this state of mind. They all fit perfectly in a closed fist, so were perfect, inconspicuous weapons as well. I pocketed them as they were meant for me alone! I felt like a VIP, and so I jumped in my little 318 BMW, and hauled ass out of Roswell, through Woodstock, and hit Interstate 75 north. I drove 100 miles an hour, right up until I was almost out of gas. I then exited, pulled into a BP station, and parked right next to a vehicle with the official markings "Military Police." I did not think this was coincidence.

I filled up, and when the MP pulled out, I followed him several miles as he cruised along, and then testing him, I passed him and he followed me well into Chattanooga. Coincidence? I thought not. It was also no coincidence that I saw a hawk over my car at all times, hovering in circles. Probably with a camera in its eye, watching my every move. Hopefully this would be the last test before I got some real orders.

Arriving in Chattanooga, I pulled into a motel with a sign

out front that stated nothing more than "Motel." I would later be questioned on the validity of this, but my brother would find my white Beamer parked in an abandoned-looking dump of a place called just "Motel." But there it was. I booked a room, went across the street to get a twelve-pack, got back to my room, popped some amphetamines, and awaited orders. The phone rang, my software client was calling, trying to finalize the last of the candidates I'd been working on placing under Scott George, the VP of Sales. We got the offer, and in my state, while trying to extend said offer to the candidate, I scared the shit out of the poor girl, and she turned it down and ran the other direction. I probably scared a lot of normal people off at this stage, but I figured, oh well, that was a distraction to the mission anyway. Besides there was money in the bank, and had been my whole life. "They" would make sure I was taken care of, whether it was CIA or Rainbow Family or both, I had faith.

After a few hours in that dump of a hotel, I called my brother, who I told I would meet at the Marriott. I didn't tell him I was staying at the "Motel," but for whatever reason, I thought it would be good to meet up. I wasn't quite sure why, but I'd know once I saw him. I got to the Marriot, ordered a Crown and Seven, went to the bookcase they had in the hotel bar room, and picked up a book on Einstein, because I was just that smart. Before my brother got there, Fox News announced that North Korea had launched several missiles without warning, and that they had either failed or been intercepted, and that became the obvious purpose to my mission! They had delivered me out of a target city like Atlanta, into a protected city like Chattanooga, surrounded by mountains, and powered by the Tennessee Valley Authority, probably not a nuclear target, and it all made sense in my head. When my brother arrived, I told him all about my missions, my undercover CIA operations, the fact that dad probably hadn't killed himself, but had probably just failed in a mission, and how they'd sent me here to tell him something of great importance. "What was it?" he asked. "That you and your wife need to have kids, to reproduce, or else you'll get drafted into this same line of work as me and dad, and if you don't have a family they'll come after you too!" "Dad had a family," he tried to tell me, but it didn't matter, I remained unconvinced. I delved deeper telling him about my recruiting efforts for the international chemical client, obviously the CIA, the terrorist plot I'd thwarted, and for a moment, even he was buying into it. I've always been a hell of a salesman. Not for long though.

We left the Marriot to dinner with his wife, where I did my best to explain the situation, while drinking about six Crown and

Sevens, on top of the amphetamines and on top of what I'd already downed, and then he began to take me back to the Marriot. At some point in the drive, I told him to please take me into the woods and shoot me, that I didn't have the courage to do it myself. That if he were a man, he would do it. He begged me to listen to myself, and I'd snap out of it for just a second, saying "Just kidding, that was just a test to see if you were an enemy of the mission." Not knowing what else to do, he took me out drinking before taking me back to the Marriot instead, probably scared to death I was going to kill myself.

We got to the bar, and on the news they were still talking about a suspected group of Hezbollah who had snuck into America through Mexico and were plotting to attack random American cities. Aha, this must be my new and adjusted mission. I would stay up as late as possible, guarding as many bars as possible. I popped some more amphetamines, and tried to make small talk with my brother and his friends, while I scanned the bar for Arabs, and watched the outside windows in the off chance that I would be the next great terrorist catcher. Who better, I thought? Eventually my brother left me at the bar near the Marriot, and I swore I wouldn't kill myself, and I promised to meet him for lunch the next day. Whatever, if it was part of the mission, I would.

Reaching the hotel room around 10 PM, I tried to rest my eyes, only to instantly receive orders. This time, I was to go and hide my cell phone in a parking garage. It didn't make much sense, but who was I to question orders from Langley? They were probably just testing the lines of communications, I thought. There's a lot of testing and training involved when becoming a psychic CIA operative. I walked around the block and saw a parking garage that fit the bill perfectly, in my mind. I went and hid the cell phone in between two huge concrete beams, and I left just before the gate was closing. I would have to return in the morning, but I would remember exactly where I placed it. There, now they were only tracking me by the microchip in my ankle. The ankle microchips were simple satellite GPS, whereas the cell phone captured audio as well, so now I was as covert as they wanted me to be.

My next orders took me to the closest bar, as usual. I drank in the bar and babbled extensively to anyone who would listen. I traveled back to my bed at the Marriot, telling the gentleman at the front desk, orders were orders, and he smiled like he was in on it. Five minutes later I was back in the lobby, telling him, I guess the mission isn't over yet. I did this three or four times, exhausted, but following orders, feeling proud of my diligence, all the while he

254

grinned like he knew, or so I thought.

When I woke up around 10 or so, I tried to eat breakfast. I popped some Adderalls, and walked along downtown Chattanooga, retrieving my cell phone on the journey, and turning it on just in time for my brother to call and give me the name of a BBQ place where we would meet for lunch. But first, I'd find a bar and down about five or six Jägermeisters to get my head straight. When around four policemen walked into that bar, and it was just me and them, I decided it was time to go. It wasn't yet noon.

Timing was perfect, though, as it was just about time to meet my brother. My brother was there just long enough for me to realize there wasn't any beer, when my Uncle Jack Bell sat down at the table with us. A set up! I knew it, I'd been ambushed. I ran outside, paranoid and delusional as I'd ever been in my life, and Jack tried to talk to me.

"We could put you in that car, Bryan. If we have to call the police, we will, but we could do this easily if you'd just come into the car and go with us. We just want to get you somewhere safe."

"That's not in the orders, Jack" and he looked at me strangely.

"Don't make us call the police, they're right around the corner, let's just do this easily, a few days, have them check you out and you'll be on your way." Uncle Jack was convincing.

"Fine," I agreed, not sure why I'd agreed, but exhausted and tired of explaining myself, tired of the voices in my head.

Three Signatures

I got into Jack's van, and we drove from Chattanooga to the Dekalb County Crisis center, where my little sister would meet us, in order to provide the three signatures required to check a grown adult into the detox center. Or, as I'd later hear it called in AA, the loony bin. The whole ride from Chattanooga, I heard conversations that I later learned never took place. We covered everything from Satan worshipping, to Freemasons, to the CIA, and we spoke about them all. When I had a few months sober, I would come to find out that those conversations never happened anywhere but inside my own deluded, swollen, chemically-fried mind.

Arriving in Atlanta, after an hour and a half of my ramblings in that ride, and my brother and uncle amusing me, rolling their eyes, and playing along with my delusions, we arrived at Dekalb County Crisis Center, where my sister met us briefly to provide the third signature. When my father killed himself, it had been 1989, and two weeks prior, three family members had checked him into a detox facility. I guess that's why my brother, sister, and uncle all looked scared. I'd sworn when my dad died never to be like him and yet here I was exactly like him. All the irony was lost on me, though. I could piece together connections that made me an undercover CIA operative, but I couldn't face any obvious coincidences about my own disease, alcoholism. I was too deep into the delusions, or as we say, I couldn't see the forest through the trees.

That's how I came to inhabit the loony bin for the first time. To be honest, it was a relief. For one thing, I'd incorporated it all into the delusions. I was so far gone into outer space my mind hadn't even accepted I was at a detox facility for drug and alcohol, but was convinced that I was really there only to be psychically debriefed by the CIA and to provide a cover story to my brother, who obviously lacked the Top Secret clearance, I had imaginarily been granted. I had babbled to my brother too much about my CIA work, and this was their way of disqualifying me, of making my brother think that everything I'd said was nuts, and that I wasn't to be believed. I checked in to that loony bin after my uncle convinced me he was there on the behalf of the mission, to quell my brother's fears, and also to debrief me. Waiting for my bed in there, I remember telling the nurse I had terrible running thoughts, and that I wanted badly to be debriefed. She told me she'd get me some Librium when I got in there, and that sounded good to me.

They took my three special rocks from the Earth, moon, and stars, and finally allowed me into the detox center, and I'd never felt more at home in a detention center in my life. I was there as part of the mission. But also, the Librium they gave me slowed the voices down, and for the first time in a long time, I slept long and hard. Not on the first dose, but once I was able to get a second, and then a third dose my first night, I wasn't as miserable. This was all part of the mission, I was here to be debriefed and to disqualify my CIA ramblings to my brother. I even found cigarettes in there, as all the crazies before me had worked out a system. Every four hours or so, we all lined up and get our meds, and for the first time in many months, my mind began to slow down a bit, and I wasn't hearing fifteen voices at any given moment. There were no more orders.

I talked to the therapist, I told them I drank too much, that I'd eaten shrooms a few days before, that I'd been taking amphetamines, and they would call my doctor and have that prescription revoked. They told me I needed to stay a week or so, and I was fine with it. After all, I was being debriefed. I remember one of the therapists talking to me, and her eyes being so crystal clear, I thought she must be an alien. Also on her form, patients were referred to as consumers, which to me was a clear indication of something sinister. Consumers, not patients it was obviously a conspiracy. I waited to be debriefed.

After a night or two, and no debriefing, I realized the debriefing must also be psychic, or that they were just providing a cover, so that my brother would think I was crazy, and not actually privy to all the top secret information I'd leaked to him. That was fine, I'd kill some time. I found a puzzle in there made of 1500 pieces, a complex collection of Christmas ornament decorations, all circular, and all silver and gold, so it was hard to tell where the pieces went. I began forming the outline of the puzzle, and before too long I had several schizophrenic patients helping me to put the puzzle pieces together. At first just the outline, but eventually we were all filling in the middle of the puzzle. Once the outline was complete, I stared long and hard for hours at the outline and the box, and to my great frustration, they simply didn't match. "What kind of psycho ward gives mentally unstable people a puzzle to put together for which the pieces don't match the box!" It made me livid, and I talked to the doctors about it. Several of them argued with me about how the outline did match the box, but no matter how many times they told me, I still couldn't see the outline, they were flat wrong. I was right, I was seeing clearly and the puzzle on the box simply didn't match the puzzle on the table we were putting together. Even once we finished it, which the doctors told me was the first time it had ever been completed, the puzzle still didn't match the box. It was close, the colors and shapes were the same, but the overall design was different by a few distinct details. Nobody but me was terribly bothered by this. They simply couldn't see what I could see. They probably weren't as smart, I decided pompously. Later I would realize everything I saw, heard, and felt was skewed, right down to my vision. Rocks becoming significant, puzzles not matching, and conversations created out of thin air, were all just a part of the insanity. But while I was in there, that was just beyond me.

Before letting me go, they gave me a list of halfway houses and outpatient centers to go to, and I even attended a meeting while in there. I got Graham Flagg, who had been sober for years, to assuage my family, and ultimately after a few days, they let me go. I promised my uncle that once out, I would go with him to check into somewhere long term. Before I was released, at some point I called Adam Archer and told him I was in the nuthouse. "From the Ritz to the Nuthouse in three days." Adam said, and I remember him laughing and it bringing me some slight comfort. "Only Jared Bryan Smith." It was still funny, I still wasn't hurting enough to take it all very seriously.

They let me go and at first I had no intention of staying sober. They'd thrown away my Adderall, and I didn't have any beer. I had my rocks though -- clearly simple, normal rocks -- I had my wallet, and, of course, my Rolex. The rocks that I'd believed were meant for me, and magical, and had fit perfectly in my hand, now looked like regular, gravel rocks. Strange, I thought, but I didn't dwell on it. I got on the train with the intention of getting to Northridge Station, to catch a cab and get to my hole-in-the-wall wreck of a house in Roswell. I couldn't even make it three or four stops before a plan to get fucked up had become the new mission. Go to Little Five, to the Pendleton Apartments where'd I'd lived with Gwen, find some hippies, drink some beer, and smoke some herb. Sounded like a good mission to me, though at three days removed from drugs, I was pretty sure it hadn't come from the CIA.

Those apartment buildings were filled to the brim with like-minded alcoholics and drug addicts, and I knocked on every door I thought might potentially be "Family" and help me get fucked up. I had a sob story about being admitted by my blood family into a loony bin, so they could steal my domain name, bigbounzyballz.biz, and take the last remaining asset I had. From the moment I conjured up that story, it became the truth in my head. It made more sense to tell people than the CIA story, and besides, I obviously needed to be careful about who I told the CIA story to, lest I get locked up again. I searched that entire complex, and the only two people I could even find the afternoon I was released from the loony bin, were the two lesbians I'd known who lived right below me. Through sheer coincidence, they were in the AA program. I told them my story, and they asked me to go to a meeting. "AHHHH!" I ran away from them, smelling a conspiracy from top to bottom, jumped back on the train and headed back to Roswell. Getting a cab from the train back to my cabin, I got a hold of Melissa Gilbreath who happened to be in town, and she and some friends were out drinking at the house of a mutual friend. I cabbed it over there, and began drinking their beer. Twelve beers later, they asked me to leave, and I was offended.

That night, my uncle showed up at 4 AM or so. My family

had come by and cleaned up the wreck of my house. My poor Aunt Becca, with three kids of her own, and having herself survived breast cancer just a couple of years before, had come over to my pigsty of broken bottles, empty pizza boxes, and stacked dishes, and had cleaned the entire house from top to bottom. I began steadily wrecking the house all over again, resenting my family's imaginary plot to steal bigbounzyballz.biz, which I'd entirely created in my head, and resenting my brother for calling my uncle in the first place, because you know, that domain name and idea was just such a gem. I decided to quit being a pussy about it, screw my family, who did they think they were? They weren't going to steal my genius ideas, and besides I wasn't hurting anybody else, only myself, I thought! The ultimate lie alcoholics and addicts tell themselves.

Family Plots and CIA Banjee

When Uncle Jack showed up that night late in the evening, I screamed at the door, "You're not coming in, and you're not taking bigbounzyballz.biz, get the hell out of here!" He yelled back that I'd promised to go somewhere long term, and I told him to "Fuck off!" He disappeared back into the night, but now I had reason to fear. At any time, not only could Al-Qaeda come to get me, but my family was after me as well. At any time, they could show up and attack, they could have me committed, they could take away my million dollar ideas! I wouldn't let them, though, I'd stand guard from here on out!

Somehow, through all that chaos, I would continue to make money. As soon as I'd begun drinking again the delusions kicked into high gear. If the CIA expected me to continue to operate, they would have to keep throwing me bones, I believed. I created a new mantra, "I will close 16k by July 31st, 2006 by being the best recruiter I can possibly be," and I dove into my work again. I still had a little bit in the bank, and so I got back to recruiting. I sprayed Arabic-speaking auditor ads all over the world again, pacing my house, awaiting the terrorists. I placed another ad for another chemical corporation, an international company not unlike my other chemical client, with international offices sprinkled worldwide, the perfect CIA cover. Within a week or two of placing their ads, I had a candidate named Anita Banjee, who I thought for certain must be a cover for the compensation the CIA was covertly sending my way. Anita Banjee I thought was certainly clever for "I need a banshee" a word my mother had used for an old gypsy woman. I had submitted one candidate, and within a couple of weeks, she was hired, and had accepted a job with this international chemical company in India, where she would begin an international assignment. How could that name not be a code!

Ha! My commission was 16k exactly, identical to my mantra I stated outloud, so certainly this had been another CIA mission, another victory for JB Smith, but this time, I'd learned to keep my mouth shut. I wouldn't tell a soul, I would just follow my orders, collect my money, and await instructions, psychic or otherwise. I felt almost like a god, I'd conquered the mantras. Whatever I needed, I could imagine, think about, and create out of sheer desire. It was working like a charm. My family was still checking in on me from time to time, but I told them I was better. I didn't need their help. In retrospect I was running on Devil's luck, carried forward, while my disease picked up its pace. Around then, I'd taken a picture of the hot stove in my house, glowing red in the night. The pattern of the burner was a spiral, I noticed. The downward spiral tightens as it draws to a close, two points closer in. The tragedies of drinking were getting closer and closer, the bouts and benders were all but continuous now, and though my superficial luck was still good and I was still closing deals, I knew deep down it wouldn't keep up.

Caroline came over once or twice after I'd been temporarily committed. By then, I always had a knife or gun in my hand. I had knives in the walls all over my house. There were broken beer bottles and trash throughout the entire place. I'd been telling Caroline the old house was haunted for the entire time we'd lived there, and we'd hear things move around all the time, and we were both just used to the supernatural events. It wasn't until a rat ran across her face as we laid down to pass out, that she finally realized it probably wasn't ghosts after all. The ancient house had spirits, but they were alive and were well-fed rats. It didn't help that we fought physically a few times before she finally called it quits on my ass, way after anyone sensible would have. One day I was bringing her back home, and we fought over the hat I'd bought her at Nordstrom's. I pulled it off her head, ripping a ton of hair right out of her head. Her father was none too happy about this. After I dropped her off at her nice country club home in east Cobb County, I peeled out through her yard, and then her neighbors' yards, off-roading the BMW into the street, and burning up a little rubber once I hit the pavement. Classy stuff.

Documentary on Afghanistan

I began meeting with the Colonel I'd met at North River Tavern more frequently, talking about putting together a documentary project to Afghanistan. He'd just gotten back in the country, was going through a divorce, was bored as hell, and unable to go back to active duty because of an injury. He claimed he could get Newt Gingrich's endorsement for a documentary project, funded by the Ad Council, and we could head to Afghanistan in a matter of months, if not weeks, as well as put some green in our pockets. The first number he mentioned was 250k. It sounded like an excellent plan to me, and we began putting the details in order. We came up with a mission critical path, and I began thinking of people I could bring. Dwayne was one of them, and I also wanted Dwayne to meet this guy, because, even then, I was a little afraid this might all be just a figment of my imagination. Dwayne met him too though, and so with the Colonel clearly existing, Dwayne and I began planning the trip to Afghanistan over three or four meetings. One time, the Colonel had me pick him up at Kennestone Hospital. I couldn't shake the feeling that he was the Devil, there to collect somebody's soul, after a long life of getting exactly what he wanted. Fuck it, I thought, what has God done for me lately?

The Colonel left a magazine at my house, and on that cover was an image of Darth Vader. I hung it over my toilet, so I could see it as I pissed out beer all day long, and thought about going to Afghanistan to kill or torture strangers for money. "Would I be willing to torture?" he asked me once. For 250k, I'd do whatever you asked, I told him. I downloaded the Star War's Imperial March song, revamped in dark and emphasizing techno music, and I listened to it obsessively. I imagined I was selling my soul to the Devil again. Take two I thought, picking up from where I'd left off at 18, right before Jake was born. I would go to Afghanistan, I would work for the CIA, I would do their bidding, and I would make some serious loot. When I returned, I would go to Hollywood and I would be just like Oliver Stone. I would be rich and famous, and when I died, the Devil could have my soul. Fuck it, where was God anyway? I was lost.

When I was 18 and the Devil tried to get me to join the Rainbow Family, it just hadn't been a good enough offer, I imagined. But this: 250k, Afghanistan, Hollywood, a Rainbow Family Captain, if you will, not just a piss-ant like back then smuggling drugs, but a real player. Well, it was about time someone recognized my genius. And after what I'd done for the CIA, I was only due. Mooney, my Rainbow Family hippie friend from Little Five, came by nodding his head in agreement as I told him my grandiose Afghanistan plans. He gave me what he called a Captain's hat, with the Grateful Dead "Steal Your Face" lightning bolt and nothing else, across the front of a gray,

261

stylish baseball cap that fit my head perfectly. It was like the Devil himself had delivered it, subtly, but powerfully, and meaningful to those that recognized its significance. I found that to be a small crowd, but there were one or two strippers who bought the story. To me, though, that hat was like wearing magic slippers, I was purely invincible. It all came together, the Devil, the CIA, The Rainbow Family, the hat, all one, and all interested in getting me to join.

I spent a lot of time that summer watching Nicolas Cage in "Lord of War". I watched the movie on a loop, drinking and pondering its meanings. I watched the movie with the director commentary on, and finally, I was able to understand and comprehend the war in Iraq. In my delusional, paranoid mind, the movie was about the major powers providing guns to the weaker nations, weeding out their populations, and making a pretty penny on the profits. It tied in with my thoughts about AIDS and HIV being population control, as well. Of course, all of this was instrumented by the CIA. And after years of reading every news article I could find about the debacle that was the Iraq war, my mind finally came up with a deep, dark strategy that we must be implementing in Iraq and Afghanistan to justify our presence there. Now, having worked for the CIA, I could grasp the higher meaning, the dire consequences of our actions, and finally I had faith in our leadership. We were in Iraq killing ALL Arabs of fighting age, and more importantly, breeding age, and suffering minor losses in the process. It was the only equation I could make work, and watching that movie over and over, it made sense. It may take a hundred plus years but we would slowly reduce their populations through this long term, sinister, malicious strategy.

With this newfound knowledge, I could watch the puppet show that was the news, and know that we were actually winning in the entire middle east. We were probably so evil that we were manipulating their birth rates. Fanatical Arabs were going the way of the American Indian, genocide, in a hidden, yet politically acceptable, agenda. It was victory with the presentation of being a constant guerilla war that made it look like we were losing. It had to be the answer, how else could we continue suffering the constant, pointless roadside bombings, and the multiple tours of troops? What looked like a strategic defeat in Iraq & Afghanistan had to be a bigger and broader victory, and watching that movie made me aware that what we saw was just the magician drawing our attention away from the rabbit. Once I'd made that realization, though, it made me sick to my stomach. Sick that I could be OK with genocide, sick that our nation would and could perpetuate it, and sick that I was going to go there and be a part of it. I began to feel guilt for my role as a recruiter for the CIA. Real guilt for my imaginary accomplishments. Hell, I'd indirectly tortured people, and worse!

The other thing about "Lord of War" that I related to was towards the end, Nicolas Cage's character having the curse of invincibility. I felt just like that. I felt like I'd been trying to die unsuccessfully for years, unable to, cursed to walk the earth forever, unable to die. He snorts a line of gunpowder and coke, and a gun gets pulled on him, and the gun doesn't work. He's miserable, he wants to die, and so did I. I'd even had a gun to my head that didn't work years before, the parallels were striking! All the patterns blinding and maddening. It was the whole escapism of heading to Afghanistan that I craved, that maybe I would die in an instant explosion, or gunshot to the head, and the suffering would end. Those scenes where he can no longer experience pleasure, where he fucks a prostitute who does or maybe doesn't have AIDS: that was me, that was my life, I was too fucked up to care about anything, but too unlucky to die, I thought. It was a parallel for how I felt, and I watched that movie over and over again, obsessively.

Invincible, I would drink for days and not eat. I would open the flu of the brick fireplace and wait as the rats would inevitably come into the house. Sitting ten yards away, I shot rounds from my .22 into the fireplace as shrapnel and the occasional ricocheting bullet buzzed past my head. I wandered around my glass-strewn house, barefoot for days on end, never getting a scratch, and I would marvel at my seemingly magical powers.

To me, it was all real. Once on the way to North River Tavern, drinking and stopping by the river to contemplate the Afghanistan adventure (and, of course, to smoke some weed), I stared at the water, waiting to see ripples, where there was no pebble tossed. Just like the Grateful Dead song "Ripple". After just a few minutes, clear as day, I could see ripples on the river's surface from seemingly nothing, wherever I wanted. I created them, I was a shaman, a Jedi, more human than human, and I looked at normal people with disdain. I was just superior, I thought.

When I begged Caroline for one of her many last shots, she came over and we made up temporarily. We watched "Wedding Crashers," and I showed her all the rainbow scenes, the imagery, the subliminal messages the Rainbow Family had put in the movie, or so I believed. She thought I was a kook, though before she'd heard me ramble on so much about the Rainbow Family and their conspiracies, she had brought me a pretty picture she'd made as a child, of rainbows. She bordered between buying into my delusions and calling me a psychopath. Her rainbow painting was pretty, though. It must have been a sign, I thought.

One day, I made her walk with me up to the closest bar, Chaplin's. She was sick of hearing about the Colonel, she was sick of hearing about my undercover work and how I was superhuman, and she was sick of walking everywhere, as I made her do once I was drunk (which was now all the time). Her parents came to pick her up at that bar, where I made Caroline pick up the tab. I told her dad I wanted to ask him a question at my house, and they came by to amuse me, I guess. I asked him to follow me into the woods, to avoid the microphones in my house, to which he raised his eyebrows and cautiously followed me into the adjoining woods. There I told him about my mission, and how the Colonel and I were going to Afghanistan to film a recruiting documentary, but that it was really an undercover CIA mission, and would he give me permission to marry Caroline? Considering it, he asked "Where would she live?" She was in her late 20's and still living at home, so he was open.

"An Air Force Base," I lied, and he said "We'll see." They took their daughter home, and she broke up with me shortly thereafter. First, she visited one last time, where I confessed to cheating. She pushed me and I reacted by punching her a few times in the stomach, telling her I was invincible, that I worked for the CIA, and if she called the police, they would laugh at her. She left for a good long while this time. I knew I'd been in the wrong, but I just dove deeper into my drinking. Deeper into madness, deeper into the dark abyss. "Sometimes when you stare into the abyss, the abyss stares back into you." Friedrich Nietzsche knew his shit. I'd stared long enough, and the abyss was undoubtedly within me, and I was dark.

Psychic Mission to Florida

I caught up with the Colonel, and we discussed our potential operations some more. He hooked me up with some morphine, and I started down that path again, briefly. Now I was drinking daily, smoking Dwayne's amazing herb, and the psychic missions picked up steam again. "Go to Florida, await instructions." I knew someone in Florida, Melissa Gilbreath. I called her, and she told me to come on down. The 16k from the chemical client placement I'd made, financed my sudden vacation down to Florida, and the plan was to meet up with Melissa and probably receive more orders once I was there. I had faith that as soon as I burned through this money, I'd just imagine up a new figure, and the CIA, or my own magic mantras, would conjure it right on up. Life was grand, in between the misery.

I bought a bottle of SKYY Vodka and a bag of weed before hitting the road to Florida. Before I got to Macon, I killed the bottle of SKYY, but for some reason, I wasn't swerving. I was on a mission at this point. Nothing would slow me down. Just outside of Valdosta, I looked down at my speedometer and saw that I was cruising along at 120 miles per hour, when BOOM, the tire popped. It felt like the car slid to the side of the road of its own force, smoothly parking itself behind a minivan on the side of Interstate 75 South. I jumped out to change the tire, got the tire out, and realized I didn't have a jack. The van in front of the Beamer was abandoned, so I opened the door and scavenged through the whole vehicle, only finding a filleting knife I would pocket. As I got out of the vehicle that wasn't mine, a Georgia State Patrolman pulled up behind my car. Without a moment's hesitation as he got out of his vehicle, I stated, "Popped a flat, officer. Do you think you could give me a ride to the nearest exit so I can buy a jack? Mine is missing."

"Hop in." He barely glanced at me.

I was shit-faced drunk, having killed the entire bottle of SKYY, I must have assaulted that cop's nose with alcohol fumes, but I didn't think twice about it. I was on a mission with the CIA, I was in training, the police were mine to order around, and I'd just ordered this one to give my drunk ass a ride. And he did. I had become the Abyss, I was able to command those whom were dark around me I thought. We got to a QuickTrip store, and I had the balls to ask him to wait and give me a ride back. He drove off, and I went inside, slightly irritated he hadn't helped me complete the task. I bought a jack, walked up to the closest group of locals in a truck and asked if they would give me a ride back to my Beamer for a hundred bucks, which they did. I fixed the tire, got back in the car, and promptly blacked out for the remainder of the ride down to Homosassa, Florida. I was heading for the exact same trailer park heaven where Gwen and I had spent time two years before. I didn't think anything of blacking out. I thought I had just time traveled. It wasn't mission-critical for me to be fully conscious on that part of the ride. I had plenty of gas, the tire had been fixed, and it was simply like having the Rolex and gold ring transported, it seemed magical, but it was all just part of the mission. I was just along for the ride, who cares if I lost a few hours or not? Time traveling was better than being bored, I thought.

Melissa, her new boyfriend (having lost the Turkish

husband), and I all went and got an eight ball my first day there. I checked into that same trailer Gwen and I had stayed in a couple of years before and we began snorting that eight ball of coke, and drinking and laughing and partying, not leaving the trailer for a day or two. I don't remember a word of what was said, but I know I talked a lot and I thought I knew everything. I had diarrhea of the mouth, I babbled on and on about my missions, about my CIA undercover operations, about God and the Devil. Eventually, Melissa left, and I laid on the bathroom floor, bleeding out of both nostrils, heart pounding, clinging to the floor, the toilet, whatever, unable to puke, unable to stop putting coke up my nose, and unable to get any more coke up my nose. I had to get rid of the rest of what I had, I had to finish the coke, but I couldn't force another molecule into my battered, bleeding nostrils. My heart banged like it had many times before on the tail end of an eight ball, and eventually I found myself on my knees, begging God for one more chance. I was utterly alone. The person I'd come to see had left, I didn't have a mission, I'd spent all the cash I intended on spending, I was utterly confused and demoralized, and I felt like I was going to have a heart attack. Somehow, I fell asleep after many hours on that floor, and woke up with a bloody rag next to my face, beer bottles all over the place, and blood splattered all over the bathroom and smeared across my face, mixed with tears and God knows what else. I was glad I wasn't dead. I was also glad the coke was gone. Even Melissa had left me, and that girl loved coke. Once there was ever any amount of that shit around, I was doing it all. There was no stopping if it was around. Same with drinking. I had beer, and so I cracked one.

Six beers into killing that hell of a hangover, I called Shane Oleander. He asked me about Afghanistan, and I said I didn't even know how real it was, but if it was real, I'd go. He thought I should. I asked Shane about sobriety. I mean, here was this guy who had been more of a fuckup than me, and he was a little over a year sober, while here I was in a bloody, disgusting trailer in Florida. He had my job, he had a little bit of time sober, more than I'd ever had, and I asked him some honest questions about AA. He told me the only way to find out was to do it. We talked for about an hour, and in all honesty, that was one of the first times I actually had some hope. If Shane Oleander could get sober, hell, how hard could it be? I would later find out that is the entire concept of AA.

When we got off the phone, the manager of the trailer resort banged on the door. I opened it up, and he took one look at my sorry ass and said "You've got to go!" I offered him money and it didn't help, he wanted me out. You have to look pretty rough to get kicked out of a trailer park in Homosassa Florida, but I must have looked it, and hell, I'd been kicked out of Tijuana before. But it did jumpstart my paranoia as well.

I drove to the closest motel, afraid to drive too far, checked in, bought some beer at a nearby gas station, and stayed holed up, turning my cell phone off so they couldn't track me, and intermittently keeping my ankle submerged in the bathtub. It would confuse the satellites, and this was probably all just part of the training. The coke bender had turned the paranoia back on with a vengeance, not that it had ever been too far out of reach. After two more days of ordering movies, radio silence, and an underwater ankle, the voices told me to head home. It was a relief, I was sick of Florida anyway.

I only got a few hours out of Homosassa when I began getting dizzy and paranoid, and I really needed a drink. I pulled of the highway, and the first motel I could find was the same exact name as the chemical client I'd represented, obviously a guise for CIA recruiting, and here was a hotel with their exact same name, ha! I'd placed Anita Banjee at the company with precisely the name as this hotel. Coincidence? I highly doubted it. I got some beers at the gas station across the street, and went to settle my nerves in that room. The cocaine sweating out of my body, the shakes starting to die down with the beer, I kept thinking demons might bust through the windows and snatch my soul. The adventure was beginning to get scary for some reason. I didn't have the same fucked up confidence I'd had when I left Atlanta, the orders were less clear, and I was plain scared. I took some Tylenol PMs and crashed out after about twelve beers.

Waking up feeling a bit better, I left the motel to get back to the rat-infested house I called home in Roswell. I found my weed, I bought some beer. Caroline was still ignoring my phone calls, but the Colonel came over once or twice, and we continued to discuss Afghanistan strategy. I was having a hard time getting into the devilish mood though. The Darth Vader magazine cover hanging on the wall was a little eerie to me now, and when I tried to play the Star Wars song, it just didn't give me the same emotional glory it had given me before. I wondered if it had anything to do with my praying to God for another chance on that bathroom floor in Homosassa, Florida. I didn't know. I remember getting drunk with Dwayne one day in late August, and writing an email to God and the Devil, and telling them both to leave me the fuck alone, I didn't want anything to do with either of them. That should settle that.

I wonder now who I really sent that desperate email to.

Swirling Down the Vortex

The drinking and the drugging raged on, despite the prayer and emails to God, despite the heart-to-heart with Shane Oleander, and despite all the obvious clues, I just kept drinking. Afraid to drive, I would walk, first to Chaplain's, then to North River Tavern, then up to the Rusty Nail, then hitch or take MARTA down to Buckhead. One particular day in the middle of a bender, things began to get very scary for me.

I'd actually driven that day, heading to the Four Seasons in midtown Atlanta, to meet up with Kristen, my bartender friend at Fuego who lived in midtown. We hung out, though she could tell I was losing my mind. We went back to her house to smoke a joint, at which point I asked her why she wouldn't be my girl, or something to that effect. She told me, "Because you're a carrier." She may have been kidding, but it put the fear of God into me. She said she had to do something later that day, so I wandered over to Joe's on Juniper, where, within five minutes of being there, I began making fun of a homosexual in full overalls. A pretty girl led me out of the place, luring me to the Vortex to go play poker. Having noticed Joe's was a gay bar and having already offended a patron, I was open to the change of venue. Before I would leave however, my racing mind would notice all the left wing, democratic party slogans underneath the bars veneer plastic. A few connected dots later a new theory made sense to me! The CIA would definitely want gay men in their ranks, able to start and stop relationships on a whim, and pushing their leftist new world agenda! You see, if Russia really was running the show, having taken over through the manipulation of the intelligence communities, and then taking over from within, the CIA could actually be the bad guys by now, subverted and turned against America! And of course socialists would obviously welcome homosexuality as it was Godless, in my mind, and as a movement would consume less overall resources. It was the perfect communist cover I thought madly! Then again maybe I was just overanalyzing it... such were the state of my thoughts, regardless of facts or common sense. Whatever, it would make it easier to follow that random chick out of the gay bar. Several shots into my buzz, now journeying from the gay bar to the Vortex, escaping the gay commie CIA agents, several of whom were wearing farmer like overalls, I was playing the big shot yet again. When passing a black man I thought to be homeless, I offered him a five dollar bill. He looked at me with dark

268

piercing eyes and said "I don't need your money." He was proud, and his statement pierced my soul. I instantly realized, this was an angel, and I was so far from God's grace, I was condemned to Hell. I'd been flirting with the Devil to sell my soul. This black man wasn't just some bum on the side of the street, he was an angel of God, and he wanted nothing to do with me. I was damned.

And then we arrived at the Vortex. I took one look at the entrance, a spooky gateway to hell type decoration, and said "Hell, no," I'm not going in there. The girl couldn't figure out why I wouldn't follow her in, but I told her, "It's the gates of hell, where I belong. I'm not going in." She went inside and eventually, after much thought and deliberation, I scooted to the side entrance of hell, as surely this would save my eternal soul. I sat down, but I couldn't shake the feeling that any minute my very spirit might ignite. I had to get out of the Vortex, it was just too creepy, and how ironic if it really was the portal into hell, I thought. I bolted hard and fast, and wandered on foot from there to the liquor store, rambling about going to hell, visiting Afghanistan, and the burdens of working for the CIA. I ended up in Little Five Points, wandering around, trying to find the Land Trust, where the Rainbow Family headquarters in Atlanta was located. I was going to pin them down once and for all, get some clarification on the Afghanistan mission, but I couldn't find the place, drunk out of my mind. Eventually I took a cab ride all the way home. But that moment with the proud black man would change things for me, my drinking, and my delusions in general.

That night I prayed to God for a long time. I begged forgiveness, for suddenly in my mind, I'd been flirting with evil, and danced with the Devil a little too closely. It had gone from a game to reality, too fast. That dignified black man refusing my money may have been an angel, a messenger of God, and he wasn't happy at all. I'd received fair warning of the consequences of my path, from the tone in his voice. I'd sobered up and felt strange that entire evening, but eventually I fell asleep. On awakening, I was grateful not to be in hell. The same creative psychotic imagination that had made me a super hero, had turned against me in a moment, and now I imagined I was a traitor to God himself.

Taking a Stand

That next day I would set things straight. First I got drunk, and then with a belly full of liquid courage, I would tell the Colonel, or the Devil, or whoever the hell he was, to go fuck himself. I would get Dwayne over to my shack, and I would have a witness, and I would turn down his offer to go to Afghanistan, take my soul, make me rich, whatever. The Colonel came over that afternoon, pulled into the driveway, and before he could even get out of the car, I screamed, much to his astonishment and Dwayne's, "Fuck you, Steven, go fuck yourself, I want nothing to do with the military, you can't take me and you can't take my soul! Go to hell, Satan!" He said fine, jumped into his car and quickly bolted out of my driveway quickly, looking enraged. Dwayne was also a little confused, but drunk as we were, he joined in the refusal, and we both were proud of telling the guy off, even if we weren't so sure as to what he had in store for us. All I knew in my heart was that it was evil, and it wasn't something we should do. I was still just wasted, not very sure, but was following the orders and whims of the voices in my head, which had gone from CIA orders to avoiding hell, which I felt was destined to appear right around the corner. From the moment the black angel in downtown Atlanta had refused my money, the family delusions, the CIA, and everything else inferred from those seemed poisoned. It was the Devil's trickery, and I'd gone too far. My imagination had become a double edged sword.

After we told off Colonel Steven McPherson, AKA Satan, I tried to get Dwayne to go up to North River Tavern with me, but he wouldn't go. I went by myself, got drunk by myself and walked all the way home, about five miles, before getting to the traffic light that was no less than 100 yards from my mailbox. The light was blinking, so being a good citizen, and former undercover CIA operative, and of course, being completely shit-faced, I began directing traffic. I did so apparently loudly enough to have one of the neighbors call the police, because they were there shortly. Roswell is fast!

As soon as they pulled up, I walked up to them and said, "Hi, I'm with the CIA and I'm here to inspect your jails." They happily obliged me and cuffed me. Then I seemed to get the gist, and begged to be released. That didn't work, so I went back to the CIA story. I was in and out of that Roswell jail cell within a couple of hours. It was my fastest visit ever, and I believed that my recent work for the CIA had had everything to do with it. That, and my ex-wife picking up the phone when I called, and coming to get me out.

She took me to her parents house, where I starting drinking again that morning. By the afternoon, I'd wandered from her parents' house back to mine and smoked some weed. That left me re-energized enough to make it back up to North River Tavern, walking the entire distance, too afraid to jump in my car, thank God. I was a little worried about getting picked up again by the Roswell Police, for walking drunk, but I decided it was worth the risk. Besides, they let me out after two hours anyway. I just wouldn't direct traffic again, no matter how badly they needed me, I thought.

Chattahoochee Mud Swim

As night fell, I found myself inside North River Tavern on the patio. I couldn't tell you what I was babbling, but I remember crying like a baby and complaining about having to go to Afghanistan, which I'd completely botched by now, anyway -- if the possibility had ever really existed. But, you know, I was so drunk at this point, I could have been crying about anything. The bouncer came up to me and told me I was banned again, this time for life, and my paranoia enveloped me instantly. It was the Devil, kicking me out of his playground! It was the CIA trying to put an end to my drinking, it was anything and everything other than my behavior.

I hopped the patio fence ran through traffic across Roswell Road in the black of night. I looked back and could see the piercing eyes of the invisible agents that were now my enemies. Now that I'd told off the Colonel, the CIA were my enemies. Hell, the CIA, Al-Qaeda, the Rainbow Family, and even my own family -- they were all after me, and they were right behind me, they were tracking me, and I had to get away. Water, I needed to get my foot in water and I'd be just fine. I took another glance back, and could see the eyes of the invisible agents. I don't remember jumping off the bridge into the Chattahoochee, but my next memory was of me thrashing and swimming down the middle of the river, lightning cracking in the sky and me headed towards the shore, as if I'd had a plan the entire time. The following days I would wonder if my father remembered pulling the trigger of that .357, or the taste of the bullet as it went through his mouth, entering his skull, or if he too had just been in and out of an episode, overly drunk, paranoid, unaware of what he was doing. Having zero control over ones actions, one can be dead in a mere moments, I would think looking back on this fateful night. Had my father killed himself in a blackout I'd wonder, as I'd just seemingly jumped off a bridge? It was possible. Or worse yet, had I died in that fateful jump? When the real insanity of detox would set in I would look back at this as sheer proof I was in hell, a ghost, forced to walk the Earth forever. But for now, I would just swim hard to the river shore. The first shore I hit, turned out to just be an island in the middle of the river. I waited, watching the top of the bridge to see if anyone followed me, keeping my ankle submerged in the cool river. The sky was flashing lightning, summer heat lightning as I crawled along the riverside. It looked like artillery flashes from "Band of Brothers", the HBO World War II series. My plan had worked, they didn't follow me. Nobody had.

I walked around the island, which I thought was the river's shore near Azalea Drive, only to find I'd reached the river again. I hopped on in again, between the island and Azalea Drive, slowly making progress across the slow moving water. I would creep to the shore to ultimately follow the river all the way down Azalea Drive, keeping my ankle in the water of course, keeping the microchips and satellites at bay, watching the lightning and actually relishing the adventure again. My invincibility was back! I'd jumped in the river for a purpose, I'd escaped my pursuers! As I crept along, the sky flashed, and a long, unidentified snake swam past, not ten feet away from me in the water. I wasn't scared, it was better than having those invisible agents on my ass. Trust me, their eyes looked like they could steal your soul, and apparently mine was for the taking.

I got out of the river slowly, watching for invisible spies. I had to make the final leg of the journey and I started jogging the rest of the way home, making sure not to stop and direct traffic anywhere. I got to my house, and drank some beer, and smoked some weed, with my foot in the bathtub, and just enough water to cover the microchips.

Prayer That Worked

Around 8 AM, I still hadn't slept. My baby sister Carrie knocked on the door and I walked outside. She had brought over some donuts and coffee. My hands had begun to shake again, and I'll not soon forget the mixture of sadness and anger in her eyes when she saw me covered in river mud. She asked me, "Why are you so dirty?"

I tried to give her a reasonable explanation for why I'd swum so many miles in the Chattahoochee River the night before, yet still smelled like a brewery and was all around insane. But reasonable explanations don't involve microchips, satellites, or the CIA. She just stopped me in my tracks and uttered one sentence that, just like the black angel's words, pierced my very soul.

"It's been so long since I've thought of you as a brother." Tears welled in her eyes as she walked away.

She began crying and jumped back in her car, leaving my gravel driveway, and me in a brief moment of clarity. In an instant all my grand delusions crashed down inside my head. Fuck it, I knew I was crazy. I had to get sober. I got on my knees and prayed to God for guidance. After that I went to the store and bought a twelve-pack. I got home, hoping to calm the shakes, the craziness and all that alcohol could cure and had been curing for the last fifteen years or so. But when I began to chug that beer, it went down my throat like battery acid. I tried to spit it back up, but it didn't want to come. I tried to drink it again, and sure enough, once again, it tasted like something used in torture. I waited 30 minutes, nervously pacing. I took a walk outside, scared, then went back to the fridge, opened a new beer and began to drink. I immediately spit it all back out. It was disgusting, it wouldn't go down, and I felt a terrible pit in my stomach. Something indescribably wrong had happened. I began to pray again, and my thoughts began to race. My solution of fifteen years plus had simply and suddenly, stopped working.

The first thoughts involved suicide. I'd wondered for years why my dad had killed himself, and now, with the only cure life had ever offered me out the window, I felt like I was in hell. Suicide finally sounded like the best option. I flirted with this idea most of the day, occasionally trying to drink more beer, always with the same result, a nasty, scolding, acidy, battery taste, with zero effect on my mind. This was indeed hell. I tried to smoke a cigarette, and I got the same result. Instead of the smooth nicotine, it felt like sinus medicine, it felt like putting my mouth to a muscle car's exhaust. I could derive no pleasure from anything I attempted. I tried to look at porn, and got no reaction, I tried to eat some food, and it tasted like rocks. I was certain I was in hell.

My mind racing, I began exploring the roots of life in general. It had all been a joke. I was angry, resentful, my mom and dad were dead, the rest of my family had left me to die here, and die I would. Perhaps all of life was a test, and the only real way to pass was to kill yourself? This thought became the theme of the next twelve hours or so of my pondering, and had been just under the surface for many years now. Maybe killing yourself proved that you had been to Earth, found it wanting, and decided to leave of your own volition? Proved that this place was insane, that war and hunger and disease and famine were all just tests, all just arrows pointing me to the ultimate direction of suicide and death, and an exit strategy? To abandon this planet and all its misery, was surely the only answer. Certainly I'd tried everything else. I held onto my .38 caliber pistol for most of the day, a gift from my Rainbow Family friend Mooney. I remember

273

thinking that right after I pulled the trigger, I would probably be instantly beamed up to a mother-ship, and would be given a medal, a congratulatory speech, and a pat on the back. They would say I'd done a fine job under the circumstances, and that most men in that same training scenario had killed themselves years before, having had their father show them the way. But I had endured the torture longer than any other soul ever sent before. Obviously I was an alien, how else did I fit into this civilization? I didn't, it was the only logical explanation.

The only thing that held me back from killing myself that day, when alcohol quit working -- the jumping off point, I would later hear it called -- was imagining putting my son through the exact same miserable pain I'd gone through when my dad killed himself. I just couldn't do it to him. Even though it made perfect sense, and I was going to receive the Alien Medal of Honor, there was simply no lie and no extraordinary stretch of the imagination, I could tell myself that wouldn't leave my son bitter, angry, confused, and alone without a father at 11 years old, the exact same age I was when my dad died. So failing to find a sufficiently delusional fiction, I got back on my knees and begged God for help.

Getting Sober for Real

When I began praying, all of the insane thoughts of the CIA, the Devil, aliens, and what have you, all left me. All I remembered was everything anyone and everyone had ever told me about AA. From my dad telling me it didn't work, to Graham Flagg when I was 17 telling me it did. Followed by Mike Rubin, Chad Major, everything Roger Henderson had ever said in those 28 days of sobriety I'd tried in what seemed like another lifetime ago. All my thoughts were directed towards AA, and at least I finally remembered a direction I could go in.

The one story I remembered above all was that of Graham Flagg, smiling zen-like, almost bragging that his first sober job was cleaning out Porta-Potty's. I remembered laughing at him when he told me this years before. Now, though, I suddenly understood his zen-like smile. If I could feel normal again, even relatively normal, or sane at all, then yes, Lord, I thought and prayed, yes, I'd be happy to clean up shit. That's why he had smiled. He'd been in this hell and gotten out, that's why he has no shame about cleaning out crap from plastic containers. I wanted what he had, to feel better, to get relief. This I've heard called the real miracle. That out of the insanity, we can have clear thoughts of a solution, not knowing that a solution exists. That I could go from thinking about justified suicide, to remembering everything everyone had ever told me about AA, was in fact the beginning of the miracle. All of that information had been discarded, I thought, but for whatever reason, that day, it all came back to me in a flash, and it stayed with me through that awful night, day one of my detox, the end of that awful Thursday, August 31st, 2006.When the morning came, I would know what to do. I would go back to AA, and this time I would do as I was told.

I didn't sleep a wink. When the morning came around, after 24 hours of shaking tremendously, and clutching my heart, through chest pains and what felt like an imminent heat attack, I awoke. My war-torn rat shack of a house, ants and mice crawling over all the trash was a disaster area. I looked around for a shirt to put on, and grabbed the closest shirt I could find. I was so out of it, I failed to realize it was one of my son's old baseball shirts. It was more than a little tight, but I was down to my lowest weight ever, 145 lbs, and looked good in a tight shirt, so I thought. I looked in the mirror, and despite my being skinnier than I'd ever remembered being, I was uglier than hell. I hadn't slept in over 24 hours, and I was incapable of eating. My face was yellow, and my eyes were tired, yet leery and watchful. I was ashamed to look at myself for too long in that mirror. It would have to do. I drove my BMW up to 8111.

I walked onto the campus of 8111, the AA Clubhouse, not like the punk that had strolled in back in November of 2005 with a marijuana maintenance agenda, to get the threat of being fired off my ass. I was in hell, and I wanted to get out. I hadn't showered, as I didn't have hot water, and was still covered in mud from my adventure through the river. I was wearing a shirt too tight, and my eyes looked more than a little insane. Last time I'd walked onto this property, I didn't want to talk to anyone. This time, I was afraid they'd call the cops on me, I looked so bad. Soon after I got out of the car and walked towards the benches, nervous, with butterflies and insane thoughts racing, a pretty blonde came up to me and gave me a huge, bearlike hug. I was astonished. I wouldn't have hugged myself, I'd recently been swimming in sewage. It was amazing that someone would hug me period, much less as dirty as I was.

"It gets better," she told me. I wanted to believe her, but I just couldn't quite grasp that yet. "Just remember, it's an inside job." That sounded like a conspiracy to me, and I walked away from her, nervously.

Within about five minutes a guy named Trevor approached me and said, "Hey, you look like you could use some help." He looked just like Faust Santino, one of my best friends in high school, who had turned out to be Pagan and Rainbow Family, and who I'd suspected had tried to steal my soul in all my paranoia.

"Yeah, man, I don't know what to do, but yeah, I want to get sober." I looked him in the eye, and he could tell I was being honest, because then we went to a second level of conversing I'd never yet approached in AA.

"Are you willing to do anything it takes?" He stared at me intently.

"You're not gay, are you?" He laughed, but I didn't think it was funny at all, at the time.

"No, man, but anything we suggest you do, you know, go to any number of meetings, get sponsees, that kind of thing."

"Yeah, sure, whatever, I just feel like shit, man, I want to get better. I can't drink anymore." I didn't mean that I shouldn't drink or it might not be prudent. I meant: I can't fucking drink anymore, I feel like I'm losing my fucking mind, please help me!

"OK, well, meet me here tomorrow morning at the 11:30 meeting, and don't drink between now and then, and we'll start working together." Faust was smiling, but I wasn't I assure you.

Detox Day Two

Don't drink between now and 11:30 tomorrow morning he told me. I drove the little Beamer home, and looked around my little house and wondered what the fuck I was going to do to stay sober another 24 hours. At this point I hadn't slept the night before so I laid down and tried to sleep. Nothing. Couldn't get a wink.

I began thinking, which is the mortal enemy of a detoxing alcoholic. I remembered telling the Colonel to go fuck himself, and then remembered that night walking along downtown, Kristen telling me I was a carrier, the black angel with his look of disdain, and my walking to Little Five Points and drinking some more. The girl who knew I'd written "I remember when I lost my mind" gave me a drink. She must have put something in the drink. She must have put some ice in it. Little Five Points, it's a gateway to hell, I told myself. I'd wandered around it, listening to the voices, growing confused, telling me to find the Land Trust, in between ordering me to go to the airport and book a flight to Afghanistan. I'd wandered all the way to Candler Park searching for the Land Trust, but it had disappeared. Fucking hippie aliens! I had wandered back to Little Five and drank with a bum in the courtyard of Little Five. Eventually I'd gotten a cab back home. They must have drugged me. It must be, because I told the Colonel to fuck off. Maybe I was dead. Maybe when I'd jumped off the bridge I'd died? Maybe worse, I'd killed someone else? Maybe this was hell. That thought didn't invade too seriously into my second 24 hours of detox, but it would.

That night, August 31st, 2006, shaking, miserable, and riddled with fear and delusions of a million different kinds, but not drinking, determined not to drink, I went back up to 8111, the AA Clubhouse, intending just to sit in the parking lot, lest I go drink. I found the Candlelight meeting though, arriving almost exactly at 10 PM. They turned the lights out, and I tried to listen to everybody, though today, I can only repeat one sentence that was said in that meeting: "I was glad to be able to show my mom I'd gotten sober before she died." It tore my heart out, but I didn't share. Eventually, at the end of the meeting, I walked up and grabbed a white chip, and returned to my seat in the very back of the room. Somebody gave me a little red Big Book that night. Everybody clapped. They obviously didn't know what a piece of shit I was. I did feel just a little bit better though. I thought I could make it without drinking until the morning at least. When I left anyway.

I went back home and tried to go to sleep. I even took four Tylenol PMs to no avail. I laid awake, shaking, riddled with chest pains, body aches, and my ankle was swollen from all the walking. But mostly I was stark raving mad, and getting worse. Why couldn't I sleep, I wondered? Maybe I was dead, I thought again? Maybe this really was hell, the inability to get drunk or die, being stuck on Earth for eternity. I deserved it I thought. I cried. I eventually tried to read the Bible, finding absolutely nothing interesting, but stumbling across almost every passage pertaining to hell there was, though I had to concentrate very hard just to be able to read, and it hurt my eyes and head both.

Finding no solace in my prayers or Bible reading, I eventually opened up the Big Book. I found some small comfort there. I decided I would do it, do all twelve steps, and if it didn't work, I would kill myself. Nobody could be expected to live in this much pain. Searching for relief, I read the Big Book that night, and did my absolute best to write down the twelve steps. On that piece of paper, all I wrote down was my mom, Jennifer Garden, a high school girlfriend I'd scammed 10 years ago, and my son. I didn't have a clue what I was doing, and all I could think about was going somewhere to get a drink, though I knew it wouldn't work, I'd tried that.

I watched TV. The thought that aliens and the CIA controlled Hollywood crept up. The thought that I was a target because I knew this came up. The actors and actresses spoke to me off and on. The thought that I was in hell and would stay feeling this awful forever stayed with me, haunting me. And I shook, cried, and prayed, and brushed away the constant ants crawling all over my skin. As soon as I rested, I would feel them crawling. The house did have ants, but to this day, I don't know if they were real or not that night. They felt and looked real, though, and through the fear, I was plagued with bugs. Ants, spiders, and cockroaches, as the night went on, joined me in my tossing and turning in that rat shack of a hellhole in Roswell, Georgia, as I sailed along into 48 hours of detox, without any alcohol or drugs, and without a wink of sleep.

Detoxing with Complete Abandon

Eventually the morning came. My third day sober, and I still hadn't slept. One remarkable thing was that I still had 10k in the bank, and wasn't completely and totally broke. I decided to rid myself of the ant and insect problem once and for all, not realizing that it was probably mostly hallucinations. I went to Home Depot and bought three huge buckets of dry ant killer, and I bought gloves, deathly afraid I would poison myself accidentally. I got home and began pouring the stuff all around my house that morning. I was probably a threat to the environment I used so much, and then I became acutely aware of the smell, all around the perimeter of my house, and how I'd probably, in fact, just poisoned myself. My mind was racing faster than it had the previous two days. It was now Friday, I still hadn't slept, and my shakes hadn't subsided. I washed my hands for about twenty minutes straight, and I jumped in the car, looking cracked out as could be, and, for some reason, drove to my mom's church, Roswell United Methodist, that I hadn't visited since her death. I think I wanted any possible solution other than AA.

I walked into the old chapel where'd I'd botched the poem at her funeral and prayed as a child, and I said a long and lengthy prayer to any God that would listen, begging for help. Then I walked into the Minister's office, told him I'd been sick for a long time and I needed to get better. Told him I was an alcoholic drug addict, and I didn't know what to do. Once again God directed me to AA. The minister told me the church had meetings once a week, but 8111, an AA clubhouse, had meetings all day every day. Feeling resentful and angry that this minister couldn't just slap a cure on my forehead, I left and went to 8111 to meet Trevor, and do anything it takes. I still hoped "anything" wasn't gay, but I wasn't sure.

Trevor was there at 8111, and I was glad, my mind was beyond sane at this point. I think my two remaining marbles were banging up against each other, coming up with ridiculous theories and plots against me. As I pulled into the parking lot, I parked against the fence, and noticed the inordinate number of squirrels running along the fence, several of them stopping their business to stare at me menacingly. Maybe that was it, maybe my punishment was to be reduced to an animal, feeling only primal instincts like hunger, sex, and cold? It wasn't unlike the last several months, and the idea I might be transformed into a squirrel seemed like a real possibility. I could take any small fear, and magnify it into the most terrible reality any horror movie had ever suggested. I had lost my mind quite completely, and was on the verge of crying real tears over potentially being turned into a squirrel. Trevor could see the fear in my eyes.

"What's next, I asked? Am I dead?" He looked at me with patience, "No, not yet." That didn't sound like good news.

"I'm glad you made it, did you drink?" He asked.

"No, drinking doesn't work, it's been three days, I haven't eaten and I haven't slept." I shared nervously.

"OK, come over here and talk to me." He began walking to the gazebo in the corner of the parking lot. Surrounded by squirrels.

I hesitated, if he were going to metamorphose me into a squirrel, that gazebo was just the place it would happen, but I didn't have much of a choice. Besides, I thought, if it were that sinister, it was going to happen anyway. I decided to walk the plank and accept my consequences, squirrel or no squirrel.

He asked me about my life, and I began telling him everything, from growing up in an abusive family, to the CIA, and he tried to slow me down, to no avail. I cried. I was insane.

"Listen, stick with us, and things will get better." He was there with a group of people and he'd introduce me, he said. We would go to a ton of meetings, and it would be a slow process, but I would get better. I didn't believe him, and I thought slow meant like how long it took for the Earth to cool, but I didn't have an option.

"Let's go to the meeting," and I followed him into 8111. I found that I could no longer read. I tried to read the steps and traditions on the wall, and found my mind incapable. I was having a hard time understanding people as well. Three days of dt's had taken a toll. I heard two things in that meeting that I held onto. The second step: "Came to believe that a power greater than ourselves could restore us to sanity." Sanity, I finally understood that step, and I wanted that to happen. I finally recognized that I was insane. Hell, I knew I was insane. To be restored to sanity sounded like a good deal. And I also heard another person share about being able to be there for their dying mother. I tried not to cry at that meeting. I tried not to get up and run out and go drink. I tried not to stare at the squirrels running along the fence, and I just hoped this wasn't hell.

From there we went to Wendy's off Roswell Road, where I told him the rest of my discombobulated story, holding back nothing. Ironically the Wendy's was right next to the gas station where the Fulton County Police had beaten me up, back when I was 16 years old, over LSD. I winced when I thought of it, that brutal cop throwing me into the back of the police car by my balls. All the billy clubs, the looks of despair from my friends, watching me helplessly get beaten. It was how I felt right now, completely helpless again. He ordered me some food but I couldn't eat. He asked if I was willing to do whatever it took. "Yes" I said, "as long as it isn't gay." He asked me if I'd stick with him for three days and let him be my temporary sponsor. "Fine," I said. He probed my whole life, my whole drug and drink history. He told me his fucked up story. He told me Complete Abandon was the only way he'd stayed sober. Though I didn't know what he was talking about then, Complete Abandon was the group he belonged to, within AA. He asked if I used needles. I told him one night in my life, and he told me that he'd seen miracles happen in this program when people did what was suggested. I assumed this meant I had AIDS. I began to think this guy was a spiritual cop. He wasn't taking me to jail, I'd gone beyond mortal laws. This man was delivering my soul to burn.

We drove down to the Triangle Club, another AA Clubhouse in Buckhead, and there we met more of his crew called Complete Abandon. A cult within the AA cult, I thought. Just like the Rainbow

280

Family, inside the deadheads. I'd run into the worst of the worst, as always, and they had plans for me, and most likely for my soul. I was certainly going to be tried, convicted, and condemned to hell. No doubt about it. I was too tired to fight it.

I remember sitting on that porch at Triangle, three days into detox, having never detoxed before, talking to another Complete Abandon kid. As soon as Trevor left, I began asking him all the crazy thoughts and fears I'd come up with.

"Seriously man, am I dead?" I asked honestly. He looked at me wildly, not like he was concerned for my sanity, but more like maybe I'd just hit the nail on the head, and my fear grew.

"Really, man, is there a bullet in my head. Did I kill myself in a blackout? Did I kill someone else? What the fuck is going on, man, I've never felt like this, am I dying, am I going to die? Help me, man!" I drew a lot of stares early on.

He went and got Trevor, and these assholes played it up. They used my delusions, and told me maybe, you'll just have to wait and see. The fuckers thought it was funny, but I had nowhere else to go. I knew they wouldn't let me drink, and I'd agreed to stay with him for three days. I went into the bathroom, to take a leak and read a poem there that hit home like no other poem I'd ever read. I had to focus to read the words, and think them through, but it struck like lightning, especially the last word:

I drank for happiness and became unhappy,
I drank for joy and became miserable,
I drank for sociability and became argumentative,
I drank for sophistication and became obnoxious.
I drank for friendship and made enemies.
I drank for sleep and woke up tired.
I drank for strength and felt weak.
I drank for relaxation and got the shakes.
I drank for courage and became afraid.
I drank for confidence and became doubtful.
I drank to make conversation easier, and slurred my speech.
I drank to feel heavenly and ended up feeling like hell.

-Author Unknown

That poem made sense, but the word that stuck out was HELL. It could even be so sinister as to mean that this was the gateway to hell. Easily, I thought, since I was beyond redemption. I couldn't remember my last spree, maybe I'd killed someone. Probably my ex-girlfriend, Caroline. Why did they ask me to leave North River Tavern anyway, surely it wasn't for crying? I must have hurt someone. I was already dead, all this was just waiting for my senses to catch up. Surely the brief moments of pain before the torturous agony of flesh ripping and flame of hell. I walked into the meeting starting at Triangle, and everything about it reminded me of a government facility. Surely the floor would open up, a courtroom of my peers would be waiting for me, I'd lose and the flames of hades would engulf me instantly. I shook and tried not to cry in that meeting, and once again, all I heard was "Restore us to sanity," and somebody talk about how proud their mother was that she'd died in peace, knowing they were sober. That was the third mother remark in 3 days of detoxing. I was fucked, and at 28 years of age I wept some more.

The gates of hell didn't open quite yet, and I followed Trevor and Complete Abandon to another meeting in Alpharetta. They told us not to cuss. Every single person in my group cussed, and I thought for sure, they were just demons here to collect my soul. But what choice did I have but to follow them around, and await my ultimate punishment? That Alpharetta meeting began at sunset and the sky had turned a crimson red. Perfect weather for soul collection, I thought. At least there weren't any squirrels. In the meeting once again, I clung to "restore us to sanity," and like God's clockwork, somebody shared about their dying mother. I wanted to attack them, I was sick of hearing about proud mothers. Mine was dead, and she'd never be proud. I'd stolen drugs from her in her dying breaths. Fuck all of you. I'm going to hell. I began to grow impatient for it.

From there, we headed to our fourth meeting of the day. "When is it going to be over," I asked one of them. "Trust me, you don't want this to end." Someone messed with me some more, fully aware of my delusions and vulnerability. To me that meant once this ends, I was condemned and the real torture would begin. It scared me, and the reality and details of hell, plagued my confused head some more. Three days without sleep, well into 72 hours, nothing to eat, and cigarettes and water tasted like shit. If it got worse than this, it must be pretty fucking bad, I thought.

We drove to downtown Atlanta. Complete Abandon's home

group met in an old church in the ghetto, or so it seemed to this upper middle class Roswell white kid. The meeting was in the basement of a church, which seemed as plausible a place as any to enter hell. Before the meeting started, I asked another guy if it ever got better. And he told me sort of, but it was different. He asked me how I felt. I told him, "I feel completely empty. Like I don't have a soul." He looked me in the eyes, and said "You probably don't. It gets better, though, there's just a lot of work ahead of you."

With the meeting about to start and darkness surrounding this shady group of characters, we all walked single file into the basement of this church. To me, the basement of a church was probably the best place on Earth God or the Devil could symbolically choose to collect souls. It was as if we'd missed the main chapel by just a hair, and we were now inevitably doomed. I walked into the basement, and this motley crew of ex-heroin addicts, crack fiends, and alcoholics all surrounded a table. It was hot and I was tired, but as one man started sharing about having a disease that was trying to kill him, and how he'd done his best, and how he couldn't have tried harder, he said but at least it's not as bad as it is for one of us at this table, who probably wouldn't survive the month, and tears flowed down his cheeks as he spoke dramatically staring me down. I automatically assumed he was talking about me. As he passed to the next person to share, tears raining down his face, my body shaking and sweating, and my mind restless, but exhausted, I looked up at the clock in this hot as hell basement to see that all of the numbers on the clock had fallen to the bottom. Cleverly written across the face of the clock was the word "Whatever." I knew then, in no uncertain terms, that the clock was a riddle for hell. What does it matter what time it is in Eternity? My heart started pounding, the sweat poured out, and when it was my turn, I fully expected to be lowered into the flames of hell, what was left of my soul to burn eternally in damnation for all of my sins. That clock set me off, it was no longer a possibility, but a reality. I was condemned.

I shared. I said I was scared, and then I passed. I didn't die. I didn't go to hell. I hadn't slept in three days, I'd eaten nothing but nibbles. I drove home with the Complete Abandon crew, where they told me they would watch me detox in shifts, so if I stopped breathing or went into convulsions, they could get me to a hospital. That sounded encouraging. I tried to eat a little bit. I drank a lot of Gatorade as they suggested, and I prayed to God for another chance. I can remember the strange delusions I had just before I went to sleep.

One was that they would transport my soul to a small Mexican village, where I would be condemned to live in the body of a frail old Mexican man, barely able to walk, and worse, married to Gwen Evere, minus her beauty, but also in the body of an elderly Mexican woman. When I awoke, I would surely be in a Mexican shanty. I was able to be frightened by this, however ridiculous it may sound now. The other was that I had been an alien experiment. There was a tumor in my head, which was why I was so off the chain nuts, and once I fell asleep they would surely come to harvest my brain for medicinal purposes. Obviously there was a connection to my mom, and probably my dad knew, and decided to blow his head off to rid himself of a brain. Eventually, the shaking slowed, my mind turned off, and I drifted into sleep.

I woke up hopeful. I'd slept. I wasn't condemned to walk the planet sleepless for the remainder of humanity's time on Earth. I was still hanging out with Complete Abandon, and they were still weird, and I still had a too-tight t-shirt on and felt like shit, but ultimately I hadn't been metamorphosed into a squirrel or an elderly Mexican man, hadn't been harvested by aliens, and more importantly, hadn't died and gone straight to hell. There was a little hope yet!

I spent Saturday and Sunday with Complete Abandon, going from AA Clubhouse to AA Clubhouse, and eventually I began calling Graham Flagg, my AA contact that I'd known since I was 17. I kept getting his voicemail, and we never stayed in any one place long enough to get a call back, as my cell phone had died that Friday and I was using other folks phones. When mine had powered down I complained to my temporary sponsor Trevor, and he said "You're an alcoholic, who do you think wants to talk to you?" He was right and I was just happy not to be in hell. My fears subsided a little, I was still able to bring them up intermittently and they would evolve in those early days of sobriety. At the end of each day, we would meet at sunset at Dunkin Doughnuts off Peachtree Industrial, where Trevor told us we would receive orders. Orders? This sounded like CIA stuff to me, and I began questioning him thoroughly about who gave us the orders. He wouldn't tell me, and it pissed me off.

The next meeting I went into with them, I began trying to read the little red Big Book someone had given me, which is basically just a small version of the standard AA Big Book, with a few minor differences. One difference is an international listing of all the meeting phone numbers worldwide in the back of the book. Noticing this, my paranoid mind raced just a bit. Just before I sat down, someone said "Keep coming back, you will be contacted."

Sounded like they knew something about my top secret background! Shit, that's what this was probably all about, my lunacy screamed at me! All this was the perfect cover for the intelligence community, come to think of it! Just like going to the loony bin before had been the perfect explanation for my brother, these meetings were the perfect places for spies to meet amongst the crazy! Why hadn't I thought of it before! "You will be contacted!" I repeated the new mantra in my head.

I opened up the little red Big Book and it fell open to those international phone numbers on cue. There they were, proclaiming my legitimacy, screaming practically that I was really an undercover operative! Meetings in Moscow, Beijing, Taiwan, Israel, Germany, you name it, with phone numbers and everything! Now it was making sense. You will be contacted! I will be, you're damn right! Hell, the OSS, which later became the CIA, had even come to power about the same time as Alcoholics Anonymous had back in the mid 1930's. I was really onto something! I turned to Trevor to whisper my revelations and before I could get too far into the madness he said "Shut the fuck up! You're just crazy, just listen to the meeting." This shut the crazy train down pretty quickly, and I remembered I was just mad. Sponsors are crucial early on. Before the meeting was over, someone would share about being at their dying mother's bedside, solidifying the reality, but further pissing me off. I wasn't a spy, or a grandiose undercover operative, I was just a garden variety drunk that had stolen, lied, and manipulated my way into one of these AA seats, so skilled at lying I was no longer able to tell the true from the false in the world. Still, reality sucked, the delusions had been more fun, and for a split second I'd believed in them again, it was creepy.

Another thing that pissed me off about Complete Abandon was they wouldn't tell me who their higher power was. Despite all my anger at God, I wasn't a Pagan, and though I thought myself the worst example on Earth, I considered myself a Christian. These guys also were so cryptic and cultish, they reminded me a lot of the Rainbow Family, and of course, I was paranoid. But I had fears that AA was a cult already, I damn sure wanted to be taken through the steps by another Christian, if for nothing else but superstition, and Trevor wouldn't for the life of me tell me he even believed in God. For all I knew, he was praying to Satan, or the proverbial doorknob. I needed God's help, not a doorknob's. He also told me to quit my job. Well, this just wasn't going to happen. I had 10k in the bank, and my own damn company. I'd just placed the Director of Audit at one of the top 10 companies in the world, and I was trying to get

Bob Greyson into that same company now, I wasn't about to quit my job and get some menial, dishwashing job just to be humble. I'd been walking around thinking I was condemned to hell in a Little League t-shirt around nothing but strangers, and I felt quite humble enough, thank you very much.

Still, I didn't trust myself to go home just yet, so I stuck around and had some interesting conversations. Once I'd finally slept, I was able to grasp, for the most part, that what I was going through was simply alcohol withdrawal, or detox. Another Complete Abandon kid and I started hanging out a lot, and it turned out he'd lived at the Samson Lofts around the same time I'd been there. He mentioned a girl I'd known, and he told me she'd died, he'd delivered her last shot of heroin, and I thought to myself, "Well, if he's not in hell, I guess I have a chance." He told me about his detox and thinking there was a watch in his forearm, and Trevor having to stop him from carving it out of his flesh with a knife. We laughed and I told him about the microchips in my ankle. Suddenly there was comedy in all this tragedy. When two people were able to share about their insanity, it softened the blow somehow, it made it human. I'm grateful for everyone in Complete Abandon that watched me while I slept and dragged me to five or six meetings a day that first hellish week of my real sobriety. They get a bad rep for their heavy recruiting style and their stance on meds, primarily telling newcomers not to take them, but for me personally, they saved my life and I'm grateful.

I'm ultimately grateful for what I heard in all those meetings they dragged me to. In every meeting I attended, someone, male or female, young or old, it didn't matter, like clockwork, would mention their mother, and how she had died, proud that they were sober. Every time I heard that it would choke me up, and force me to examine what a colossal fuck-up I had really been. That I wasn't just a fun-loving good guy, but that this disease had taken me to the level of stealing from my dying mother. It hurt, but I needed that pain.

Museum-Quality Home

Eventually, I got in a screaming match with Trevor after he didn't want to take me home that Sunday, and I blasted him for telling me it was OK to be a temporary sponsor, and that yelling at the top of your lungs at sponsees was definitely not cool. Especially when they have only a few days sober. I was really missing home, and was pretty sure he was either a Rainbow Family sober guy, or a CIA operative, and I wasn't sure which, but I didn't want to stick around to find out. He weirded me out and I wanted to go home. The Complete Abandon experience had been nice, but these guys were all broke, and I had 10k in the bank and my own company, my ego was still capable of rearing its head, and my delusions were far from gone. I did think, though, that having gotten the worst of the dt's over with, I could make meetings at 8111 and stay sober, using the Complete Abandon strategy of just going to meetings all day long. And I'd call Graham Flagg and ask him if he was Christian, which I was pretty sure he was, and whether he'd be my sponsor, which I was pretty sure he would be, but I couldn't get him to call me back at payphones. I would charge my phone at home.

I walked up to the front door of my little rat shack cabin in Suburbia, opened the door, and saw the insides of a place I felt I'd never visited before. I remembered a conversation I'd had with my ever so patient Uncle Jack a few months back, about the writings on the wall, the lamp I'd made, and other such oddities. I vaguely recollected telling him I was an artist. His ever witty reply was, "Yeah, Bryan, they'll probably turn that house into a museum." At the time I didn't register the sarcasm, but actually thought, well, maybe they would, I am quite the genius, and such is what I thought of the lamp I'd created out of a bicycle tire, two government flags, and a whole lot of glue. Museum-like also, I believed, were the writings covering all the walls of my home, genius in nature, eccentric at worst, but obviously treasures, in my own deluded head. The empty refrigerator box I'd kept in the kitchen, filled almost to the top with empty beer, vodka, and whiskey bottles, was riddled with bullet holes, as I would drink and blast holes into the cardboard, to enjoy the sound of shattering glass and shrapnel flying all over my house. It had all been a part of the cosmic way of things a short week ago, but suddenly, I was seeing this house for what it was, with sober eyes. It was a fucking disaster. It was a war zone. It was a loony bin unto itself.

Every wall was covered with ramblings, incoherent writings, that only I, at one time had understood, and now I couldn't tell you what they said. Drawings a five year old could compete with were everywhere, and that God-awful, ugliest lamp on Earth I'd been so proud of, and had spent days piecing together without sleep, the one I was sure was a masterpiece. It was a piece all right, but not of the master type. It was like I'd been living in a different dimension. A dimension of hell that this shit, this wasteland had been acceptable, and just five days of sobriety had ripped me from the delusion. From the madness. The next thing I noticed was how disgusting it was outside of the décor. The dishes were piled up, there were pizza boxes everywhere, and beer bottles, broken, and half empty, all over the entire house. A few rats scurried away, right when I had opened the door, and the smell was something to behold. I'd never noticed the rats, or that smell, in fact I'd told myself I had ghosts, and believed it for over a year. How I'd lived like this for so long was beyond me. My aunt had cleaned it spotless just a few months back when I first visited the looney bin. I got enraged with myslef, and I decided to clean.

I took one small step into the grimy cluttered cabin, and within one step, a chunk of glass sliced the side of my foot open and I began bleeding all over the kitchen floor. I laughed, though. The "curse of invincibility" was gone. I'd been living like this for months on end, without one scratch, with glass all over the house, from the bottom of the toilet seat, to the couch itself, and not once had I gotten so much as a splinter. Five days sober, one step into my house, and I sliced my foot open. I laughed, but I also worried a little about what other hell to pay there would be.

I began panicking about the days preceding my five day sober adventure. I couldn't remember for the life of me what I'd done to get kicked out of North River Tavern. I couldn't remember why I'd jumped off the bridge, or when this hellish time exactly had started. I was mad, sweaty, pacing, frantic, and I freaked out. My phone was still dead, so I walked up to Kroger to the pay phone and began making calls. Somehow I began to think maybe I'd even killed my ex-girlfriend Caroline, and this was all a sequence of events leading up to my entrance into hell. I kept remembering The Brothers Karamazov, which I hadn't read, but had heard was about a man who'd killed a woman and how guilty he had felt. I was nuts. I called her dad, and asked if she was OK. "Yes, she's fine, why?" I didn't know what to say so I just hung up on him, slightly relieved. Then I called North River Tavern and asked why I'd been kicked out. "Did I hurt anyone?" "No, you were just crying, and we were just sick of it. You also knocked over a chair, I think." I walked back home, the paranoia and delusions abating for a moment. I would just clean up my house and ignore my thoughts, I told myself. I was capable of getting worked up over absolutely nothing.

I cleaned the entire house as best I could. I mowed the yard. I tried to clean the dishes but they were beyond repair, stinking of death, and rats and waste, I had to throw them all away. After that I went for a jog. I didn't make it 100 yards before I had to stop and walk, and when I got back to the house, I laid on the floor and cried like a baby. I felt so fucking awful. I thought after all that physical

288

exercise, I would have sweated it out, but I hadn't. I still felt like shit, and I couldn't believe that after five days sober, I still felt that bad. I cried, and then it hit me. I remembered where I'd hidden that quarter bag of weed.

The irony of this was that when my friend Logan had been at my house not a month before, we'd gotten into a fist fight in my living room over him stealing this weed. I was absolutely positive he had. Apparently, I owed Logan an apology, because when I reached into my computer, and felt between the hard drive and the CD-ROM, there was a big ol' fluffy bag of $125 a quarter ounce bud, and Logan hadn't stolen it after all. He'd tried to send me the hospital bill for dislocating his shoulder over that incident. Years back, he'd made fun of me for using club flyers as toilet paper in my apartment at the Pendleton after Gwen had left me car-less and rent-less, with one good foot. When he called to tell me he'd send me the hospital bill, I told him to please hurry up and send it, so I could wipe my ass with it. He wasn't amused, but everyone he told the story to thought it was hilarious.

I grabbed that weed, and stared at it, thinking. On the one hand I'd earned five days sobriety, and didn't want to start over. On the other hand, maybe this shit would make me feel better. Before I could pontificate any longer, my sister and her fiancé Skip pulled up into my driveway, and before I could think it over too much, I walked outside and handed her the bag of weed, and begged her to give it away. It was good weed, and she lived downtown, I was sure she could find someone. It was another God shot for me. Had she not been there, I'd have surely smoked it up, and been drunk again in weeks, if not days. I'm grateful she pulled up, unannounced, both this time, and the time before.

We talked a bit about how hard it was, her not really understanding, having only read a few books about alcoholism but trying at least. I just couldn't put into words how bad I felt. It meant something to me that she'd read about it though, that she was attempting to understand, not just condemning me as useless, as I'd felt for years. Again I was glad she'd stopped by, I wasn't completely alone in this.

Getting Sponsored

After Carrie left, I went up to a meeting. I tried to share for the first time, and I remember having something clear cut and simple to say, but when I opened my mouth, I simply starting bawling tears.

They were tears of frustration, sadness, mourning for my mother, tears for Gwen leaving, for my divorce, you name it. Everything and nothing. They say that when you drink constantly for years on end, you never really experience the emotions of anything you go through, so that when you sober up, you literally play catch-up on all the terrible things that happened that you had buried and numbed out since you began. It all came out, and I cried like a baby, and didn't get a word out. Several people came and hugged me. I resented them for it. I was a mess. But afterwards, I actually felt a little better.

My friend Graham Flagg showed up, and I told him what was different about my house, about me, about giving away the weed, about needing a Christian sponsor. He had a huge wooden crucifix on his neck, hanging from what looked like a simple, humble string, not gold or anything pretentious. It's exactly what I needed to see. I got my first real hope, and I promised him I'd do whatever it took to get sober, if he could promise me real relief, that it really got better. He swore it did, and I believed him. Hell, I'd known him since I was 17. I finally, truly had a little bit of hope. I still felt like ass, but felt that maybe it would get better. He told me to begin praying in the morning, on my knees, exactly like this, "Lord, please give me the strength to stay sober." And at night to pray, "Lord, thank you for giving me the strength to stay sober." This time I wanted it. I was willing to do whatever it took, including praying on my knees, humbly. I wasn't alone.

I went home and slept in my clean house, and I was pretty sure I'd wake up in the morning. I said a prayer of gratitude to God for keeping me sober that day, and I would say another prayer to God asking for strength to stay sober tomorrow morning, just like my sponsor had told me to do. Graham knew his shit. This time I was teachable, and this time I wouldn't try the marijuana maintenance program, which hadn't worked anyway.

I hadn't spent much time with my son Jake and I felt terrible about that, as well as everything else, but Anne Marie kindly brought him over now that I had five days sober, and the house was relatively clean. He brought over a board game, Stratego, and I did my best to play with him. It was another solid indication of just how warped my mind had become. My brain was so damaged I couldn't grasp the rules. I could barely read the box enough to find that the game was OK for kids 7-9 years of age. I was 28 and lost. The magnitude of my years of drinking began to weigh in like it never had before. I pretended that I understood the rules, and I remembered my dad never playing games with me ever, despite my begging. At least I was here, I thought, regardless of whether I could fathom the elementary rules or not.

Anne Marie picked him up after a few hours and the visit had been good for my soul. I tried to sleep after Anne Marie and Jake left, after a long first day home and found my thoughts dark, strange, and racing. I tried to imagine a large switch in my head. One that was just turned in the wrong direction, that all my thinking was wrong, and that I needed to sober up and stay sober to turn the switch back. Still, the darkness and silence assaulted my thinking as if purposefully trying to make me see how evil I'd become. Eventually, I would picture myself being slain, execution style, by a masked firing squad, all firing automatic AK-47's. I dreamed of dying from gunfire often, and somehow this was the best thinking my mind at that stage had to offer to calm me down. Death by firing squad offered me rest and comfort, and I finally fell asleep. I would use that imagery to fall asleep well into my first year of sobriety. It seemed more likely to give me solace than actually being cured of alcoholism.

And so I woke up with a six day head start on real sobriety. I was still a mess, for sure, but it could have been worse, I thought. I had my Beamer still, and I still had 10k in the bank. So, thinking that God would surely reward my good behavior with success in business, I relocated my home office to a nice swank office in Tower Place, the heart of Buckhead, for a large down payment on the office and a huge $1200 a month nut. Grandiosity never escaped this alcoholic. But I wasn't worried, I had faith, I'd be just fine, now that I was sober. A week sober. I had failed to run the plan by my sponsor, but it was OK, I'd make it happen. I'm still working on grandiosity. It is said not to make any major decisions your first year, other than of course, getting sober. It's ok, I've seen worst year one decisions, tattoos, pregnancies, joining the military, all rank up there as major decisions I've seen people jump into while clearing their heads in their first year.

I began calling my Fortune 10 client with a new vigor, sharing with them my new office address, and pushing Bob Greyson's resume on the Global Controller there, because Bob was literally the perfect candidate for an internal audit job there. I was even greeted with some success, and in that first 35 days of real sobriety, was able to slowly get the ball rolling on getting my own company on a Fortune 10's permanent vendor list, which had been a huge goal of mine for years.

I would talk to my brother regularly for the first time in years. I shared with him that the most immediate results of quitting drinking had been solid craps. For years on end, I'd had the runs. We laughed and he said that yeah, he valued a good bowel movement too much to drink like that. I was also able to recollect old hobbies I'd loved and given up, like fishing.

I spent a lot of time fishing in the lake across the street from my little house. In my first two weeks of sobriety I caught the biggest bass I'd ever even seen, probably weighing in around eight or nine pounds, though I let it go before I could weigh it. I couldn't help but think this was another God shot. A little blessing, sign of things to come, reward for putting down the drink.

I made it to the 10 PM candlelight meeting every single night, and I chalked every single passing day on the wood above my toilet, like a prisoner in an ancient dungeon. I didn't share much in the meetings, but I did begin talking to a few select people after the meetings. Rene Broussard had a mellow, almost Buddhist approach to the program that I really liked, and Tanner was able to convince me it did actually get better. Tanner was an older guy, maybe 55, who reminded me of a CEO or an Officer in the military, bald, and always wore a white T-Shirt. He told me, and I hope I never forget it, "Give this thing a year, and if you still want to drink after a year, I'll buy you your first drink. But I promise you, you won't want it." That sounded like a good plan, but I wasn't quite sold on it all just yet.

That first attempt at real sobriety, without pot, was more painful than description allows. Ironically, the book I'd read, Think and Grow Rich, helped me to justify the meetings. Not really realizing the full meaning of the spiritual side, or the psychic change all the AA'ers promised, I was able to rationalize the use of the meetings by remembering the book's defense of the collective consciousness. This is the theory that where two or more people joined in a common cause, that stated that cause daily, they were more likely to achieve it. AA is definitely two or more people. Before I would have a spiritual experience, or a psychic change, I would buy into the collective consciousness being able to at least amplify my odds of quitting drinking, God or no God. That made sense. I wanted to be relieved of the obsession to drink and everyone said it was a God thing. I mostly believed there was a God, I just didn't know that he cared to help me. I would also try and go to church to increase the odds of his helping me out, to RUMC where my mom had forcefully dragged me against my will. Regardless of my theories or doubt, it made sense that a group trying to quit drinking, or two or more people, stood a better chance than me alone.

Early on, I visited my Aunt Becca, my mom's sister, and a cancer survivor. Something she said helped me out a lot. I was entertaining the committee of voices in my head that all alcoholics in church seem to host, debating this time the relevance of the New Testament. Being a history buff, I thought I knew a lot about the randomness in which certain books of the New Testament had made it into the Bible, and certain books had been thrown aside by the Vatican, or by Constantine or others. She said to me "The Bible is exactly as it is in your hands as God wants it to be. God is omnipotent." Later that Sunday, in an AA meeting someone said "God is everything or God is nothing." Coincidence, maybe, but it was a crack in my defenses, and the wall would soon simply crumble.

I looked around that meeting and saw people with five years, ten years, and even twenty-plus years sober. The Big Book of Alcoholics Anonymous had sprung up in the 1930's after 20,000 years of civilization and alcoholics destined to die of their progressive disease. We just happened to be born in the 70 years of human history in which there was some sort of solution. Just as the Bible was exactly as God wants it to be when I put it in my hands, so too was the Big Book of Alcoholics Anonymous. He had led me to AA, even the church, RUMC, had pointed me there, and here I was, and the knowledge was free, and exactly as God wanted me to find it. I began to really feel the answer really was through the twelve steps of AA, the Big Book, and the collective consciousness of all of us drunks trying to accomplish the same goal. A few days later, I was reading the New Testament, and as if for the first time I read where Jesus says "For where two or three are gathered together in my name, there am I in the midst of them." I was sold. AA isn't Christian affiliated, but that principle is wisdom, timeless, and shared by almost all religions.

Celebrating Thirty-five Days Sober

Somewhere deep down, I clung to the idea that I would still be able to drink like a normal person. Apparently that is common. And I missed Caroline, or so I thought. Towards the end of that first 30 days, I called her several times and begged her to get sober with me. She wouldn't hear of it. She wanted nothing to do with it or with me. I talked to my sponsor about "loving" her, and he told me it was my disease fucking with me. He said I'd be better off going to an Asian massage parlor than calling her again, that nothing led to relapse faster than pussy, and he'd seen it a million times. What did he know?

I heard Viper Eric speak, another middle aged alcoholic I'd met, so named because of the beautiful car he drove, and I identified with what he called "wet brain". That made sense, as I was still only able to read so many emails a day, before they would all go fuzzy. And I had the shakes that entire first two to three weeks of sobriety. At one point, on the way in to work, I remember calling my sponsor to dispute whether or not I was an alcoholic, and how I'd been thinking it over while in the shower that morning. He responded, "Do you think regular drinkers wake up and think about whether they are alcoholics or not at 8 AM?" That made some sense. Still I wanted to believe after not drinking for a month or so, my liver would go back to normal. Who cared if I was yellow, that was probably just my old age of 28 anyway?

My brother, sister, uncle, ex-wife and son were all happy I was finally getting sober, but it was hard for me to explain just how awful I felt still on occasion. I would speak to them briefly, and resent their conversations more than I'd let on. They didn't understand. Fortunately, other alcoholics did, and the meetings kept me going. Everything else in life pissed me off though. I wasn't drunk at my son's ballgames that fall, though, and not hyped up on amphetamines, I'm sure I wasn't as obnoxious either.

I remember thinking when I picked up my 30-day chip that I could drink again, and it would probably be OK. I was pretty impressed with myself for getting 30 days, yeah, but I still wanted a drink. It was still all I fucking thought about. I was still obsessing like hell, and I didn't see an end in sight, but I couldn't find a reason good enough to drink. I wanted to drink at 30 days, but I'd found I was able to get to the next day using the meetings. I hadn't started any actual step work, though, and I was still focused more on placing Bob Greyson into my Fortune 10 client, than I was on starting my first step work assignment. It seemed relatively easy, but I guess I just wasn't ready yet. I was calling my sponsor every day, but I still hadn't bought in entirely.

Cold-calling was definitely more difficult without the Adderall, though, and eventually I talked myself into going to get the prescription I still had, filled one last time. Just to jump start the business, I swore.

At 30 days or so, I went to court to answer to the drunk and disorderly charge from my directing traffic incident in Roswell, days before I came into the program. The judge ordered probation, and a mandatory 90 meetings in 90 days. I chuckled a little at this, as I was already doing a 90/90 per my sponsor's orders. To celebrate not getting locked up, I remember popping a few Adderalls, of course, deciding against telling my sponsor. It was a prescription anyway, I lied to myself.

And as will happen to any alcoholic not fully wearing his armor, an opportunity presented itself. Caroline called me the next day while I was in the office cold-calling, and she sounded drunk. She wanted me to pick her up and take her back to my house, and said she missed me. I got a hard-on while she was talking. Without calling my sponsor, without even thinking about it, I drove to pick her up in East Cobb at her parents, and before I'd even decided what was going to happen, found myself stepping foot into one of my old hot spots, O'Shaunassy's. As I stepped into the bar, my phone rang. It was my sponsor, Graham.

"Is everything OK?" he asked.

"Uh, yeah, I'm fine." I stepped back out into the parking lot and wandered how the fuck he knew.

"Ok, just checking, hadn't heard from you in a couple of days." I could feel him smirking.

"No, everything is good. I'll call you later." It was weird, and I wouldn't forget it, but it wasn't about to stop me from drinking. 30-day chip or not, sponsor calling me or not, they say you relapse days before you actually drink, and that was true for me, as I stepped back into the bar to throw away 35 days of sobriety.

I remember hoping I could just have a few beers, but the stark reality hit me between the eyes. If I was controlling my drinking, I wasn't enjoying it, and if I was enjoying it, I sure as hell wasn't controlling it. Caroline and I finished off a couple of midday pitchers of beer, then went and bought a twelve-pack, and went back to my house.

We wasted no time before we were in bed going at it, and not having had sex in over a month, and feeling like I loved her drunk ass, I was way too excited, and finished entirely too early. Earlier than I'd even predicted, and I ended up coming inside her, which was one of the first times I'd ever not been able to time it to pull out, since I'd been a teenager. Funny how that works. Or sometimes doesn't, just quite right.

After we were finished, we laid in bed for about 20 minutes and I began to be disgusted with myself. Her cell phone rang, and she grabbed it and started talking to someone that was obviously her lover. She then looked at me, and said "Where's my underwear? Oh my God, did we have sex?" It was a bullshit lie her conscious was forcing her to tell, or something psychotic, but it pissed me off something fierce.

"Oh, bullshit!" and I still believe I called that one right.

"I don't remember us having sex, I want to go home." She pouted.

"Fine, whatever, get the hell out of here, then!" and I called her a cab.

She left, the romance and lust gone, I was left with what remained of a twelve-pack, a head full of AA and a belly full of beer. But, I thought, at least I'd given myself a 35-day break. I would be able to keep it under control from here on out. No benders, I swore to myself. This time it would be different. I went to sleep early that night, and promised myself I'd go to work tomorrow, and accomplish a ton with the Adderall, and not drink myself into oblivion.

By lunchtime the next day, sitting in my office, my heart pounding from the Adderall, all I could think about was a drink. I didn't want to cold-call whatsoever. Around 1:00 PM, I went to the bar across the street and began drinking. I hadn't told anyone that I'd started drinking again, so Anne Marie was still trusting me to pick up Jake and watch him for the night. Not to let her down, I drove drunk to Roswell, picked up my son, and avoided her, so she couldn't smell me.

That night, I took him to the movie theatre where I could drink, in downtown Buckhead, next to my office in Tower Place. I drank something like six Guinness's in the theater, and then drove him back to the house. We sat on the couch for a few hours, and we shot the .22 at the fireplace, killing the rats that would drop from the chimney into the kitchen looking for food after I opened up the flue. This didn't strike me as wrong at all, in fact, quite the opposite. My son was enjoying drunk dad way more than he had sober dad. Fuck the world, this was better.

For a brief moment that Friday night I recalled feeling better sober while fishing, than I felt than this while drunk, which was a first. I brushed it aside with force. I'd drink and use Adderall and close 100k like I'd done while at CV Confidential, except for this time, I'd have my own company by God, I raged belligerently, trying to bring back the magic when it had worked just months before! The chemistry would work again, I lied to myself.

Re-Detoxing

Anne Marie came to pick Jake up the next day, and within a few hours, she called and told me to quit drinking, that I couldn't watch my son and drink, and that if I ever wanted to get him again, I needed to quit drinking forever. I went to the liquor store, filled with anger, resentment, and a thirst like I'd never had before. I bought a huge bottle of Grey Goose Vodka, a case of beer, and a carton of cigarettes. I came back to the house, put "Wedding Crashers" on a loop, and began drinking Saturday, like I'd always wanted to drink. For oblivion. I unplugged the alarm clock and I just smoked, and drank the nights and days away.

Eventually my phone rang. It was October 11, 2006. My brother sounded pissed.

"What the fuck are you doing, why aren't you at work?" he blasted at me.

"Fuck you, I don't have to be at work on Monday, I own my own company, I can go in on Tuesday, go fuck yourself!" I righteously informed him of the facts.

"It's Thursday, you moron, get your ass to work."

Shit. I hung up the phone. How could it be Thursday? What had happened to the time? Had I time traveled again? That lie wouldn't even work anymore. I was disgusted with myself. I couldn't even muster up the energy to start the delusions and insanity. I knew I hadn't time traveled. I was just a garden variety drunk, and I'd just blacked out, pure and simple, for longer than ever before.

I went to grab a beer out of the refrigerator, and when I pulled a sip out, it went right back to that moment where alcohol no longer worked. Battery acid. I was in hell again. Impossible to describe how beer can taste like such poison, impossible but real and scary, and somehow, I'd thrown away the miracle that had restored my sanity enough to eat, and even smoke cigarettes, but

I had, and I was back to square one. Shaking, miserable, unable to consume anything, once again, I got in my car, and cried the whole way up to 8111. It was beyond words, I'd re-condemned myself back to hell. I'd been given a second chance, and somehow thrown it all away. I was miserable, ashamed, and scared, once again, that this was my lot, to walk the earth unable to eat, smoke, or drink. God was omnipotent, unfortunately he just kept fucking me over, I thought.

Kevin B. was at 8111, and I told him what was going on. I'd blacked out for a few days, I'd gotten back on Adderall. His mother had set herself on fire in a deluded Adderall bender, and he said he would help me. He had about nine months sober, and that was better than me. We drove back to my house, and he flushed all the Adderall. He found the rest of my beer and flushed that down as well. On the way to detox, his sponsor called and told him not to flush all the beer, but to leave me one or two to nurse myself down, lest I die of cardiac arrest, and so I melodramatically awaited a heart attack. I didn't want to detox with Complete Abandon again, I wanted some fucking Librium, and this time, I would stay sober, I never wanted to feel like this torture again. I remembered feeling good at 30 days, not great, but way better than this.

For the first time, I craved sobriety like before I'd craved a drink. I wanted it back. I prayed for it to come back. I was as desperate as the dying can be...finally.

Arriving at Dekalb County Crisis again, the looney bin, but this time aware of why I was there, I sat out in the lobby and waited. Kevin got a ride back to 8111, and I waited in the lobby for them to get a bed ready, this time alone, without my brother, sister, or uncle. I'd gone right back to where I started 35 odd days ago. I was right back to not being able to see the light, to feeling like pure evil. I was disgusted with myself. I'd been shown the door out of hell, and I'd willingly gone back in, and my delusions and paranoia were all back with a vengeance. After about an hour of waiting, a tall black man, not unlike the black angel who'd snapped fear into my soul a month or so before on the streets of downtown Atlanta, came in to the waiting room and eyeballed me, staring me down like I was a peasant, like I was a POW in a foreign prison camp. I saw him pace the floor, never taking his eyes off me for more than a minute. Every hour or so he would go to the phone, dial a number, and then talk into it, and I could swear, I heard him say more than once, "No, he's still here, looks like he's checking in." He was obviously there to watch me, and he was obviously either CIA or an angel... possibly a demon. My insanity, quelled at 35 days sobriety, had come right back from where I'd left it.

I kept going outside to try and smoke, but the smoke wouldn't go down. It was just like before, I couldn't eat, smoke, or even drink water, I was in hell. About the third time I came in from trying to smoke, I noticed that the sky had suddenly gotten as dark as night. Thunder began clapping, and then as I stared out of the lobby, looking right at where I'd just been standing, lightning struck the precise spot, followed by a long, ominous, thundering roll. It was obviously a sign. If I didn't get it this time, I would surely die, and I would surely go to hell.

And as bad as it was, feeling similar to the last time I'd been here in hell, there was something different. There was hope. I knew that if I did the same things I'd done before, I could get better. I could get sober again, and enjoy food, water, and smoking, and ultimately not be consumed by the obsession to drink. I could get out of this hell. The last time, I was afraid I would be condemned to feel like this forever. This time, at least, I knew there was a way out. It just wasn't an easier softer way, there was only one way for me, and it was the Twelve Steps of Alcoholics Anonymous. This time, I would give it my all.

Me and the undercover black operative were admitted into the same room. They gave us some Librium, and this time it didn't take me three doses to finally fall asleep. This time it was a little easier, though the black man woke me up, speaking gibberish several times in the night, I was able to push him away, yell at him, and finally get him to go to sleep, or to at least leave me alone. I woke up feeling refreshed and much better. I had a mission. Stay sober, and it had come down from high. Both God and the CIA wanted me sober. This black agent was proof, I thought.

This time while in there, I actually picked up a Big Book and read it for dear life. I read all the stories in the back of the Big Book, and for some reason that go round, I could really relate to the stories. The one in particular was Acceptance was the Answer. This guy, was an alcoholic, but also a Dr. and an opiate addict like me, cross addicted to hell and back, and had successfully gotten sober. Reading his story, I could really relate, and also see, that I hadn't been different after all, that there were addicts and drunks more bad off than even me, that had gotten sober. His story was a gut check to my ego, and remains one of my favorite.

Third Time's the Charm

Inside detox, or the looney bin as we call it now, I checked my voicemail and had several messages from my Fortune 10 client in regards to setting up Bob Greyson for interviews from the hiring managers, and a couple from HR in regards to getting on the permanent vendor list. I convinced the doctor, who I'd previously been certain was an alien, to let me out, that my Fortune 10 client needed me, and eventually, later that day I was released. I got out, went home, called my sponsor, and set up a time for us to begin step work. I was done fucking around.

It was definitely easier that third go round of getting sober, because I knew it got better. Every time before when I'd come in, I'd had no faith that it would improve. The look of fear in my father's eyes all those years before proved to me that it didn't work, but I now saw that I was wrong. There had been moments of happiness and peace in that last 35 days, and I wanted more of them. It was nowhere near as hopeless as detoxing with Complete Abandon had been, and I began hearing everything everyone was saying in those meetings. I listened to the similarities, instead of the differences. And ultimately I began my step work.

My first meeting back at 8111, I was on the back porch whining about detoxing after relapsing for a week. A beautiful blonde named Michelle with 10 years sobriety, which may as well have been 100 years to me, said loudly and bluntly, "You only drank for a week, suck it up, you big baby!" Then she walked away. I named her Mighty Michelle, she was right, and I was in love. I'm very grateful for the beautiful strong-willed women in AA, even though they made me feel like a pussy early on. Early on they helped keep me coming back, and they never watered it down. That was exactly what I needed to hear, and it wouldn't be the last time an easy-on-the-eye's lady would point out with simplicity and with their very presence, that it just wasn't that complicated, that even they had gotten sober once. I called my sponsor and he came over after that meeting and we read the 1st step out of the <u>Twelve Steps and Twelve Traditions</u> book. Lo and behold an even further look into this sobriety business, and another book I'd previously not known existed, but which turned out to be crucial for my sobriety.

Step One: "We admitted we were powerless over alcohol, that our lives had become unmanageable."

My first step work consisted of writing down everything in my life, every experience that had been adversely affected by drugs and alcohol. Eight pages into bad experiences, drama, and self inflicted tragedies, I was pretty convinced I was an alcoholic. My sponsor heard me read it aloud when I said I was done. He told me when you finally realize that to get in the ring with Mike Tyson is to get knocked out, you've completed the first step, I had a real sense of relief. Things began to get better. I'd never really known there was work behind each step, and how simple it was. I'd never surrendered to it.

I wasn't out of the woods yet, though. I beat myself up pretty bad about that relapse. I had to start over on the Roman numerals above my toilet, keeping track of my sober time. I'd almost blown the Fortune 10 deal being in detox while the flurry of phone calls had come in. I'd blown some more trust with my family, and I was generally appalled that I could have relapsed that quickly, over nothing, over a girl who would claim she didn't even remember us having sex. I promised myself if I relapsed again, I would check into a halfway house, that if I couldn't stay sober on my own, I'd do whatever it took, though I really didn't want to. It was a good motivator to stay sober, though, and so was my company Seek and Employ, Inc. So was my sanity. A few days after I was out of the detox facility, having gathered my bearings a bit, I realized, that my new sobriety date was October 12, 2006, the two year anniversary of my mom's death. Her last words to me were to get sober. It was another God shot, and some more motivation, as if I should have needed any.

At the meetings, I ran into an old high school friend, Brent Giles. I asked him if it had gotten any better when he'd gotten the most time he'd ever had of nine months. He teared up, and said, "A little." That scared me, but others were more positive. Tanner, Viper Eric, and Rene all talked about this gift of sobriety, and as bad as it was, I had to believe it would get better. And I also began speaking to Shane Oleander a whole lot more about sobriety. He had my old job, sure, but he was a prime example of it getting better and I'd known him since we were 5 years old. He'd been as bad as me, for sure, and he was killing it at CV Confidential, my old employer, making money hand over fist, and now had over a year of sobriety. He was proud of me for starting my own company, but encouraged me to stay sober. We talked a few times a week about the meetings, about sobriety in general, and about business. He kept clinging to the idea, though, that one day he would drink like a normal person, once he was off probation. I, on the other hand, wasn't convinced I could. I was pretty sure my drinking days were done for good.

This second serious round at AA was definitely easier than

my first 35 days, but it was by no means a breeze. I began obsessing over Caroline and began calling her, begging her to get sober with me. Codependency and alcoholism apparently go hand in hand, as well as obsession. She wanted nothing of it and then worse, just to add a little more stress into my life, she claimed she was pregnant. So when I'd relapsed and slept with her that one time, she'd gotten pregnant, 20 more years of child support, and this time with a raging alcoholic like myself I feared. Not the sweet-as-pie Anne Marie, mama bear, but a sheer alcoholic, lunatic, which in early sobriety put the fear of God in me. My sponsor would walk me through these fears and my obsessions to get Caroline sober by telling me there was nothing I could do about it, I had no power, and worry helped nothing. All I could do was the next right thing, which was stay sober myself, work my twelve steps, go to work and meetings, and do God's will. I didn't know what God's will was, but I damn sure knew what it wasn't, and that was for me to drink, in my mind, God had made that blaringly obvious by now. Still I would obsess and stress and want to drink until eventually two or three weeks after she'd told me she was pregnant, she told me she'd had an abortion. I still don't know if any of that was true, but it certainly dialed up the tension in my early sobriety. Maybe what everyone said about early sobriety relationships was true. They certainly didn't assist my case at all. I stayed sober, though, and good things did begin to happen.

Illusions Crumble Slowly

In that second round of AA without drugs, and actually working the steps, I soon found that even 30 days into it, I was still delusional. I was working my ass off as a recruiter, and I thought I was dressing the part, with nice slacks, leather black shoes, and collared shirts. But at the 10 o'clock candlelight meeting one night, I met a beautiful woman by the name of Tara Begonia. I watched her in the meetings and would always sit near her, so we could end up holding hands at the end of the meeting when we said the Lord's Prayer. She was from Alpharetta, and I was from Roswell, and I thought I dressed much nicer than the rest of the people in the rooms. We were the same age, and both pretty damn good looking. "Hell," I thought, "I'm Jared Bryan Smith, of course she wants me, that's why she always holds my hand at the end of the meetings. Sure, sure, everyone does, but I mean, she's always next to me. Must mean something," I thought.

I'll never forget one night in particular. I was looking good I was sure, and I was going to ask her out that night, in all my early sobriety wisdom. At some point during the meeting, she leaned over and said "Did you know you have a huge hole in your shoes?" and she giggled a little bit. I was horrified. For one thing, no, I did not know that, and secondly, I'd been dead wrong about her intentions. Maybe, just maybe, she didn't want me, as impossible as that seemed to my ego. Sure enough, though, I'd been walking around now for months thinking I at least dressed better than these other whackos in AA, only to find I'd been dressing worse. It was like the rocks, or the puzzle in the looney bin, I was still clearly insane. Things were not as I thought. I called my sponsor and he said it was all right, I just wasn't sane yet, but at least I was getting better. Some help. What's worse I didn't have extra money to go buy shoes, I would have to simply be humbled and be aware of the holes in my shoes, another early lesson in humility.

I'd also really begun to run out of money, finally.

Personal Journal, October 20, 2006:

"I'm 29, and I relapsed, ending up quicker than ever in the depths of spiritual HELL. There is no other option, no softer easier way, and I'm happy about it. I can just keep my company, make some placements and I'll push through, I'll feel much better. I'm down to 1k with 1k rent due in a couple of weeks, and my only asset is my car...during winter. Thy will be done, but it will hurt."

The next couple of days, I came up with the idea of getting a second job and selling my car. The Fortune 10 deal was looking good and I had some other strong Big 4 candidates in the loop. So, as long as I could stay capitalized, I'd have some big money coming down the pipeline in no time. I got a part time job at an office supply store, working nights and weekends, and I sold my BMW on craigslist for $3,000. A year before I had paid 6k and also spent 3k on fixing the air conditioning that summer of insanity, but cash flow is paramount when running a business on sheer cash, and zero credit. I should have never been driving a beamer in the first place, that's what's called in the program a dress upped trash can. I was living in a rat infested shack, but in my head I looked good in my BMW. Asinine! But by selling the car, I was able to pay the corporate rent that I obviously couldn't afford, and my Uncle Jack sold me his beat up old 1991 Nissan Pickup truck for a small amount. I'm blessed my family was still speaking to me, much less working me favors. It would keep me afloat for the rough times ahead, as I worked harder than I'd worked in several years, cold-calling 40 hours a week in my office at Tower Place, and going to the office supply store to work until 9:30, only to haul ass to the candlelight meeting at 10:00 PM. At the office supply store on my smoke break, I would look over at The Tavern, where Caroline and I had drunk so much and I would crave a drink. But knowing the meeting was right around the corner, ultimately, I would persevere. And the meetings would kill the cravings. Things were headed in the right direction, I felt.

Personal Journal, November 26 2006:

"44 days into sobriety and physically and mentally I feel good. I escaped insanity, illusions of the mind, trickery of the Devil, what the fuck ever you want to call it, life is back to normal and I'm very thankful. It's a daily battle for sure, but I'm a fighter and I'm better than my dad. With God I am strong. Through God I can help the world, left to my own devices I'm nothing but a pest to society, helping only myself."

I felt like things were finally getting better, I'd surpassed the 35 days I'd had before and I could string a few hours together where I wasn't obsessing about drinking. The Fortune 10 deal was moving along, and selling my car and getting the 2nd job had helped out tremendously. Now it all hinged on closing this deal with my Fortune 10 Client, and staying sober. I was apprehensive, but hopeful. I called my sponsor daily with what-ifs and paranoid fears. But still, they were nowhere near the magnitude of being an Al-Qaeda target or CIA operative. I'd cleared my mind of those grandiose illusions by now. They'd simply left me, for the most part.

At one point, though, almost 60 days into sobriety, as I was trying to fall asleep, I heard clear as day, someone run through my house, stomping across the entire floor, shaking the house to the foundations. I got out of bed and ran to my truck. I called my sponsor, and he told me if it was that bad, just go to a motel for the night. Almost 60 days into sobriety, and I was still delusional, and still capable of hallucinating entire scenarios in my head. But they were getting fewer and farther between.

Personal Journal, December 7th, 2006:

"I did it. I persevered and closed 18k with my client.

(Fortune 10) With God's help and strength I've yet again accomplished what most would have believed impossible."

I had placed Bob Greyson at literally one of the top 10 companies in the world! I had set out to do business with them several years before. I had finally made a little progress while at CV Confidential, but received no credit for it, because of getting fired before it would yield results. But I had stuck with it and placed a stellar candidate with an amazing company, and I thanked God, and was thrilled for my sobriety and future riches! Little drunk fuck-up Bryan Smith's company had closed an 18k deal with a Fortune 10, the once #1 company in the world. I could accomplish anything I set my mind to now. Now that I was sober, I would never be poor again! Now that I could be consistent, I would run my own company forever, I would be successful! Nothing would hold me back now! Seek and Employ would be a success! Before the Christmas holiday, I would even make another placement at another top Atlanta company, with another Big 4 candidate Brian Smith. Since getting sober on October 12, 2006, I'd closed 36k in business, and I gave all the credit to God's grace and my getting sober. Life would be a breeze from here on out. Hell I'd probably even become a scratch golfer!

Hall Pass for Losing a Friend

Friday morning, December 22nd, 2006, Brian Huff called me asking me if I knew where Shane Oleander was. I told him I talked to him the night before, and I was a little irritated with him pumping me for information about our mutual client, a Fortune 100, but that I hadn't talked to him since. Two weeks earlier, Shane and I had eaten at Dantanna's, where he told me that once he moved into his new house, he would be able to drink a couple of glasses of wine with dinner from time to time. I nodded OK, but inside I thought that didn't sound too good. I didn't think much of the call from Brian that morning, until Brent Giles called me a few hours later, and said, "Man, I've got some bad news."

"What?" I said.

"Shane Oleander died last night, man."

"Bullshit." I didn't believe Brent for a second. Just a week before, someone had told me Shane was in jail for six months, Roswell was rampant with rumors, and Shane had been the high school quarterback, everyone knew him and everyone loves bad news and gossip. I thought for sure it was just crap.

"No, man, I heard it from James Price, who talked to Mrs. Oleander."

I hung up the phone and called James Price's mom, as we had all grown up together, James Price, Shane Oleander, and me. She answered and told me it was true, and I cried like a baby. It wasn't fair, I lost everyone I knew, I thought, how could God do this to me? He was one of my only sober friends. Life just wasn't fair.

I drove to the Oleander's house, a huge mansion in Alpharetta, and I was reminded of when my Dad died, and the first place I went to was the Oleander's house. Ford Oleander, Shane's father, came to the door, and he was crying. He said Shane is dead. Then his face filled with rage, and he told me "Now, Bryan, if I found out you had anything to do with this, I will make you pay for this! Do you understand, Bryan? I'll make you pay!" He slammed the door in my face.

I'd had nothing to do with it, shit, I was just as shocked as him, but I guess in Ford Oleander's mind, I was still that little punk that got Shane mixed up with drugs back in ninth grade, selling him weed. Hell, following that thought, it was my fault Shane died, he smoked his first joint when I passed it to him. I cried and cried all the way home. I'd lost a brother-in-arms. We were fighting this shit together, and I'd lost him, I felt for sure he'd relapsed. A year and a half sober and he'd gone out one night and died.

Brent Giles came over, and we drove the truck up to the Morgan Falls Dam, and we watched the river for a little while. The crazy thing was, after losing my friend from first grade to drugs and alcohol, all I wanted to do was take a fucking drink, or twenty. I called my sponsor, and it didn't help, the craving was still strong. I went to a meeting, I shared, got very pissed off when it didn't help, and Brent and I drove up to Startime, sat at the bar in Whirlyball and after 77 days of sobriety this time, I drank. I told myself, it was a hall pass. That I would only drink when God took my closest loved ones. Evan Woodward, a friend from middle school served us, and Brent and I got good and drunk. I didn't go straight to hell, and the beer didn't taste like battery acid and we got pretty toasty. That night we would go over to Chris Tulane's house, where James Price would ramble on and piss me off, as usual. He talked as if he was the expert on sobriety and drug addicts, not knowing the first thing about real sobriety, but claiming to have all the answers. He didn't know shit, but I smoked his weed, and eventually Brent and I left. I drank about twelve beers that night, smoked some of James Price's herb as he enlightened us, and as Brent and I got back to the rat shack we would try and sleep it off.

The next day I woke up, and the obsession that I'd fought 77 days to keep at bay, was back with a vengeance. Just like the last time, and I hated myself for letting any reason make me drink -- or allow me to drink. The craving was there at 9 am upon awakening though, and there was beer in the fridge, so Brent and I drank the rest of the day, hitting a bunch of bars nearby and finding absolutely nothing of interest. When we got back home, I actually emptied the last of the beer that I had, told Brent I was done, that I didn't even enjoy the drunk, and Shane was still dead. I went to sleep, and Brent stole my truck as I slept and didn't return until four in the morning. He told me he went to North River Tavern, but I suspected he'd tried to sell my truck in the ghetto for some rock, to no avail, it being the ugliest vehicle on God's green Earth. That truck looked like it had survived Baghdad, been stolen, reworked in Guatemala and driven hard straight through to Atlanta. I smiled at the thought of the crack dealers laughing at Brent's attempts. The next day, I kicked Brent out of my house, where he'd been staying temporarily, and I vowed to quit drinking once again, as well as keep it a secret that I had even relapsed. Besides, it didn't count, God had given me a hall pass, and I actually sold myself that line.

I wasn't invited to Shane's funeral. George Oleander, Shane's older brother would later thank me for being such a good friend to Shane, getting him that job and what not, but I never heard anything else out of the Oleander family. I'm sure they were simply distraught beyond words. He was the all-American kid, and it was a tragedy. Christmas Eve, 2006, was my first full day sober, and I began keeping two sets of dates in my head: the 79 days sober everyone thought I had, and the one day sober I really had. I would do this for my full first year, convinced it was OK, given the hall pass God had given me. One person caught me on this bullshit, and that was Dylan Valentine, who'd got sober a few months before I entered AA, and who had called me that Friday night and heard me answer the phone drunk. I wouldn't admit it to him, but he knew.

With Shane Oleander's death came the absolute certainty that I could not drink again, after that one last brief relapse, of course. Officially, it was ruled as a cardiac arrest, and the Oleander's sued the hospital, but no matter how you look at it, the amount of drugs he'd done to damage his heart up until that point couldn't have helped. The official story out of the Oleander camp was he was taking Hydroxycut, an over-the-counter weight loss pill that has since been warned against by the FDA. Now I think those bastards sell skin cream. Shane had mixed it with two Percocets, they said, and the mixture had given him a heart attack. The hospital should have caught his low potassium levels, but let him go home instead where supposedly he died in his sleep. Maybe that it is what happened, but had he not done more cocaine than I'd ever seen any man on Earth do in one sitting those many times, years before, his heart could have probably handled the challenge. Furthermore, the guys he was living with knew he was on Hydroxycut, and if they hadn't coddled him over that, maybe he'd be alive today. The recovering addict shouldn't be taking any kind of borderline pills like that, that amp you up, for weight loss or any reason at all. It's just not a good idea. The Percocets themselves would definitely have been considered a relapse, though. Freakish as it may have been, the years of abuse leading up to it, made it very believable. And it could have just as easily happened earlier, many times over, and it could have easily happened to me, many times over. I mean, hell, I knew I'd had a heart condition, and was still walking this Earth. Shane Oleander's death put the real fear of death into me.

I went to his grave a few weeks after the funeral, and saw where all my Roswell friends had held a funeral after the family had, and I'd still not been invited. They were just trying to be nice. It wasn't about me, I knew, and hell I probably wouldn't have gone anyway. They put a picture on his grave that he would have hated as well. He hated being called "Shaney," and that was on the grave. It reminded me that once you're dead, you don't get a say in the way things happen on Earth anymore. More eerily, not 100 yards away, was my father's overgrown grave, ignored, and almost hidden. He, too, had lost his right to complain about the way things were done down here. I'm sure he wouldn't have wanted my mom to live in that house with my stepdad, and then have Dan Jones end up with it all after she died. But that's what happens when you're dead, you lose all control on Earth.

Working the Steps

Christmas has been weird for my whole family ever since my mom died in 2004. That year was no exception, as I would have one day of sobriety, but was lying and telling everyone I had almost three months. My stepdad bought my brother and both sisters iPods, and he got me a video game I already owned. Caroline was infuriated by my stepdad's obvious favoritism, but, honestly, I was used to it and barely felt worthy of being invited to Christmas anyway. Still,

I'd only done one of the Twelve Steps, and my resentment towards my stepdad were still heavy. We played nice, but just beneath the surface, there was always a palpable tension. Back then, I was only there for my brother and sister, as justified or not, I was still angry with him for innumerable perceived wounds, as well as being equally ashamed for endless harms I'd caused him and my mom. It was uncomfortable, to say the least, but we were both trying.

I went back to work in the new year with a fervor, and got down to work with my sponsor as well. Within a couple of weeks, we'd had a falling out and I got Rene Broussard to be my sponsor, the Buddhist petite man from New Orleans. He had 18 years sober, and had ridden his bicycle out of New Orleans before Katrina hit, and was one of the most likable guys I'd ever met. His style was softer and more laid back, and we just got along a little better than Graham and I had. I'd done steps one and two with Graham, but with step three, I felt like Graham had gotten a little more creative than the Big Book suggested, and that worried me. I did it regardless, but for the rest of the steps, I decided I would work with Rene. There are no concrete rules on the twelve steps, and for that I'm grateful as well. What I had believed was rigid is actually very flexible within Alcoholics Anonymous, in fact it is all just suggestions, not rules or laws. Before I switched to Rene as a sponsor though, Graham and I read over Step Two, again from the <u>Twelve Steps and Twelve Traditions</u> book and then he assigned me some work.

Step Two: "Came to believe that a power greater than ourselves could restore us to sanity."

This is the step that had grabbed my attention when I'd come in back in August, that promise of restoration to sanity. It had spoken to me, I'd been aware, in my miraculous moment of clarity, that I'd in fact gone off the reservation insane, and upon coming into the rooms I'd clung to this. The work behind the step however, was different than I'd imagined. It consisted of writing down all I desired my Higher Power to be, a list of ten to twenty characteristics that I could expound upon. I liked this step a lot, it made my whole idea of God easier for me. It began my changeover from fearing God to loving God, but that wouldn't happen overnight. It had been a good start, though. We then moved on to Step Three.

Step Three: "Made a decision to turn our will and our lives over to the care of God <u>as we understood him</u>."

This is where my first sponsor and I disagreed. Graham

wanted me to write down all the negative thoughts I had on a daily basis, one page a day, for two weeks, every single negative thought. This pissed me off, because, being borderline OCD, I thought, I felt like it was going to make me think negative thoughts. Also, when I shared what my step work was with other AA'ers, they said Graham was off his rocker, that that wasn't in the Big Book, so I shouldn't have to do it. I tended to agree, and though I did the work, I decided I would get a new sponsor moving forward for some of the more work-intensive steps coming up.

Graham did more for me than I can ever repay though. He'd spoken to me about God was I was 17, and we'd talked on and off for over 10 years. He made me want what AA had to offer by showing me serenity and peace by example. When I came in, he taught me to quit debating, quit fighting, socialism versus capitalism, God versus no God, and so on -- that it just didn't matter, that all I needed to focus on was sobriety. He guided me easily and when I told him I wanted a new sponsor, he took it with grace, and even told me to keep calling him when I needed to anyway. That's what the program of AA is about. Giving without expecting a return on your investment, but for the sake of giving, for the sake of love. Without him, I couldn't have survived my first six months or so, I'm sure. Hell, I wouldn't have even been there in the first place. He shared his experiences, and how crazy he'd been early on as well, and he'd make it OK for me to feel like shit, to be crazy, and feel foolish. As long as I didn't drink, it would get better he said, and I believed him.

For all the good Graham was for me early on, though, Rene was the perfect sponsor for me moving forward. Our third step was simplified from the more complex way Graham had suggested, to simply reading the chapter out of the Twelve Steps and Twelve Traditions book, and upon completion, getting on our knees, holding hands with my new sponsor Rene, which wasn't easy for me, but I did anyway, and saying at the same time, the 3rd Step Prayer:

The Third Step Prayer

from page 63 of the Big Book of Alcoholics Anonymous

God, I offer myself to Thee-
To build with me
and to do with me as Thou wilt.
Relieve me of the bondage of self,
that I may better do Thy will.
Take away my difficulties,

that victory over them may bear witness
to those I would help of Thy Power,
Thy Love, and Thy Way of life.
May I do Thy will always!

Moving forward I would use Rene to do my fourth and fifth steps with as well. He didn't use a spreadsheet where you listed your sex and fears lists, like a lot of sponsors did. Instead, he simply told me to answer all the questions out of the <u>Twelve Steps and Twelve Traditions</u> book, which were pretty meaty questions, and that appealed to my literary mind much better than building a list or a chart, as the Big Book has laid out. It worked for me, and I'm glad I found Rene.

Step Four: "Made a searching and fearless moral inventory of ourselves."

The big deal for me, and one of the reasons I hadn't completed the steps the first 28 days when I had been in 2005, was the stealing morphine from my mom while she lay dying. I was very afraid to ever admit that to another human being, and certainly I couldn't complete Step Four without being thorough and honest about it. But by now I'd gotten 35 days under my belt, went back out drinking and it got worse, faster, as fellow AA'ers had promised me it would. Then I'd gotten 77 days and gone back out when Shane died, and woke up with the obsession to drink just as bad as the day I'd quit. I had to abandon the idea that I would ever be able to drink like a normal person. I'd researched it, I'd given my body time to flush out the poisons, only to drink again and immediately begin feeling like I'd felt, the last day I drank. I finally believed what I'd been told, that it was a spiritual disease, centered in my mind. I could never drink like a normal person again, and in fact after that last outing, throwing away 77 days of sobriety, I finally didn't want to. I felt better sober, better without the obsession, and I wanted that feeling back.

Also, in those 77 days of sobriety, I'd closed two major deals with a Fortune 10 and with another top 100 Public Company in Atlanta, 36k that would all be going in my pocket, and had I been drunk or high, I'd never have accomplished that. I wanted more goodies like that. It didn't hurt that I'd met a girl as well. Sweet Tara Begonia, though never once interested in me, probably doesn't know how much her very presence got me back into those meetings. There are beautiful girls in AA, and they aren't trying to kill themselves, like so many women I'd dated in my twenties. In fact, quite the opposite, they are survivors, trying to beat a disease.

So I sucked it up, and I did my Fourth Step. It was easy, I wish I'd done it earlier, it was just a matter of writing down all the questions in the corresponding chapter in the <u>Twelve Steps and Twelve Traditions</u> book, and being thorough and honest about them. I was tired of running, I would just do it.

Step Five: "Admitted to God, to ourselves, and to another human being the exact nature of our wrongs."

Rene also made this step easy. It's basically just reading the work you did on your Fourth Step. I flirted, egotistically, with going to a monk who'd vowed silence, that is an actual option in Georgia, as well as going to a shrink or lawyer, who by law, must keep it confidential. But the truth was, after I'd written it all out, most of my transgressions just didn't seem as bad as they had in my head. Sure there was the big one about stealing from my dying mom, and some with Gwen Evere that were rough, but I'd already run them by Graham and Rene, and so I knew they wouldn't judge or condemn me on those. After being in the rooms this long in fact, I'd heard much worse. I ended up going to the riverside at the park, near where I'd jumped just a few months back, and sharing my whole Fourth Step with Renee. I received instant relief.

With Rene, in the first few months of 2007, I felt better than I could ever remember feeling. It was beyond words. For so many years, I'd felt awful, only feeling halfway good while fucked up, and, all of a sudden, I was free. The promises began to come true for me. The tenth step promises even came true for me. We read the ninth step promises every single meeting, but the tenth step promises mean the world to me as well. Both sets of promises are copied below, and both came true for me surprisingly quickly, once I finally became teachable, and began doing what was suggested within AA.

9th Step Promises

If we are painstaking about this phase of our development, we will be amazed before we are halfway through. We are going to know a new freedom and a new happiness. We will not regret the past nor wish to shut the door on it. We will comprehend the word serenity and we will know peace. No matter how far down the scale we have gone, we will see how our experience can benefit others. That feeling of uselessness and self-pity will disappear. We will lose interest in selfish things and gain interest in our fellows. Self seeking will slip away. Our whole attitude and outlook upon life will change. Fear of people and of economic insecurity and will leave us. We will intuitively know how to handle situations which used to baffle us. We will suddenly realize that God is doing for us what we could not do for ourselves.

When I came back after those 77 days of sobriety, having heard those promises in 77 plus meetings, and having not really heard those promises, I listened, because I was desperate. I needed every word, because the obsession had returned, and I knew of only one way for it to end. The words rang true. Every single word of those ninth step promises had come true for me, in the short time I'd been sober. Those promises are real. I dare anyone who doesn't believe them, to work the twelve steps, alcoholic or not, and test them. See if you build a relationship with God, see if those statements don't come true. If my father had known or better yet believed in them, he'd be alive today. So would a lot of people.

So with Rene, I'd worked through my big steps of four and five. The steps are in order, they say. If I hadn't been a little bit sober, with a little bit of sanity returned, there is no way I could have found my part in every one of my resentments. Doing steps 1-3 made it possible for me to grasp the meaning of 4-5, and to see them as just another part of the steps, not a huge anvil hanging over my head. I wished I'd just done them earlier, and stopped fighting it. They work.

My resentments included: number one, myself. Then, my biological father, my mother, my former wife, Gwen Evere, society, government and, of course, my stepdad, brother, sister, and even aunts and uncles. I carried around heavy anger and imposed much misery upon myself with just that shortened list of major resentments. Working steps four and five cleared my mind of all of them. It made me high. I'd been angry and miserable for so long, and I had no idea why. Four and five opened up the gates of hell and let me out, as I'd heard it said in the rooms of AA. I forgave everyone wholeheartedly for everything, real or imagined, and though it didn't affect them one bit, I was a brand new man for it. After I read my fifth step, all the promises came true for me, but especially important to me, the tenth step promises came true. I didn't even know they existed, though I'd heard them several times in meetings, and read over them as well. They just didn't have meaning until I heard them read aloud after they had occurred to me. This is the miracle, beyond a shadow of a doubt. And I didn't do it, I just did what I was told, and it happened.

10th Step Promises

> And we have ceased fighting anything or anyone – even alcohol. For by this time sanity will have returned. We will seldom be interested in liquor. If tempted, we recoil from it as from a hot flame. We react sanely and normally, and we will find that this has happened automatically. We will see that our new attitude toward liquor has been given us without any thought or effort on our part. It just comes! That is the miracle of it. We are not fighting it, neither are we avoiding temptation. We feel as though we had been placed in a position of neutrality – safe and protected. We have not even sworn it off. Instead the problem has been removed. It does not exist for us. We are neither cocky nor are we afraid. That is our experience. That is how we react so long as we keep in fit spiritual condition.

I find it hard to summarize the magnitude of those words to this man, who, before coming in, thought he was condemned to die and go to hell. Who had seen his father, the grown man he'd spent 11 years idolizing, in tears, crying, ashamed at his inability to quit drinking and be a normal dad, and who months later ended his own life with a .357, blowing his head clean off rather than sober up, because he just didn't believe it was possible. To him it wasn't possible. To me, it wasn't possible. Coming in to AA, going through detox, I'd finally just resigned to feeling miserable for the rest of my life. I was just commiserating with the other men and women of AA, and was trying not to cry when I asked Brent Giles if it ever got any better, and he teared up and said "A little." For those promises to come true, that I could quit thinking about, or wanting to, or obsessing over alcohol and drugs, is a sheer miracle. Hell, why hadn't anybody said so? And of course they had, I just hadn't listened. Awash in doubt, the miracle crept up on me regardless.

And there is the paradox. People had been saying so for so many years, and I just didn't believe them. When I saw my dad kill himself rather than do the AA program, there had to have been a reason. I just really believed it was all a lie, that it never got better. But it did! It happened, those exact promises, and the ninth step

314

promises as well, happened precisely as they are written in the Big Book. Who would have figured? Not me. It turned out the millions who had sobered up before me were onto something. This God thing worked, this life really was better all of a sudden.

If my dad knew about these promises, or better yet believed them to be possible, he would never have shot himself, abandoning his three kids here on Earth, and inflicting untold psychological scars upon them all. Never in a million years. He killed himself because he thought his plight was hopeless, and that we as a family were better off without him. What a world of massive delusions addicts set up for themselves in order to justify suicide, and yet it is all too common. Almost all suicides involve altered states of being. I guess I'm just lucky I realized it was a lie, before it was too late.

I wish -- probably because I'm an addict at heart -- that you could put in a pill the way I felt after working up to step six, and could give that pill to suffering alcoholics and addicts, and let it last for one hour. The way they would feel for that hour would make them want to get sober no matter what the pain. Basically we got high and drunk because we liked the instant effects it produced, but the effects of sobriety FELT BETTER. Who knew? I'd been torturing myself for years. To the normal Earth person, this probably sounds so foreign, and that's ok. But to those who have sobered up, they know exactly what I'm talking about. I just didn't believe it got better. I thought to get sober meant no more fun, no more sex, no more life. I didn't know it meant a better life than I could have ever imagined.

In the Ninth Step Promises, I love the sentence "We will comprehend the word serenity and will we know peace." Prior to working the twelve steps, I hadn't a clue what serenity or peace meant. Even before I'd drank, I thought of suicide. As a child, I'd contemplated self extermination. I never felt comfortable in my own skin, ever. I always felt different, out of place, and not a part of the whole. Alcohol had fixed it for many years, and then it stopped working and I needed it constantly, and it made my life worse and worse. As Mario likes to say, "Alcohol gave me the wings to fly, and then it took my sky away." And then, 29 years into my life, sober no less, I felt just fine in my own skin. I felt amazing. I felt high permanently. I still do, three years into it, but man, for those first few months of that feeling, I was flying. They refer to it as the pink cloud. I wish I'd followed all the suggestions earlier, because it felt better than any binge, any trip, and coke banger weekend. It was fucking phenomenal, it was permanent, and all I had to do was go to meetings to keep it.

I remember Rene telling me "Bryan, the only person you're doing any favors staying sober is yourself. Society will survive with or without you." It's true. Addiction is America's voluntary concentration camp. Alcoholics are constant criminals in the United States, and gone are the days when the courts and the law would tolerate alcoholism with a wink and a smile. Multiple DUI's and consistent public intox violations are prosecuted to the full extent of the law, and basically, you'll either get busy living or get busy dying, a criminal in the eyes of your fellow man. He was right, it's like I'd said all those years before, "Fit in the grid or die." Either help society out, and serve, or get busy killing yourself, maybe slowly at first, but fast in the end, the downward spiral picks up speed towards the end, and you will be society's burden no more. Choose life.

Swimming the Hippopotamus Sea

So the beginning of 2007 was looking strong! I closed another deal two months into 2007, placing Deborah Weinstein with a major multimedia client, and earning a hefty 17k fee. I was flying high. I started playing a ton of golf, and even began leading meetings a bit. Since I still hadn't admitted my 77 day relapse, most folks thought I had around six months clean. A funny thing kept happening though. I'd go for a week or two of normality, and then I would sleep for almost a complete day. I knew I was burning it at both ends of the candle, working the office supply job and running Seek and Employ, Inc. But once the insurance kicked in from the office supply job, I went to the doctor to check up on everything, to make sure I didn't have cancer or AIDS or something. The sleeping bouts were strange, and I was still pissing dark brown, which sadly was an improvement from my drinking days when sometimes it had been straight almost black.

During the Men's Meeting on Wednesday night, I heard a guy named Austin mention "Hippopotamus Sea" several times. The first few months I'd been there, I was still just gathering my bearings and not listening to, or able to comprehend every word of every meeting. Besides, Austin kind of mumbles. But in the early months of 2007, I finally made out what this old hippie was babbling on about: hepatitis C. I laughed at myself for thinking he had been talking about a safari, or an ocean near Africa. Man, I'd been shot out, I was lucky not to have "wet brain". He was talking about a disease, a junkie disease no less, and it affected the liver. And wasn't there something about my liver I'd been completely ignoring? I must have known, and in fact, my sponsor pointed out later that I was scared of it the moment I heard Austin clearly in that meeting.

So finally, armed with health insurance and a few months sobriety, I thought I would face the music, and see if quitting drinking had cured the liver problems they'd told me about a year before. I would also specifically ask them to check for hepatitis C, having finally translated "Hippopotamus Sea," and knowing all too well it would only make sense to check for it. Austin had shot heroin for years, and I'd only shot up one night in my life, but it only takes once, and, hell, if life were fair, I'd be dead and in hell.

I told the doctor to check for hep C, and he told me, "Oh no, that's a drug addict's disease, not an STD, you don't have to worry about that." This was the same doctor who the year before had prescribed me the Adderall that had done me so many wonders. "Go ahead and check it out, Doc." I pushed adamantly.

Three days later, I had my son for the weekend, and we were eating Japanese when the doctor called. He said, "Bryan, the HIV came back negative, but the hep C came back positive. Call me on Monday and we'll discuss the next steps." My world crashed down upon me in an instant. I thought my life was over. I thought I'd never have sex again. I thought I'd die. I was mad at myself, ashamed, scared, everything. I felt like I deserved it. I felt dirty and disgusting. I felt hopeless again, and psychosomatically, I instantly felt stabbing pains where I knew my liver was, from the ultrasounds a year before.

Personal Journal, March 7th, 2007:

Sitting in the Dr's office today scared to me death and I thought "I have a disease that can kill me. I'll have to tell potentially everyone about an almost guaranteed deal killer if I'm to stay honest, if I'm to stay good, which I want. Otherwise it's potentially attempted murder. I feel like my life is about to suck. That or drugs, damn it. God please have mercy, God please give me a miracle, God please forgive my selfishness, cure me of this shit, and let me move on with a normal life. FUCK, Bryan, you've really fucked up this time." What sucks too, is you can't point to one thing, but a myriad of sin, irresponsibility, and so called partying, all of which are indicative of this bullshit. God has upped the ante on

317

living a good life, but in his omnipotence you should have faith. He's brought you this far from the insanity of your mind, why doubt this isn't for the better as well? It's not convenient. It's embarrassing, it's worrisome, and it's not fatal...yet. I don't think, but I guess that's why I'm here: I'm scared. God I'm scared, give me strength to beat this Lord, please dear God, cure me of this bullshit, in Christ's name I pray."

I'd really turned up the panic.

That doctor told me, in his attempt to cheer me up, "Well, HIV would have killed you faster." Some pep talk. I got a different doctor after that visit. This may just be me, but I like Jewish doctors, call me superstitious. I found a Jewish liver doctor named, Feldman, and sure enough, he looked just like Woody Allen. He told me that first, I would need to get a biopsy to see how much liver damage had been done, though he didn't suspect much, as my viral load was 150k, which was relatively low. Most people discover they have hep C when their viral load count is in the millions. He told me that because I had hep C, I should drink in moderation. I told him, if I could drink in moderation, I'd have never had a needle stuck up my arm over a redhead. He smiled and said "At least you know that about yourself, you'll stand a much better chance of curing it."

"Curing it?" I asked, skeptical, since most of the things I'd read about online talked only of remission.

"That's right, we can cure it in about half the cases, especially when we catch it early like we have in this case. If it's still gone for six months after treatment, it will be cured. Also, Bryan, it's not an STD, it spreads blood to blood only, so you got it either from straws or needles. I've known married couples that have been together decades, even had children together, that didn't spread hepatitis C."

The straws threw me for a loop. I hadn't thought of that, but I'd used straws with dozens of people snorting meth, ice, and cocaine over the years of partying, never thinking twice about it. They left that out of health class, I suspect. Still, I couldn't shake remembering the one night Gwen and I had used needles, right as my mom lay dying. I suspected it was from that night, though I wouldn't have the courage to tell her or Caroline, the only two women I'd been with since, for some time yet.

I had to get started with the treatment. It became my new

mission, and Seek and Employ, Inc. instantly became priority number two. Dr. Feldman, one of the kindest, gentlest doctors I'd met, scheduled a biopsy before we would start my treatment. He asked me if I wanted any sedatives, and I had to tell him no. I wanted the sedatives, hell, I wanted a whole bag of heroin by this point, I was scared, but deep down, I really didn't. I didn't want to go back to that hell. I was glad, despite it all, that I was sober, the obsessions gone, and the sanity had returned. I was glad I was no longer in the CIA, and glad nobody was following me anymore. I wasn't going back to that, so we did the biopsy with only local anesthetic.

I thought I was tough, but then I saw the needle. Needle is the wrong word. Sword is better. Eiffel Tower could work. It was huge, like a foot long. I watched the whole thing, and he did it with precision.

"Don't move or I'll have to do it twice." That wasn't reassuring, so I didn't move. He did it once, and it worked smoothly, and then when the needle, or skyscraper came out of my side, the blood began trickling out, and I was struck with a piercing, stabbing pain, the likes of which I haven't felt in my life. It was rough. I wanted to cry, but I didn't. I had to sit there for an hour, not moving, allowing the liver to clot back up, I guess. It was a painful, boring hour. I wanted to cry, but I wouldn't just yet. I would wait to get home and my sponsor would have me pray and apologize to God this time, for doing damage to "my temple." After that prayer, I would cry like a baby. I couldn't believe what I'd felt I'd done to myself, and ultimately had. This was all one more self-inflicted tragedy, months after I'd actually sobered up. The wreckage of our past, as they say, was still haunting me, reminding me of how badly, how wrongly I'd treated myself for so many years.

Eventually he came to me and gave me a prescription for Interferon, which he told me would feel like a heavy case of the flu, and to wait to fill it once the results of the biopsy were back. I went to my office supply store job with the Band-aid near my rib cage. I showed my manager the wound and told him I had cancer, and would need medical leave. I still had some money in the bank, and I had a feeling I wasn't going to be able to work retail through my "flu-like symptoms" while taking Interferon. I felt bad about lying, but cancer was just broader, easier to explain, and, of course, isn't associated with junkies or promiscuous sex.

I went to my office at Tower Place, moved all my equipment into my house, and prepared to work from home. With these flu-like symptoms, I didn't need to be paying $1500 a month for corporate office space. They would come after me hard for breaking the lease contract, but fortunately, when you have absolutely zero assets, very few people will sue you, though they'll research the hell out of you. You just need to tell them that if they find anything, let you know and you'd be happy to split it with the bastards! They give up after a while. I didn't have a pot to piss in or a window to throw it out of. Well, the rat shack had windows, but they were all boarded up to keep the rodents at bay, and it wasn't my shack to begin with.

I waited for the biopsy results. All the while, I doubled up on meetings, I prayed extra hard, and I talked to my two sponsors about it. I was now talking to both Graham Flagg and Rene Broussard, as I needed all the insight I could get. They both just kept telling me to do the next right thing. Continue down the path of treatment. Thank God, I'd just qualified for health insurance through my office supply job. Thank God, I'd caught it early. Thank God it wasn't cancer or HIV, and I continued to thank God every single day that I was sober. No matter what, I never had to drink again. It wasn't even a battle. Had this happened a year before, I would have cursed God. I would have raged that he'd taken my mom, dad, inheritance, best friend, and had now given me a junkie disease. I would have most likely killed myself, unable to handle such a heavy truth. Instead, I was grateful. I understood the word serenity and I knew peace, despite having to battle a life-threatening illness in my first six months of sobriety. More than that, I had faith that I would feel better, get through it, and be even more grateful. I can't put it into words. I just felt it. I knew somehow it would get better, and I had a real calm about me that I really couldn't explain, given the circumstances, other than that I'd already changed considerably since getting sober and working some steps. I was able to accept the situation.

Personal Journal, April 8th, 2007:

The beauty of it all, of all your character defects, of all your faults, is that you're sober. Your life is getting proportionally better, despite the added struggles, the bondage of drinking has been released. There is a freedom in following instructions. A joy in doing the right thing, serving your Lord by being the best man you can be. You need to get more focused, yes, but congratulate yourself so far on a job well done. Good is great, but God is greater, even though this guy leading this meeting is a jackass. Well, to each his own, live and let live. You're going to be ok.

Tara Begonia flirted back and forth in my journal in between these two writings. It was insignificant stuff, but fun and lively, a romantic visit to Nepal we spoke of. It wasn't much, but it was enough to make me appreciate sobriety, and the new people I'd met, the new relationships I could form with healthy people, not the sick. Nothing would ever come of it, but she gave me hope of a new life, with new people. As I was going through all this struggle alone, God spoke through others, and for me, she was constantly a conduit, and still can be to this day.

Personal Journal, April 27th, 2007:

Despite all the loneliness, the pain, the flashbacks, all the hallucinations, the paranoid delusions and terrible shakes and sweats of my first 90 days, this serenity, this PEACE, is priceless. I'm a free man to do whatever I want, but I choose to follow God and match his will as best as possible. Thank you God for this miracle of sobriety. Please don't ever let me let go of this peace and happiness, no matter what happens. I want what I've got right here, right now. I love you God. Thank you.

I think the main thing that happened to me at about the halfway mark of working the twelve steps was the change in my relationship with God. I went from fearing God to loving God, with all my heart and soul. Our relationship evolved, and it was a beautiful thing for me. It was necessary. I could have never faced the prospect of a year of feeling like shit on Interferon, if I hadn't had that relationship. I didn't even know what the treatment was going to feel like yet, but I heard enough in the meetings to know it was going to be OK.

I told barely a soul about my struggling with the hellish treatment. I told Rene and Graham, and that was it, at first. Somewhere deep down, though I acknowledged that I'd mostly imagined the CIA and all the nonsense, something in me continued to lie and tell myself that the hep C was punishment for not doing the job right, for not going to Afghanistan. Or perhaps, all agents had to go through Interferon once, in order to show them how they would be punished, should they fuck up in the field. Death was too good, they would make them suffer for a year. Hell, even Jesus only suffered three days on the cross, my mom had gone five years on chemo, and I was about to have to do a year of Interferon. I would snap out of this thinking quickly by now, but it could still come back from time to time and rear its imaginative head. Plus, it actually made it easier for me to face the year ahead. I had hep C as part of my continued training. Nobody else could know, buhahaha! This may sound silly to you, and even to me now, but occasionally that fantasy would make it easier to bear. The difference is that I wasn't living in those fantasies daily, and I knew it wasn't real.

The results of the biopsy came back fine. I didn't have any liver damage at all, and there was no cancer, as I was at risk of having, now that I was a "carrier" as ol' Kristen the bartender had once prophetically called me. The sooner I started the Interferon, the better, the doc said. I'd moved my offices into my rat shack humble abode, and I'd even closed another deal with another Fortune 50 headquartered in Atlanta, so I was ready to begin. I took the prescription for Interferon down to the local CVS, and they told me they didn't have it, try Wal-Mart. They also looked at me rather funny, I thought. Wal-Mart repeated this process. Target said they would order it for me to which I said "Fine," and I'm sure I complained all the way out of the store, eager to begin my year long tour of duty on Interferon.

Target called a couple of days later, and said they had the medicine, but that my insurance only covered 50 bucks a month of it, and the prescription cost $2500.00 dollars a month. WTF! Where was God now? $2500.00 a month! I didn't have that kind of money, hell, who does? What is the point of the insurance, if it doesn't pay for what you need done, you may ask. Well, so did I. I was pissed, infuriated, and even this time, a little angry at God. What did he expect from me?

My sponsors Graham and Rene, both told me they were sorry, but to keep trying. Not to give up but to find a charity or something. That sounded farfetched to me, but, hell, what choice did I have? I began calling around. I probably applied to five different charities, and finally applied directly to Roche Diagnostics, the makers of Interferon. That showed some potential. I had to send in my doctor's reports, the biopsy, the strain of hep C, the viral load counts, and my tax returns for the past years, proving I was poor. That all took several stressful weeks. Finally, by the grace of God, and the generosity of the big bad pharmaceutical company I'd been cursing by name for weeks, I received an entire year's worth of treatments of Interferon, at absolutely zero cost to myself. They were going to send me the Interferon and the ribavirin combination for me to take, on a monthly basis and I would begin my hellish treatment, in the hope that I would be on the good side of the 50/50 odds the doctor had given me. A miracle indeed.

Interferon Hell

As if God hadn't given me enough, I closed two deals with a major Fortune 50 the week before I started treatment, totaling somewhere near 30k. Living rent free in the condemned rat shack, only having to pay my bills, food, and gas to and from the AA Clubhouse, it was looking like I might make it all work after all. I had a little bit of hope as I awaited my first shipment of Interferon.

And then hell opened its gates again. I was shocked that the Doctor advised I inject myself with the Interferon. He said that I could come in and have him inject them, but knowing my financial situation, this of course would mean many more Dr's visits, and again, I had my insurance but it was limited. He calmed me by explaining that you just injected them into your stomach or thigh and that it was really easy and foolproof. I was skeptical, but I didn't really have a choice. I was operating on pure faith at this stage, and the Doc assured me it was fine and it was how most patients treated themselves, because the shots were so frequent. For 48 weeks straight, quite a daunting number, and far too many to have a professional inject them at an average of a few hundred bucks a visit. The medicine arrived, and on a Thursday, I injected myself with my first shot of Interferon, and took my first three pills of Ribavirin. The dosage would be one injection, once a week for 48 weeks, and five pills of Ribavirin daily. This was the ultimate irony, since needles and pills had gotten me into this fine mess. He also advised I take Wellbutrin for the emotional rollercoaster I was going to be riding. I declined, again thinking drugs had created this monster, and I wanted nothing more to do with mind altering chemicals, ever.

It would be two months of hell before I realized how much Tylenol could dull the pain, every four hours at least. But nothing in that entire year would be as bad as that very first shot of Interferon. Flu-like symptoms doesn't begin to give justice to how awful I felt. Within an hour, I was curled up on my bed, crying like a little baby, wondering how on Earth I could feel this bad for a year. It was the worst headache, worst fever, worst shaking and sweating I had ever felt in my life -- worse than detox. I cried in bed for a few hours, and then finally passed out, either from the pain or exhaustion, I don't know which. I was afraid it would be like that all year, but fortunately, I'm just a dramatic alcoholic. When I woke up, I felt bad, but nothing like I had the night before. I was alone though, and it wasn't lost on me, that nobody was there to help me. That regardless of my sobriety, over the long haul, I had driven everyone close to me away, to the point that I'd not even told anyone about my sickness but my sponsors.

The cycle would continue monotonously for the entire year. I would inject the poison, ironically using needles, the source of my disease, to deliver the Interferon. I would be nervous that it wasn't working, anxious that I hadn't gotten enough liquid Interferon in my belly, as sometimes the injection wound would bleed, "rejecting" the medicine, I thought. I would be neurotic and paranoid that the temperature of my refrigerator wasn't accurate, and I did actually have to adjust the settings for it to be in line with what the medical documents told me about Interferon. It made me wonder if my mom's chemotherapy medicine had ever been stored properly.

I would forget whether I'd taken the ribavirin accurately, hell, I'd forget if I'd eaten or not. I would eventually have to develop a checklist that I would use for the majority of the year, marking off the Ribavirin, the Interferon, the Tylenol, and my vitamins, with the slow progression of the weeks going by. I would pray constantly, begging God for a miracle. I would take the shot, then run a fever for the first few days afterwards, then try to work at my desk, painfully and slowly. The first few days my head would be too cloudy to move off my couch very far, although I'd try to make it to a meeting daily, for fear of relapse. I stuck to that pretty rigidly, despite the pain.

I didn't tell anyone for the first few months, but eventually Anne Marie complained about how I wasn't living up to my responsibilities as a dad, and accused me of being a bad father. I broke down and told her. She cried like a little girl, and I felt terrible. I told her I'd be fine, I just needed her to be patient, and she cried some more.

I told my brother, my sister, and my stepdad, just so they wouldn't hear it from Anne Marie, and I don't think they knew what to make of it. I was in too much pain to be embarrassed, though I still wouldn't tell most of my friends, and God forbid that I let any women know that I'd gotten it.

I put a lot of debate into going back and telling the women I'd been with, especially the one who had probably given me the disease. Ultimately my sponsors weighed in that regardless of whether it was an STD or not, it was still the right thing to do, no matter how painful. I told Caroline first, and she went and got tested and was fine. Hell, she'd been pregnant with my child and was fine, so I guess it really wasn't an STD, as the doctors had told me. Telling Gwen Evere was a little more dramatic, as always.

She screamed and cussed me out. She wished she'd never met me. I was too exhausted to be upset. I told her to get tested, and that no matter what, I wasn't angry with her, as she hadn't invented the virus. Nobody had, it just happened, and that now, the only thing to do was the next right thing, to get treatment. I also asked her to tell me her viral load count. At first she told me it was in the 250k range, but three months after that, she admitted it was in the millions. So, it was no longer a suspicion. I'd identified where I'd gotten hep C from. The only God-forsaken night I'd ever stuck needles up my arms. Austin, from the AA Clubhouse, had been a junkie 20 years, and I'd used needles one night, but I'd suffered the same consequences. Except, Austin was cured of hep C, and I still had a year to go before I would know my results. Once again, life isn't fair, I guess. If it were, I'd be dead.

It became harder and harder to keep in good spirits. Feeling like shit for that long is so hard on you mentally, that I didn't know if I could make it. After my Aunt Becca knew, I asked her how she'd done chemotherapy, and gone through a divorce, and still defeated breast cancer. She summed up the bravery of all patients who undergo these types of things, though I don't claim that Interferon is worse, just similar. She said "I didn't have a choice, Bryan." She was right. You do it because you have to, much like sobriety: by no great, valiant choice, but by sheer necessity. But even to keep that mindset, you must stay sober. I know many alcoholics and addicts with hep C that can't get there, because they are still so deep in denial. It is very sad.

The pain was so brutal those first two months that I didn't write much in my journal. I still forced myself to work, and to play golf once a week, I was determined not to be in the hospital at the end of my treatment as Austin had been, and though I hated playing golf and working while on it, I needed the exercise, and I definitely needed the money to keep coming in. My first journal entry was nine weeks into the Interferon treatment, after I'd finally told Gwen about the situation.

Personal Journal, August 20th, 2007:

I don't know why I haven't been writing more in one of the most trying times of my life but it's true and I should write

more. Hep C treatment, low-level chemo, as Dr. Feldman calls it, is hell. Exhaustion, lethargy, paralysis from being sick prevents me from being even half the man I was, going into what is now my 9th week of treatment. Treatment that is scary, as only a percentage are cured, a large percentage, but a percentage nonetheless.

Meanwhile the world still spins, bills still must be paid, clients still demand fresh blood, yet my focus and concentration are fuct. But all the while, I'm happy and grateful to be sober.

No matter what happens, I'm not miserable and waiting to die. I'm happy and willing to accept God's will. Even when it hurts. Gwen Evere tested hep C positive as well and I've done what I can do, which is not much, hopefully just being honest with her about it in the first place, honest about viral loads, etc, regardless of outcome, was the right thing to do. Despite all the hell we put each other through, I can't help but see the continued coincidence, synchronicity of our lives. Both of us now fighting hep c, staying sober, thousands of miles apart, yet a parallel life story, almost. I guess, truth be told, I'm just still in love with that red headed woman. Instead of being mad at her for giving me this God awful malady, I just wish she were here, instead of fighting it all alone. Telling her about the hep c was tough, but hopefully, ultimately, it will save her life.

I pray I'm beating this virus. I pray my business stays alive. Most of all I pray I stay sober to be a good father, brother, son, etc. Thank you God for the miracle of my sobriety and please help me beat this hep C.

Personal Journal, August 21st, 2007:

Well in 1989 today or tomorrow my dad supposedly blew his head off with a .357. Alcoholics, always overdoing things. A .45 would have been fine. I hate this day, week whatever. Power of thought is crucial, but damn, some things are just hard to be positive about. Hep C treatment, which primarily attacks one's ability to fucking think, is difficult to stay positive about. House crawling with ants, 80 degrees inside, hot, sticky, and dirty, I'm fucking miserable. Why do I choose to live here you say? Who fucking knows. Ex-wife and kids I guess. Damn I love them all to tears. Even lil Patrick. Good people, I'm a lucky man.

5 Things I'm Grateful For:

Jake Smith (my son), Anne Marie (former wife), her whole family, my sobriety... hope.

Whenever I would call my sponsor bitching, he would make me write that list. That must have been one of those days, but I am still grateful for those people. They have done a lot for me in my life, and had I not had a free place to live, even in a rat shack, I don't know how it would have all worked. So many variables had to come together just perfectly for me to get sober, go through treatment, and stay sober, it's just undeniably a miracle.

So much of those early days of treatment, like the early days of my sobriety, were blurry. I'm glad I wrote as much in my journal as I did, though I could have written more. This next passage is moving in more ways than one.

Personal Journal, September 25th, 2007:

Ran into Nathan Lester at the 10 o'clock meeting, wild. He's new and you could tell he was still hurting. So I led the 10 PM meeting and it went real well. Strong God shots.

Can't find my sponsor Rene. Laying in bed about to fall asleep and I just hallucinated his spirit voice in my head. Told me he was moving along, that everything would be OK, and he told me to read <u>Course of Miracles</u>. Clear as day his voice sounded in my head. Wild.

Waiting on blood results to see if hep C treatment is working or not. I'm praying for good news, but the meeting I led was on acceptance. I'm ready for whatever God has planned. I'm still hoping for the best, though. God please let this stuff be working.

I told my friend Luis about the voice I heard the next day, and he said to call Rene at work. I called his work number and found out that Rene really had passed away. Incredible, I'd known it since hearing his voice as I'd laid to down to sleep the night before. My sponsor had died after taking me through the first six steps, and for the first time, I felt OK with someone dying in my life. I mean, his death was more like a reunion with God than any other death I'd ever experienced. I'd known Rene, I'd known how spiritual he was. He wasn't afraid of God, but was in love with God. I would miss him, yes, but I was happy for him, I had tears of joy that he'd been in my life period. I loved that man.

The other significant thing I wrote in that journal entry was running into Nathan Lester. He died within a year of that candlelight meeting. We had been friends when I lived at my first house and he drank at my house many a night. He'd been a Marine, and we'd spent many nights talking about drinking too much. His was just another sad story of drugs and alcohol. I swear this disease kills more than anything else out there, when you count in accidents, suicides, and the like. It touches every part of our society.

So Rene had died. Instantly I remembered the hall pass I'd given myself, or that in my deluded mind, God and I had agreed on, that I could drink when my closest friends died. A funny thing had happened, though. I had absolutely no desire to drink. In fact, the very idea repulsed me. It sounded like hell. I knew then and there, that I would be OK for the rest of my life, and that as long as I stayed in fit spiritual condition, I would never drink again. Just for today, absolutely, but as long as I stayed in fit spiritual condition, kept doing the things I'd been doing basically, I would be ok permanently. The 10th step promises had become true, and were now a part of my life, beyond a shadow of a doubt. It was a major victory, and although Rene died, I was actually of service for the first time when a friend or family member died, instead of feeling massive amounts of pity for myself, or using the death to justify a drinking or drugging spree, or other terrible behavior. I got hold of Rene's parents, who had already held a service for him, and told them that Rene was a huge fixture within the AA Community, and I think that it brought them a lot of joy. I had really loved Rene, in a way I didn't know I could love another man. He was peaceful, laid back, kind and fallible all at the same time. One of the last meetings I heard him speak in he coined a phrase that I love and try to hold onto to this very day. He said, no matter what happens, whether your enemies spit in your face or drag your character through the mud, we should always practice "Kindness Regardless." It was a very Buddhist sentiment I thought, but one that Christ himself would have taught as well. I bought the domain name that night, and later I would write a poem mentioning his statement he'd originated, and read it at his funeral.

328

What kind words. We held a memorial for my sponsor Rene in the same Cathedral where we'd held one for my mother, three years earlier. Except this time, I wouldn't be high on Xanax and I would speak clearly when reading a poem I had written:

Kindness Regardless

Kindness regardless,
Wise words from the subtle sage.
Deny your primitive instincts,
And crush the momentum of rage.
Fear, Pain, and Agony,
No war is worthy of wage.
Idealistic Consciousness,
But this dreamer stands not alone.
Daily sharing a vision of light,
Truth finds ways to be shown.
We did not lose this unique, kind soul.
This spirit was here but on loan.
Blessed to have felt these moments of peace,
He surely didn't die, but went home.

-JB Smith

I organized the entire memorial. I was able to look people in the eye, and was sober through the entire event. I was participating in life instead of being thrown around it like a rag doll. It was a monumental turning point for me. I knew I wanted and had sobriety, and would keep it, even through the Interferon treatment, even with just nine months sober. Life had changed dramatically for the better already, and it was getting even better. I was still waiting on the first set of test results to give me an indication of whether or not the treatment was working, but I felt good about it. Maybe Rene had gone on ahead to God, to ask him for a miracle. I hoped, anyway.

Personal Journal, October 3rd, 2007:

Test results were good, <50k viral load, which means I'm responding to the meds, but not sure precisely if that means it's gone or not, Dr's appt 10/12 to clarify (my mother's

anniversary of her death). Liver enzymes back to normal. That is fucking great news! 16 weeks, 4 months of hell, rough medicine, low level chemo as the doc says, and I finally have good result! Victory is sweet, not out of the woods yet but getting there.

The obvious lesson is to listen to your doctor verbatim. I had postponed going to the doctor to get that test, and had gone at sixteen weeks instead of eight or twelve, because, frankly, I was scared shitless the news was going to be bad. Apparently, though, if my doctors had that early information, they could have found out whether I was an early responder or not, and could have lessened the amount of time I needed to stay on Interferon overall -- which, I assure you, would have been greatly appreciated. Because I was scared and didn't get tested until sixteen weeks, though, my doctor suggested I go through the entire 48-week course, just to be sure. I wish I'd known that before, but I thought I was just being extra thorough or something. There was a lot I didn't know about Interferon going in that I found out the hard way. If this book saves one person from repeating that mistake, it will have been successful. Following your doctor's suggestions verbatim can mean less treatment, which means less pain, if you are or are planning on going through Interferon. The more accurate data they have the better. Don't procrastinate blood work or doctors visit like I did foolishly, there are significant long term benefits to doing exactly as your doctor recommends, I learned this, like so many damn things, the hard way.

It felt great to get the good news, though, the blood work found no hep C in my system. It felt like a miracle so far, four months in. Even the treatments had stabilized a little, or the symptoms had, to the point where I knew which days would be the worst. Those were usually the first two or three after the shot, followed by the less painful four to five days after the shot was wearing off. Still, I could get severe headaches out of the blue that would put me in the bed indefinitely. By this time, too, anytime I ate, I would get indigestion badly, as well as having pretty constant diarrhea, insomnia, and, of course, the urinating. Jesus, I had to pee every 30 minutes. I couldn't make it through a one hour meeting at AA without having to get up and go piss once or twice, and of course that was embarrassing. You don't have the energy to feel embarrassed, though. You also barely have the energy to put up with anybody's bullshit. You feel like the most stressed and irritated you've ever been, the entire time you're on the meds. You can't deal with corporate phone calls, waiting on hold for the bank, or listening to a woman ramble on about nothing, you simply just don't have the patience. For an ex-addict, I guess the best metaphor would be that you feel like the day after an eight ball and a three day bender, all the time, for a year straight.

Dull headache and nauseating, persistent flu-like symptoms were the mainstay of Interferon treatment, but it wasn't without its own unique quirks. I don't know if this has ever happened to anyone else, as I wasn't able to find it listed as a side effect anywhere online, but my fingernails and toenails actually began growing into my cuticles, causing infections and severe pain. One week I looked down at my hands to see three fingernails infected, all with nails growing sideways into my fingers -- the wrong direction. I would operate on them myself with razors, fingernail clippers, and tweezers, only to find my other hand would have the same problem a few days later, followed by my toes. It sounds like a small thing, but I assure you that constantly digging jagged edges out of your cuticles gets old fast, and only added to the unique misery. That special kind of hell persisted throughout the entire year, and stopped abruptly once I quit Interferon. It was no fun, and it reminded me of my mom chewing down on her fingernails when she went through chemo. It sucked, but Neosporin, Tylenol, and removing the actual nails with makeshift self-surgery made that aspect bearable.

The irritation and frustration is so great though, that I couldn't even handle maintaining my health insurance, given the flurry of weekly calls it would take to stay up-to-date with everything. Between the office supply job, my leave of absence from the part-time gig that had given me health insurance, and the calls to the insurance company for paying the premiums, I would almost go mad. Besides it hardly covered shit anyway. The office supply job wanted verification that I was sick, which I must have sent about five times. The insurance company required me to call weekly to pay the premiums, and each time I did, it was like I was doing something outside of the realm of this dimension for employees I spoke with. The Interferon and Ribavirin were free from Roche, but I still needed visits to the liver specialist doctor, of course. I also began having chest pains again, so insurance was crucial, but literally impossible for me to keep current by myself in that state of mind, and I was of course too stubborn or ashamed to ask anyone for help, like I should have.

I repeated the process, calling and faxing the office supply company over and over and making the premium payments by phone, until finally the office supply company fired me, saying I hadn't sent the form I'd sent so many times. I just gave up. I just didn't have the strength or patience to deal with it all. It was just too complicated for someone in my state. Such is the mind of an Interferon patient. I would use my insurance cards fraudulently and even be sued by my cardiologist before it was all over. Still, that was better than all the phone calls. The frustration level of dealing with the office supply company and the insurance company while on Interferon is beyond words. I have the utmost empathy with patients worse off than me, on chemo or dying, having to converse with low-level morons from major medical insurance companies. It was beyond frustrating, and though I don't know of any alternative, and would fear the Government handling health care just as much, the process seemed hellish. My suffering wasn't terminal, and I wasn't on my deathbed, so I can only imagine the frustration of someone who is dying being told to hold, repeatedly. Going through the bureaucratic hell I experienced, it's amazing more people don't just go postal on these bureaucracies.

After four months, though, and the good news of the viral load being under 50k, I was committed to finishing out the rest of the treatment. Hell, I was going to beat it, it looked like! But around that time, I began running out of money. I didn't have anybody to ask for money I thought, so I painfully began working again. Up to this point, I'd mainly watched TV and played computer games when it wasn't too awful. It made the time pass, and that's a blessing, while on treatment.

Through begging and pleading, Becca Chair, the Manager of Human Resources at my Fortune 50 client, had gotten her huge corporation to pay little old Bryan Smith's recruiting company in 30 days, which usually took about 90 days. My telling her that I was going through low-level chemo I'm sure played no small part in it. I lied through my teeth and told her in one emotional, long email that my being able to afford cancer treatment depended on her and her company paying on my invoice early. It worked but I do feel like I owe her a huge apology, and everyone else to whom I alluded that I had cancer, though it was fewer than a handful of professional contacts. My doctor called it low-level chemo, and, quite frankly, it was just too damn embarrassing to tell people I had hep C, especially while I was going through the pain of that treatment, though that doesn't make it right. Most people think of it as an STD instead of a blood disease, and there is a negative connotation that goes along with it. It's also much easier to write and talk about once it is actually gone and I'm cured. I am sorry that I alluded to low-level chemo and let a few select people think I had cancer, but I felt justified in doing so. I felt

332

like I was in a fight for my life. Ultimately, it was deception, though, and it did eat me up quite a few nights. Using that strategy, though, my Fortune 50 client, notorious for taking over 90 days to pay, sent me my check, signed by the VP of Audit within 30 days, and I am very grateful for that, as it got me through those first four months of my Interferon treatment, as my bills never stopped rolling in.

As I began to run out of that money in late October, God provided me another deal that I by no merit earned. I had picked up a job order with another publicly traded technology company, and I was so mentally exhausted that I just stuck a free ad on Craigslist. For a recruiter, that is the laziest method of recruiting there is, and usually you get only limited success. I received one good resume, and I didn't even meet the candidate. She went through four rounds of interviews with the publicly traded technology company, and started in early December of 2007. My ratio for interviews to offers has usually been around 10 to 1. Somehow, through good luck, God, or even sheer coincidence, I was almost flawless during my entire Interferon treatments. The publicly traded technology company paid me right before the Christmas break, just as my Fortune 50 client money ran out. I was becoming more and more stressed about money, but it was all for naught. When I had $100 dollars left of the $30k the Fortune 50 client had paid me six months before, the publicly traded technology company money came in. God carried me through with grace, undeserved love.

Any recruiter or salesman knows that it's a numbers game. You make a certain number of cold calls to get a percentage of people calling you back, a percentage of clients responding to you, and so on. During my treatment, in pain though I was, I was running at almost 100% candidates presented to candidates hired. Maybe a fraction less or so, but for the most part, all the work I did was rewarded. I was poor, I was living in a hovel, and I was too exhausted to even speak most days, but my treatment was free and I was taken care of. Hand to mouth, I broke into 2008 with high hopes that things were going to continue to look up.

Personal Journal, December 17th, 2007:

Money should be in the bank by tomorrow. Felt OK most of the day despite the panic over cash-flow, but now I feel pretty rough. Bad diarrhea, and I'm super itchy all over my body. Didn't sleep last night, so I'm running on 29 hours no sleep as well. Laid in bed tossing and turning through the

entire night, not a wink. Itchy everywhere, feels like my skin is majorly dehydrated, though I do nothing but chug water constantly, and piss, let's not forget taking 1 billion pisses a day, and now I'm on the toilet just pissing out of my ass for the 5th or 6th time today. "Soon this will all be over" I once said to my mom as we picked her up from Northside Hospital. I was right about it then, and I'm right about it now, just hopefully in a different way this time, though. Keep it up JB, if nothing else, your 12th stepping helps folks at meetings. Stay alive!

Picking Up the Pieces

After Rene died, I went back to being exclusively sponsored by Graham Flagg. I couldn't have done it without him. He encouraged me, free of charge, as sponsors do, to keep marching through the pain, do the next right thing, and to be OK with just being in pain, that it would pass. We spoke daily, and I owe this man my life. It built a bond, a trust, and for the second time in my sobriety, I loved another man. Not in a gay way at all, but just a spiritual connection that I had not created, but wouldn't be the same without. I felt like I'd take a bullet for the guy, and I called him every day to whine and bitch about the pain and frustration. Somehow, it lightened the burden, as did moving through the steps no matter how little I wanted to, the act of progress kept my momentum in sobriety.

Step 6: "Were entirely ready to have God remove all these defects of character."

Working with my sponsor, from my already completed previous fourth and fifth step, I was able to come up with a fairly extensive list of my character defects, not uncommon to most other human beings on Earth, but a real first assessment of what I struggle with, and what could be improved. I was taught that I ought never say never, but be willing to one day give up all my defects of character. I honestly just made a beginning, a perfect ideal for myself, and I continue trying on that ordeal. It was more important that I try, than that I do this perfectly. Nobody removes all their defects of character all at once, but to be ready to have them removed is an ideal I was able to agree to.

Step 7: "Humbly asked him to remove our shortcomings."

The emphasis on this step is humility. I was barely able to

understand a lot of these concepts as I marched through Interferon and the step work, but just continued to do the next right thing, as pointed out by my sponsor. For this step we kneeled down and prayed from the Big Book.

The Seventh Step Prayer
from page 76 of the Big Book of Alcoholics Anonymous

My Creator,
I am now willing that you should have all of me,
good and bad.
I pray that you now remove from me
every single defect of character which stands in the way
of my usefulness to you and my fellows.
Grant me strength, as I go out from here,
to do your bidding.
Amen .

Step Eight: "Made a list of all persons we had harmed and became willing to make amends to them all."

I had feared this step as well, just as I had the Fourth Step, primarily because I didn't know what it entailed either. I had imagined my having to confess to the FBI, my family, all the women I'd ever wronged, etc. This was wildly incorrect. In fact, there is no approaching anyone at all in this step, but simply making a list of people, based on what I'd written and shared in my fourth and fifth step. And being as desperate as the dying can be, I did just that and made the list. My sponsor told me to be fearless and thorough and so I was. He told me, accurately, that when it was all said and done, I would probably only need to make direct amends to about a third of the people listed, and to just get it done so we could move forward. Not wanting to stall out, while suffering through Interferon, I just did the work.

Step Nine: "Made direct amends to such people wherever possible, except when to do so would injure them or others."

And so we went over my Step Eight, and began to list, by priority, who I could begin making amends to. My family came first, as it was most obvious. Many coworkers and friends followed that.

I became willing to work on this for a lifetime if need be. It wasn't a race, but to be willing, made the difference. Many of the amends I couldn't make immediately, but being willing, I was granted the spiritual reward, keeping the obsession to drink at bay, which had happened around Step Five or so for me.

I don't list these steps to be an example of shining AA 12 Steps perfection, but to show, that even with my mangled, Interferon laced, brain dead thinking, the steps were still able to work, even as half assed as I worked them. I am more pointing out that this approach, working with a sponsor, and the collective consciousness of AA performs miracles, even when you are as slow, and mentally and physically taxed as someone going through low level chemo. I know fully that I need to go through the steps more thoroughly, but I only point out that even handicapped to a certain extent, the steps worked on me, and kept me sane, sober, and moving away from a drink, rather than towards one. If I could stay sober on Interferon, and do the steps while as tired as I was, anyone, really anyone, should be able to do the same thing, under more ideal conditions.

On December 23rd, 2007, my sponsor gave me my real one year chip. He threw it to me in the side room, adjacent to the main room at 8111, from about 15 feet away. I swear on my life, it curved strangely two or three times, then seemed to glide directly in between my fingertips. It felt like magic. It was damn sure magic that I'd stayed completely sober for whole year. Even though I'd already lied and picked up my one year chip on 10-12-2007, my sponsor had said to me earlier in the week "Aren't you coming up on a year?" I finally just admitted it. I still can't get anything past the guy!

This is a little ridiculous, but I did think that once I had a year, the woman at AA would line up to get this stud! When I'd gotten my first one year chip in 2007, it seemed like nobody even noticed. Can you imagine, I mean how could these women let such a catch go by? I'd let it go at the time, being on my treatment and all. But by the genuine anniversary date, I had come to terms with the fact that nobody was really keeping an eye on my sobriety date but me and my sponsor. And for damn sure, there were no women holding their breath for me to get a year in, though I'd found that very hard to believe. It was irrefutable, as the second picking up of my year chip produced the same results as the first on the woman front. None.

My sister invited me to her December 23rd engagement party for both her and Madison Stafford at the Stafford's house, an 11k square foot mansion in Roswell. Being there made me feel like a peasant, living in a rat shack hovel, and quite rightly. This was not their fault, of course, but still, on Interferon, running a fever, and head aching, the last place on Earth I wanted to be was at a mansion watching happy, successful people smiling and embracing one another while I suffered. My sponsor walked me through it, and told me to forgive all my resentments, and to be there for my sister and be thankful I was still invited to these types of events, period. I went, I watched, and I tried to mingle as my entire family, including my 86 year old grandmother, drank beer and laughed heartily. I even managed a smile or two, but I was miserable every last second of the event. Social is the last adjective you would use to describe someone going through Interferon, and it was good my brain was too fuzzy to put together how much I resented being forced to go to this engagement party. By the time I realized I resented it, I would be through it and it would be over. A lot of things in sobriety seemed to be like that. If I just kept doing the next right thing, regardless of how uncomfortable it was, I'd get through it sooner rather than later. I'm blessed to be included in my family's life, but at that engagement party, I assure you I didn't feel blessed.

Madison told me that at eight, they would open up the bourbon, but until then it was just beer. Thanks, but no thanks. I had just picked up a one year chip, and I didn't miss drinking at all. I just missed my life, missed not being on Interferon, missed the pink cloud I'd felt from three months to six months of sobriety. The drinking didn't appeal to me at all anymore, but feeling better did. I left the engagement party after exactly two hours, and went home and wrote resentful things in my journal, things that the poor write about the rich. I couldn't help it, I felt awful. Good thing I was lying to myself, though, the last journal entry of 2007 I wrote was "Four and a half months left of treatment. I'm getting there. God thank you please give me strength." I had until May, so it was much longer than that, closer to six months than to four and a half, but I guess I needed to believe it was almost over. The last half of treatment went by much slower than the first, as I continued to scratch down the weeks on the wood above the toilet. At least my lying to myself was about better things now.

So picking up my year had produced no women, and neither had the mansion engagement party. That was OK, though, because the lulls between bouts of pain, maybe on a Wednesday or Thursday, the last days before giving myself the Interferon shot, were the best I could hope for. That didn't leave me much time for chasing skirts or wanting a relationship. The pain and enhanced irritation of any regular conversation were too much to bear in general. There simply wasn't the strength to muster up to try to date anybody, period. The few occasions of hooking up I had were mostly with other girls in AA. I was always safe, and the relationships never really went anywhere.

I was safe in those few incidents, despite my doctor telling me it wasn't an STD. Despite the numerous couples he knew where the husband had hepatitis C, and the wife had borne children and breastfed, and never gotten the disease. It isn't an STD, yet, still, it's not something that anyone wants to talk about on a first date, either. It has a social stigma, as does any disease, I guess, but worse because it's associated with drugs as well as sex. Regardless of the validity of that fear, I was safe with the handful of girls I was with. I'd feel better after the virus was gone for six months without the treatments, so that I could declare it cured, as my liver doctor had told me.

Helping and Not Helping

So 2008 rolled in with a whimper. I was too weak to party, and I got Christmas with the family over as soon as possible. I just didn't have the strength to socialize or even relax anywhere but my own home, lest I be overwhelmed with the runs, a massive headache, or what have you.

Jacob, my best friend in the program at this time, began relapsing quite regularly and began coming to crash at my house at the end of his weekend-long cocaine benders. Man, I could feel his misery. The dead look in his eyes, the panic, the futility. He'd had nine months sober before, and he'd thrown it away, and now his very presence made me feel uncomfortable, not that I'd been feeling great to start with. I put up with it a few weekends in a row in January, just trying to preach the Big Book and AA literature. I spoke about how I felt so much better than he did, even though I was on Interferon, just knowing that I was on the right side of God's plan, and no longer was an adversary, and so on. I spent hours talking to him, but eventually I realized I was just being a crutch to him. He was using me as a place to crash after his binges, and I wasn't helping him get sober at all. In AA, we call it denying someone their bottom. I told him he was negatively affecting me and to not come by again until he'd gotten a little time sober, that he was making me feel a little squirrely. A funny adjective AA'ers use to describe feeling uncomfortable, especially hilarious in my case considering my 1ˢᵗ week while detoxing, specifically fearing squirrels!

After a few weeks, he agreed to check into some long term rehabilitation, but it hadn't happened over night. For a few weeks there, it was touch and go with this guy coming in and out of my house, fucked up, eyes shifting, the lies piling up, rationalizations, and just general sickness. It's hard to describe how that makes an ex-alcoholic feel, but it's like you have to be on your toes around it. It's like the Devil is in them, so you've got to call up God in you. It feels like spiritual warfare. As long as you remember to arm, you're fine, or if you simply outnumber the sick as you usually do in meetings it's ok, but if you start to buy into the bullshit, you can easily slip into the old thinking. One night after trying to talk sense into Jacob all night, after he left, I kept thinking that smoking a joint would sure make my stomach and nausea feel better. I had to call my sponsor, I had to tell him what was going on, and he told me flat out I wasn't prepared, in my current condition, to do that kind of twelfth step work. He said to let Jacob know he couldn't just stop by any more. It was good to have a sponsor and some strategic advice. It made sense after he said it, but I didn't think it through as it was going on. It was all good, though. Jacob agreed to long term rehab and I took him to the airport and dropped him off.

The treatment dragged on. Without the meetings, I'd have never made it. I told barely anyone in AA that I was sick, and that was stupid, there was so much help available at 8111, but I just marched on in silence, telling only my sponsor and a select few people. The deal with the publicly traded technology company had put a fat check in my bank account just before the Christmas break, and I somehow managed to stretch that money all the way up until around March. Around that time, I did a ninth sep amends with Brian Huff and Christopher Stanley, regarding my ratting them out to Everett Monahan years before and within a couple of weeks of that amends, God granted me a deal that Brian and I would split with a Big 4 MBA candidate, placing him in an M&A role with a regional accounting firm here in Atlanta. It happened just as my other deals had happened, in the nick of time, and I received the money just as I was down to a hundred bucks in the bank again. It was incredible. As Ralph Waldo Emerson stated "The whole course of things goes to teach us faith. There is guidance for each of us, and by lowly listening, we shall hear the right word." Once again, moving through the twelve steps had provided me with a miracle. If I hadn't done my ninth step, I wouldn't have closed that deal with my old boss, splitting a fee. I had come into the rooms of Alcoholics Anonymous hopeless and scared, and now I'd almost made it through the entire year of treatment without once needing a drink or a drug, and had been provided for at every corner and every step.

I'd been delivered through the entire course of my treatments by May of 2008, and I'd kept my business afloat, closing just enough deals to survive, and keep the roof over my head, the lights and energy going, and I'd barely even worked that entire year. It was a straight miracle, and even a doubter like myself couldn't deny God's grace at work within me.

I attended my sister's wedding, exhausted and visibly drained, as all the wedding photos attest. Though I was tempted to be resentful that they couldn't wait until I felt better, I knew in my heart that that was ridiculous, and that it was a privilege to be there, period. My sister was beautiful as always, and regardless of feeling like shit, I was very glad to have attended that glamorous event, and grateful I didn't wuss out and not show up. I was lucky to still be included with my family, at all.

The last few months had been brutal. There are countless pitiful journal entries complaining of diarrhea, headaches, nausea and the like. But every time I would be at a breaking point, I would go to a meeting, and like clockwork I would see Logan S., who'd been sober six months before finding out he'd gotten leukemia. He'd been given six months to live about the same time I came into the rooms, and though his treatment was probably ten times what I was going through, he was always stronger and happier than me, it seemed. He always embraced that no matter what happened, he was sober, and more than that, he was going to beat it. I didn't believe for a second that he would beat it, but it was hard to feel sorry for myself with such an example of courage and faith in his eyes. Every single time I felt so weak I was planning on quitting the treatment, I walked into a meeting to see his completely bald head and the sparkle in his eyes. He has remained sober and cancer free to this day, just another, now commonplace, miracle I've witnessed in the rooms of AA.

I'd found a doctor at Duke who specialized in hepatitis C. While I was torturing myself over the decision to stop taking treatment two weeks early, I'd sent him an email. Ironically he didn't send me anything back until six months later, on the exact day I was waiting on the final test results, to see whether I was officially cured or not. I'd asked him simply what he thought my odds of beating the virus were. He responded the day I would receive my test results back, six months later, "The thin do better than the fat, the young do better than the old, and the strong, do better than the weak." He was right, I was young, thin, and strong as I could be after seventeen years of drinking and drugging abusively. I got the test result back that day, and I was clear of the virus, or under 50k viral load. Cured as Dr. Feldman would pronounce. What a miracle, just a year and a half earlier I'd thought my life was over.

When I received that word in October, 2008 that I was cured of hep C, Logan C. also received word that his cancer was completely in remission. Despite all the medical advice over the previous two years that he was terminal. If God be with us, who can be against us?

Bearing Witness

This book is an attempt to bear witness to those that I would help. I came into AA literally insane. The second step required that I believe a Power Greater than Myself could restore me to sanity. I did not, but I didn't have a choice, I had to believe it would work, or else I was fucked. I came, I came to, I came to believe, as it's said in the rooms I used to think so threatening, that not only turned out to be harmless, but in fact miraculous.

I clearly remember to this day the fear in my father's eyes the last time I saw him, when he said "AA doesn't work." Fortunately, someone told me early on, "There isn't anybody too stupid for AA, but I've met a lot of people who were too smart." Had it not been for my dad's example of failure, and where I would end up if I didn't surrender to the program completely, I know I wouldn't have made it. I came in a wretched, delusional, insane person, unable to go a single day without drinking, right up until drinking literally stopped working for me, tasting like battery acid and giving me zero results. I suffered through the pain of early sobriety, but the people in the meetings swore it would get better. Lo and behold, it did.

In October, 2008, I had been given an amazing second chance. The hepatitis C was completely gone. I was one and a half years sober, with my two year mark coming up on Christmas Eve of 2008, and I'd never felt better in my life. The treatment took a long time to get over, and I'm sure I have an amends or two for implying it was cancer when I passed on what my doctor told me, that it was low-level chemo. But I didn't tell anyone it was cancer, and I denied it when they asked. Still, I did feel bad about using that line, "low-level chemo", I just didn't know what else to say. I am still human, and I still have my character defects. I just don't drink over them anymore.

Alcoholics Anonymous has saved my life, given me a brand new one, and given me hope for a better life as well. At three years sober now, I've made peace with everyone in my life, whether those resentments be real or imagined. I've no reason to quarrel with anyone. I've even learned how to forgive when someone just blatantly wrongs me.

When my Nana's husband Harry died, my stepdad asked me to go to the funeral. Nana, my stepdad's mom, had been close with my mom, and is one of the sweetest ladies on earth. I went, still a little resentful that I had to attend such family events still feeling like an outsider, and an amazing transformation took place. I'd included Dan Jones on my resentments list, and I'd worked through the major emotional baggage I carried for so long. But at Harry's funeral, I really saw and felt how good a man he really is. We had just been two unwitting passengers in life's journey, thrown together by circumstances, as he had been with Harry. More than that, though, he'd actually tired to be close to me, where I had purely and emphatically rejected his presence from day one. It was actually me and my anger and resentments, that made our relationship difficult! What a revelation! He'd spent his late 30's and 40's taking me and my brother camping, on countless vacation trips, fishing expeditions, and trips to the movies. We even loved the same things: movies, computer games, golf, women, you name it. I began to see my entrepreneurial attempts had been sought after with faith, having watched his success.

Unwittingly and miraculously, I realized I loved Dan Jones, not as my stepdad but as my dad, my real dad. I'd always called my biological dad my real dad and I'm sure it was always a thorn to Dan, though the man never said a thing about it. But Dan Jones was as close to a real dad as I'd ever had, warts and all. The major resentments I'd built around the time of my mom's death about our supposed and imagined inheritance, as well as my anger at his dating soon afterwards, faded away at that funeral. I'd prayed over those resentments a lot in my first year and a half of sobriety, but only when I forgave him in my heart, 100%, did I begin to really see him for who he is. He'd put up with my bullshit my whole life and was still there. When he'd given me money to run away, it was out of desperation, not cold malice. I was an uncontrollable terror at the time. The inheritance was all delusional, based on a

342

few statements from my brother taken as fact, and from my mom, who was so capable of exaggeration. In reality, my mom was broke after five years of cancer, no matter how much my biological father had left her. She'd raised three children, some of them problematic (especially me), and thus more expensive.

The thorn my brother and sister had the hardest time dealing with, his early dating, was actually the easiest of all his perceived faults for me to accept. The poor man was lonely. He stuck by my dying mother's side through her entire cancer, and most certainly spent 20 times more time with her than I had. That is more than I can say for many modern men who've left their cancer stricken wives. I loved and love Dan Jones as my father now, and amazingly, as soon as I started loving him regardless of my perceived notions of how he felt about me, our relationship went from strained and forced, to mutual acceptance and understanding. And we are changed by the act of unconditionally loving, regardless of that person's feelings of it. The act of loving, is never a bad thing. Ironically, as the cosmic joker God would have it, we are closer now than we've ever been in either of our lives. That would have never happened if I'd kept drinking. I'd have never looked at my part in it, or even cared to work on the resentment at all. Clarity and truth seeking go hand in hand in Alcoholics Anonymous.

As far as Gwen went, she too took a while to forgive, both her and myself. It was hard not to be angry with her as I suffered through the Interferon for the blood disease she'd given me, because of the heroin we'd done together that one fateful night. Ultimately, though, I forgive her. After all, she didn't invent the disease, and she didn't intentionally get me sick. I choose to shoot up with her that night, she didn't force me. My first sponsor Rene asked me to quit sending her money to San Diego where she'd moved to become an actress, and I did finally. She'd blamed me for giving her hep C when I was just three months into Interferon treatment, and that had been another slap, and a tough one. Regardless, I loved her then greatly, and love her to this day. Once again, the act of loving one unconditionally, changes the world about you. When we were together, my love was conditional, and though I've not spoken to her in years, I am no longer ashamed of the love I offered, we were both unwell. There was nothing wrong with the love I felt, we were both just sick souls on a sinking ship, and we had to get away from each other, or we'd have sailed around the Bermuda Triangle of addiction rudderless, aimless and eventually dying an alcoholic death. Separately it's amazing we both found the rooms. I wish her all the success in the world.

343

It took a while for me to be OK with the love I felt and still feel for Gwen. I was so alone and depressed after my mom died and my anger for Gwen grew and grew after she left me, weeks after my mom's death. Now I don't feel any anger at all towards her. I do sometimes get angry with the disease of alcoholism, the same disease that killed my biological dad and hers and millions of others. I'm OK with the love I have and had for her now, because I was right about her: deep down she's brilliant, creative, kind, and loving. Life is too short to live bitter, wounded, and scarred. And in God's omnipotence all things are possible, even love.

For me, attempting to come to peace with my mom really began at her bedside those last few months of her life. My Uncle Owen had suggested that before she died, I go to her bedside and make amends. She had been unconscious, but I'd cried and apologized for everything as well as forgiven her for every perceived wrong she'd ever done me, as her death had forced the issue earlier. Still, I'd known this whole time what she wanted was simply for me to get sober, so that in itself brought about a lot of peace with her in my mind. I still owe her a former amends though, a letter to leave at her grave site, and one I'll share with the reader, as the finale of my first time through the 12 Steps. It is the only step I've yet to complete and will do so to end this book.

I had carried around anger towards her for my father's death, for marrying Dan Jones, for throwing me into Outward Bound, and for throwing away every personal belonging I owned after returning. When she denied custody of me and had me sent away to Juvenile Hall, I was enraged and stayed that way for years. When she didn't visit Anne Marie and me when our son was born, and didn't even see my son that first year of his life, I'd harbored incredible lasting resentments that did neither of us any good. I thought I'd forgiven her for all of those things and had apologized for all my wrongdoings as well. But it was two entirely different things to do all that at her bedside while she lay unconscious and dying while I was still drinking and drugging, and to write it all down in my fourth step after several months of real, drug-free sobriety. By then, I had added resentments to the list, being angry that she'd left everything to Dan Jones, bitter that she'd blown 750k of my dad's life insurance in the course of her life, and just angry in general she'd left the planet, whether she wanted to or not.

Working through all of that with a competent sponsor, I came to realize a few things. She did her absolute best at all times, because she was a fighter. She loved us all, and every action of hers, right or wrong, had been done in love, and what she thought would yield the best results, no matter how accurate, or occasionally delusional, those actions were. In the long run, lo and behold, those tactics worked, as here I am today stone cold sober. I was a messed-up kid, and though her methods were harsh, I didn't leave her many options. As far as the perceived inheritance that didn't actually exist in the first place, who leaves money to a drug addicted alcoholic? I had only myself to blame. She fought cancer long after the doctors had written her off, and she had loved me until the end, after almost everyone had written me off. She told me to quit drinking or it would kill me in her last words to me. She was right. And then after receiving the blessing of finding AA, and the complete and total relief of the obsession to drink and drug being lifted, by example she showed me how to suffer through painful medical treatments and fight to the last breath.

My poor fighting mother raised three children on her own for a year when her husband turned psychotic and threatened to kill us all. She braved the real estate industry without so much as a start in a sales career, she fearlessly entered and succeeded in one of the toughest businesses in the world. She fought cancer tooth and nail with everything she had and raised herself up from a hospital bed with only weeks to live to attend my brother's wedding. Anytime I felt sorry for myself during that year of Interferon treatment, I had only to look at her shining example of courage and bravery in the face of death and extreme pain to find inspiration. Mine was but a mild discomfort by comparison. When I didn't want to go to one of my son's ball games during treatment because I was nauseous with a headache, I'd remember my mom, mid-chemotherapy after just having ribs and portions of her lungs removed, showing up to the last few innings of my son's baseball game, shaking and clutching a blanket, but cheering and smiling, glad to be alive, fighting for every last moment of her life. By her example, I fought.

If it weren't for her beating it into me that alcohol would kill me, I'd be dead today. Knowing her, when she got to heaven she probably told God personally to make alcohol quit working for me, and she probably didn't stop until he did it. God didn't stand a chance, folks. I miss my momma, but I know beyond a shadow of a doubt that she knows I'm sober, and she's proud of me.

As for the government, society, and religion, who was I to change any of them? I am a teardrop in the ocean, I can't affect any of those things. I have ceased fighting anything and everyone, for by this time, sanity has returned. I can watch and I can even be a cynic, but if I spend too much time disgusted, it will affect my sobriety, my serenity, and my calm, and I value that above all else.

I'm a brand new man. My thinking is entirely different. I'm no longer perverse. I no longer fall asleep to thoughts of death by firing squad. I'm positive and think of my dreams and goals and spirituality. I don't have to die of alcoholism, or of hepatitis C, or even be angry at anyone, ever again, and if I do get angry I don't have to stay that way for days, weeks, or years. I know how to deal with it now. I haven't punched a single wall since I've been sober. The ole rat shack didn't have a single door without a fist hole in it, not one. That is not a sign of happiness.

AA has saved my life. I think my being a Christian to start with did help me to embrace it, and I have my mom and stepdad to thank for that. But ultimately, it was the twelve steps that got me closer to God, not reading the New Testament, and I know of people in almost all religions who've gotten sober, even Pagans, through the Twelve Steps, it doesn't exclude a soul. Anyone is welcome, and that is about as Christian as I can imagine any group can possibly be. The only requirement for membership is a desire to stop drinking. That's as good as it gets.

I still continue to get God shots, or coincidences winking at me as Einstein referred to them. On my 32nd bellybutton birthday, (AA'ers must distinguish sober birthdays and real ones) I was leading a meeting on gratitude, grateful that I'd made to age 32 quite frankly. It was at 8111, the clubhouse in which I'd found sobriety, and where I know most of the folks. We do get a ton of transients as Atlanta is a major hub, and a visitor was in there that evening. When we gave out the chips that night, it just so happened a man from New York City was picking up his 32 year sobriety chip. To me that's God smiling down on me, still, even after the storm has quelled, if I listen, I can hear him.

I had come in to AA thinking I was an undercover CIA Agent, thinking that maybe I was in hell, that my family and the whole world hated me, and thinking a million other insane thoughts, and I've been saved from all that delusional thinking. The urge to drink and drug has completely left me. I'm happy and usefully whole. All of the AA promises have come true for me. Every last one of them.

Looking back, I still don't know if there was really a demon standing over me after Josh Daugherty and I fooled around with that Ouija boards and his mom woke up so panicked. I don't know whether the Rainbow Family was ever interested in my soul, standing in for the Devil, or whether the Colonel from the Marine Corp was even real at all. Perhaps just being raised Christian makes all my worst fears demonic, Pagan, or Satanesque, and thus when drugged out and delusional, that's where my base fears go. It's funny that when people lose their minds, it's all relatively unoriginal: the Devil, aliens, the CIA, germs, ghosts, and so on. It's never really unique, but is all just magnified fear. With AA, I've replaced my fear with faith. Regardless of the validity of the fears or lack thereof, God conquers all, and faith has definitely begun to conquer fear in me. And when any fears do crop up, I have tools to manage and work through them. One of my mom's favorite sayings was "If you're going through hell, keep going."

Having researched every drug combination possible, from hallucinogens to cocaine, muscle relaxants to opiates, and, of course, the ever-present marijuana and alcohol -- King Alcohol, which I began and ended every adventure with -- I ultimately found the mystique to be nothing. It was a deceit, a constant lie that had evolved me from a rational, sane, intelligent boy to an insane person barely capable of reading and speaking. The allure had been a lie that had lasted 15 plus years. The person I had become at the end and the person I really was, kept growing farther and farther apart, eventually driving me into psychosis. AA showed me the reality of what a drunkard I had been. I'd thought I was a nice guy. The more sober I got, the more drunk I realized I had been. All the magic, all the sexiness of drugs and alcohol had been lies. The music event scene, all lies. The Grateful Dead, Jim Morrison, Janis Joplin, Jimi Hendrix, and countless others, all beautiful artists that represent a lie, years of wasted life and ultimately death. The Rainbow Family delusions, the CIA, the inflated sense of ego, all of it supported my drinking and drugging and all of it had been irrelevant lies. Without AA, I would either be dead or still living in a delusional fantasy land, insane, and unable to differentiate the true from the false.

It all started with that lie, that it will be different this time. This time I'll control my drinking and drugging, knowing damn well that every shred of evidence pointed to the contrary. I'm still capable, despite the pages of evidence presented here, to occasionally hear my mind tell me that this time, it will be different. I'll just drink on the weekends. I'll only smoke mid grades (less potent weed), and so on. The difference is that now I know it's a lie. I know to combat it with an AA meeting. I have tools to use, that work against this insane thinking. Before AA I had no defense against that first drink and no clue what would happen afterwards.

I continue to go to meetings five to six times a week, not because I have to, but because I love it. I can feel the pulse of God inside the rooms of AA. I love seeing the sick get better, and I love to help in any way I can. I love our traditions, and wish the U.S. Constitution were subject to the same type of unfaltering principles, that we might still enjoy some of the freedoms we had in 1776. AA will continue to live and grow, because we can't change it, or worse, amend it death, and that's a great thing.

I really didn't know I could get any better. I didn't know that quitting drinking was an option. I watched my father die of this disease and many others, and I just thought I was destined to die an alcoholic addict, of either a car crash, a suicide like my dad, or maybe an overdose, but I thought it was inevitable. God saw fit to save me from that destiny, but I had to be willing to go into AA and give it a shot. Here are just a few of the names of people I've known, just since I got sober, that either didn't make it to AA, or made it to AA, and were too smart for the program, and didn't give it their all, because I've never known a single person to give it their all and fail:

Shane Oleander
Noah Driver
Nathan Lester
Patrick Floyd

That is just in the three years I've been in the rooms, and I knew all of those people well. I could add an additional three names of people who died of hepatitis C. This disease is out to kill, and it does the job well, and unfortunately it is a progressive disease, always getting worse, never better. I was at the end of my rope, as far low as I think was humanely possible, just a few shades away from complete and total wet brain. I may have caused irreparable brain damage for all I know, and yet still I was able to pull out of the nosedive, repair my body, and lead a happy and usefully whole life.

If I can do it, get sober and defeat hepatitis C, anyone can. And it's about to get even easier. If you are suffering from hepatitis C, then definitely google Telaprevir, as I've read it increases the odds of beating the virus, as well as reducing the amount of time it takes to be on Interferon. Had I known this drug was awaiting FDA approval, I may have waited before going through treatment. So though it is tough now, there is hope for a better way.

A grateful heart will never drink. Thank you God for curing

me of my hepatitis C, and thank you above all else, for my sobriety. I love you with all my heart and soul, and hope that this book helps at least one alcoholic on Earth, that it may bear Witness to Thy Power, Thy Love and Thy Way of Life.

-Jared Bryan Smith

Epilogue: Living Amends to my Mom

Hey mom, how is heaven? Has to be better than those last few years here on Earth, in all that physical and emotional pain. When you are the focal point and glue of an entire family, it must make it that much harder to up and leave, knowing damn well the damage it would do, the vacuum it would create. God it was tough when you finally passed in October of 2004. Six whole years ago. My already inflamed alcoholism reached new heights, my self destruction amplified. I'm sure you were in God's ear on more than one occasion and saved my ass. Eventually alcohol and drugs quit working. I was certain that was you and God's work, who did he think he was up against?

Three and a half years into sobriety, all of my major amends behind me, this last amends to you remained. Six years since your death and I'm just now making it to your grave. The story of that timeline is interesting in itself. Two times I came on my own, expecting the 1st to remember the location in this vast cemetery and not being able to find it after hours of searching and the 2nd on my own, when Dan Jones told me of course, the office would be open on a Sunday, as that was a prime visiting day. He was wrong. In 2008, my third try, Dan and I tried to make it down here for your birthday, but he too requires no map, and knowing a famous one of his "short cuts" we were completely lost before even finding the cemetery. Yesterday was literally my fourth attempt at trying to visit your grave. I planned it all out, made sure the office was open, as it was a Saturday this time, and the weather looked like it would hold, so my hopes were high. I left Roswell, made it to Westview Cemetery in south Atlanta and went straight to the office, and got a perfectly accurate map, with X marking the spot of your gravestone. I drove through the mostly empty, miles wide and long cemetery, all the way to section 42, incidentally Jake and I's favorite number thanks to the Hitchhikers Guide to the Galaxy, and as I came over that last hill, confident I was mere moments from writing down my last amends, I see the one and only funeral taking place in all of Westview, and sure enough the audience at said funeral were all standing on and around your grave! What the hell?! Four legitimate, sober tries, all failures. I headed home frustrated, stressed out, and over analyzing the meaning. Recalling your last looks at me at Carson's wedding. That utter disdain and perfect look of disappointment, I headed

350

home, imagining your old, familiar anger with me, even stretching into the infinite beyond.

Mom you'd be amazed with me. I not only quit drinking and drugging three and a half years ago, I even quit smoking cigarettes in August of 2009, and I run. Up until yesterday maxing out at about 6.4 miles, as the loop we used to run together in Brookfield West is about 3.2 miles, and I'd gotten up to running it twice. So emotional and upset after returning from the cemetery yet again empty handed, I set out to run it off, as far and as long as possible. When I got to nine miles or 3 laps, I still felt pretty good and decided to continue on, one last lap, miles 10, 11 and 12, as it were and that would surely be the longest I'd ever run in my entire life. Not bad for someone who just 3 years before was drinking and drugging himself to death, smoking 1-2 packs a day while pissing a brownish black, as my liver headed towards a permanent shutdown. As I ran those last 3 miles, 10, 11 and 12 I was reminded of so much of my past in that neighborhood. I ran past the place where I made the conscious decision to pick up a half a cigarette butt out of the gutter and smoke it, because I wondered what it was like to be addicted to something, at the age of 12 years old. My sister watched me with morbid fascination, telling me not to. I'd ignored her then. I ran past Shane Oleanders house, now dead to addiction, and remembered all the times we played tackle football in that front yard. Past Corey Black's street, and that long friendship lost due to my actions while drunk and high on hash, and past the road that leads to Dylan Sublime's parents house, where I participated in felony breaking and entering, just to get high for a few hours. Past the street corner where I held a knife to Doug White's throat as a teenager after his friend Justin robbed me of that quarter pound, I'd borrowed money from my high school girlfriend to buy, and I thought about how much worry all that bullshit must have put you through. Our entire relationship, altered, skewed, from the moment I began chasing my addictions. That lie, that we only hurt ourselves, is one of the biggest in the barrel. We, mother and son were changed forever by my behavior. As I finished that last mile, mile 12, my knees hurt, my ankle they said would make me limp for life and didn't was sore as hell, and all my leg muscles ached, and I thought about how mile 12 was the toughest. Come to think of it, so was Step 12, in fact 10, 11 and 12, the maintenance steps, or the last miles in recovery were sometimes the toughest for me in the last 3.5 years, but also

351

now, how I maintain my spiritual condition, which keeps me safe and secure and the burden to drink and drug at bay. The obsession lifted, and I don't ever want it to come back.

Step 10: "Continued to take personal inventory and when we were wrong promptly admitted it."

For me mom this isn't as difficult as it sounds, but just to write in my journal every day, looking back over the day, examining whether I participated in any of my character defects, and if I did, to keep them in check for tomorrow. This self examination is just not something that happens when you're drinking and drugging. You're too busy living in the delusion. In sobriety I seek truth and this personal inventory, thinking about my day, admitting my wrongs, helps me beyond words. It's another one of those things you reap more of the results by completing the action than by reading or analyzing it. Much of the 12 steps are like that.

Step 11: "Sought through prayer and meditation to improve our conscious contact with God as we understood Him, praying only for knowledge of His will for us and the power to carry that out."

I began praying the moment I came into AA, but what I've learned about prayer and meditation since then surpasses anything I ever knew. I pray every morning and every night, no matter what. "God give me the strength to stay sober", and then at night "God thanks for keeping me sober". I meditate every so often and I pray throughout my days now mom. There is room for improvement in all the steps, but I think this one, for me, is the one I'd like to work on most. I think there is a real value in listening to God, for His will, rather than trying to tell him what it should be. Foxhole prayers included. The serenity that prayer and meditation give me now are real and tangible, not superstitious ramblings as were the prayers of my drinking days. And still there is much room for improvement here.

Step 12: "Having had a spiritual awakening as the result of these steps, we tried to carry this message to alcoholics, and to practice these principles in all our affairs."

For me, working with others can be the most taxing and as

such the most rewarding, as has been, writing this book. God gives each and every one of us strengths, and mine, I believe is writing, which is why I believed it was God's will for me to finish this book about recovery and be bold enough to talk about having hepatitis C. Otherwise, I would have much rather preferred keep this struggle to myself.

As I finished mile 12 mom, I simply couldn't ignore the correlation and significance between my running those last miles and continuing to work ALL the steps to the very last mile, incorporating them in everything I do.

After I finished my longest run ever, I called my sister Carrie, an amazing athlete herself, to tell her about my accomplishment. I then told her how the emotional turmoil of the day had led to such a long run, and that deep down I thought perhaps the universe was keeping me from mom's grave because she was still mad at me. In an instant, as my sister has done so many times in my life, she told me like it really was. "Don't you think that for a second JB. Mom would be so proud of you. You've done everything and more than mom would have ever asked you! I know she's proud of you right this second, and you just keep it up."

I believe my sister. Good or bad, she never sugarcoats it, and this time she was right, and I'd earned it. I know you would be proud mom. And though it took me five times to get here, sitting at your grave, I write by your headstone now, as the sky is blue and birds sing to me, knowing that my past forgiven, I am a good man, a good father, brother, and good son. That I finally got the help I needed and more. Your words, God, the program of Alcoholics Anonymous, Jake and his whole family, all pointed me to sobriety and with those 12 Steps, I'll stay sober one day at a time, to be the good man and son you would want me to be.

My living amends isn't to sit here and apologize for every nuance and infraction I ever committed against you, but rather to live as you would have had me live all along. I remember you used to tell me you only wanted for me to be happy. I thought it was a lie or a trick. We used to argue about the Bible and even bending for my obtuseness you would say "Well even if it isn't ordained by God, couldn't you at least agree it teaches some common sense values."

I didn't listen, even later when I would run into Graham Flagg, who would later become my sponsor, and he would argue the exact same point, word for word, that perhaps there was value in a 5,000 year old piece of literature, regardless of whether God wrote it or not, and again I would ignore the advice. At 3.5 years sober, I look at such common verses as:

Obey thy father and mother, treat your body as a temple, lying, throwing the first stone and love thy neighbor, and to love God above all else, and I realize that yes mom, you really did only want me to be happy. I just thought I knew better. If I'd obeyed you, and followed such simple advice as was laid out for me centuries before I stumbled across it, yes my life would have been easier and I would have been happier, sooner. My amends to you, mom, is to never forget that lesson. Youth is wasted on the young as they say though, you simply can't go back, but moving forward, I can hold that lesson near.

Emerson said "People are their own biggest shadow." Sobering up gave me so many gifts. The relationship with God is indescribable. Where there was fear, now there is love. Repaired family relationships mean the world. I've never been this close to my brother and sisters. Carson is joining the Marine Corp, Officer Candidacy School mom, and going off to war as a 1st Lieutenant with 40 men under his command. I'm damn proud of him. We spoke about it for months before he ultimately made the decision on his own, but that closeness, did not exist in my drinking and drugging days. Dan Jones and I talk daily, and considering we went years without, that too is remarkable. Things I imagined impossible even a year or two into my sobriety continue to shock me. God is omnipotent, and truly forgiveness knows no bounds. Ultimately he's already healed more wounds than I knew existed.

Mom, I was locked up, beat up, stitched up, and ultimately just worn down before finally surrendering to alcoholism and asking anyone at all for help. As Mark D. in the rooms says, cancer patients get chemo for just the chance of getting better, alcoholics go to meetings and do all the steps and are guaranteed recovery. It works if you work it.

There are more gifts in sobriety than I knew existed mom,

I forgot how much I loved books for instance. I hadn't read a good novel in years before coming in. We rediscover the things we love once we come in from the rain, reading and writing are God given gifts I'd completely forgotten about.

My living amends to you mama is my continued happiness. My sheer utter gratitude for you, for God, whom you introduced me to, though we met kicking and screaming, and even for AA. You told Dad to go and though he didn't fight, or work the steps and ultimately killed himself rather than face sobriety, when the time came, I knew where to go, and you were the first person in my life to have ever mentioned the words AA. Now I just feel incredibly lucky. For 20,000 years or so of human history, borderline civilizations have had alcohol, and it has killed men and women rampantly. I fully believe alcoholic bodies treat alcohol differently, and throughout all of history, men and women afflicted with alcoholism die, usually hated and shunned to the bitter end. For centuries and millennia there was no cure, just a slow, sometimes quick descent into death and hell. I was just blessed enough to be born in the 75 year time frame that Alcoholics Anonymous existed. The sliver of human history that a couple of guys named Bob and Bill, a doctor and a stockbroker, put together a group who have by now saved millions of lives collectively. I'm eternally grateful for Alcoholics Anonymous mom, and for you for pointing Dad that direction all those years before I would need to follow. For all your prayers and of course, for the demands I'm quite certain you immediately put upon God for me to quit drinking, the very second you had his ear.

Thanks mom, for everything. I love and miss you and will continue to do God's will which I know for me is to stay sober, and be an integral part of Alcoholics Anonymous. You can give God a rest, we're talking daily now. In the big scheme of things, I'm sure I'll see you soon. Tell the big guy to watch out for Carson in whichever theatre of war Uncle Sam deploys him to. I know you'd be proud of us all. We are all fighters, and we were taught by the best. Rest in peace mama, I love and miss you.

-Jared Bryan Smith

www.ingramcontent.com/pod-product-compliance
Lightning Source LLC
Chambersburg PA
CBHW020507100426
42813CB00030B/3151/J